Investment Pricing Methods

Investment Pricing Methods

A Guide for Accounting and Financial Professionals

Patrick Casabona, Ph.D.
and
Robert M. Traficanti, CFA, CPA

John Wiley & Sons, Inc.

ISBN 0-471-17740-7

Printed in the United States of America.

10 9 8 7 6 5 4 3 2 1

Patrick:

To my dear wife, Frances, for her patience and understanding and my two loving children, Amanda and Patrick Jr.

Robert:

To all accounting students. I hope this book will help you understand the types of risk management issues that your soon-to-be clients are dealing with on a daily basis.

Foreword

This volume explores pricing techniques commonly used by investment analysts as they determine prices for investment-related financial instruments. Because all standard setters have agreed to and are taking steps to implement fair value accounting guidelines for financial instruments, the Financial Instruments Joint Working Group of Standard Setters requested the Financial Accounting Standards Board (FASB) to have this volume prepared to assist accountants in understanding how the marketplace arrives at investment-related fair values. Although the research presented in this book was sponsored by the FASB, the opinions expressed herein represent those of the authors.

Often investment fair values are observable in the marketplace. However, private investments, such as private-placement loans, commercial mortgages, forward contracts, and interest rate swaps, may not have observable fair values. Pricing techniques often obtain inputs from publicly traded investments (that have observable prices) and then utilize those inputs and other estimates in various models to determine the investment's fair value. This book is intended to make the "nonanalyst" familiar with the techniques that analysts use, but in no event should one interpret this volume as establishing accounting guidelines for investment pricing.

Robert Traficanti
Patrick Casabona

Contents

Preface

Accounting guidelines are evolving in response to the growth and complexity of investments. As a result, fair value concepts are becoming part of measurement and disclosure accounting guidelines, and, therefore, accountants must understand the fundamentals of investment pricing methods. This book was written to provide accountants with a practical understanding of how investment analysts price common financial investment instruments, such as commercial mortgages, private placement bonds, mortgage-backed securities, private and public equities, derivatives, and joint ventures. As a part of understanding investment pricing, one will need to become familiar with investment terminology that may, at times, seem confusing or have different meanings depending on one's frame of reference. For example, initially we used the word "valuation" rather than "pricing" in the title of this book. However, in discussing this topic with analysts, we were told that some investment analysts view *investment valuation* as a process of comparing one investment with another to determine the best relative buy, while pricing means determining an investment's current or fair market value. We therefore use the term "pricing" to avoid confusion.

To reinforce pricing concepts, we illustrate certain public security pricings, since these are often less complex than private investments. We then apply those concepts to pricing private investments. Our goal is to familiarize readers with those pricing concepts so that they will understand how investors are compensated for assuming risks and how this impacts pricing. Readers then will be able to understand the inputs used in the appropriate investment pricing model (including the basic valuation formulas), how changing market conditions impact fair values, and why certain internal control processes are important in arriving at reasonably accurate and consistent estimates of prices for private investments. We also would like readers to appreciate the limitations of such pricing procedures.

This book also introduces certain derivative hedging transactions that may be useful to accountants who are involved in reviewing similar types of transactions. Those types of transactions have become pervasive, and derivative pricing may be better understood when hedging concepts are also explained.

After reading this book, one should have a sound understanding of the foundations of investment pricing procedures and be able to apply these building blocks to evaluate the reasonableness of investment pricing calculations observed in practice. One also should be well positioned to explore more in-depth material, such as that presented in the recommended references included in this book.

Accountants and other business practitioners should have a basic understanding of the following concepts that are typically used in investment pricing procedures.

Fixed-Income Instruments

- Term structure of interest rates
- Inverse relationship between interest rates and prices of fixed-income investments
- Pricing fixed-income investments using yield curves specific to the investment type
- Composition of fixed-income yields into the risk-free rate, sector risk premium, credit risk premium, and other costs
- Credit rating categories and a process for determining such ratings
- Duration as a measure of the sensitivity of financial instruments to interest rate changes
- Convexity as a measure of the rate of change of duration and its relationship to prepayment features and call provisions
- Make-whole provision formulas and the impact of changes in interest rates
- Structures of mortgage-backed securities and asset-backed securities
- Types of loan covenant provisions and their importance in protecting value
- Common terms included in mortgage and note contracts
- Common fixed-income derivative types used for hedging instruments
- Pricing concepts and models for various fixed-income derivatives

Equity Instruments

- Common pricing methods such as price multiples and discounted-cash flow models
- Measuring risk and factoring it into the pricing model
- Components of free-cash flow in business pricing
- Impact of earnings growth rates on equity pricing
- Impact of changing discount rates on equity pricing
- Importance of covenant provisions to protect private equity investors
- Impact of control premiums or discounts in pricing private equities
- Pricing concepts and models for equity derivatives

This book begins with a discussion of the term "structure of interest rates," which is provided for those who may require a review of those fundamental concepts. Readers already familiar with those concepts may begin with Chapter 2.

Note that the FASB has issued Concepts Statement No. 7, *Using Cash Flow Information and Present Value in Accounting Measurements.* Concepts Statement 7 outlines the framework for using present values of future cash flows in accounting measurements. In paragraph 25, the Board describes the objective of present value in the following terms: "The only objective of present value, when used in accounting measurements at initial recognition and fresh-start measurements, is to estimate fair value. Stated differently, present value should attempt to capture the elements that taken together would comprise a market price if one existed, that is, fair value."

As the name implies, a Concepts Statement addresses broad principles rather than specific techniques. However, there is no conflict between the conceptual discussion in the Concepts Statement and the pricing methodologies and concepts presented in this book.

In paragraph 23, the Board describes the five elements necessary to fully describe economic differences between various assets or liabilities:

a. An estimate of the future cash flow, or in more complex cases, series of future cash flows at different times
b. Expectations about possible variations in the amount or timing of those cash flows
c. The time value of money, represented by the risk-free rate of interest
d. The price for bearing the uncertainty inherent in the asset or liability
e. Other, sometimes unidentifiable, factors including illiquidity and market imperfections. [Footnote reference omitted.]

This book is devoted to describing tools that investment professionals use to assess those elements.

A CD-ROM PowerPoint™ presentation is available to assist those who wish to teach this material. Please go to *www.wiley.com/go/investmentpricing* to download this file.

Acknowledgments

The following institutions, investment analysts, and other business professionals provided significant assistance in creating this book. We wish to express our sincere thanks for their efforts to ensure that this book informs and educates readers about how actual investment pricings are performed in practice.

American Business Financial Services, Inc.
  Anna M. Bucceroni
Bear Stearns
  David Zion, CPA, CFA
  Raymond Lee Katz, CFA
BondCalc
  Donald C. Wiss
Canadian Institute of Chartered Accountants (CICA)
  J. Alex Milburn, Ph.D., FCA
  Ian Hague, CA
Conning Investment Management Company
  Karen Kelleher
Deloitte & Touche LLP
  Thomas Hewitt, CPA, Ph.D.
  James Mountain, CPA

Financial Accounting Standards Board
  Timothy S. Lucas
  James J. Leisenring
  Edward Trott
  Wayne Upton
  Amy Tenney
  Glen Kudlicky
  Ana Thiers
  Mary Huydic
Intrinsic Value Associates
  Gerald Bollman, CFA
Massachusetts Mutual Life Insurance Company
  Douglas Janik, CPA
Principia Partners
  Brian Donnally
Times Square Capital Management Inc.
  Philip Spak, CFA

The following individuals also provided assistance: Kenneth Andersen, former department head of Private Placements, Connecticut Mutual Insurance Company, and Theodore Kappler, mortgage-backed security consultant.

Investment Pricing Methods

Chapter 1

Pricing Concepts and the Term Structure of Interest Rates

INTRODUCTION

This chapter explains the basic building blocks of investment pricing methodologies.[1] Those building blocks include the basic present value formula, the term structure of interest rates, and an introduction to the concept of *duration*.[2]

We have referenced for certain examples the keystrokes entered on a financial calculator (for our use, the Hewlett Packard™ Model 12C) to reinforce the steps in computing present values. This may help individuals remember key present value determinants, such as the periodic interest rate, payments, the number of periods, and the present or future values of cash flows.

A glossary is included at the end of this book.

PRESENT VALUE FORMULA

The prices of financial instruments that are publicly traded are determined in the marketplace by supply and demand conditions but may be estimated by pricing techniques. Pricing techniques are especially important in the determination of estimates of the prices of nonpublicly traded financial instruments, since market exchange prices are not readily available.

In general, the price of any financial instrument is equal to the present value of its expected future cash flows discounted by an appropriate rate of return that compensates investors for bearing risk. The key pricing technique is the following discounted cash flow (or present value) model:

$$\text{Present Value} = \sum_{t=1}^{T} \frac{CF_t}{(1+r)^t} = \frac{CF_1}{(1+r)^1} + \frac{CF_2}{(1+r)^2} + \ldots + \frac{CF_n}{(1+r)^n}$$

Where:
- CF_t = the expected cash flow for period t
- r = the required rate of return or discount rate used to compute the present value of the future cash flows
- n = the final period

Variations of this formula will be applied in subsequent pricing calculations, but, first, this formula will be applied to the simple example presented in Exhibit 1-1.

Effect of Interest Rate Changes on the Value of a Treasury Note

Exhibit 1-1 illustrates the effects of changes in market (effective) rates of interest on the price of a Treasury note with a $100 million par value, five-year term, 6 percent coupon rate, and semiannual payments. When market participants demand a 6 percent return on money, they may invest in this hypothetical Treasury note; the price of this Treasury note is $100 million—the present value of the expected cash flows. The yield to maturity (YTM) of the note also is 6 percent; that is, if investors hold those notes until the final payment is made (maturity), they receive a 6 percent return on the $100 million that they invest.

What happens if the market demands an effective interest rate of 7 percent on the day a Treasury note is issued? If the Treasury note offers only 6 percent interest (coupon rate), the market will not pay $100 million for this note. The price of the note, when the market's required effective yield is 7 percent, is $95,841,696—the present value of the contractual payments discounted at 7 percent (more than $4 million less than the par value of the note).

Exhibit 1-1   Effect of Interest Rate Changes on Treasury Note Pricing, $100,000,000 5-year, 6 percent Treasury Note Issued at Par, Pricing Assuming Interest Rates Shift 100 Basis Points (1 percent).

		Present Value or Price		
Period	Cash Flow	6% YTM	7% YTM	5% YTM
1	3,000,000	2,912,622	2,898,550	2,926,730
2	3,000,000	2,827,788	2,800,532	2,855,443
3	3,000,000	2,745,425	2,705,828	2,785,798
4	3,000,000	2,665,461	2,614,327	2,717,852
5	3,000,000	2,587,826	2,525,920	2,651,563
6	3,000,000	2,512,453	2,440,502	2,586,891
7	3,000,000	2,439,275	2,357,972	2,523,795
8	3,000,000	2,368,228	2,278,235	2,462,240
9	3,000,000	2,299,250	2,201,193	2,402,185
10	103,000,000	76,641,672	73,018,637	80,463,435
		$100,000,000	$95,841,696	$104,375,932

Price change for a 6 percent Treasury note with 5 years remaining as rates:
    Increase from 6% to 7%   −$4,158,304
    Decrease from 6% to 5% $4,375,932

In contrast, what happens if the market demands an effective interest rate of 5 percent on the day the Treasury note is issued? Since this Treasury note offers 6 percent interest (coupon rate), the market will pay $104,375,932 for this note. The price of the note when the required yield is 5 percent is $4,375,932 more than the present value of the contractual payments discounted at 6 percent (more than $4 million more than the par value of the note).

Shown below is an illustration of the present value formula, which is used to price the bond in Exhibit 1-1, assuming that the effective yield is 6 percent and has 10 periodic 3 percent semiannual coupon payments, and a par value of $100,000,000 to be received at the end of year 10.

$$P = \frac{3,000,000_1}{(1+.03)^1} + \frac{3,000,000_2}{(1+.03)^2} + \frac{3,000,000_3}{(1+.03)^3} + \ldots + \frac{103,000,000_{10}}{(1+.03)^{10}} = 100,000,$$

Note that the numerator and denominator subscripts reference the end of the period in which the cash flow is received.

To calculate the note's price using a financial calculator and now assuming a 7 percent YTM and a 6 percent annual coupon rate (3 percent, semiannual interest payments), one would enter the following keystrokes:

6[PMT], 7[i], 1.012000[ENTER], 1.012005[f][PRICE]. This then calculates a price of 95.8417. (The keystrokes "1.012000" and "1.012005" represent a method of inputting the note's term of 5 years. Dates can actually be entered. The back of the HP 12C provides instructions.)

There are several important relationships to recognize when evaluating non-callable fixed-income instruments:

- If one knows the note's effective yield, par value, periodic interest payments, and maturity, one can solve for its price, as illustrated above.
- If one knows the note's price, par value, periodic interest payments, and maturity, one can solve for its effective market yield as follows:

95.8417[PV], 6[PMT], 1.012000[ENTER], 1.012005[f][YTM]. This calculates a yield of 7.

- The effective market yield or the YTM is the rate that equates the present value of all of the note's cash flows (discounted at this rate) with the note's current price.

Key Elements of the Discounted Cash Flow Formula

Note from the above illustrations that key elements of the Discounted Cash Flow (DCF) formula are the estimated future cash flows and the appropriate discount rate used to compute the present value of those cash flows. Cash flows may vary depending on the type of the investment and the current economic conditions. For example, both a Treasury bond (term greater than 10 years) and a Treasury note (term between one to 10 years) have known fixed cash flows because they are not generally called in before maturity and do not have any default risk. Therefore, one can refer to the terms of the note or bond to obtain the contractual cash flows. Other types of fixed-income investments have less predictable cash flows. For example, a mortgage-backed security has cash flows that may be impacted by prepayments as interest rates decrease and homeowners repay their residential mortgages prior to the end of the loan's scheduled amortization term. Investment analysts use models to forecast expected cash flows of mortgage-backed securities, net of prepayments. Those investments are covered in Chapter 4. In contrast, a common stock may be priced by estimating the uncertain future "free cash flows" of the enterprise that are expected to grow at projected rates (rather than remain constant, like many bonds) and then discounting those cash flows by a risk-adjusted rate or a blended-average cost of debt and equity capital. Enterprise cash flows are difficult to estimate because they involve estimates of growth rates in cash flows and a higher degree of uncertainty related to the magnitude and timing of the future expected cash flows. This topic is covered in Chapter 5.

The discount rate used to calculate the present value of an investment's cash flows depends on the risks associated with the investment's cash flows. For example, a default risk-free rate is appropriate for a Treasury bond or note, whereas the rates used to discount cash flows related to a credit-sensitive corporate bond or commercial mortgage require that various risk premiums be added to the risk-free rate. The market prices default risk and sector risk (other types of risks to be discussed below) as a yield spread over certain benchmark rates that are risk free. Historically, financial markets in the United States have used comparable-term U.S. Treasury rates. Although a Treasury bond has interest rate risk (i.e., fluctuations in price in response to changes in interest rates), as shown in Exhibit 1-1, the rate on this instrument is referred to as the risk-free rate, as no other risks (other than interest rate risk) are associated with this instrument. As markets are evolving, other benchmark rates may be used, such as London Interbank Offered Rate (LIBOR) swap rates. This will be addressed later in this book.

Yield Curve and Term Structure of Interest Rates

In the example provided in Exhibit 1-1, the assumed discount rates used to calculate the present values of the cash flows of a five-year Treasury note ranged from 5 to 7 percent. In the case of a Treasury note, the discount rate (or effective yield) can be observed in the market or derived using a *spot-yield curve* constructed from observed rates of *zero-coupon* Treasury securities of different maturities. The following discussion will illustrate this process. A key aspect of the yield curve is the relationship between time until maturity and yield; differing maturities of similar quality investments may have different yields. One reason for those differences may be due to the market's preference for liquidity (i.e., shorter-term bonds). This liquidity factor is one type of risk premium. The yields may therefore vary in what is termed an upward-sloping yield curve, where rates increase in relation to the investment's term, or where rates decrease in relation to the instrument's term—a downward-sloping yield curve. An upward-sloping yield curve is illustrated in the graph in Exhibit 1-2. (The upward-sloping yield curve is most common.)

The following concepts are important to an understanding of yield curves and other pricing concepts.

Key Interest Rate Mechanics

Interest rates are an essential part of any model used to compute an estimate of the price of an investment's future cash flows. In the absence of an active market for the priced instrument, the selection of an appropriate interest rate requires considerable judgment and must be founded, in part, on an understanding of the following interest rate mechanics. Interest rates indicate the market's assessment of what a fair return for a debt investment should be, given the current supply and demand for funds. That assessment includes an evaluation of the risk associated with a particular investment alternative at a given point in time, which includes consideration of various micro- and macroeconomic factors.

Benchmark Risk-Free Rate

A Treasury note is a risk-free asset, which means that a Treasury note does not have default risk. For the pricing of instruments that have default risk, the Treasury rate corresponding to each instrument's maturity historically has been used as a reference discount rate. A yield spread (risk premium) is added to compensate the investor for *default risk* and to arrive at the risk-adjusted discount rate used in the present value calculation. However, in early 2000, investors predicted[3] a shrinking Treasury debt supply and that the U.S. markets may use other benchmark risk-free rates to build discount rates. For example, fixed interest rate swap rates with corresponding LIBOR-based variable legs also are being referenced (referred to as the LIBOR swap rate). (Interest rate swap pricing is illustrated in Chapter 7.)

For present value calculations illustrated in this book, the Treasury rate is used as the base rate. (But remember that this rate is not the sole benchmark risk-free rate and that market preferences may be changing.) Integral to the process of pricing private placement investments is the reference to quoted public security yields and the related spread or risk premium over the risk-free rate. A public security spread over the benchmark risk-free rate often is used as a reference point in discounting the cash flows on comparable-quality, private fixed-income instruments after adjusting it by adding another risk premium, for their lack of liquidity, to arrive at the appropriate risk-adjusted discount rate. This is discussed further and illustrated in Chapter 2.

Yield to Maturity

Yield to maturity is the internal rate of return that equates the present value of an investment's estimated periodic future cash inflows (discounted at this rate) with its current price. Exhibit 1-1 illustrates 5 percent, 6 percent, and 7 percent yields to maturity that, when used as the discount rates, equate the present values of the estimated future cash flows with the note's prices.

Spot Rate

For debt instruments, the *spot rate* refers to the prevailing rate of interest on a zero-coupon instrument with a given maturity. A zero-coupon instrument is purchased at a discount, has no coupon interest payments during the instrument's term, and matures at par value. Spot price in the market refers to the price related to immediate, as opposed to future, delivery. The spot price may also be calculated for securities such as Eurodollar deposits contracts (U.S. dollar-denominated deposits held in foreign banks). When performing present value calculations, the spot rate for a particular maturity may be used to determine the present value of a cash flow received in the corresponding future period. Exhibits 1-3 and 1-4 illustrate this concept. A zero-coupon rate is used to calculate present values because it makes no assumptions about reinvestment rates associated with the receipts of any intermittent cash flows, since zero-coupon bonds do not have such cash flows.

Forward Rate

For debt instruments, the *forward rate* refers to a rate of interest required today, for delivery of an investment in a future time period. It is the rate of interest specific to a security between two future dates, such as a two-year rate one year from today. The forward rate is sometimes referred to as the implied forward rate because it is computed from (i.e., implied by) successive spot rates. Spot rates may be used to compute the implied forward rate for a future period. (This is done when an actual security does not exist for this period.) Note that for nondebt instruments, there can be forward prices, analogous to forward interest rates, such as the forward price of corn or oil. In that particular case, the forward price represents a price for future delivery, whereas the spot price is the price for immediate delivery or transaction.

The relationship between spot rates (SR_t) and forward rates (FR_t) is depicted by the following formula (where t = time period):

$$FR_t = [(1 + SR_t{+}_1)^{t+1} / (1 + SR_t)^t] - 1$$

What Does This Information Tell Us about the One-Year Forward Rate?
Assume that the one-year spot rate is 6 percent and that the current two-year spot rate is 7 percent. One can calculate the one-year spot rate that is expected one year from today, at 8.01 percent, as follows:

$$FR_1 = [(1.07)^2 / (1.06)] - 1 = 0.0801 \text{ or } 8.01\%$$

To verify that the two-year spot rate is indeed 7 percent, note that the spot rate is the geometric mean of one plus the related forward rates minus one:

$$SR_2 = [(1.06)(1.0801)]^{1/2} - 1 = .07 \text{ or } 7\%$$

If this relationship did not hold, there would be arbitrage opportunities. For example, if the forward rate was greater than 8.01 percent, the arbitrager would buy the one-year spot and one-year forward and sell the two-year spot. Alternatively, if the one-year forward was less than 8.01 percent, arbitrager would sell the one-year spot and sell the one-year forward, and purchase the two-year security. Arbitrager in the market will trade until the above relationship holds. The spot and forward rates are important because those rates will be used in pricing securities. For example, when pricing an interest rate swap, the swap's variable-leg cash flows may be forecasted based on the forward rates implied by the spot-yield curve. Also, the swap's fixed-leg and variable-leg cash flows are discounted by the applicable period's spot rates observed in the marketplace, to arrive at a present value (price). This is covered in Chapter 7.

Yield Curve (Term Structure of Interest Rates)

The yield curve is a graph of the relationship between the yields on Treasury securities or some other homogeneous group of fixed-income securities and the time to maturity. The yield curve is also referred to as the *term structure of interest rates*. Different fixed-income investments are priced using yield curves specific to their characteristics. The spot-rate term structure or spot-rate yield curve is a set of spot rates related to an instrument (i.e., a U.S. Treasury note), arranged by maturity.[4] A spot-rate yield curve is shown in Exhibit 1-2. Note that a spot-yield curve is not a predictor of future interest rates but is used to infer the forward rates based on the current yield curve derived from spot rates.

Another yield curve is the Eurodollar futures yield curve, commonly used to price LIBOR-based interest rate swaps. This is covered later in this chapter.

How Is the Spot-Rate Yield Curve Derived?

The spot-rate yield curve may be derived from the current market prices of zero-coupon Treasury securities and coupon-bearing Treasury securities, appropriately

Exhibit 1-2 Spot-Yield Curve.

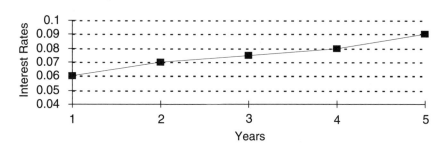

adjusted. In constructing this yield curve, on-the-run issues, which are current-issue Treasury securities, should be used because they have greater liquidity than off-the-run securities, which are older issues and require higher yields because of their lower liquidity (although off-the-run securities may be used). Adjustments also must be made to factor in the various points on the curve for which there is no corresponding Treasury instrument. Such adjustments are based on the estimated implied forward rates.

What Factors Determine the Shape of the Yield Curve?

The shape of the yield curve as it extends out in time is influenced by the market's expectations about the future. The principal component of those expectations is inflation and its likely impact on the real value (or purchasing power) of an instrument's future cash flows. Expectations of potential rising future inflation generally will cause yields in the future to be higher than current rates and, hence, will produce an upward-sloping yield curve. Expectations also include the market's assessment of future political policy, the relative attractiveness and availability of funds both domestically and abroad, and the projections of current economic trends. Those factors are assessed in the marketplace where buy-and-sell orders bring the price of an instrument into equilibrium. Also, investors may have a preference for liquidity. Therefore, the demand for shorter-term securities will tend to drive their yields down.[5]

Yield Curve Applications to Bond Pricing Procedures

The spot rates making up the yield curve in Exhibit 1-2 are used by investment analysts to calculate the present value (PV) factors (discount factors). Those present value factors are used to compute the present value of an investment's cash flows that are expected in the related periods. Exhibit 1-3 illustrates a discount factor curve corresponding to the spot rates in Exhibit 1-2, which are also presented in Exhibit 1-4.

For those using an HP12C, the following keystrokes solve for the denominator when raising to a power:

1.09[ENTER], 5[yx]

This equates to 1.5386 and is then entered as 1/1.5386 to arrive at the .64993 PV factor.

Exhibit 1-4 shows the present value factors calculated using the spot rates applicable to each period. Those present value factors are used in Exhibit 1-5 to illustrate price differences between different types of 9 percent bonds.

To reinforce those concepts, Appendix A illustrates an actual calculation of a U.S. Treasury bond curve performed with a vendor's application, which is available on the Internet. In this application, actual off-the-run Treasury note prices were identified and used to build a U.S. Treasury bond yield curve. A demonstration of

Exhibit 1-3   Present Value Factor Curve of Spot Rates from Exhibit 1-2.

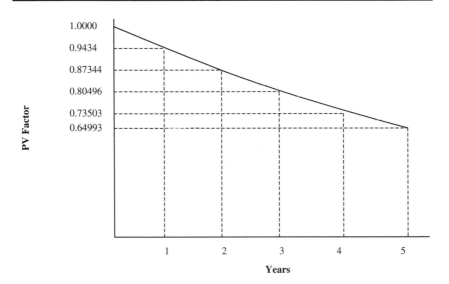

Note that the Present Value factors are calculated as follows:

$$\text{PV factor} = \frac{1}{(1 + \text{spot rate})^{n \text{ period}}}$$

$$\text{PV factor for period } 1 = \frac{1}{(1 + .06)^1} = .94340$$

$$\text{PV factor for period } 5 = \frac{1}{(1 + .09)^5} = .64993$$

Exhibit 1-4   Rates and Present Value (PV), 1-Year Factors.

Period	Spot Rate	Forward Rate	PV Factor = $1/(1+SR)^n$
1	0.0600	0.06000	0.94340
2	0.0700	0.08010	0.87344
3	0.0750	0.08507	0.80496
4	0.0800	0.09514	0.73503
5	0.0900	0.13093	0.64993

Where:
- SR = spot rate
- n = period

this application, which may be used to build yield curves and price various bonds and swaps, can be obtained at *www.fincad.com.*[6]

The forward rates are shown in Exhibit 1-4 to emphasize that they are derived from two successive spot rates. The forward rates are not used in the following calculations. However, it is important to understand the spot-forward rate relationship because the forward rate often is used in pricing investments, such as interest rate swaps and fixed-income *forward contracts* (covered in Chapter 7).

Assume that a zero-coupon bond, a coupon bond, and an amortizing bond each have a five-year life and a 9 percent annual stated interest rate and are not subject to prepayment risk. The cash flows associated with each bond are shown in Exhibit 1-5. Discounting each cash flow by the PV factor applicable to each period, calculated by using the PV factor derived in Exhibit 1-4, provides the following prices for each instrument.

Question: In the above example, the yield to maturity and the stated interest rate are the same yet the present values are different. Why are the present values different?

The present values differ because the given set of spot rates favors early payments over later payments. In other words, in a normal (upward-sloping) yield-curve environment, cash flows received in early periods are present-value weighted at larger amounts than those received in later periods.

Exhibit 1-5 also shows that the yield to maturity or internal rate of return is calculated by equating the current market value of each bond (computed using the spot rates) with the present value of its future cash flows, calculated with the appropriate yield to maturity as the discount rate. Each bond provides a different

Exhibit 1-5   Present Value of Various 9 Percent Bonds (Interest Calculated on an Annual Basis).

		Zero-Coupon Bond		Coupon Bond		Amortizing Bond	
Period	PV Factor	Cash Flow	PV	Cash Flow	PV	Cash Flow	PV
1	0.94340	0	0	9,000	8,491	25,709	24,254
2	0.87344	0	0	9,000	7,861	25,709	22,455
3	0.80496	0	0	9,000	7,245	25,709	20,695
4	0.73503	0	0	9,000	6,615	25,709	18,897
5	0.64993	153,862	100,000	109,000	70,842	25,709	16,709
Present Value			$100,000		$101,054		$103,010
Yield to Maturity			9%		8.73%		7.87%

yield to maturity and demonstrates key bond-pricing concepts previously discussed:

- If the term, cash flows, and market yield to maturity are known, one can solve for the bond's price.
- If the term, cash flows, and price are known, one can solve for the bond's yield to maturity.

Those relationships are also shown on the back of the HP12C calculator as an aid in calculating bond prices. Those concepts are used in discussing bond pricing in later chapters.

Why Does the Yield to Maturity Equal the Spot Rate Only for the Zero-Coupon Bond?

The yield to maturity and spot rate for a specified maturity are the same only for the zero-coupon bond because there is a single cash flow at maturity. The yield to maturity for the amortizing bond and the coupon bond differs from the spot rate because their yields are weighted by the different intermittent spot rates that exist when their cash flows occur.

From a pricing perspective, yield to maturity is a difficult statistic to interpret. It is a better indicator of effective market yield than the stated rate or coupon rate because it equates the security's price with the present value of its expected future cash flows discounted at the yield to maturity. Yield to maturity, however, is deficient as a pricing tool because it represents an average return on each cash flow which reflects the average, rather than the individual spot rates on the related term structure of interest rates, discussed above. In addition, it assumes that interim cash flows received are reinvested at the yield to maturity. No such assumption is made with zero-coupon spot rates. As an average, the yield to maturity has no direct relationship to any point on the spot-yield curve.

Yield to maturity can be used, however, to determine an average spread relative to the risk-free yield curve, such as the yield curve for U.S. Treasury investments. The average spread to the yield curve can be determined by computing the yield to maturity based on price and comparing it with the yield to maturity based on the risk-free spot rates or on the yield to maturity of a similar duration risk-free investment. When reviewing the illustrations of bond pricing in Chapter 3, it is important to be aware that, in practice, bonds often are priced using one yield applied to all cash flows rather than the theoretical methodology shown here, in which each period's cash flow is discounted by its applicable spot rate. The yield that is used as a discount rate is the yield applicable to similar quality and similar average-life investments. (Note that *average life* refers to the time it takes for the present value of a bond's cash flows to return one-half of the current price. This is a common term used to describe an important aspect of fixed-income investments.) This methodology and its divergence from theory is explained in Chapters 2 and 3. Understand that when pricing investments, such as private placement bonds, market-yield spreads are not publicly available and market transactions may be infrequent. Therefore, the precision from estimating, for example, each yield curve for each cash flow related to a 10-year bond may not produce any more pricing accuracy than obtaining one yield curve related to its average life and quality. Furthermore, this methodology is simpler and easier to calculate.

Eurodollar Futures Yield Curve

The Eurodollar futures yield curve is constructed using the forward rates of interest quoted in Eurodollar futures contracts. This yield curve is used to determine the fixed LIBOR interest rate in interest rate swaps (explained in Chapter 7). The fixed LIBOR swap rate quoted in varying term swaps is also referenced as a base default-risk-free rate of interest (even though the rate does have some credit risk since it is LIBOR based). An explanation follows on the development of the Eurodollar futures yield curve. The basic building block is the rate set in Eurodollar deposit contracts.

Eurodollar deposit contracts represent U.S.-dollar-denominated deposits held in banks outside the United States. The deposits are transacted at par with stated interest rates and terms ranging from one day to 10 years. Those rates are quoted on pricing services, such as Telerate. The rate set in the Eurodollar short-term contracts is identical to the LIBOR rate. Eurodollar futures contracts (*EUCDs*) are priced using the spot Eurodollar deposit rates for various terms, in calculations that estimate the forward LIBOR three-month spot rate at the contract's expiration. EUCDs are issued for three-month terms, specifying an underlying forward rate of interest. At the contract's expiration, the contract is net settled based on reference to the actual three-month LIBOR rate (set on the Monday preceding the contract's expiration on the third Wednesday of the month). This is compared to the locked-in forward rate agreed to at the contract's inception. The three-month futures contract forward interest rate is priced at 100 less the futures contract price.

Exhibit 1-6 illustrates a five-year EUCD yield curve used to price an interest rate swap. (Swap pricing is covered in Chapter 7.) The curve is constructed from EUCD prices observed in the market for contract terms ranging from December 13, 1999, to September 13, 2004, as detailed in column 5 (refer to Bloomberg prices in Appendix B). Those prices, such as the December 13, 1999, price of 94.050, are converted to a forward rate by subtracting this price from 100 (column 6). The forward rate is then converted to a spot rate in column 7.[7]

As the availability of U.S. Treasury securities diminishes, LIBOR swap rates are increasingly being used as a benchmark risk-free rate. Tim Bridges, an analyst at Goldman Sachs, has explained why LIBOR swap rates are used rather than Treasury-based rates:

- LIBOR resets daily; Treasury bills only reset weekly. This alone would cause significant liquidity and pricing issues.

- LIBOR supply is unlimited, whereas Treasury bill supply is limited and is becoming more so. Thus, the Treasury bill rate is subject to significant supply and demand price movements, whereas LIBOR is not. LIBOR, therefore, is a much easier rate to hedge (and therefore cheaper for end users).
- LIBOR is hedged with Eurodollar futures, for which, again, the supply is unlimited. (Contracts are cash settled.) If the market switched to a Treasury bills index and hedged in Treasury bill futures, supply and demand imbalances would exist as Treasury bills would need to be delivered to settle the contracts. Again, the supply of Treasury bills is limited. (As a benchmark, the open interest in Eurodollar futures far exceeds the supply of Treasury bills so that there could be a disrupted market).
- BBA (British Banking Authority) LIBOR is in many ways a risk-free or low-risk index. Only the debt of the best banks can be in the index, and if a member bank's credit deteriorates, it is removed from the index.
- This topic is also discussed in the September 4, 2000, Barron's article, "Swapping Curves, Will Interest-Rate Swaps Replace Treasuries as the Benchmark Yield Curve," by William Pesek, Jr. (p. 34). The author concludes that, due to the Treasury Department's accelerating campaign to slash the federal debt, interest rates swaps are becoming the new international debt standard.

DURATION AND OTHER FIXED-INCOME PRICING CONCEPTS

Duration as a Measure of Bond's Interest Rate Risk

Investment analysts consider duration an important characteristic because it is a numerical indicator of the price sensitivity of a fixed-income security or portfolio of securities to changes in interest rates (yields). Duration also can be calculated for real estate or equity securities, although this is a less common application. Modified duration indicates the approximate percentage change in the price of a bond or bond portfolio to a 1 basis-point change in yields. For example, if a bond's modified duration is five and interest rates decrease by 100 *basis points* (or 1 percent), one would expect a 5 percent increase in the bond's price. (Since the bond has fixed cash flows at higher rates, the bond is more valuable as rates decrease.) A common duration statistic is termed Macaulay duration (which is also used to estimate modified duration). The Macaulay duration measure is equal to the summation of the present values of a bond's cash flows, discounted by the bond's current yield to maturity, weighted by the time periods it takes to receive those cash flows, divided by the current price of the bond. Exhibits 1-7 and 1-8 demonstrate how to calculate both duration and modified duration.

Important duration concepts include:

- The ratio of Macaulay duration to one plus a bond's effective yield $(1 + r)$ is commonly referred to as modified duration. Modified duration is used to measure the price sensitivity of a bond to a specified change in yield.

Exhibit 1-6 Determining the 5-Year EUCD Curve and Swap Rate.

Analysis Date   09/15/99
Notional $1,000,000

The swap rate is the single rate that will produce fixed cash flows whose present value equals the present value of the floating rate cash flows, when both the floating and fixed cash flows are discounted by the spot rates implied by the EUCD futures strip.

Five Year Swap Rate >>>>>> 0.06532 <<<<<< Trial and error. Enter rate that forces the PV of the fixed rate cash flow to equal the PV of the floating rate cash flow.

(1) Period	(2) EUCD Contract	(3) EUCD Contract Maturity	(4) EUCD Contract Daycount	(5) EUCD Contract Price	(6) EUCD Forward Rate Act/360	(7) EUCD Discount Factor (Spot Rate)	(8) Floating Cash Flow	(9) PV Floating Cash Flow	(10) Fixed Cash Flow	(11) PV Fixed Cash Flow
1	One Day Cash LIBOR				5.352%	1.00000				
2	Dec99	12/13/99	89	94.050%	5.950%	0.98695	13,529	13,352	16,329	16,116
3	Mar00	03/13/00	91	94.115%	5.885%	0.97233	15,040	14,624	16,329	15,877
4	Jun00	06/19/00	91	93.935%	6.065%	0.95700	14,876	14,236	16,329	15,627
5	Sep00	09/18/00	91	93.800%	6.200%	0.94255	15,331	14,450	16,329	15,391
6	Dec00	12/18/00	91	93.635%	6.365%	0.92801	15,672	14,544	16,329	15,153
7	Mar01	03/19/01	91	93.640%	6.360%	0.91331	16,089	14,695	16,329	14,913
8	Jun01	06/18/01	91	93.560%	6.440%	0.89886	16,077	14,451	16,329	14,677
9	Sep01	09/17/01	91	93.515%	6.485%	0.88446	16,279	14,398	16,329	14,442
10	Dec01	12/17/01	91	93.405%	6.595%	0.87020	16,393	14,265	16,329	14,209
11	Mar02	03/18/02	91	93.420%	6.580%	0.85593	16,671	14,269	16,329	13,976
12	Jun02	06/17/02	91	93.360%	6.640%	0.84192	16,633	14,004	16,329	13,748
13	Sep02	09/16/02	91	93.315%	6.685%	0.82803	16,784	13,898	16,329	13,521

14	Dec02	12/16/02	91	93.205%	6.795%	0.81427	16,898	13,760	16,329	13,296
15	Mar03	03/17/03	91	93.215%	6.785%	0.80052	17,176	13,750	16,329	13,072
16	Jun03	06/16/03	91	93.160%	6.840%	0.78702	17,151	13,498	16,329	12,851
17	Sep03	09/15/03	91	93.120%	6.880%	0.77364	17,290	13,376	16,329	12,633
18	Dec03	12/15/03	91	93.000%	7.000%	0.76042	17,391	13,225	16,329	12,417
19	Mar04	03/15/04	91	93.000%	7.000%	0.74720	17,694	13,221	16,329	12,201
20	Jun04	06/14/04	91	92.935%	7.065%	0.73421	17,694	12,991	16,329	11,989
21	Sep04	09/13/04	91	92.885%	7.115%	0.72132	17,859	12,882	16,329	11,778
								277,888	=	277,888

Calculated Rate		
Market	Offer	0.0653
Market	Mid	0.0654
Market	Bid	0.0650

Notes:

(1) Time period.

(2) Euro Dollar Futures Contract (EUCD).

(3) Maturity of EUCD futures contract.

(4) Number of days in the EUCD period.

(5) EUCD futures price.

(6) Forward rate = Futures Rate. 100.00 – EUCD futures price.

(7) Discount factor in previous period / [1 + (forward rate in previous period × number of days in period / 360)] = Spot Rate.

(8) (Forward rate previous period × number of days in period / 360) × notional.

(9) Floating rate cash flow multiplied by EUCD discount factor.

(10) Determine fixed swap rate that when multiplied by notional and discounted by EUCD discount rate produces a present value equal to the floating rate present value. Trial and error process.

(11) Fixed rate cash flow multiplied by EUCD discount rate.

Source: FHL Bank, Chicago, Illinois.

- Other things being equal, the longer the maturity of a bond, the more sensitive the bond's price is to changes in interest rates and, hence, the larger its modified duration (hereinafter referred to as "duration").

- Any two bonds with the same maturity and yields may have different durations if the magnitudes of their coupon interest payments are different. The bond with the smaller coupon payments will have a higher duration and, hence, will experience larger percentage price changes in response to a given change in interest rates.

- Duration is impacted by call or put provisions. For callable bonds, a separate calculation of duration is performed, known as option-adjusted duration. (This topic is beyond the scope of this book.)

- The concept of duration is important to understand when evaluating fixed-income investments and risk-management strategies. One of the investment portfolio manager's key objectives may be to balance the duration of assets and liabilities in a given portfolio, such that irrespective of interest rate changes, the price changes of assets and liabilities are offset. Therefore, the portfolio produces approximately no net gain or loss as interest rates change. For example, if a bond portfolio has a duration of five, and it is invested to fund a liability that also has a duration of five, one would expect no net over-all gain or loss in the assets and liabilities as interest rates change. As rates decrease by 100 basis points, the assets should produce a 5 percent gain, while the liabilities should produce an offsetting 5 percent loss. (Note that credit changes may cause differences.) When this balance is met, analysts consider the portfolio to be *immunized* against interest rate changes. It is important to note that although duration matching is an important process, it is an approximation, and a perfect offset rarely occurs in the context of a large portfolio due to such factors as the nonparallel shifts in the yield curve and large moves in interest rates.

- The numerical value for duration associated with a bond or portfolio, when multiplied by the basis-point yield change caused by a change in the yield to maturity, provides an approximation of the investment's price change due to the movement in rates. For example, the five-year Treasury note illustrated in Exhibit 1-1 has a duration of 4.267 years. (This is illustrated in Exhibit 1-6.) As the risk-free rate changes by 100 basis points, one would expect a gain or loss (depending on the direction of rates) of 4.267 percent (4.267 × .01), or $4,267,000 (.04267 × $100 million). In actuality, Exhibit 1-1 illustrated a change of +$4,375,932 for a decrease in rates, and a change of -$4,158,304 for an increase in rates. An understanding of duration (discussed next) provides an explanation for the difference in these price changes.

Duration Illustrations

Exhibit 1-7 shows how to calculate both Macaulay duration and modified duration for a five-year Treasury note.

Exhibit 1-7 Macaulay Duration, 5-Year Treasury Note, 6 Percent Yield to Maturity.

Period (n)	Cash Flow	PV of Cash Flow @ 6 %	(n)(PV)
1	3	2.91	2.91
2	3	2.83	5.66
3	3	2.75	8.25
4	3	2.67	10.68
5	3	2.59	12.95
6	3	2.51	15.06
7	3	2.44	17.08
8	3	2.37	18.96
9	3	2.30	20.70
10	103	76.63	766.40
		100.00	878.65

Macaulay duration in periods = sum of the (n)(PV)/bond price = $878.65/100 = 8.79 periods
Macaulay duration in years = duration in periods/periods per year = 8.79/2 = 4.395 years
Modified duration = Macaulay duration in years/ (1 + periodic interest yield) = 4.395/1.03 = 4.267

One can expect that for a 100-basis-point shift in the yield curve, the Treasury note will gain or lose approximately 4.267 percent in price; for a 200-basis-point shift in the yield curve, the Treasury note will gain or lose approximately 8.534 percent in price.

Exhibit 1-8 illustrates how to calculate duration and modified duration for a higher coupon bond. Note the lower duration of 3.956, as compared with the five-year Treasury note above (duration of 4.267). This difference in duration is caused by the effect of the B-quality bond's higher coupon.

Duration concepts are important in the evaluation of hedging strategies. For example, Appendix F (located after Chapter 7) provides examples of hedging the benchmark risk-free rate using hedge ratios that are determined based on duration.

Duration versus Convexity

As discussed above, modified duration measures the sensitivity of the price of a bond to changes in interest rates. Although the rates of different maturities can change in complicated ways, it is assumed in the following analysis that the entire yield curve shifts by a uniform amount, Δr, for all maturities, where r equals the yield to maturity.

The modified duration of a bond is defined as follows:

$$D_M = \frac{D}{1+r}$$

Exhibit 1-8   Macaulay Duration, 5-Year B-Quality Bond, 9 Percent Yield to Maturity.

Period (n)	Cash Flow	PV of Cash Flow @ 9 %	(n)(PV)
1	4.5	4.31	4.31
2	4.5	4.12	8.24
3	4.5	3.94	11.82
4	4.5	3.77	15.08
5	4.5	3.61	18.05
6	4.5	3.46	20.76
7	4.5	3.31	23.17
8	4.5	3.16	25.28
9	4.5	3.03	27.27
10	104.5	67.29	672.90
		100.00	826.88

Macaulay duration in periods = sum of the (n)(PV)/bond price = $826.88/100 = 8.27 periods
Macaulay duration in years = duration in periods/periods per year = 8.27/2 = 4.135 years
Modified duration = Macaulay duration in years/(1 + periodic interest yield) = 4.135/1.045 = 3.956

Where:
• D = the duration of the bond
• r = its yield to maturity

Modified duration[8] adequately measures the percentage rate of change in a bond's price for a small shift in yields. If one were to graph the price of the bond as a function of its yield to maturity, the slope of the resulting curve should be shown as $- P \times D_M = -$ (Price) × (Modified Duration). This is illustrated in Exhibit 1-9. (Note that this diagram applies primarily to noncallable bonds.)

Suppose that the yield curve shifts so that the yield to maturity of the bond changes from r to r + Δr (that is, from r_1 to r_2). If the change in yield is small, the straight line drawn tangent to the price curve in Exhibit 1-9 is a very good approximation of the actual price curve, and the new bond price is approximately P − Δr(−P)(D_M); where Δr = r_1−r_2.

Note, however, that the actual change in the bond's price is depicted along the curve and not the straight line. Thus, for larger percentage changes in yield, the change in price estimated using the modified duration formula (− Δr(−P)(D_M), indicated along the straight line in Exhibit 1-9, will produce increasingly larger errors.

The differences between the actual change in a bond's price (P) and the estimate based on modified duration are caused by the fact that the graph of (P)

Exhibit 1-9 Noncallable Bond Price-Yield Relationship.

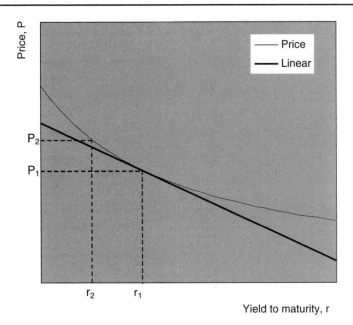

against the yield is curved or convex. Therefore, the straight line drawn tangent to any price on the curve is only a good approximation of the curve for very small changes in yield. One can get a better estimate for the change in the price of the bond if *convexity* is taken into account.

Convexity

Instead of explaining the rather complex formula for *convexity* here,[9] convexity can be thought of as the percentage rate of change of dollar duration (i.e., of the quantity (Price) × (Modified Duration)) for a given change in yield. It can be shown, using calculus, that the quantity (i.e., PC = (Price of a bond) × Convexity)) represents the rate at which the slope of the straight line that is tangent to the curve in Exhibit 1-9 changes as yields change. The convexity can be used to determine a quadratic curve that approximates the bond's price curve more accurately than the tangent line for a wider range of changes in yield.

Those ideas can be summarized to involve duration and convexity in the following formula to calculate a percentage change in a bond's price in response to changes in the risk-free rate, as follows:

The duration- and convexity-based bond price approximation is:

$$\% \text{ Price change} = \Delta r(D_M) + \frac{1}{2}(C)(\Delta r)^2$$

Where:
- P = the current bond price at yield to maturity y
- D_M = modified duration
- C = convexity
- Δr = the change in yield, positive for an increase in yield or negative for a decrease and expressed as a decimal, not as a percentage
- P^+ = the bond price after the shift

Therefore, if a bond's duration is five and its convexity is 15 and interest rates increased 200 basis points, the expected interest rate–related price change is calculated as:

$$.02(-5) + \frac{1}{2}(15)(.02)^2 = -9.7 \text{ percent}$$

To hedge a bond or portfolio of bonds successfully, one should hedge the convexity in addition to the duration, particularly in volatile interest rate environments. (Note that if one only uses duration, the change would have been -10 percent. In this case, the positive convexity minimized the loss.)

Concept Checks

Question: What is the Macaulay duration of a five-year noncallable zero-coupon bond and a five-year bond paying LIBOR with a semiannual rate reset?

Answer: The Macaulay duration of a noncallable zero-coupon bond is equal to its term, in this case five years, because no cash flows occur during the term of the bond. As a result, this type of bond has the highest sensitivity to interest rate changes. This is advantageous from a bondholder's viewpoint as rates drop. In contrast, a three-month LIBOR instrument has a duration of nearly zero because the rate frequently resets to market interest rates.

Question: Fixed-income asset and liability portfolio managers also use duration as a tool to manage price sensitivity related to interest rate changes.

Immunization strategies track and match asset and liability durations to eliminate the effects of interest rate volatility. As long as a portfolio's asset and liability durations are equal, the portfolio's net assets will not change in market value (excluding credit risk considerations) as interest rates change, since the asset and liability market value changes will offset each other. If management's policy was to eliminate a portfolio's interest rate exposure and the duration of the portfolio of assets was shorter than the duration of the portfolio of liabilities, what are possible actions to match the durations?

Answer: Because the assets (in this example) are less price sensitive to interest rate movements than the liabilities, the portfolio manager needs to lengthen the asset duration or shorten the liability duration. The portfolio manager could enter into a receive-fixed interest rate swap or a long position in Treasury note futures contracts to lengthen duration based on a calculated contract term and level of notional principal. (Swap characteristics are explained in Chapter 7.)

Question: What is negative convexity and what type of securities in the 1990s surprised analysts with higher than expected negative convexity?

Answer: Negative convexity refers to the event in which appreciation of fixed-income securities (most notably, mortgage-backed securities) does not occur as interest rates decline. This is generally caused by embedded prepayment options in the loan terms that permit borrowers to prepay their principal prior to the loan's contractual maturity. During the 1990s, mortgage-backed securities experienced unplanned principal repayments as interest rates declined. Therefore, those securities did not appreciate in value. This caused large losses at certain institutions that planned on meeting fixed-liability cash outflows by earning higher returns from mortgaged-backed security investments. This topic is covered in Chapter 4.

Exhibit 1-10 illustrates the difference in price changes of noncallable and callable bonds as interest rates change.

Exhibit 1-10 Difference in Price Changes of Noncallable and Callable Bonds as Interest Rates Change.

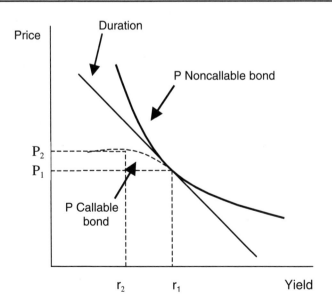

Notice how the price of the callable bonds does not increase significantly as interest rates decrease from r_1 to r_2, due to the call feature. That is, as interest rates fall, the issuer will eventually utilize the call option and recall the bond, thus limiting the investor's potential gain. In contrast, the noncallable bond has significant price appreciation as rates decrease. Investment analysts price the bonds to compensate the investor for assuming this call option risk. This pricing may be accomplished using option models that consider prepayments as rates change (discussed in Chapter 2).

Duration and Convexity Concepts Useful for Accounting Applications

Hedging

One key use of duration is its application to fixed-income instrument hedging strategies. The duration (price sensitivity) of the hedged item and of the hedging instrument are used to formulate a hedge ratio. The hedge ratio determines the quantity of the hedging instrument that is required to offset price changes in the hedged item. This topic is discussed and illustrated later in Chapter 7.

Reasonableness Check of Prices

Accountants involved in reviewing fixed-income investments may use duration as a reasonableness check of the portfolio or bond price change from period to period. For example, assume that a $100 million portfolio with a duration of 4.267 lost $10 million during a period in which interest rates increased 100 basis points. It may be assumed that approximately $4 million of the loss was due to changes in the yield, while the $6 million loss resulted from other causes, such as credit deterioration. If the client cannot explain the change, perhaps a pricing error occurred.

CONCLUDING REMARKS

The pricing concepts discussed in this chapter are applied to pricing certain fixed-income instruments and decomposing market yields through several methodologies, which are discussed in Chapter 2. A private-placement bond quality ratings process is also explained.

NOTES

1. A portion of an earlier version of this chapter is available on the FASB website and in the FASB derivative training course on FASB Statement No. 133, *Accounting for Derivative Instruments and Hedging Activities.* Available at *www.fasb.org.*

2. Words defined in the Glossary at the end of this book are set in *italic type* the first time they appear.

3. Gretchen Morgenson. "Shrinking Treasury Debt Creates Uncertain World, *New York Times,* February 22, 2000. Available online at *www.nytimes.com/00/02/17/news/financial/treasuryplace.html* [February 24, 2000].

4. Portions of the following discussion dealing with the spot yield curve were adopted from Deloitte & Touch LLP, *Financial Instruments: Fair Value Considerations—Implementing SFAS 107* (New York: Deloitte & Touche LLP, 1996).

5. In theory, various explanations exist for the shape and steepness of the yield curve (e.g., the market segmentation theory, where investors have a demand for certain term investments, such as 10 years).

6. To access the demo of this application, one must register with fincad.com. Once you have accessed the fincad homepage, click on "Manage Financial Instruments on Excel" and then click "Download Now." Download "fincad.xl." Once this is complete, you can find the above information by clicking "Term Structure Model."

7. Bill Miller of the Federal Home Loan Bank provided this schedule. For a complete explanation of Eurodollar futures contract pricing, refer to *Eurodollar Futures and Options* by Burghardt, Belton, Cane, Luce, and McVey (New York: McGraw-Hill Publishing, 1991).

8. Portions of this discussion were provided by Thomas Hewett of Deloitte & Touche LLP, Capital Markets Group.

9. $C = \dfrac{1}{P(1+r)^2}\left(T_1(T_1+1)V(F_1) + T_2(T_2+1)PV(F_2) + \ldots + T_N(T_N+1)PV(F_N)\right)$

Calculation of U.S. Treasury Bond Yield Curve

Benchmark Bonds

date adjustment | next good business day

This data is input and calculated on the sheet "Bond List"

Must be in ascending date order	Settle Date	Maturity Date	Coupon	Clean Price	Accrued	Yield
6.125 US TR NT01	16-Feb-2000	31-Dec-2001	6.125%	99.15625	0.79087	6.60635%
5.875 US TR NTS 2004	16-Feb-2000	15-Nov-2004	5.875%	96.73438	1.50103	6.68658%
6 US TR NT 2009	16-Feb-2000	15-Aug-2009	6.000%	95.39063	0.01648	6.66272%
6.125 US TR BD 2029	16-Feb-2000	15-Aug-2029	6.125%	96.81250	0.01683	6.36582%
None						
None						
None						
None						
None						
None						
None						
None						
None						
None						
None						
None						
None						
None						
None						
None						
None						
None						
None						

Source: "Integrated Zero Coupon US Treasury Bond Curve Calculator" has been printed from fincad™ XL by Permission of FinancialCAD® Corporation, Copyright © 1991–1999. For more information, visit *www.fincad.com* or telephone 1-800-304-0702.

(continued)

Integrated discount factor and Spot Rate curve

Grid dates	Discount factors	spot rate
15-Feb-2000	1.000000	6.6926%
30-Jun-2000	0.976151	6.6926%
02-Jan-2001	0.944453	6.6926%
02-Jul-2001	0.914595	6.6926%
31-Dec-2001	0.885524	6.6926%
15-May 2002	0.863979	6.7244%
15-Nov-2002	0.835566	6.7490%
15-May-2003	0.808528	6.7657%
17-Nov-2003	0.781654	6.7782%
17-May-2004	0.756223	6.7876%
15-Nov-2004	0.731619	6.7950%
15-Feb-2005	0.719958	6.7843%
15-Aug-2005	0.697017	6.7810%
15-Feb-2006	0.674444	6.7783%
15-Aug-2006	0.652953	6.7760%
15-Feb-2007	0.631808	6.7740%
15-Aug-2007	0.611675	6.7723%
15-Feb-2008	0.591867	6.7708%
15-Aug-2008	0.572904	6.7695%
17-Feb-2009	0.554153	6.7683%
17-Aug-2009	0.536495	6.7673%
16-Feb-2010	0.520743	6.7350%
16-Aug-2010	0.505618	6.7060%
15-Feb-2011	0.490772	6.6795%
15-Aug-2011	0.476518	6.6555%
15-Feb-2012	0.462451	6.6331%
15-Aug-2012	0.448946	6.6128%
15-Feb-2013	0.435694	6.5938%
15-Aug-2013	0.423039	6.5765%
18-Feb-2014	0.410350	6.5599%
15-Aug-2014	0.398626	6.5453%
17-Feb-2015	0.386733	6.5309%
17-Aug-2015	0.375501	6.5179%
16-Feb-2016	0.364475	6.5056%
15-Aug-2016	0.353889	6.4941%
15-Feb-2017	0.343443	6.4831%
15-Aug-2017	0.333467	6.4729%
15-Feb-2018	0.323624	6.4631%
15-Aug-2018	0.314224	6.4540%
15-Feb-2019	0.304948	6.4453%
15-Aug-2019	0.296091	6.4371%

Integrated discount factor and Spot Rate curve

Grid dates	Discount factors	spot rate
18-Feb-2020	0.287210	6.4291%
17-Aug-2020	0.278868	6.4217%
16-Feb-2021	0.270680	6.4146%
16-Aug-2021	0.262818	6.4079%
15-Feb-2022	0.255102	6.4014%
15-Aug-2022	0.247692	6.3953%
15-Feb-2023	0.240381	6.3894%
15-Aug-2023	0.233399	6.3838%
15-Feb-2024	0.226509	6.3783%
15-Aug-2024	0.219894	6.3731%
18-Feb-2025	0.213299	6.3680%
15-Aug-2025	0.207205	6.3634%
17-Feb-2026	0.201023	6.3587%
17-Aug-2026	0.195184	6.3543%
16-Feb-2027	0.189453	6.3500%
16-Aug-2027	0.183950	6.3459%
15-Feb-2028	0.178549	6.3420%
15-Aug-2028	0.173335	6.3381%
15-Feb-2029	0.168218	6.3344%
15-Aug-2029	0.163333	6.3309%

Eurodollar Futures Yields

```
<HELP> for explanation.                              DG21 Comdty CT
<PAGE> now scrolls 17 contracts.     Enter # <GO> to scroll contracts.
Session:D                    Contract Table
90DAY  EURO$  FUTR
   Exchange N              Pricing Date: 9/15/99      Price Display: 2
Chicago Mercantile Exchange                          --AS REPORTED 9/15 --      1
Grey date = options trading                          2753411 477657
   Symbol   Last  2Pct Chg  Time   Bid 1 Ask    Tic OpenInt TotVol         Open
 1]EDV9 Oct99 94.0425s unch  Close 94.043 94.045  397  .45302   7528       94.0300
 2]EDX9 Nov99 94.0500s +.01% Close 94.045 94.050  114    5726    232       94.0550
 3]EDZ9 Dec99 94.050s  unch  Close 94.045 94.050  860  530400  76840       94.040
 4]EDF0 Jan00 94.255s  +.02% Close 94.255 94.270  183    5866    367       94.230
 5]EDG0 Feb00 94.165s  +.01% Close 94.165 94.180   67     353    100
 6]EDH0 Mar00 94.115s  +.05% Close 94.115 94.120 1677  460805 129660       94.070
 7]EDJ0 Apr00                                             0       0
 8]EDM0 Jun00 93.935s  +.07% Close 93.935 93.940 1506  305719  84085       93.865
 9]EDU0 Sep00 93.800s  +.09% Close 93.800 93.805 1589  224765  56238       93.715
10]EDZ0 Dec00 93.635s  +.11% Close 93.635 93.640  972  195218  23798       93.530
11]EDH1 Mar01 93.640s  +.11% Close 93.640 93.645  667  139305  20823       93.540
12]EDM1 Jun01 93.560s  +.11% Close 93.560 93.565  454  112467  13168       93.455
13]EDU1 Sep01 93.515s  +.11% Close 93.510 93.515  435   84697  12071       93.405
14]EDZ1 Dec01 93.405s  +.11% Close 93.395           61   84098   6603       93.305
15]EDH2 Mar02 93.420s  +.10% Close 93.410           46   74658   6259       93.325
16]EDM2 Jun02 93.360s  +.10% Close                  52   56073   6192       93.270
17]EDU2 Sep02 93.315s  +.09% Close 93.315           43   53524   6366       93.230
Copyright 1999 BLOOMBERG L.P.  Frankfurt:69-620410  Hong Kong:2-977-6000  London:171-330-7500  New York:212-318-2000
Princeton:609-279-3000   Singapore:226-3000   Sydney:2-9777-8686   Tokyo:3-3201-8900   Sao Paulo:11-3048-4500
                                                            I643-14-1 20-Oct-99 12:45:13
```

```
<HELP> for explanation.                               DG21 Comdty CT
<PAGE> now scrolls 17 contracts.     Enter # <GO> to scroll contracts.
Session:D                    Contract Table
90DAY EURO$ FUTR
   Exchange N          Pricing Date: 9/15/99     Price Display: 2
Chicago Mercantile Exchange                      —AS REPORTED 8/15 —        I
Grey date = options trading                      2753411 477657
   Symbol      Last   2Pct Chg Time   Bid 1  Ask   Tic OpenInt TotVol    Open
 1 EDZ2 Dec02  93.205s  +.09% Close 93.195        53   53045   3468    93.115
 2 EDH3 Mar03  93.215s  +.08% Close               49   51593   3899    93.145
 3 EDM3 Jun03  93.160s  +.08% Close               49   41741   3295    93.080
 4 EDU3 Sep03  93.120s  +.08% Close               52   45761   3984    93.040
 5 EDZ3 Dec03  93.000s  +.07% Close 93.000        48   26891   2375    92.940
 6 EDH4 Mar04  93.000s  +.07% Close 93.000        44   27026   2691    92.935
 7 EDM4 Jun04  92.935s  +.06% Close               39   20611   2500    92.875
 8 EDU4 Sep04  92.885s  +.06% Close        92.890 42   12557   2766    92.830
 9 EDZ4 Dec04  92.775s  +.06% Close 92.750        25   13568    132
10 EDH5 Mar05  92.775s  +.06% Close 92.750        25   10392    212
11 EDM5 Jun05  92.725s  +.06% Close 92.700        24    9322    132
12 EDU5 Sep05  92.685s  +.06% Close 92.685        23    7884    237    92.680
13 EDZ5 Dec05  92.580s  +.06% Close 92.555        20    5459    203
14 EDH6 Mar06  92.580s  +.06% Close 92.555        20    5642    203
15 EDM6 Jun06  92.530s  +.05% Close 92.510        20    4708    203
16 EDU6 Sep06  92.495s  +.05% Close 92.475        20    3936    203
17 EDZ6 Dec06  92.395s  +.05% Close 92.375        18    3951     67
```

Bloomberg PROFESSIONAL

Fixed-Income Pricing Matrix and Decomposing Yields

INTRODUCTION

Chapter 2 introduces many pricing concepts that will be used throughout this book and provides an illustration of the process of rating the quality of private-placement bonds. The importance of this ratings process is emphasized, since it determines the risk premiums that should be added to the risk-free rate in estimating an appropriate market discount rate for an investment. As seen in Chapter 1, this required rate of return is used to discount the future cash flows expected from investments in order to estimate their prices.

A framework is provided for determining the discount rate for both public and nonpublic investments through several methodologies. Those discount rates for various fixed-income investments, determined at a specific date, will be used in various pricing illustrations presented throughout this book.

Summary of Cash Flow Characteristics and Determination of Discount Rates by Investment Type

Exhibit 2-1 introduces the types of investments that will be explained and priced throughout this book and summarizes their major characteristics. Compare each investment's cash flow attributes and the components of their discount rates.

Before one reviews the ratings processes, one should understand that a significant portion of this book is devoted to fixed-income investments because those types of investments make up a large percentage of institutional investor assets. Regulatory capital constraints may limit private and public equity investments. Therefore, the entities may be required to match fixed or predictable liabilities with fixed-income–type assets.

DETERMINING THE DISCOUNT RATE

Discount rates that approximate an effective market yield for a specific investment can be obtained in a number of ways. As discussed briefly in Chapter 1, they

Exhibit 2-1   Investment Valuation Characteristics.

Investment Type	Cash Flow Characteristics	Method of Estimating Cash Flows in DCF Model	Discount Rate Comprising the Following
Fixed-rate, noncallable public corporate bonds, private-placement bonds (excluding asset-backed), and whole commercial mortgage loans	Contractually determined per note agreement, such as 7 percent semiannual coupon, principal due at maturity	Follow note's contractual terms	The risk-free rate applicable to investment term adjusted for credit and sector risk, special features, and certain expenses
Fixed-rate, public corporate bonds, and private placement bonds with stated call provisions, and in the case of private placements, sinking fund-requirements	Variable—depending on issuer's exercise of call options	Follow note's terms and determine an expected average life depending on estimates of cash flows after considering call options	The risk-free rate applicable to investment term adjusted for credit and sector risk, special features, and certain expenses
Mortgage-pass-through securities	Variable—depending on prepayments and, in some investments, credit losses	Determine an expected average life using analysts' models estimating expected cash flows without adjustment for credit losses	The risk-free rate applicable to investment term adjusted for prepayment and credit risk (credit risk does not apply if federally sponsored)
Collateralized mortgage obligations and asset-backed securities	Variable—depending on prepayments and, in some investments, credit losses	Determine an expected average life using analysts' models and estimating expected cash flows without adjustment for credit losses	The risk-free rate applicable to investment term adjusted for prepayment risk and credit risk (credit risk may not be applicable if federally sponsored programs)
Bonds with monetary default	High risk—extremely variable depending on extent of credit losses	Determined based on analysts' best estimate of recovery	Although this does not represent fair value, in practice, cash flows may not be discounted, and the investment may

Exhibit 2-1   *(continued)*

Investment Type	Cash Flow Characteristics	Method of Estimating Cash Flows in DCF Model	Discount Rate Comprising the Following
			be written down to its expected recovery value and carried as nonearning. However, fair value estimate would require discounting the cash flows at a risk-adjusted rate
Equity investments	Variable—depending on enterprise's free cash flows	Determined based on analysts' best estimates	The risk-free rate adjusted for systematic (undiversifiable risk related to interest rate levels, economic, and other market fluctuations, etc.) and nonsystematic risk, such as company-specific business and credit risk
Derivatives	Variable—depending on changes in underlying variables	Depends on type of instrument	Depends on the risk-free rate and characteristics of derivative instruments

can be constructed by building each component of the rate, starting with the benchmark risk-free rate and then adding risk premiums and other spread factors. The Treasury-yield curve or LIBOR *swap* rate frequently is used as a starting point in the selection (or estimation) of a discount rate because each is considered to be risk free (with respect to credit or default risk and other firm-specific uncertainties). Certain security yield spreads over Treasuries can be obtained directly from market interest rates of comparable public corporate bonds. Public corporate and government bond information is provided by various services, such as *Bloomberg* or *The YIELDBOOK.* For example, the bottom chart in Exhibit 2-2 illustrates that over a 10-year period, the 10-year, A-1 quality-rated financial-sector public corporate bonds were priced between a range of 53 to 190 basis points over 10-year Treasury notes.

Exhibit 2-2　　Historical Yields on A-1, Medium Term, Public Corporate Debt and Comparable Term Treasury Notes.

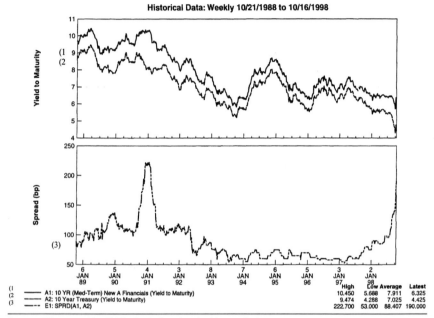

Source: File created by Philip Spak. Reprinted with permission.

　　Exhibit 2-2 provides historical yields on 10-year, A-1 rated public corporate bonds and identical-term Treasury notes. It is important to observe that the top chart is not a yield curve but rather a chart illustrating yields at different points in time applicable to an A-1 rated public corporate bond from the financial sector and a similar-term Treasury note. In contrast, a yield curve illustrates yields applicable to the same security type with different terms, observed at a point in time. Review Exhibit 1-2 if this is unclear.

What Factors Explain the Spread over Treasuries to Arrive at the A-1 Rated Bond Yield?

A bond's yield includes a return equal to the risk-free rate, in addition to risk premiums for factors such as credit, sector, and the bond's unique characteristics. Sector risk premiums relate to the entire industry that the entity is in, such as the financial or automotive sector. Credit spreads relate to the entity-specific default risk premium applicable to credit rating. Unique characteristics relate to call features, conversion privileges, and other factors that affect yield. Consider the following price-yield spread relationships as applied to pricing an investment:

- An increasing yield spread above the risk-free rate has the effect of decreasing a bond's price because contractual cash flows are discounted at higher required market yields (or discount rates). A narrowing spread has the effect of increasing a bond's price because the contractual cash flows are being discounted at a lower discount rate and, thus, have higher present values. (Exhibit 1-1 illustrates this effect.)
- The credit risk premium for higher-quality rated bonds is lower, relative to the risk premium charged for lower-quality bonds. Therefore, purchasers of lower-quality bonds demand a higher total yield because of the higher required risk premium to compensate for the higher default risk.

A bond quality-ratings process can be used to estimate the default-risk premiums specific to a certain investment. It is imperative to understand this process in order to apply these concepts to nonpublicly traded bond pricing. Similar principles also will be applied to equity valuations, which are analyzed later. Further discussions also will include the factors that independent credit-rating agencies utilize in arriving at entity-specific credit ratings that may be used to estimate default-risk premiums. Those factors generally pertain to the entity's ability to honor its debt service requirements. Credit ratings are a key indicator of credit risk and drive the amount of credit-risk premium spread over the benchmark risk-free rate of interest (often Treasuries).

CREDIT RATING CATEGORIES AND DETERMINATION

Independent rating agencies rate public and certain private debt to provide an assessment of an entity's creditworthiness. The credit rating is a significant factor in determining the entity-specific credit yield spread required to be added to the risk-free rate for pricing purposes (in addition to such features as liquidity, sector or minority groups, and name recognition). Most private-placement loans and all commercial mortgage loans are internally rated by the lender without the benefit of public ratings. The methodologies that may be used in this process are discussed below. The following table summarizes two nationally recognized rating agency categories.[1]

Credit Rating Categories

	S&P	Moody's
Investment grade:		
Highest rating, strongest ability to pay interest and principal	Aaa	AAA
Very strong capacity to pay debt service	Aa2	AA
Strong capacity to pay interest and principal	A2	A
Adequate capacity to pay interest and principal	Baa2	BBB

	S&P	Moody's
Noninvestment grades (high yields):		
Speculative characteristics regarding ability to pay interest and principal	Ba2	BB
Currently identifiable vulnerability to default	Caa	CCC

Each of these categories has subcategories that may include a plus (+) or minus (–) sign to show the relative standing within the category. The ratings consider only the borrower's ability to repay the principal and interest, not the risk of early repayment due to interest rate changes. Ratings are driven by a multitude of factors, and different rating agencies may use different approaches. To reinforce the relationship of credit premiums and bond quality ratings, review Exhibit 2-3, which illustrates increasing credit premiums as bond quality decreases. Also notice that as the term increases, the spread over Treasuries increases due to increasing interest rate risk and the upward-sloping shape of the yield curve (that existed at this time).

The bond credit ratings process is a combination of qualitative and quantitative methods. Important considerations in bond ratings are the analyst's view of items, such as:

- Quality of management
- The operating plan, including cash flow and net income projections

Exhibit 2-3

COMPARISON OF RECENT CREDIT PREMIUMS OVER VARIOUS TREASURY MATURITIES
(Basis-Point Average Credit Spread)

	AAA	AA	A	BBB	BB+	BB/BB-
			September 1999			
1-Year	35	40	78	132	243	304
5-Year	89	106	133	187	301	327
10-Year	110	133	154	209	325	336
			June 1999			
	AAA	AA	A	BBB	BB+	BB/BB-
1-Year	26	37	65	111	200	260
5-Year	68	85	109	155	258	295
10-Year	87	105	128	173	282	310
			September 1998			
	AAA	AA	A	BBB	BB+	BB/BB-
1-Year	54	56	73	102	154	252
5-Year	79	98	118	156	216	365
10-Year	88	114	135	176	240	411

Note: Data as of month end. Some measurement error may occur because of differing sampling rates (daily for Treasuries versus weekly for corporate bonds).

Source: DRI McGraw-Hill; Banc of America Securities LLC.

- The competitive environment in the industry sector
- Industry environmental issues
- Entity market share
- Planned capital expenditures
- Financial ratio analysis

Bond Credit Ratings Process Illustrated

To bring all those factors together and arrive at a quality or credit rating, examples of rating grids used by a private-placement investment rating department have been provided (Exhibits 2-4 through 2-9).[2] Recognize that many fixed-income instruments are not rated by a public rating agency. Therefore, one must understand the type of process that investment analysts use to arrive at quality ratings. This process will vary depending on the preferences of different investment departments. This type of process also is used to arrive at a quality rating that is then compared with public ratings, if they are available. An analyst then may try to determine why the quality ratings are different and, at times, use the lower quality rating for pricing decisions.

Exhibit 2-4 outlines the actions required to complete each step in the analysis in order to evaluate and rate each investment. Exhibits 2-5 through 2-9 illustrate rating grids applicable to the industrial and retail industries and differentiate between investment-grade and noninvestment-grade investments. Analysts' rating grids and processes to derive at bond quality ratings vary because the ratings process involves weighing many factors and exercising judgment as to how they impact the overall rating. An understanding of those factors that affect credit ratings may be difficult to conceptualize because there are many entity-specific financial factors to consider. Furthermore, a standard set of ratios or other indicators available to automatically classify an entity into a certain rating category does not exist. In addition, a forward-looking approach is needed to determine an entity's future financial performance, taking into account all the above factors. A methodology called a *matrix approach* permits adjusting a bond's quality rating for factors, in addition to financial ratios, calculated using historical financial information. (Certain bond indenture terms that are used are fully explained in Chapter 3.)

Information related to public rating agency ratings is available from the rating agencies. For example, Standard & Poor's monthly publication, *Credit Week,* provides this type of information. The credit profile in Exhibit 2-10 was prepared by Philip Schank, regarding an upgrade on the EMC Corp. credit rating.

As illustrated by the above private and public bond rating processes, key quality-rating determinants are obtained through a thorough understanding of sources and quality of an entity's cash flows and the quality and integrity of its management. That type of information is gathered by interviewing with the management, having a complete understanding of the business, tracking down the sources of cash flows, and assessing future changes that may impact the business.

Exhibit 2-4   Private-Placement Underwriting Process.

A.   Underwriting Focus on Procedures

Prior to any loan transaction being recommended, an exhaustive study (frequently four weeks in length) is conducted by the assigned staff member. Each underwriting step is part of an integrated credit risk assessment. Individual or incomplete procedures by themselves can lead to vastly incorrect conclusions. Consequently, each step is part of an assessment methodology and a formal comprehensive report is the final product. At a minimum, the basic underwriting procedures would include the following:

1. *Evaluation of Industry Risk.* What is the strength of the industry within the economy and the current economic cycle? Is the industry stable, declining, volatile, capital intensive, regulated or deregulated? Does the industry require heavy fixed capital investment (Steel Industry) or is it driven by receivables, inventory, or high service?

2. *Borrower's Market Position.* The borrower's historical market position is evaluated, the protection of its market position is considered, and the borrower is compared to its primary competitors. The borrower's operating efficiency is critical (i.e., high cost/low cost producer).

3. *Management Evaluation.* Each analysis includes a one- to two-day face-to-face meeting with the borrower's senior management to include a detailed discussion of past performance, the planning process, and a detailed review of the borrower's financial statement to include, at a minimum, a five-year historical income statement, balance sheet, source and application of funds, and projections with full assumptions for at least three years. All financial statements must be audited and include footnotes.

4. *Accounting Quality.* A close analysis reveals understated or overstated performance and industry norms. In many cases, a meeting with the borrower's auditors is required.

5. *Financial Ratio Analysis.* As one part of the overall risk assessment, industry specialization allows the use of rating grids to numerically capture the general credit quality of a borrower, based on audited financial statements. Those grids are used in addition to numerous qualitative factors. Rating grids vary greatly by industry.

   However, the objective is to measure, at a minimum, the following financial characteristics of a borrower:

   - Earning protection through a fixed charge coverage of interest
   - Leverage and asset protection through capitalization ratios of various classes of debt
   - Cash flow adequacy to service debt and meet capital budgets
   - Profitability through operating margin and return on capital
   - Staying power and financial flexibility

Source: Private-Placement Underwriting Process (Kenneth D. Anderson, Private Placements, Connecticut Mutual Life Insurance Co.).

Exhibit 2-4 *(continued)*

In all cases, rating grids are utilized by the staff to measure credit risk. The rating grids are subject to change because of the annual dynamics that impact all industries. Also, some industries (electric utilities, telephone, gas transmission and distribution, airlines, and transportation) are presently rated to a large degree by the rating agencies. In those cases, initially accept the rating agencies rating unless it is believed that the rating should be lower; then, for purposes of analysis, the company will be rated lower. In no cases will a company be rated higher than its recognized agency rating.

The attached exhibits contain rating grids for the following industries:

- Exhibit 2-5 Industrials
- Exhibit 2-7 Retailing

6. *Loan Documentation.* Each investment is documented by internal and external legal counsel. Although this is a legal function, the business financial covenants are structured by the Staff in negotiations with the borrower with the conceptual objective of controlling credit risk.

Covenants are generally structured to capture a borrower's existing credit quality. In most cases, the following financial covenants are viewed as favorable:

- Negative pledge
- Debt maintenance
- Cash flow maintenance

B. Credit-Watch Process

Monthly. Credits that are on or candidates for the watch list, potential problem loans, or problem loan lists are contacted at least monthly to ascertain their condition and progress toward meeting established goals.

Monthly financials, if applicable, are reviewed and variances from the projected budget are analyzed.

Quarterly. For each quarter, financials are analyzed to verify adherence to covenants, determine trends, and identify areas for further discussion with management. Calculations of standard ratios and the A-Score Probability of Financial Difficulty are used to facilitate the financial analysis.

Biannual. A comprehensive review of each credit is performed biannually, including visits with management to discuss projections, business plans, and financial needs. Particular emphasis is placed on factors that could impact the timely repayment of outstanding principal.

C. Sector Analysis

Biannual. Top-down sector review of major investment sectors. Review to include review of sector characteristics, issues/risks, and key success factors.

Annual. Portfolio review of private portfolio to include a detailed discussion of each credit to identify emerging upgrades/downgrades, sectors of opportunity, and shifts in investment strategy.

Exhibit 2-5 applies those concepts to an industrial bond credit rating analysis.

Exhibit 2-5   Industrial Rating Grid.

A. Introduction

Unlike other industry specific grids, the Industrial Grid requires even more reliance on qualitative factors by the investment officer in that hundreds of different subindustries by necessity become combined into a single rating system. As an example, the Grid considers $3 billion sales to be a major strength. For a hearing aid manufacturer, $3 billion in sales would be a monopoly position, but for an auto company it would indicate a marginal competitor. Similarly, a higher debt to capitalization ratio is more acceptable in a stable business than a cyclical one.

B. Investment Grade Rating Grid

The Investment Grade Industrial Rating Grid considers size, profitability, leverage, and cash flow as rating criteria. More specifically, the grid determines its rating by calculating the arithmetic average of the points assigned the following parameters based on a company's financial statements:

1. *Net Sales*—The assumption is made that the larger the company's sales volume, the greater its relative competitive strength as well as financial flexibility.
2. *Debt Ratio (long-term debt/long-term debt plus equity)*—A traditional measure of financial leverage comparing long-term debt to total capitalization. The greater the percentage of the debt, the more vulnerable the company is to operating declines, and the less the creditors receive in a liquidation.
3. *Total Debt Ratio (long-debt plus short term debt/long-term debt, short-term debt, and equity)*—A second leverage ratio that reflects the use by most companies of a portion of short-term debt for long-term needs.
4. *Interest Coverage (earnings before interest and taxes/interest)*—A key indicator of borrower's ability to service debt.
5. *Cash Flow to Long-term Debt (net income, depreciation, amortization and deferred taxes/long term debt)*—An additional measure of the borrower's ability to service debt with an adjustment for noncash charges.
6. *Operating Profit Margin (operating earnings/sales)*—A measure of a firm's profitability in relationship to its long-term capitalization.

    After calculating the composite rating based on the average of the above factors, the grid provides an adjusted rating that reflects the relative ratings of items 2, 3, and 4 versus the other ratings.

Source: Private-Placement Underwriting Process (Kenneth D. Anderson, Private Placements, Connecticut Mutual Life Insurance Co.).

Exhibit 2-5   *(continued)*

Example: *XYZ Company*

		Points
Net Sales	$24 billion	10[a]
Debt Ratio	32.3%	7
Total Debt Ratio	37.4	8
Interest Coverage	6.5×	8
Cash Flow/Long Term Debt	65.0%	7
Operating Profit Margin	11.9%	8
Return on Capital	14.4%	10
Average Points		8.3

Composite Rating: A-1   Adjusted Rating: A-2   Moody's: AA   S&P: AA

Qualitative factors such as product lines, competitive position, earnings stability, management ability, production capacity, labor history, regulatory environment, lack of technological risk, etc., could all account for Moody's higher rating.

C. Noninvestment-grade Rating Grid

The Noninvestment Ratings Grid is very similar to the Investment Grid with a greater emphasis on preferred stock and cash flow.

1. *Net Sales*—See above.
2. *Total Debt Ratio*—Same as #3 above except preferred stock is treated as debt.
3. *Interest Coverage*—Same as #4 above except preferred stock is treated as interest expense.
4. *Gross Cash Flow Interest Coverage (net income, depreciation, deferred taxes, and amortization/interest expense)*—Since earnings are lower for weaker credits, total cash flow becomes a more likely measure of the ability to repay.
5. *Gross Cash Flow/Total Debt (net income plus depreciation plus deferred taxes plus amortization/long-term debt plus short-term debt plus preferred stock)*—Same as #5 above except preferred stock included.
6. *Gross Cash Flow Profit Margin % (net income before interest, taxes, depreciation, and amortization/sales)*—A profitability measure similar to #6 above except for the addition of noncash charges.
7. *Return on Capital*—A measure of the return as a percentage of invested capital.

[a] Exhibit 2-6 illustrates point scoring.

Exhibit 2-6 Industrial Investment Grading Grid.

Rating	Points	Net Sales (000,000's)	Debt Ratio % LTD / LTD+SE	Total Debt Ratio % LTD+STD / LTD+STD+SE	Interest Coverage X's EBIT / Int	Cash Flow to LTD % N1+Dep+DefTax+Amort / Ltd	Op. Profit Margin % *Operating Earn/Sales	ROC% NI / LTD+SE
AAA/Aaa	10	>3,000	<20.0	<32.0	9.0X	>100	>15.0	>13
AA/aa	9	2,500-3,000	20-25	32-37	7.5-9.0	80-100	12-15	11-13
A-1/A+	8	1,750-2,500	25-29	37-41	6.0-7.5	65-80	10.5-12.0	10-11
A-2/A	7	1,250-1,750	29-33	41-45	5.0-6.0	50-65	9.5-10.5	9-10
Baa-1/BBB+	6	750-1,250	33-37	45-49	4.0-5.0	35-50	8.5-9.5	8-9
Baa-2/BBB	5	250-750	37-41	49-53	3.0-4.0	25-35	7.5-8.5	7-8
Baa-3/BBB2	4	150-250	41-45	53-57	2.0-3.0	20-25	6.5-7.5	6-7
**Ba/BB	3	<150	>45	>57	<20	<20	<6.5	<6.0

Source: Private-Placement Underwriting Process (Kenneth D. Anderson, Private Placements, Connecticut Mutual Life Insurance Co.).

Industrial Noninvestment-Grading Grid

Rating	Points	Net Sales (1)	Total Debt Ratio % $\frac{LTD+STD+PS(2)}{LTD+STD+PS+SE}$	Interest Coverage X's $\frac{EBIT}{PSDIV+Int}$	Gross Cash Flow Int Cov X's $\frac{CFBIT\ (3)}{Int\ Exp}$	Cash Flow to LTD % $\frac{N1+Dep+DefTaxes+Depl}{LTD+STD+PS}$	Gross Cash Flow Profit Margin % $\frac{CFBIT}{Sales}$
Ba-1/BB+	3	>150	<61	>2.5	>3.0	>25	>20
Ba-2/BB	2	150-100	61-70	1.5-2.5	2.0-3.0	15-25	14-20
B-1/B+	1	100-50	70-100	1.0-1.5	1.0-2.0	5-15	8-14
B-2/B	0	<50	>100	<1.0	<1.0	<5.0	<8

*Excludes Depreciation

**If the composite rating falls into the Ba category, use the noninvestment-grade grid. (1) DO NOT USE Net Sales category for LBO Financings. (2) PS—Preferred Stock (3) CFBIT—Cash flow before interest and taxes.

Composite Rating: Arithmetic average of the seven ratios. If the composite is X5 or above, round up to the higher rating category (i.e., 4.5 = Baa-2); if the composite is X.4 or below, round down to the next lower rating category (i.e., 4.4 = Baa-3).

Adjustment Factor: After figuring composite rating, if ratings for interest coverage, debt ratio, and total debt ratio are higher than the composite rating, round up one rating category (e.g., Baa-1 to A-2); if ratings are lower than the composite rating, round down one category.

43

Exhibit 2-7   Retail Industrial Rating Grid.

A. Introduction

The retail industry includes three broad segments: apparel; general merchandise; and supermarket. In today's environment, good supermarket retailers and discount apparel and general merchandise retailers are continuing to report strong operating results.

Stores are a retailer's most important asset. However, retailers often lease their stores instead of owning them outright. This may result in a relatively unleveraged balance sheet when compared to a retailer that owns many locations. Therefore, when evaluating a retailer we capitalize operating rental expense by a multiple of 8 in order to get a true picture of a retailer's leverage. The definitions of long term debt and total debt include rents $\times$ 8 in the rating grid.

B. Rating Approach/Grid

In addition to the ratios listed below in the rating grid, other factors that help to determine the credit quality of a retailer include: market share position; quality of fixed assets; inventory management; technology; geographic location; and covenant quality. The Retail Rating Grid considers size, profitability, leverage and cash flow as important rating criteria.

1. *Net Sales*—The assumption is made that the larger the company's sales volume, the greater its competitive strength, as well as financial flexibility.

2. *Long-Term Debt Ratio*—A traditional measure of financial leverages comparing long-term debt to total capitalization. The greater the percentage of debt, the more vulnerable a company is to operating declines, and the less creditors receive in a liquidation. Due to the inclusion of operating rents in the debt definition, a retailer can tolerate additional leverage when compared to an industrial credit.

3. *Total Debt Ratio*—A second leverage ratio that reflects the use of a portion of short-term debt for long term needs by many companies.

4. *Fixed Charge Coverage*—A key indicator of the borrower's ability to service debt.

5. *Cash Flow to Long-Term Debt*—An additional measure of the borrower's ability to service debt with an adjustment for noncash charges.

6. *Operating Profit Margin*—A measure of the profitability and operating efficiency of a company. The grocery industry reports lower profit margins than the department store industry but benefits from higher inventory turnover.

7. *Return on Capital*—A measure of a firm's profitability in relationship to its long-term capitalization.

C. Examples

ABC Company

		Points
Net Sales	$22.2 Billion	10
Long Term Debt Ratio	76.6%	2
Total Debt Ratio	76.9%	2
FCC	1.7×	3
CF/LTD	4.1%	2
Operating Margin	3.2%	2
ROIC	3.2%	2
Average		3.3
Internal Rating: Baa3 per grid		

Source: Private-Placement Underwriting Process (Kenneth D. Anderson, Private Placements, Connecticut Mutual Life Insurance Co.).

Exhibit 2-8 Retail Investment Grade Rating Grid.

Rating	Points	Net Sales ($ millions)	Long-Term Debt Ratio (%)	Total Debt Ratio (%)	FCC (×)	CF/LTD (%)	Operating Income Margin (%)	ROIC (%)
Weighting		0.15	0.125	0.125	0.25	0.20	0.075	0.075
Aaa/AAA	10	>5,000	<35	<40	>5.00	>50.0	>15.0	>7.0
Aa/AA	9	4,000-5,000	35-40	40-45	4.25-5.00	40-50	12-15.0	6.5-7.0
A-1/A+	8	3,000-4,000	40-45	45-50	3.50-4.25	30-40	0-12.0	6.25-6.5
A-2/A	7	2,500-3,000	45-50	50-55	2.75-3.50	25-30	9-10.0	6.0-6.25
A-3/A-	6	2,000-2,500	50-55	55-60	2.25-2.75	20-25	8-9.0	5.5-6.0
Baa-1/BBB+	5	1,500-2,000	55-60	60-65	2.00-2.25	15-20	6.0-8.0	5.0-5.5
Baa-2/BBB	4	1,000-1,500	60-70	65-70	1.75-2.00	12.5-15	4.5-6.0	4.5-5.0
Baa-3/BBB-	3	500-1,000	70-75	70-75	1.50-1.75	10.0-12.5	3.5-4.5	4.0-4.5
*Ba/BB	2	<500	>75	>75	<1.50	<10.0	<3.5	<4.0

* If result is less than 2.5, use noninvestment-grade grid below.

Source: Private-Placement Underwriting Process (Kenneth D. Anderson, Private Placements, Connecticut Mutual Life Insurance Co.).

Exhibit 2-9 Retail Noninvestment Grade Rating Grid.

Rating	Points	($ millions) Net Sales	(%) Long-Term Debt Ratio	(%) Total Debt Ratio	(×) FCC	(%) CF/LTD	(%) Operating Income Margin	(%) ROIC
Weighting		0.15	0.125	0.125	0.25	0.20	0.075	0.075
Ba-1/BB+	10	<500	<75	<75	>1.50	<10.0	<3.5	<4.0
Ba-2/BB	9	350-500	78-85	75-85	1.35-1.50	5.0-10.0	3.0-3.5	3.0-4.0
Ba-3/BB-	8	250-350	85-90	85-90	1.20-1.35	2.5-5.0	2.0-3.0	2.0-3.0
B and Below	7	<250	>90	>90	<1.20	<2.5	<2.0	<2.0

Long-Term Debt Ratio: $\dfrac{\text{LTD} + (\text{Rents} \times 8)}{\text{LTD} + (\text{Rents} \times 8) + \text{Net Worth}}$

Total Debt Ratio: Includes short-term debt

FCC: $\dfrac{\text{Pretax Income} + \text{Interest} + \text{Actual Rents}}{\text{Interest} + \text{Actual Rents}}$

CF/LTD: $\dfrac{\text{Pretax Income} + \text{Depreciation} + \text{Amor.}}{\text{LTD} + (\text{Rents} \times 8)}$

Operating Income Margin: $\dfrac{\text{Operating Income}}{\text{Net Sales}}$

ROIC: $\dfrac{\text{Net Income}}{\text{LTD} + (\text{Rent} \times 8) + \text{Net Worth}}$

Source: Private-Placement Underwriting Process (Kenneth D. Anderson, Private Placements, Connecticut Mutual Life Insurance Co.).

Exhibit 2-10

EMC CORP.

Analyst: Philip Schrank, New York (1) 212-438-7859

UPGRADED

CREDIT PROFILE

ISSUER CREDIT RATING

EMC Corp.

Corp credit rtg   BBB+/Stable/—

REVISED RATING

Data General Corp.

Sub debt (Gtd: EMC Corp.)   BBB

March 28, 2000 Standard & Poor's raised the corporate credit rating on EMC Corp. to 'BBB+' from 'BBB'. At the same time, Standard & Poor's raised the rating on Data General Corp.'s subordinated debt, which is guaranteed by parent EMC Corp., to 'BBB' from 'BBB-'.

The ratings upgrade reflects the company's proven track record of execution and its strong business and financial profiles, despite ongoing technology challenges and very competitive industry conditions.

The ratings on EMC reflect the company's solid profitability, conservative capital structure, and strong market position. Hopkinton, Mass.-based EMC manufactures innovative high-performance data storage products. Near-term earnings momentum is expected to remain strong, fueled by new product introductions in the mainframe and open systems environments. Also, the company's expanding installed base enhances earnings stability.

Although EMC's profitability measures are very strong for the rating category, with return on permanent capital averaging above 35% for the past three years, revenues are largely tied to a narrow product line that is vulnerable to market shifts and rapid technological change. Standard & Poor's also anticipates that gross margins, currently in the low-50% area, may moderate over time as similar product offerings become available from larger

competitors, and due to continued price volatility and product mix shifts.

Capital expenditures are expected to remain moderate, in the $400 million area, as the company mostly outsources its key components. Despite its high growth rate, the firm has generated sizeable free operating cash (free operating cash flow has averaged more than $400 million over the past five years). Minimal debt levels, and cash and investments in excess of $3 billion, should help fund the increasing cash requirements necessary to support EMC's growth as well as cushion any near-term volatility.

OUTLOOK: STABLE

The outlook anticipates that EMC will maintain its market position and a financial profile in line with the current rating. The company has ample financial flexibility to fund its strategic initiatives.

Source: Standard & Poor's *Credit Week* (April 5, 2000), p. 121.

PROCESSES FOR DECOMPOSING BOND YIELDS

The concepts of the discounted cash flow model, the risk-free rate, credit-quality ratings, risk premiums for credit (or default) risk, sector risk premiums, and required yields on bonds have all been introduced. In applying those concepts to the pricing of fixed-income investments, remember the following relationships introduced in Chapter 1:

- If the investment's cash flows, yield, and term to maturity are known, one can solve for its price.
- If the investment's cash flows, price, and term are known, one can solve for its yield.

Before one moves on to Chapter 3, where all of this information is used in investment pricing examples, we provide a process for determining private-security market yield spreads for different types of fixed-income investments and decomposing the yields into their components. The matrix provided in Exhibit 2-10 will help one visualize the components of bond yield spreads and the factors that the market uses to determine them. (The resulting yields are used to value fixed-income instruments.) Once this is done, the question of whether the factors are realistic and the related fixed-income securities are fairly priced can be asked. A similar approach also will be used in valuing equities.

Explaining Fixed-Income Risk Premiums Expressed as Yield Spreads

An important point to recognize is that the market's view on risk premiums is not clearly spelled out but rather is embedded in the total required market yields. Therefore, the only publicly available market reference rates are the risk-free rate and the total market yields for publicly traded securities. To explain the yield spread concept, we illustrate several methodologies, including a continuum of spreads applicable to a BBB-rated bond, and a normalized-yield pricing matrix.

Continuum of Spreads Applicable to a BBB-Rated Bond

As of February 1, 2000, a publicly traded, BBB-rated bond, priced at 100 (meaning that it is trading at 100 percent of par), had a quoted market yield of 8.4 percent. Exhibit 2-11 illustrates that the market determined this yield as a bundle of risk premiums added to the benchmark risk-free rate.

Exhibit 2-11   Continuum of Spreads Comprising an Interest Rate Applicable to a BBB-Rated Borrower.

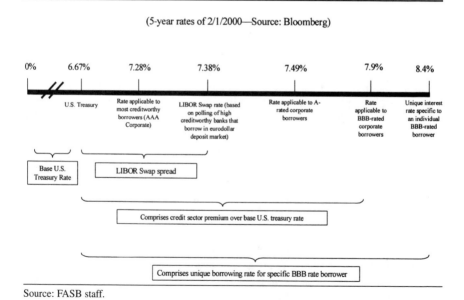

(5-year rates of 2/1/2000—Source: Bloomberg)

Source: FASB staff.

Notice that the benchmark risk-free rate was the 6.67 percent U.S. Treasury rate. The following risk premiums were added to arrive at the 8.40 percent market rate for BBB-rated bonds:

- 71 basis points above the U.S. Treasury rate attributable to the LIBOR swap spread (7.38–6.67)
- 11 basis points above the LIBOR swap rate to arrive at an A-rated bond (7.49–7.38)
- 41 basis points above the A-rated bond to arrive at a BBB-rated bond (7.9–7.49)
- 50 basis points due to credit risks specific to the issue (8.4–7.9).

Analysts may use this type of spread information when determining the discount rates for private bonds. For example, a private BBB-rated bond may be assigned a yield of 9 percent, determined as the 8.4 percent public yield plus 60 basis points attributable to the liquidity risk premium related to the private security.

NORMALIZED-YIELD PRICING MATRIX

Another method to decompose and understand the risk premiums that make up the differences between the benchmark risk-free rate and the total market yield for a particular security is a "normalized-yield matrix approach" that may be designed for a specific investor's portfolio. Such a matrix is provided in Exhibit 2-12. Some caveats are needed:

- Some bond portfolio managers have stated that, at times, such as in October 1998, bond yields are extremely volatile and this type of matrix is less than reliable because the market yields are so volatile or because very few transactions occurred.
- Some analysts combine the sector and credit-default-risk premiums into one credit-risk premium.
- It is our belief that the matrix in Exhibit 2-12 is useful as an aid in explaining and documenting the components that make up total market yields. However, other types of matrices may be used in practice. For example, some analysts may use the continuum-type matrix shown above.

The following analysis is a snapshot of market yields of various 10-year fixed-income investments hypothetically estimated at October 1998. For purposes of this analysis, assume that the portfolio comprises $1 billion of each of those six asset classes shown in Exhibit 2-12. The market yields documented in this matrix will be used in Chapter 3 to value a 10-year public corporate bond, a 10-year private-placement bond, and a 10-year commercial mortgage loan. Therefore, this tool is used as a model to illustrate how those yields may be developed. Certain investors may use this type of process to document and compare their views on specific risk premiums with those of the market's. In this manner, an investor may decide that certain investments are priced fairly, overpriced, or underpriced. The analysis also can be used as a reasonableness check to compare yields of similar-quality public and private investments to verify the reasonableness of risk premiums used in the valuation process. For example, a private-placement bond normally would be priced at a slightly higher yield than an otherwise comparable-quality public corporate bond due to a liquidity-risk premium. However, other favorable factors, such as a private-placement covenant protection provision, may help to reduce the yield.

Review Exhibit 2-12 to identify the different types of risk premiums and inter-relationships of various spread factors. Notice how the process begins by building each yield with the risk-free rate applicable to a 10-year Treasury bond rate. (Note that a 10-year average life was assumed for the collateral mortgage obligation [CMO] and mortgage-backed security [MBS].) Note that based on developments in early 2000, the base risk-free rate may evolve to a LIBOR swap rate.

Bond yields also will be affected by specific features, such as call options or equity-conversion features. An explanation of how the above risk premium factors were derived follows.

Exhibit 2-12   Analysis of Yields for 10-Year Term Fixed-Income Instruments as of October 1998 (Average Life for the CMO and MBS of 10 Years).

Normalized Yield Factors	A-1 Financial Corp.	BBB Indust. Private	B Indust. Corp.	AAA PAC CMO	BBB MBS	A-1 Commercial Mortgage
Benchmark Risk-Free Rate	4.43	4.43	4.43	4.43	4.43	4.43
Default Risk	0.07	0.07	2.50	0.00	1.00	0.15
Management Expense	0.10	0.17	0.10	0.05	0.05	0.25
Liquidity	0.05	0.25	0.50	0.01	0.05	0.10
Option Return	0.00	0.00	0.00	0.25	0.30	0.00
Covenant and Event Protection	0.00	−0.22	0.00	0.00	0.00	0.00
Sector Risk Premium	1.55	2.10	4.00	1.60	2.00	1.45
Target Normalized Yields	6.20	6.80	11.53	6.34	7.83	6.38
Current Market Yields	6.33	6.93	12.00	6.33	7.68	6.40
Internal Pricing Premium or Deficit	0.13	0.13	0.47	−0.01	−0.20	0.02
Spreads over Benchmark Risk-Free Rate	1.90	2.50	7.57	1.90	3.25	1.97

A-1 Public Corporate Bond

The A-1 financial-sector corporate bond is publicly traded, and therefore its yield is readily available to investors. The yield quotes provided in Exhibit 2-13 (i.e., the latest yield quoted for A-1 financial-sector bonds is 6.33 percent) were obtained from the *YIELDBOOK* Service.

During the period January 1989 through October 1998, A-1 financial-sector corporate bond spreads over comparable-term Treasury bonds ranged from a low of 53 basis points (1994) to a high of 223 basis points (1991). This corresponds to the flight to quality during 1991 and the economic expansion in 1994. One would expect the A-1 whole-loan commercial mortgage yield to be somewhat similar, as shown in Exhibit 2-12, at 197 basis points over Treasuries. Important aspects of the risk premiums for A-1 financial-sector corporate bonds include:

- The default-risk premium is estimated at seven basis points, indicative of high-quality loans with low default risk. This reflects the portfolio manager's expectations of low future default charges specific to bonds in this portfolio and is based on various factors, such as analysts' expectations about the economy,

Exhibit 2-13   Treasury Spreads.

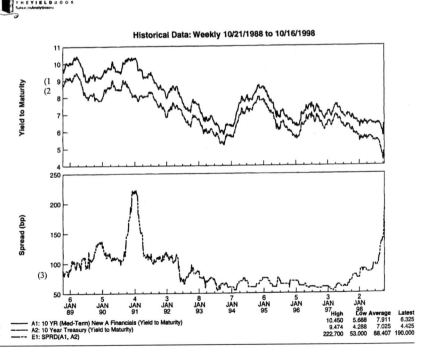

Source: File created by Philip Spak. Reprinted with permission.

interest rates, and the quality of the specific creditor's management team. A seven-basis-point default-risk premium means that the portfolio of A-1 financial corporate sector bonds is expected to experience a seven-basis-point loss each year due to specific bond defaults and the resulting loss of principal and interest. While conceptually this makes sense, it is not a perfect analysis, and the timing of defaults has a huge impact on this methodology. For example, assume that one has a $1 billion portfolio of A-1 financial bonds and that those bonds have 10-year bullet maturities (meaning that all the principal is repaid at the end of year 10). That seven-basis-point loss is expected to occur evenly over the term at $700,000 per year. The expected loss is therefore $7 million over this term. Since it is known from the analysis that 190 basis points over Treasuries are being earned by A-1 public corporate bonds, this loss is easily absorbed by the $19 million of yearly income in excess of the risk-free alternative of investing in the Treasuries. However, to the extent defaults occur unevenly, and especially early in the 10-year term, the risk premium can be understated.

• The management expense charge is estimated at 10 basis points. Compared with private investments, public investments are less expensive to manage because information is readily available and transaction costs are lower. This means that for a $1 billion portfolio, it will cost $1 million each year for management expenses, such as salaries for the investment analysts managing the portfolio, accounting costs, and transaction costs.

• The liquidity charge is estimated at five basis points. Compared with private investments and lower-quality public investments, the A-1 financial corporate bond is very liquid and the spread over Treasuries is accordingly narrow. Therefore, for this $1 billion portfolio, the investor is demanding an additional $500,000 per year to compensate for lower liquidity than a Treasury bond.

• The sector risk premium is estimated at 155 basis points. This means that the market demands an extra return over the Treasury rate to compensate for non-specific A-1 bond risks related to the industry sector factors that include supply and demand and investor perceptions of the overall default risk in this sector. For example, the A-1 financial bank sector risk premium differs from the B-industrial corporate bond sector risk premium of 400 basis points (shown in Exhibit 2-12) for various reasons, such as the industrial peer group's overall higher default risk.

A-1 Commercial Whole Loan Mortgage

The A-1 commercial whole loan mortgage is not publicly traded, and the 6.40 percent market yield was obtained from an institutional lender. It represents an interest rate on newly issued 10-year A-1 quality whole commercial mortgages offered by a specific lender. Other lenders may be offering a different rate; however, generally, the market rates are comparable when similar characteristic and sector loans are compared, such as A-quality office buildings, A-quality shopping centers, and A-quality apartment buildings. Important aspects of the risk premiums include:

- The default-risk premium is estimated at 15 basis points. This is indicative of the portfolio manager's expectations of future default charges specific to mortgages in this portfolio. This is based on various factors, such as analysts' expectations about each mortgage loan's loan-to-value ratio. The loan-to-value ratio is calculated as the ratio of the loan balance to the fair value of the supporting loan collateral. (This is covered in Chapter 3.) Other factors impacting default risk include the loan's terms (i.e., amortization and capital improvement reserves), economic conditions, occupancy rates, and growth trends in the location of the loan collateral and the general level of interest rates. To illustrate the importance of a default assumption, consider the commercial real estate depression that first began in the mid-1980s, as the Southwest real estate markets plunged. At the same time, demand remained high for new investments, yielding large spreads over Treasuries. Many investors ignored the actual commercial mortgage default losses in the Southwest markets and associated default-risk premiums that were 200 basis points and higher. They continued to estimate default-risk premiums at 25 basis points for commercial mortgage loans with collateral located in other markets, such as the Northeast. The impetus behind this thought was that oil-related factors had caused the Southwest mortgage-related defaults, whereas other areas were immune to those forces. Certain analysts looked at the 25-basis-point default-risk premium and refused to accept this amount. They believed that the risk premium would have been at least 250 basis points higher if the markets were reflecting more realistic property cash flow assumptions. History has proven that the latter view was correct as tax law changes and economic downturns drove real estate prices down and commercial mortgage loan defaults (and associated risk premiums) increased significantly.
- The management expense charge is estimated at 25 basis points. Commercial mortgage loans are expensive to administer because information is transaction-specific and public information is not available. This means that for a $1 billion portfolio, it will cost $2.5 million each year for management expenses, such as salaries for the investment analysts managing the portfolio, accounting costs, loan servicing fees, and transaction costs. Notice that this type of portfolio is more expensive to administer than the public corporate bond portfolio that has a 10-basis-point management expense charge.
- The liquidity charge is estimated at 10 basis points. This means that for this $1 billion portfolio, the investor is demanding an additional $1 million per year to compensate for lower liquidity than a Treasury bond. (Note that some analysts may therefore include liquidity charges as part of the sector risk premium.)
- The sector risk premium is estimated at 145 basis points, by basically plugging in this amount to balance the market yield. This means that the market demands

an extra return over the Treasury rate to compensate investors for nonspecific A-1 commercial mortgage risks, including supply and demand and general business risks related to the sector. At times, the sector risk premium can be very volatile and therefore readily identifiable based on market conditions. For example, during October 1998 the commercial mortgage sector risk premiums widened dramatically in response to market expectations that demand for new commercial mortgages would decrease because the commercial mortgage-backed securities market would be impacted by a lack of investors willing to hold the riskier tranches. Chapter 4 discusses how many types of loans may be used as collateral to support securities that are sold to investors, thus providing market liquidity. However, during October 1998 several key players in the commercial mortgage-backed securities (CMBS) market experienced financial difficulty. Those players had created the CMBS market by buying the support tranches.[3] As a result, investors believed that new CMBS issues and, hence, demand for commercial mortgages would decrease.

B-Corporate Industrial Bond

The B-corporate industrial bond (a noninvestment-grade security) is publicly traded, and the yield for a specific secured credit issue was obtained from the *Wall Street Journal.* Note the significant spread over Treasuries. Noninvestment-grade bond yields vary widely, as do the bid-offer spreads. Important aspects of the risk premiums include:

- The default-risk premium is estimated at 250 basis points, indicative of the related expected lost income and principal associated with these lower-quality loans. It reflects the portfolio manager's expectations of future default charges for specific public bonds included in the portfolio.
- The management expense charge is estimated at 10 basis points. Since those securities are publicly traded investments, information is readily available and the asset class is less costly to administer than commercial mortgage loans.
- The liquidity charge is estimated at 50 basis points, indicative of high-liquidity risk associated with lower-quality loans. This means that for this $1 billion portfolio, the investor is demanding an additional $5 million per year to compensate for lower liquidity than a Treasury (.005 × 1 billion + 5 million).
- The sector risk premium is estimated at 400 basis points, indicative of the market's demand for a high return due to supply and demand and loan-loss risks unique to this sector. At times, the sector risk premiums applicable to noninvestment-grade bonds are extremely volatile. For example, in the early 1990s the noninvestment-grade sector spreads widened, causing noninvestment-grade bonds to be the worst-performing (as measured in terms of total return) fixed-income asset class for a particular year. However, in the following year, the noninvestment-grade sector spreads narrowed, causing this asset class

to be the best-performing fixed-income asset class. Compare this 400-basis-point risk premium in Exhibit 2-5 with the other asset classes that ranged from 145 to 210 basis points.

The timing of loan losses is critical; the later the better. The timing of defaults has a large impact on the total return; in fact, this is one of the key factors that must be considered when analyzing the return. The issue of defaults in the context of noninvestment-grade bonds is not whether defaults will occur but rather at what point in the investment term the defaults will occur.

BBB-Industrial Private Placement Bond

The BBB-industrial private placement bond is not publicly traded, and the 6.93 percent market yield was obtained by surveying new money rates applicable to comparable-quality and average-life investments issued by other institutional investors. Important aspects of the total risk premium include:

- The default-risk premium of seven basis points is in line with that of the A-1 financial public corporate bond. This favorable loss expectation is a result of the portfolio manager's expertise in managing the portfolio and reflects low credit losses in the past and expectations that this trend will continue.
- Management expenses of 17 basis points is indicative of higher management expenses in connection with monitoring the borrower's financial performance (i.e., obtaining and reviewing private financial information and enforcing covenants).
- A liquidity charge of 25 basis points reflects the higher costs and greater time required to sell the private investments. Compare this with high-quality public investment liquidity charges, which range from 1 to 5 basis points.
- An offsetting risk premium of −22 basis points reflects the covenant and event protection provided by this bond. This will be discussed below and in Chapter 3.
- A sector risk premium of 210 basis points reflects the non–loan-specific default risk and liquidity charges related to this asset's sector.

AAA Planned Amortization Class Obligations

The AAA planned amortization class (PAC) collateralized mortgage obligation bond is assumed to be publicly traded at a 6.33 percent market yield. Important aspects of the risk premiums include:

- No default-risk premium is provided because the loans are government insured as to principal and interest. This asset class is fully explained in Chapter 4.
- Management expenses of five basis points are indicative of low management costs because information is publicly available from sources such as Bloomberg. This is illustrated in Chapter 4.

- A liquidity-risk premium of one basis point is due to the publicly traded nature of mortgage-backed securities.
- An option risk premium of 25 basis points is to compensate investors for the prepayment risk associated with mortgage-backed securities. This is fully discussed in Chapter 4.
- A sector risk premium of 160 basis points (again a plugged amount) relates to prepayment and other sector risks since defaults are not applicable.

BBB Mortgage-Backed Security

The BBB mortgage-backed security (MBS) is assumed to be publicly traded at a 7.68 percent market yield, based on similar quality and average-life investments. Important aspects of the risk premiums include:

- The default-risk premium of 100 basis points, unlike the AAA PAC security, has higher default risk because it is assumed that the mortgages are nonconforming. This means they do not meet government guarantee guidelines.
- The liquidity-risk premium of five basis points is relatively low due to the publicly traded nature of mortgage-backed securities. Note that this risk premium is higher than the AAA PAC because of its lower quality.
- The option-risk premium of 30 basis points is higher than the AAA PAC because the PAC has more predictable cash flow patterns. This concept is explained in Chapter 4.
- The sector risk premium of 210 basis points relates to high prepayment risks and sector risk factors.

Other Observations of the Normalized-Yield Methodology

Market yields for nonpublicly traded securities may not always be available from institutions because spreads become so wide that no one is issuing or selling the securities. This lack of liquidity can be overcome by using and adjusting the yield of comparable-quality public bonds. For example, in October 1998 the yield for B-quality commercial whole loans tracked the B-quality public bond yields that were 757 basis points over Treasuries. Certain bond analysts may believe that due to this wide yield spread of 757 points, using this information in the normalized-yield methodology may produce questionable results. However, many analysts believe that the normalized-yield methodology is a useful tool to explain and decompose risk premiums. The yield for a given investment can and will change because the overall yield is impacted by the risk-free rate, entity-specific credit spreads, and sector spreads, all of which can move independently. However, the normalized-yield methodology still provides reasonable results under the circumstances.

Note that analysts also use documented yields to decompose yield changes into price changes. For example, assume that the risk-free rate rises 100 basis points (from the initial rate of 4.43 percent as shown in Exhibit 2-12) and that a $100 million, 6.80 percent coupon, fixed-rate, 10-year, semiannual Baa-industrial private-placement bond sector narrows by 80 basis points (excluding changes in the risk-free rate), while credit spreads are unchanged. Because of those changes, the bond lost $1.42 million. The components of this loss, as illustrated in Exhibit 2-14, are attributed to several factors:

- An increase in the risk-free rate amounting to a $7.11 million loss.
- A narrowing (reduction) of sector-spread yield amounting to a $5.69 million gain.

The main point is that one should recognize that the yield components that are used in determining a bond's price can move independently of each other. Also understand the concept of spreads widening and narrowing and the impact on bond prices. For example, during October 1998 market-yield spreads between high-quality and low-quality investments widened. The widening spreads were due to a flight to quality investments, which drove market prices down for riskier investments. The lack of buyers in the bond markets at this time (excluding Treasuries) increased bid-offer spreads, which drove market prices down.[4]

Exhibit 2-14 $100 Million, 6.8 Percent, Fixed-Rate, 10-Year Bond, Calculation of Changing BBB Private Rates Assuming Yield Changes upon Issuance at Par.

Yield Factors	Initial Yield	Basis Point Change	New Yield	Dollar Impact ($ Millions)
Risk-free rate	4.43	1.00	5.43	−7.11
Credit spread	0.07	0.00	0.07	0
Sector yield spread	2.30	−0.80	1.50	5.69
	6.80	0.20	7.00	1.42

The above price changes may be calculated on an HP12C calculator as follows:

Change in the risk-free rate = 500[PMT], 3.5[I], 20[n], [PV] = 7.11.

Note that the amounts are semiannual and the amount is negative because yield rose. The 500 PMT is derived as 1% × $100 million/2.

Change in the sector yield spread = 400[PMT], 3.5[I], 20[n], [PV] = 5.69. The 400[PMT] is derived as .80% × $100 million/2.

Total price change due to 20 basis point yield curve shift = 6.80[PMT], 7[i], 1.012000[Enter], 1.012010[f] [Price].

CONCLUDING REMARKS

Chapter 3 will apply the above concepts to public and private placement bonds and whole commercial mortgages.

NOTES

1. Refer to Equity Analytics, Ltd. Available at *www.e-analytics.com/bonds*.

2. Reproduced with the permission of Kenneth D. Andersen, former department head of Private Placements at Connecticut Mutual Life Insurance Company.

3. To understand the widening sector risk premium, refer to David D. Kirkpatrick, "Credit Markets: In Commercial-Mortgage Issues, Players Are Locked in a Freeze," *Wall Street Journal,* October 23, 1998, C–1. The article discusses how Wall Street securities firms held more than $30 billion of risky bonds on their books waiting to be sold and that Criimi Mae Inc. had bought nearly half of the riskiest bonds issued in recent years.

4. Greg Ip, "Illiquidity Is Crippling Bond World," *Wall Street Journal,* October 19, 1988, p. C–1.

Chapter 3

Public Corporate Bonds, Private-Placement Bonds, and Whole Commercial Mortgages

INTRODUCTION

This chapter explains bond terminology and the key characteristics and pricing considerations related to public corporate bonds, private-placement bonds, and whole commercial mortgages. These asset classes make up a significant portion of institutional invested assets, yet they do not generally have the complexity inherent in mortgage-backed securities and equity investments because their cash flows are more predictable. The concepts discussed in this chapter will also be used later in this book as more complex asset classes, in which prices are impacted by such items as prepayment risk (mortgage-backed securities) and fluctuating free cash flows (equities), are addressed.

KEY TERMINOLOGY

Bonds are long-term promissory notes issued by businesses or governmental units. Mortgage notes are long-term promissory notes entered into by home-owners or owners of commercial real estate. To understand how the cash flows and resulting bond and mortgage values are determined, the following terms need to be defined:

Amortizing bond   This type of bond requires scheduled principal repayments over the life of the bond. The entire principal or a portion of the principal may be repaid over the life of the bond, depending on the bond's provisions. From an investor's standpoint, amortization will decrease credit risk, since the loan balance is being repaid more quickly, but it will increase reinvestment risk, since the portions of principal repaid may require reinvestment at a time when interest rates are declining. However, if interest rates are increasing, amortization payments can be reinvested at higher rates.

Average life   This term refers to the period of time it will take to receive cash flows from a fixed-income investment that have a present value equal to one-half of the investment's current cost or price. This term is an important factor in evaluating fixed-income investments that have principal cash flows throughout the investment term (as discussed in Chapter 2). An important consideration when evaluating an investment's average life is to realize that this measure is often an estimate, since the timing of cash flows may vary significantly depending on the contractual terms and economic factors.

Bond price   Analysts quote bond prices as a percentage of par. For example, a bond price of 100 equals 100 percent of par; a price of 102 equals 102 percent of par, etc.

Bullet bond   A bullet bond receives the entire principal repayment at maturity (also referred to as a *balloon payment bond*). Because a bullet bond's principal cash flows cannot be repaid prior to maturity, this minimizes reinvestment risk arising from declining interest rates (although the coupon cash flows may require reinvestment at the lower rates). European investors historically have preferred bullet (and variable-rate) bonds over amortizing bonds in part because of this protection. Bullet bonds may include make-whole provisions, as discussed above.

Call provision   This allows the issuer the option of paying off the debt prior to maturity. For example, if interest rates decline and a debt instrument has a call option, the issuer can issue new debt at lower rates and use those proceeds to call (and retire) the original debt. The buyer of the callable bond therefore charges a premium for this option that equates to a higher coupon rate than for a similar bond that is noncallable. The key concept of a call provision is that from the issuer's standpoint, the exercise of the call option as rates decline is economically advantageous. This is in contrast to the issuer's paying off a loan and paying a premium due to a make-whole provision (discussed below).

Coupon interest rate   This is the stated dollar amount of interest to be paid annually (or semiannually) divided by the par value of the bond. If, for example, the par value of the bond is $1,000 and the stated coupon interest rate is 10 percent, then the bond will pay interest of $100 per year, or $50 every six months.

Loan covenant   A loan covenant is a contractual stipulation included in the indentured agreement to protect the investor. Common loan covenants include requiring that the borrower maintain a minimum net-worth ratio, prohibiting certain cash outflows, such as dividends, and prohibiting the issuance of new debt, or mergers and acquisitions. A loan covenant is critical to protecting the investor in private-placement transactions (as discussed below). In contrast, public debt indentures generally do not include loan covenants other than a change-of-control provision (i.e., they prohibit a change in control without bondholder approval).

Lock-out period   A provision prohibiting principal repayments for a specified period, such as the first five years of a loan. From an investor's standpoint, this provision eliminates interest-related reinvestment risk for a period of time.

Make-whole provision   This provision is a contractual stipulation that requires the borrower to pay a premium to the investor if the borrower repays the loan prior to its stated maturity. The investor is compensated for reinvestment risk by a payout formula, such as discounting the remaining contractual cash flows at the current Treasury rate plus a specified level of basis points. A common amount is 50 basis points. An illustration of a make-whole payment is covered in the private-placement bond section of this chapter.

Maturity date   This is the specified date on which the par value must be repaid.

Noncallable bond   This is a bond that does not have a call provision. This type of bond is protected against reinvestment risk arising from declining interest rates (although the coupon cash flows may require reinvestment at the lower rates).

Par value   The par or stated value of the bond is often set at $1,000, although other multiples are also used. Par value represents the amount of money the firm borrows and promises to repay at some future date. Par value also may be called the *principal* amount of the loan.

Recourse versus nonrecourse   A recourse loan provision permits the lender to seek recovery of principal and interest from the borrower. Therefore, for example, if a loan was secured but operating cash flows or secured assets did not satisfy the loan's conditions, an investor could seek repayment from the borrower's other assets that were not designated as assets that secured the loan. In contrast, a nonrecourse debt provision bars an investor from seeking recovery from the borrower. In those situations, the investor is repaid from operating cash flows and specified secured assets.

Secured position   This type of position gives the investor a claim to specific assets in the event of default. For example, commercial mortgage loans are generally secured by a first lien on real estate, and the loan repayment depends on a borrower's either selling or refinancing the property. The security feature is therefore important in assessing the loan quality and, in the event of a monetary default, the level of impairment. Related to this discussion is the concept of recourse and nonrecourse loan provisions, as discussed below.

Senior versus subordinate   The relative position of debt is critical to the lender's ability to recover principal and interest when a monetary default occurs. A senior position must generally be repaid prior to subordinate positions receiving any cash flow. A secured lender, however, may have a claim to a specific asset or assets and therefore have a claim that must be met before senior debt holders receive payment. It is also common that all lenders in a class (i.e., the senior debt) share equally in the liquidation proceeds.

Sinking-fund provision   The term "sinking fund" has several meanings. Investment analysts often refer to a sinking-fund provision as requiring actual periodic principal repayments during the loan term. Those payments reduce default risk and may help match an investor's cash flow requirements. Notes without sinking-fund provisions are referred to as *bullet*-type loans, meaning that the entire original principal is repaid at maturity. (If the borrower cannot refinance at this time because of an economic or business downturn, repayment may not be possible.) A sinking-fund provision also may entail a requirement that the borrower legally set aside funds in an escrow account that will be used to retire the debt; however, the investor does not immediately receive the amounts. This provision is included in certain serial bonds to ensure that sufficient funds have been set aside for repayment of the bond when it matures.

Type of default   Default may be monetary, meaning a contractually required payment was not made on time, or nonmonetary, meaning that a covenant breach occurred. For example, a certain required current ratio was not maintained. This may contractually trigger an acceleration of the debt repayment, such as being due immediately.

Yield to call   A yield measure that assumes the bond will be called at the earliest specified call date. Therefore, the yield calculation assumes the principal is received at this call date.

PUBLICLY ISSUED CORPORATE BONDS

Corporate debt securities that are issued to the public must be registered with the Securities and Exchange Commission (SEC) and listed on an exchange before they can be traded. As a result of being exchange traded, those securities generally will be more marketable, since they have readily obtainable prices in the marketplace. This also means they will be more liquid. It is interesting to note that investments in corporate bonds provided excellent returns during most of the 1990s, due to the fact that many of the bonds were call protected. Therefore, as interest rates declined, their prices increased further and generated larger capital gains than they would have if they were not call protected. Exhibit 3-1 reproduces the 1998 *Merrill Lynch Bond Index Returns Summary* for separate index funds comprising public corporate bonds, mortgage-backed securities, and asset-backed securities. As one can see by reviewing each year's actual total return amounts, U.S. public corporate bonds outperformed asset-backed bonds and had similar total returns to the Government National Mortgage Association (GNMA) pass-throughs. As discussed in Chapter 4, investment analysts normally expect to earn higher yields by investing in mortgage-backed and asset-backed securities because those asset classes pay a higher yield to compensate the investor for prepayment risk. Therefore, if the analyst believes that this index is representative of the industry, it could be concluded that over this time period, the models for mortgage pass-throughs and asset-backed investments did not lead to better risk-adjusted returns than plain-vanilla public corporate bonds. This can be attributed to actual prepayment rates in excess of modeled prepayment amounts, as discussed in Chapter 4.

Exhibit 3-1 Merrill Lynch Bond Index Returns Report for the Period 1989 to 1998.

Asset Class	1998	1997	1996	1995	1994	1993	1992	1991	1990	1989
U.S. Corporate A–AAA	9.49	10.06	3.19	21.38	–3.62	12.12	8.82	18.05	7.97	14.15
GNMA mortgage passthroughs	9.37	11.95	5.33	19.88	–3.67	14.95	6.68	20.33	11.69	15.93
Asset-backed, fixed rate	7.19	7.38	5.52	12.26	.73	6.86	7.83	15.75	N/A	N/A

Key Characteristics of Public Corporate Bonds

Public corporate bonds have the following characteristics that are important to consider when valuing those securities:

- They are highly liquid because they are exchange traded with readily available prices.
- They have publicly available information such as Securities and Exchange Commission (SEC) reports, audited financial statements, and brokerage firm analyst reports.
- Public corporate bonds generally provide semiannual fixed-rate interest payments.
- They may have a sinking-fund feature.
- They are often unsecured.
- They are typically of high credit quality; however, credit quality may range from AAA to the high-yield (junk bond) category.
- Public corporate bonds usually have long durations and often are noncallable or have lock-out periods during which repayment is prohibited. Therefore, they offer a potential for large capital gains and losses as interest rates change, as was observed in the 10-year Merrill Lynch corporate bond index report reproduced in Exhibit 3-1.
- These bonds contain limited financial covenants (in contrast to private-placement bonds). A common covenant found in public corporate bonds is a change-of-control covenant that requires bondholder approval for a change of control.
- Payments of principal and interest on public corporate bonds are contingent on the issuer's financial strength; credit risk is the primary risk.
- Supply and demand for these bonds in the market varies, and therefore, new corporate security investments sometimes are unavailable. This occurred, for example, during mid-1997, as companies opted to raise capital in the equity markets rather than issue debt.

PUBLIC CORPORATE BOND PRICING

The prices and yields to maturity on publicly traded corporate bonds are available in the marketplace. However, to illustrate their pricing, the price and fair value of a hypothetical noncallable public bond are calculated below.

Price Calculation of ABC's Noncallable, A-1 Credit Rated Bond

Assume that in October 1992, an investor purchased at par a $10 million, 8 percent, fixed-rate, A-1 rated, noncallable bond, maturing in October 2008. The bond pays interest on a semiannual basis. Assume that the bond maintains its A-1 credit rating. It is now time to calculate this bond's price at October 1998, assuming that the market yield for this type of bond is 6.33 percent and that the semiannual payments are due October 1 and April 1. It has been assumed that interest on the bond has been paid through the valuation date, in order to keep the calculation simple. (Refer to Exhibit 3-2 where the above information is used to value this bond.)

Exhibit 3-2   ABC Noncallable 8 Percent Fixed-Rate Bond, 10/1/98 to 10/1/2008, Yield to Maturity = 6.33 Percent.

Period	Principal Balance	Coupon Rate	Cash Flow— Interest	Cash Flow— Principal	Present Value
1	10,000,000	0.08	400,000		387,728
2	10,000,000	0.08	400,000		375,833
3	10,000,000	0.08	400,000		364,303
4	10,000,000	0.08	400,000		353,127
5	10,000,000	0.08	400,000		342,293
6	10,000,000	0.08	400,000		331,792
7	10,000,000	0.08	400,000		321,613
8	10,000,000	0.08	400,000		311,746
9	10,000,000	0.08	400,000		302,182
10	10,000,000	0.08	400,000		292,911
11	10,000,000	0.08	400,000		283,925
12	10,000,000	0.08	400,000		275,215
13	10,000,000	0.08	400,000		266,771
14	10,000,000	0.08	400,000		258,587
15	10,000,000	0.08	400,000		250,654
16	10,000,000	0.08	400,000		242,964
17	10,000,000	0.08	400,000		235,510
18	10,000,000	0.08	400,000		228,285
19	10,000,000	0.08	400,000		221,281
20	10,000,000	0.08	400,000	10,000,000	5,576,808
Present Value					11,223,528

The bond's fair value is calculated by discounting the bond's remaining contractual coupon interest cash flows, plus principal at the current market yield of 6.33 percent. This amounts to an $11,223,528 fair value, calculated as indicated in Exhibit 3-2.

A bond's price of $11,223,528 is quoted as a percentage of its par value, or 112.23528 percent of par. Why is the market yield to maturity for this term's investment being used to discount cash flows instead of the individual spot rates (not shown here) applicable to each period's cash flow? The reason is that the market's customary practice is to price bonds based on the yield to maturity of comparable-term and quality bonds, despite the fact that this methodology may produce a different result from discounting the cash flows at the applicable spot rates (described in Chapter 1).

Using the basic bond-pricing formula previously discussed and the above data, one can solve for the bond's price on an HP12C calculator by using the following keystrokes:

6.33[i], 8[PMT], 1.012000[ENTER], 1.012010[f] [PRICE]

This produces a price of 112.2353 percent of par. Therefore, the fair value of the $10 million par value is $11,223,530. (The $2 difference between the value shown in Exhibit 3-2 and this amount is due to rounding.)

How Would This Calculation Change If the Bond Was Callable?

The theoretical concept of pricing a callable bond is that the investment comprises two components:

1. A noncallable bond
2. A sold call option

The formula can be expressed as:

Price of callable bond = price of noncallable bond – price of call option

Industry practice determines the price of the callable bond using an option-pricing model, such as an option-adjusted spread (OAS) model. An OAS model calculates the bond's price as an average of expected prices that are modeled assuming various interest rate shifts. This model considers the probability that the call option will be exercised eventually as rates change.[1] Accountants should understand the following concepts related to callable bonds:

- A bond issuer buys the call option from the investor. The option provides the issuer the right to buy back the bond from the investor at a specified price, such as at par or 110 percent of par.

- Generally, the call option is not effective immediately. For example, a 10-year callable bond may have a noncallable period in which the option cannot be exercised for a specified period, such as the first five years.
- The issuer generally will not call the bond until it is economically advantageous to do so from an interest rate perspective. For example, interest rates decrease below the coupon amount and the issuer can then refinance at a lower rate of interest.
- The investor is assuming reinvestment risk, since the issuer may exercise the call option when rates decrease. Therefore, the investor requires a higher yield over comparable noncallable bonds to compensate for the risk that bond proceeds will be reinvested at lower interest rates.
- Call option prices are influenced by the term of the option, the appropriate volatility measure (specific to the type of OAS model), the bond's issuance size (this impacts refinancing expenses), and the option's exercise price, as specified in the note.
- Analysts use an option-pricing methodology where they first solve for the callable bond's price using the OAS model. A yield is then derived by using the bond's price, coupon, and maturity. The OAS model also solves for the call option price. It is common to determine the callable bond's yield, assuming that the issuer will call the bond at the earliest date permitted. This yield is referred to as a yield-to-call basis.

Exhibit 3-3 presents a bond with characteristics that are identical to the noncallable bond presented in Exhibit 3-2. The bond is also a $10 million par value, 10-year, semiannual, 8 percent coupon bond, callable at the end of year 5, and currently priced at 107.896. The following keystrokes can be used on an HP12C calculator to illustrate how one can solve for this bond's yield to call:

107.896[PV], 8[PMT], 1.012000 [ENTER], 1.012005 [f] [YTM]

This calculation produces a yield to call of 6.142 percent. An investor may consider this yield realistic when interest rates are decreasing and it is likely that the issuer will call the bond. (Note that, in practice, accrued interest would exist and require consideration in the pricing. The accrued interest was omitted in order to keep the example simple.) The yield to call can also be calculated as indicated in Exhibit 3-3.

Exhibit 3-4 illustrates the conceptual call option pricing relationship. Remember that the price is a percentage of par (e.g., the $433,900 call option fair value = $10 million times 4.339 percent). Given this conceptual framework, Exhibit 3-5 compares and contrasts the terms and pricing for the noncallable and callable bonds discussed above.

Note that the OAS of 184.7 applicable to the noncallable bond is a result of an analysis of the spread across an entire yield curve rather than a point on the

Exhibit 3-3   ABC Callable 8 Percent Fixed-Rate Bond, 10/1/98–10/1/2008, Callable at End of Period 10, OAS Derived Yield of 6.142 Percent.

Period	Principal Balance	Coupon Rate	Cash Flow— Interest	Cash Flow— Principal	Present Value
1	10,000,000	0.08	400,000		388,082
2	10,000,000	0.08	400,000		376,519
3	10,000,000	0.08	400,000		365,301
4	10,000,000	0.08	400,000		354,417
5	10,000,000	0.08	400,000		343,857
6	10,000,000	0.08	400,000		333,612
7	10,000,000	0.08	400,000		323,672
8	10,000,000	0.08	400,000		314,028
9	10,000,000	0.08	400,000		304,672
10	10,000,000	0.08	400,000	10,000,000	7,685,442
Present value					10,789,601

Note: 6.142 = OAS Derived Price of 107.896, That Is Then Used to Derive Yield Assuming Bond Will Be Called at End of Period 10

yield curve. The OAS measure is an analytical tool used in determining relative bond values.

We will now summarize some of the key characteristics of noncallable and callable bonds, illustrated using the previous calculations and the fundamental concepts discussed in Chapters 1 and 2:

- A callable bond has a higher yield to maturity than a noncallable bond to compensate the investor for the reinvestment risk assumed. Note that the 6.894 percent yield to maturity reported in Exhibit 3-5 for the callable bond can be derived on an HP12C calculator as:

  107.896[PV], 8[PMT], 1.012000[ENTER], 1.012010[f] [YTM]

Exhibit 3-4   Price of ABC $10 Million Callable Bond, Noncallable Bond, and Call Option.

Price of callable bond = Price of noncallable bond – Price of call option
$$107.896 = 112.235 - 4.339$$

Fair value = $10,789,600
Fair value of noncallable portion of bond = $11,223,500
Plus fair value of call option = $433,900

Exhibit 3-5 Comparison of Noncallable and Callable Bonds, Priced as of October 16, 1998.

Terms	Noncallable Bond	Callable Bond
Coupon (semiannual)	8.00	8.00
Maturity date	10/15/08	10/15/08
Call date	N/A	10/15/03
Call price	N/A	100.00
Price at 10/16/98	114.090	108.134
Yield-to-maturity	6.330	6.894
Yield-to-call	N/A	6.142
10-year Treasury rate	4.43	4.43
Spread/benchmark over Treasuries	190 bps/10-year	247 bps/10-year
Market value	11,223,500	10,789,600
Duration	7.08	5.14
Convexity	0.64	−0.31
Volatility assumption used in OAS	N/A	14
Option price	N/A	4.339
Option-free price	N/A	112.235
Option-free yield	N/A	6.324
OAS	184.7	187.7

Calculation provided by Michael Mutti of Bear Stearns

- Analysts commonly refer to the call option price calculation as a yield spread over a benchmark rate. In this example, the 57-basis-point-yield spread was derived in the OAS calculation. It represents the premium that the investor required as compensation for selling the call option to the bond issuer. This can be used to calculate the call option fair value ($406,892; difference from Exhibit 3-4 due to rounding) as follows:

    28,500[PMT], 3.45[i], 20[n], [PV]

Where:

- $28,500 equals the periodic cash flow resulting from a 57-basis-point change, that is, 57 basis points times $10 million/2. (The 57 basis points equal the difference between the callable benchmark spread of 247 basis points less the noncallable spread of 190 basis points. Note that this approximates the difference between the yield on the callable bond of 6.894 percent and the 6.228 percent yield on the nonconvertible bond.)

- The 3.45 equals the periodic yield derived as half of the 6.90 yield benchmark (4.45 risk-free rate plus 247 basis points).
- The callable bond's duration is lower than the noncallable bond's duration because the call feature causes the callable bond to have a shorter expected maturity. It also causes less price appreciation when rates decrease.
- The callable bond has negative convexity—as rates decrease, the call option will limit the bond's price appreciation.

Other Yield Measures

Analysts also may calculate a yield-to-worst basis. Under this practice, the bond yield is separately calculated using the current price, assuming that the call provisions are exercised (yield to call) and then assuming that the bond is not called (yield to maturity). The method that produces the lowest yield is referred to as the yield to worst and provides investors with an indication of the yield that may be achieved over the investment term. For example, if the current bond yield exceeded the bond's coupon, a yield to maturity would produce the lowest value. This yield statistic is also useful in determining relative bond values. Appendix C at the end of this chapter illustrates Bloomberg functions for calculating yields using different methodologies for a public corporate bond.

Bond Pricing—Monetary Default

If a bond defaults, the investor's goal is to recover principal. Since public bonds lack the typical covenants that are part of private-placement bond agreements, the process is somewhat simple. It ultimately comes down to evaluating the situation and forming the best estimate of the amounts that will be recovered. For example, the company may commit to a plan in which assets are sold with the proceeds used to pay off the bond holders. The market would then factor the risk and time value of money into the yield to maturity and expected cash flows and discount those expected cash flows to arrive at a fair value. Defaulted public corporate bonds are publicly traded and therefore easier to price. However, the analyst's task is to evaluate whether the market is fairly pricing the bonds and to take action based on this evaluation. A monetary default of a private-placement bond is illustrated later in the chapter.

Noninvestment-Grade (Junk Bond) Bond Pricing Considerations

A junk bond's price depends on the performance of the issuing entity. The investment provides high coupon rates to accommodate their low credit rating; otherwise, the bond would sell at a deep discount. This link in pricing to the entity's performance is why some analysts view junk bond investing as a form of an "equity substitute." The investments are generally of shorter term than typical institutional bond investments (i.e., public corporate bonds and private-placement bonds). Therefore, analysts often buy these bonds when issued at par and hold them for their high-interest coupons. Certain analysts have explained that junk bonds are usually paid off by the issuer within three to four years, or they default. Exhibit 2-12 illustrated an October 1998, B-1 bond yield of 12 percent, or 757 basis points above comparable-term Treasury notes at that time. It can be assumed that with this large a risk premium, the marketplace was pricing for a high level of default loss. However, one of the main pricing variables is the timing of those losses, with later being better.

PRIVATE-PLACEMENT BONDS

Private-placement bonds are not registered with the SEC, nor do they trade on any exchange. (However, Section 144A private-placement loans trade among large institutional investors.) Private-placement bonds therefore are transacted directly between an issuing entity and an institutional investor or group of investors. Entities that may be thinly capitalized or are new to the market or that do not want to publicly disclose financial information about the company may seek funds in the private-placement market. Those loans are similar to commercial bank loans except that they tend to be of longer term. Private-placement loans generally have the following characteristics:

- They originate privately through investment bankers, and, therefore, detailed public information is often not available for the company. For example, annual reports are not filed with the SEC if the company is privately held.
- They generally provide fixed-rate, semiannual interest payments.
- The borrower provides management representations and warranties to a lender. For example, management may provide a representation that the financial information provided as a basis for the loan is materially correct.
- They may provide make-whole provisions that compensate the investor if the borrower pays off the loan before its contractual maturity. If prepayment occurs, the lender is compensated for reinvestment risk by a pay-out formula, such as at the greater of par or a price determined by discounting the remaining cash flows at the current Treasury rate plus 50 basis points. The key concept of a make-whole provision is that from the issuer's standpoint, it is never economically advantageous to exercise a make-whole provision based on interest rate movements. (This is because yield spreads for this type of loan will not narrow below a specified spread over Treasuries.) Generally, issuers subject to make-whole provisions may prepay anyway because they want to be free from the note's restrictive covenant requirements (i.e., prohibiting changes in control).
- They may include sinking-fund provisions, which require periodic principal repayments to the investor. Those payments minimize credit losses and lower

the bond's required yield because the principal is systematically paid off before maturity (unlike a bullet loan).

- They generally have significant covenants that protect the investor. Common covenant provisions include requiring the borrower to provide the investor with quarterly financial information and annual financial statements that are audited by an independent certified public accountant. Covenants also may require contractual limitations against the payment of dividends, minimum working capital and fixed-charge coverage ratio requirements, and limitations on the issuance of additional debt, such as limiting senior-debt levels to 200 percent of net tangible assets.[2]
- They may be secured or unsecured, depending on the type of loan. They may share assets in the same proportion as other creditors, in the event of any liquidation distributions. They may also be on a recourse or nonrecourse basis (as discussed earlier in this chapter).
- Their credit risk is generally the most significant aspect, although private asset-backed securities (discussed in Chapter 4) also may have prepayment risk.

Key Aspects of the Underwriting Process

Recall that in Chapter 2 a summary was provided of a private-placement underwriting process that entailed an analyst's evaluating the borrower's industry-related risk, market position, management, financial projections, and ratios. The end product of this process is the creation of an investment recommendation report that summarizes the transaction and the key aspects of the underwriting process. This report usually is presented to a loan review committee as part of the formal loan approval process. Furthermore, investment professionals who are chartered financial analysts (CFAs) are bound to a code of ethics requiring that:

- The decisions reached in research reports, investment recommendations, and actions are justified with appropriate records to support a reasonable and adequate basis for the recommendation. The report must be prepared with diligence and thoroughness.
- Portfolio recommendations and actions must be appropriate and suitable for the client's risk profile, taking into account the needs and circumstances of the client and the basic characteristics of the investment.

VALUING A PRIVATE-PLACEMENT BOND

In valuing a private-placement bond, an understanding of its risks and expected returns is essential. Therefore, one should thoroughly read the analyst's investment report and observe:

- Total dollar amount of debt issuance
- Issuer's expected use of debt issuance proceeds
- Principal terms, such as interest coupon, par value, term, average life, call period, and make-whole provisions
- Internal and independent quality ratings (in many cases the borrower will not have a public debt rating)
- Business summary, describing borrower's business lines, market share, management team, and other relevant factors
- Hurdle or required rate of return on investment specified as a yield spread over comparable-term Treasuries (or LIBOR swap rate) and comparable-term and quality public corporate bonds
- Key strengths of the investment, including an evaluation of management's track record, profit margins by product line, business plans, and financial ratios (including such ratios previously described in the rating grids provided in Chapter 2)
- Key risks of investment, such as industry cyclicality, competition, potential for takeover or industry consolidation, and exposure to general economic fluctuations
- Ability to withstand a cyclical economic downturns (e.g., the ability of the company to adjust staffing or other costs in response to business changes while maintaining profit margins)
- Collateral guarantees (if any)
- Summary of restrictive covenants
- Present holdings of the company's debt issues by the investor (if any—e.g., the investor may hold a public bond issued by the company, and this may increase portfolio risk due to diminished diversification)

Valuation of a Hypothetical Private-Placement Loan

An existing $50 million private-placement loan, originally issued on October 1, 1992 with the characteristics provided in Exhibit 3-6, is priced next.

Value of Loan at October 1, 1998

Assume that at October 1, 1998, the loan is in good standing with a credit rating of BBB, that 10 years remain until maturity, and that the market yield for this credit rating and term is 6.93 percent, as shown in Exhibit 2-12. The loan's current book value is $50 million. Exhibit 3-7 illustrates how the fair value of this loan is calculated to be $55,239,638.

By using the yield spread components from the normalized-yield grid in Exhibit 2-12, it can be estimated that the $5,239,638 unrealized gain ($55,239,638 fair value less $50,000,000 book value) is the result of the factors illustrated in Exhibit 3-8:

Exhibit 3-6 RJW Private-Placement Loan.

Date of issue	10/1/92
Par value	$50,000,000
Maturity	10/1/08 (16-year term)
Coupon rate	8.40 percent
Interest payment	Semiannual
Original yield spread over Treasuries at issuance (risk-free rate of 6.65 percent)	175 bps
Original yield spread over comparable-quality public corporate bonds at issuance	75 bps
Sinking-fund provision	None
Internal quality rating	BBB
Collateral	Equipment
Call features	None
Prepayment make-whole provision	Treasury plus 50 bps

Exhibit 3-7 RJW Private-Placement Bond, Yield to Maturity = 6.93 Percent.

Period	Principal Balance	Annual Coupon Rate	Semi-Annual Cash Flow— Interest	Cash Flow— Principal	Present Value
1	50,000,000	0.084	2,100,000		2,029,672
2	50,000,000	0.084	2,100,000		1,961,699
3	50,000,000	0.084	2,100,000		1,896,003
4	50,000,000	0.084	2,100,000		1,832,506
5	50,000,000	0.084	2,100,000		1,771,136
6	50,000,000	0.084	2,100,000		1,711,822
7	50,000,000	0.084	2,100,000		1,654,493
8	50,000,000	0.084	2,100,000		1,599,085
9	50,000,000	0.084	2,100,000		1,545,532
10	50,000,000	0.084	2,100,000		1,493,773
11	50,000,000	0.084	2,100,000		1,443,747
12	50,000,000	0.084	2,100,000		1,395,397
13	50,000,000	0.084	2,100,000		1,348,666
14	50,000,000	0.084	2,100,000		1,303,499
15	50,000,000	0.084	2,100,000		1,259,846
16	50,000,000	0.084	2,100,000		1,217,654
17	50,000,000	0.084	2,100,000		1,176,875
18	50,000,000	0.084	2,100,000		1,137,462
19	50,000,000	0.084	2,100,000		1,099,369
20	50,000,000	0.084	2,100,000	50,000,000	26,361,401
Present value					55,239,638

Exhibit 3-8   Attribution of Gain on Bond.

Period	Principal Balance	Value of Gain on Risk-Free Rate (−222 bps)	Present Value of Gain on Risk-Free Rate (−222 bps)	Value of Loss on Sector— Rate (+75 bps)	Present Value or Loss on Sector Rate (+75 bps)
1	50,000,000	555,000	536,413	−187,500	−181,221
2	50,000,000	555,000	518,449	−187,500	−175,152
3	50,000,000	555,000	501,086	−187,500	−169,286
4	50,000,000	555,000	484,305	−187,500	−163,617
5	50,000,000	555,000	468,086	−187,500	−158,137
6	50,000,000	555,000	452,410	−187,500	−152,841
7	50,000,000	555,000	437,259	−187,500	−147,723
8	50,000,000	555,000	422,615	−187,500	−142,775
9	50,000,000	555,000	408,462	−187,500	−137,994
10	50,000,000	555,000	394,783	−187,500	−133,373
11	50,000,000	555,000	381,562	−187,500	−128,906
12	50,000,000	555,000	368,783	−187,500	−124,589
13	50,000,000	555,000	356,433	−187,500	−120,417
14	50,000,000	555,000	344,496	−187,500	−116,384
15	50,000,000	555,000	332,959	−187,500	−112,486
16	50,000,000	555,000	321,809	−187,500	−108,719
17	50,000,000	555,000	311,031	−187,500	−105,078
18	50,000,000	555,000	300,615	−187,500	−101,559
19	50,000,000	555,000	290,548	−187,500	−98,158
20	50,000,000	555,000	280,817	−187,500	−94,871
Total		11,100,000	7,912,923	−3,750,000	−2,673,285

Note that the above cash flows were discounted at a 6.93 percent yield.

- A $7,912,923 gain caused by a reduction in the risk-free rate from 6.65 percent to 4.43 percent (a reduction of 222 basis points)
- A $2,673,285 loss caused by sector spreads widening by 75 basis points

Effect of a Make-Whole Provision

Assume that the borrower in the RJW private-placement loan decided to repay the loan at October 1, 1998. Assuming that the Treasury bill rate was 4.43 percent, as illustrated in Exhibit 2-2, and the make-whole provision required discounting the bond's cash flows at the Treasury rate plus 50 basis points, a fair value of $63,568,417 would be calculated for this loan, as shown in Exhibit 3-9.

The borrower may be willing to incur a prepayment fee because of business reasons, such as a merger or leveraged buyout, and desires to be relieved of any restrictive covenants. The fee is not economically beneficial from a pure interest rate perspective for the borrower, since the bond's yield spread generally will be

Exhibit 3-9 RJW Private-Placement Bond, Make Whole Prepayment Calculated Using a 4.93 Percent Discount Rate (4.93 = 4.43 Risk Free Plus 50 Basis Points).

Period	Principal Balance	Annual Coupon Rate	Semiannual Cash Flow— Interest	Cash Flow— Principal	Present Value
1	50,000,000	0.084	2,100,000		2,049,480
2	50,000,000	0.084	2,100,000		2,000,176
3	50,000,000	0.084	2,100,000		1,952,058
4	50,000,000	0.084	2,100,000		1,905,097
5	50,000,000	0.084	2,100,000		1,859,266
6	50,000,000	0.084	2,100,000		1,814,538
7	50,000,000	0.084	2,100,000		1,770,886
8	50,000,000	0.084	2,100,000		1,728,283
9	50,000,000	0.084	2,100,000		1,686,706
10	50,000,000	0.084	2,100,000		1,646,129
11	50,000,000	0.084	2,100,000		1,606,528
12	50,000,000	0.084	2,100,000		1,567,880
13	50,000,000	0.084	2,100,000		1,530,161
14	50,000,000	0.084	2,100,000		1,493,350
15	50,000,000	0.084	2,100,000		1,457,425
16	50,000,000	0.084	2,100,000		1,422,363
17	50,000,000	0.084	2,100,000		1,388,146
18	50,000,000	0.084	2,100,000		1,354,751
19	50,000,000	0.084	2,100,000		1,322,160
20	50,000,000	0.084	2,100,000	50,000,000	32,013,034
Present value					63,568,417
Loan fair value at 10/1/98 (Exhibit 3-7)					55,239,638
Economic gain from make-whole provision					8,328,779

above the required make-whole provision spread over Treasuries. From a fair value standpoint, make-whole provisions in an otherwise nonprepayable bond have no effect on the value, since the bond is priced assuming an average life without the make-whole provisions being exercised. However, if a bond contract did not include a make-whole provision and the issuer had the right to call the bond at par, the bond would most likely be issued with a higher coupon rate than comparable noncallable bonds to compensate investors for this risk.

PRICING BONDS THAT HAVE SINKING-FUND PAYMENT REQUIREMENTS

As with call options, sinking-fund payment requirements cause a bond's expected average life to decrease. Therefore, the yield used to discount the contractual cash flows is generally different from the yield used to discount a similar quality bond that has the same contractual term. To illustrate this concept, assume that the RJW private-placement bond contractually provides for the issuer to pay $1 million of sinking-fund payments to the investor each period and that the market yield for a comparable-risk and average-life investment is 6.50 percent. Note that this yield is lower than the noncallable yield illustrated in Exhibit 3-6 (6.93 percent). This is because the sinking-fund payments reduce credit risk. The pricing would be as indicated in Exhibit 3-10, assuming the present book value is $38 million ($12 million of sinking-fund payments had already been made, thus reducing the book value from $50 million to $38 million on October 1, 1998).

Present value is lower than the $55,239,638 determined in Exhibit 3-7, because of the decreasing principal balance which reduces the semi-annual interest cash flow, even with the higher coupon rate. In contrast, if the issuer had the ability to call the RJW debt at par on October 1, 1998, the fair value of the loan would be equal to its $38,000,000 par value. (Its average life would be one day.) The

Exhibit 3-10   RJW Private-Placement Bond, Semiannual Sinking-Fund Payments Yield to Maturity = 6.50 Percent.

Period	Principal Balance	Annual Coupon Rate	Semi-annual Cash Flow— Interest	Semi-annual Cash Flow— Principal	Present Value
1	38,000,000	0.084	1,596,000	1,000,000	2,514,286
2	37,000,000	0.084	1,554,000	1,000,000	2,395,746
3	36,000,000	0.084	1,512,000	1,000,000	2,282,178
4	35,000,000	0.084	1,470,000	1,000,000	2,173,385
5	34,000,000	0.084	1,428,000	1,000,000	2,069,181
6	33,000,000	0.084	1,386,000	1,000,000	1,969,383
7	32,000,000	0.084	1,344,000	1,000,000	1,873,817
8	31,000,000	0.084	1,302,000	1,000,000	1,782,317
9	30,000,000	0.084	1,260,000	1,000,000	1,694,720
10	29,000,000	0.084	1,218,000	1,000,000	1,610,872
11	28,000,000	0.084	1,176,000	1,000,000	1,530,623
12	27,000,000	0.084	1,134,000	1,000,000	1,453,830
13	26,000,000	0.084	1,092,000	1,000,000	1,380,355
14	25,000,000	0.084	1,050,000	1,000,000	1,310,066
15	24,000,000	0.084	1,008,000	1,000,000	1,242,833
16	23,000,000	0.084	966,000	1,000,000	1,178,535
17	22,000,000	0.084	924,000	1,000,000	1,117,054
18	21,000,000	0.084	882,000	1,000,000	1,058,275
19	20,000,000	0.084	840,000	1,000,000	1,002,090
20	19,000,000	0.084	798,000	19,000,000	10,442,876
Present value					42,082,419

loan's fair value is equal to its par value because the issuer would most likely exercise the call option, retire the debt, and issue a new loan at the then lower market interest rate (i.e., 6.50 percent in this case) to reduce interest expense. (Call options are generally not included in an instrument that has a make-whole provision.)

Efficiently Pricing a Private-Placement Portfolio

Given the procedures involved in calculating the fair value of a single private-placement loan, one can see the need to automate this process. Many institutional investors use vendor software packages to price and analyze their bond portfolios. For example, many life insurance companies use BondCalc® Corporation's software to internally price and analyze private-placement bonds and mortgage portfolios. The software is capable of quickly processing bond prices when the following information is input:

- The Treasury or LIBOR swap-rate (risk-free) yield curve details the corresponding rate for each bond's average life.
- The spread over the benchmark risk-free rate corresponds to each bond's internal-quality rating and sector. Note that certain bonds are publicly rated. This rating may differ from the analyst's internal rating because the analyst may believe that the bonds trade at a different yield-spread from the one used in its internal rating analysis. For example, an AA-quality publicly rated airline bond may trade at BBB spreads because the sector is judged by the analyst to be more risky.
- An automated portfolio file details each bond's characteristics, such as cash flows (including sinking-fund payments), coupon payments, maturity, and call dates. (Note that most analysts do not price the impact of make-whole provisions being exercised because this is difficult to do. However, software programs can model make-whole premiums based on the implied yield curve and assumed dates when the make-whole provision is expected to occur.)

Appendix D at the end of this chapter provides descriptions of selected portions of BondCalc's software program and a discussion of the program's functionality and available reports. This information is provided to illustrate the breadth of pricing and analytical information that is available and widely used.

How Reliable Are the Values Obtained Using the Pricing Methodologies Discussed Above?

As long as the assumptions are reasonably accurate and *applied on a consistent basis* from period to period, the pricing concepts discussed in this chapter should fairly reflect market conditions. For example, assuming that the internal rating process arrives at an accurate rating, reasonable and comparable spreads are estimated, the bond cash flows are accurately projected, covenants are not waived, and changes from prior spreads and quality assumptions are valid, bond and mortgage values derived with the pricing methods described earlier should provide reasonable estimates of bond prices.

PRICING DEFAULTED BONDS

When a borrower defaults on its contractual obligations, including a violation of a covenant provision (representing a nonmonetary default), the investor must identify and evaluate existing alternatives to maximize the return from the investment. The type of default and reasons for the borrower defaulting will significantly impact the investor's strategy. For example, the typical credit problem with a private-placement loan begins with a covenant-type violation, such as the borrower not meeting a net worth test. At this point, the company still may be financially viable and may be able to take action to correct the problem. Recall that in Exhibit 2-12, the risk premium was reduced for private-placement loans because of the covenant protection feature. The violations of covenants provide an early warning of trouble and give the investor the right to force the borrower to correct the situation or trigger repayment acceleration via legal actions. A common approach that the investor may take is to require that the loan is paid off in full within a specified period or else the lender will demand payment through the court system. In this case, a borrower may find it preferable to sell off assets or take other financing steps to pay the loan off and avoid publicity and litigation. In these situations, the investor estimates the value of the loan by estimating the net realizable value of the loan resulting from all possible actions that may be taken, such as selling off portions of the company or a complete liquidation of its assets. In practice, this involves estimating cash flows that may or may not be discounted based on the timing of the liquidation. Values are estimated based on data obtained from the borrower's financial information and information available in the marketplace. Factors entering into a value determination include:

- The type of default and the extent of the borrower's financial problems. For example, a nonmonetary covenant default is generally less problematic than a monetary default. This is because a borrower is generally in a better financial position at the time of a nonmonetary covenant default than when the borrower actually stops making payments on the debt (as in the case of a monetary default). Therefore, at this time, more options may be available to remedy causes of financial problems. For example, if operations appear normal, sales continue to be good, and the staff remains in place, the borrower may be able to arrange alternate financing to liquidate the investor's debt. In contrast, by the time a monetary default occurs, operating problems may have gone on for some time, eroding working capital, and impacting the going-concern ability of the entity.
- Collateral availability and the seniority of the lender's debt. A senior secured position generally ensures better chances for recovery than a junior position.
- The extent of covenant protections and the going-concern ability of the borrower. A financially viable business with temporary cash flow problems, com-

bined with the lender's being protected by covenants, would provide better chances for principal recovery.

- The extreme importance of the quality of the borrower's management. For example, an innovative and well-intentioned management team would be beneficial in working out a temporary business problem, as opposed to a management team that lacked integrity and required immediate replacement.
- The benefit of a cooperative working relationship of a lender group formed to work out the collection process with the borrower. Subordinate lenders may present an obstacle to reaching a final liquidation plan and require some payment to facilitate general plan acceptance.

A bond investor cannot take actions that could be construed as managing the borrower's business. Doing so could result in the borrower alleging lender liability by blaming the lender for creating the problems and bringing a litigation claim against the lender. This is in contrast to equity investment situations, in which investors can be insiders. As an insider, the investor can better monitor the progress of his or her investment. Private-equity investment covenants are discussed in Chapter 5. For example, private-equity investors frequently hold seats on the board of directors.

Illustration of Pricing a Loan in Default

The data in the RJW private-placement loan will be used to illustrate how covenant and monetary defaults affect valuations.

Nonmonetary Covenant Default

Assume that at October 1, 1998, the RJW Company was in a nonmonetary covenant default on its $38 million loan (as illustrated in Exhibit 3-10, $38 million book value, $42,082,419 fair value), because its net-worth balance fell below a level specified in the note covenants. The default was caused by lower profit margins, triggered by increased competition and an economic slowdown in the sector. Based on this negative trend, the investor opted not to grant a covenant waiver but rather to seek repayment as soon as possible. Although the lender has the right to demand immediate repayment and therefore place RJW in default, the lender agreed to grant RJW 90 days to obtain alternate financing. Based on the assessment that RJW has other financing alternatives available, the lender expects to recover the principal and interest within the stated time frame.

Question: What is the fair value of this loan at October 1, 1998, assuming:

- The October 1, 1998, interest and sinking-fund payments were made?
- A 7.50 percent yield to maturity is the market rate for this investment's risk class and its term (which is higher than the yield used in Exhibit 3-9 when there was no default)?

- The lender has agreed to waive the make-whole provision, provided the loan is repaid within 90 days and not assuming that the loan will be repaid at December 31, 1998?

Answer: The fair value is $38,083,926—calculated in Exhibit 3-11. (Note that this is in contrast to the previously calculated $42,082,419 fair value that assumed the loan performed without a default.)

The cash flow is discounted by the factor .98160, calculated as:

$$\frac{1}{(1+.01875)^1}$$

Where .01875 represents the periodic yield corresponding to a three-month period. (Be careful when discounting less than a semiannual period.)

Note that it is common for the lender and borrower to resolve certain covenant defaults by the lender agreeing to waive the covenant provision violated in consideration of an additional fee or increasing the interest rate, providing that the borrower is still trustworthy and financially viable.

Monetary Default

Assume that at October 1, 1998, the RJW Company (as illustrated in Exhibit 3-10) could not make its scheduled interest payment and told the lender that its business had declined materially from its forecasts, due to increased competition and declining demand for its product. Meetings between RJW management and the lender group resulted in obtaining new cash flow projections and revised financial forecasts. The investment analyst summarized this problem as resulting from changes in business operations, as opposed to excess leverage (which may be addressed through a debt restructuring), and recommended negotiating a discounted payoff as soon as possible. A plan submitted by RJW management was to shut down certain operations, sell equipment, and make a discounted payoff of $28 million in full satisfaction of the debt by April 1, 1999. The analyst supported that alternative as the best approach to maximize the investment's recovery.

Exhibit 3-11   RJW Private-Placement Bond, Covenant Default, Yield to Maturity = 7.50 Percent.

Period	Principal Balance	Annual Coupon Rate	3 Months Cash Flow— Interest	Cash Flow— Principal	Present Value
12/31/98	38,000,000	0.084	798,000	38,000,000	38,083,926

Because RJW's management was dealing in good faith, it avoided costly litigation and stopped the company from depleting funds that would otherwise be used to repay the debt.

Question: What is the fair value of this loan, assuming that no cash flows are received on this loan until the $28 million payment occurs at April 1, 1999?

Answer: The fair value is $26,415,094, calculated as the present value of $28 million to be received in six months, discounted at a 12 percent semiannual yield (see Exhibit 3-12). The 12 percent yield was estimated based on yield of non-investment-grade bonds. This process of determining a discount rate requires judgment and should represent the discount rate that an unbiased investor would seek in a similar situation.

Monetary Default—No Prospect for Recovery

It is extremely rare that a monetary default on a private-placement loan would lead to no recovery. The following is an example of an underwriting deficiency; it illustrates why ratio analysis cannot be relied on entirely and why understanding the sources of cash flows from future operations is so important.

Assume that the RJW loan was issued to a foreign entity that manufactured specialized industrial equipment. Each manufactured item required approximately 18 months to build. The loan was subordinate to bank lines of credit. The loan was made based on the strong market position of the builder and existing orders in place that were scheduled for delivery in one to two years. The orders were from foreign entities, and partial down payments were made for the construction in progress. Subsequent to the loan funding, these problems impacting the entity's ability to continue as a going concern surfaced:

- Construction and quality-control problems created large unfavorable production cost variances related to the work-in-process inventory.
- The entity incurred unanticipated losses on foreign exchange derivative hedges.
- The company's main source of operating cash flows was from leases of certain company-owned equipment; however, most of the leases were canceled after the loan was received. Those leased cash flows were crucial to the entity's continued ability to fund construction in progress.

Exhibit 3-12   RJW Private-Placement Bond, Monetary Default Yield to Maturity = 12 Percent, Valued at 10/1/99.

Period	Principal Balance	Coupon Rate	Cash Flow— Interest	Cash Flow— Principal	Present Value
4/1/99	28,000,000	0	0	28,000,000	26,415,094

- Since the entity could not make the required debt payments, it therefore entered into a bankruptcy and liquidation plan.
- The liquidation proceeds were estimated to be sufficient to cover only the existing bank loans, not the private-placement loan.

Based on those facts, no liquidation proceeds were left for the private-placement lender, and the fair value of the RJW loan is zero. The point of this example is that the assumptions determining future cash flows and the risks associated with those cash flows must be reliable, since they are the primary factors determining the loan's fair value. This is extremely important when analyzing what may be out-of-the-ordinary investments, such as foreign loans, because risks are higher. For example, the lender may have no knowledge of what is going on in the foreign marketplace and how that market reacts to changes. In addition, important documents, such as leases and other financial investments, which impact cash flows, may not be written in English. Therefore, many factors can impact the due diligence process and result in the investor's incomplete understanding of the investment's cash flows.

WHOLE COMMERCIAL MORTGAGE LOANS

Similar to public and private loans, the pricing of whole commercial loans is determined based on discounting expected cash flows by a risk-adjusted rate, which includes a spread over comparable-term Treasuries. The spread generally is derived based on surveying market transactions for similar quality and term loans. Institutional commercial mortgage lending has gone through cycles ranging from a real estate depression in the 1980s to the recovery in the 1990s and has been impacted by a number of occurrences:

- Falling interest rates have favorably impacted residential and commercial building sales and prices.
- Other economic conditions were favorable (i.e., income levels and inflation) during the 1990s, including a booming stock market.
- A slowdown or moratorium on new construction during the early 1990s reduced the supply of real estate and permitted the market to absorb vacant space. Many financial institutions stopped real estate lending transactions until market conditions improved.
- Credit spreads narrowed through much of the 1990s. This narrowing was driven in part by the liquidity brought to the market by the creation of the securitized commercial mortgage-backed market (discussed in Chapter 4). This also provided investors with an alternative to owning whole-commercial mortgage loans.
- The sharp price decline of commercial mortgages in 1998 was due to the widening of sector yield spreads.

A predominant characteristic of this asset class is that those loans have credit risk related to the value of real estate collateral, in contrast to private-placement loans, which are often unsecured and repaid from operating cash flow or refinancing. Significant characteristics are:

- Public information is generally not available, although certain tenants may be public companies. The borrowers generally are private entities or individuals.
- Payments are generally fixed rate and are made monthly.
- The lender usually is secured in a senior claim position on the real estate.
- These loans are generally nonrecourse, which means that the borrower is not personally liable for the loan repayment. As a result, in the event of default, the lender must seek recovery by obtaining the title to the property and liquidating it.
- Make-whole provisions may be included to protect the investor from interest-rate–related reinvestment risk, should the issuer prepay the debt. If prepayment occurs, the lender is compensated for reinvestment risk by an amount calculated with a pay-out formula, such as discounting the remaining cash flows of the loan at the current Treasury bill rate plus 50 basis points. (Refer to Exhibit 3-9.)
- A loan contract can provide for full amortization of principal for all or a portion of the loan; however, bullet maturity is common.
- The loan agreement may require the borrower to provide the lender periodic lease and other financial information and give the lender or its agent the right to inspect the property for purposes of loan monitoring and valuation.
- The value of the *underlying* real estate collateral is the main determinant of the loan's quality and risk premium and, hence, fair value.

The loan quality-rating process that determines the risk premium over Treasuries considers many factors and may vary by lender. Recall the private-placement underwriting process summarized in Chapter 2. This process focused on the entity's ability to generate cash flows and repay the loan. In contrast, the real estate loan underwriting process focuses on the real estate's ability to generate cash flows to repay the loan. Items that have a significant impact on the loan's quality rating are:

- Debt service coverage (calculated using the property's net operating income [NOI] derived as revenue less cash expenses before debt service, and excluding capital improvements, divided by the sum of the interest plus principal amortization payment requirements). A ratio equal to or larger than 1.25 times is viewed as high quality, similar to an A-bond rating.
- Loan-to-value ratio (calculated as the loan's carrying value divided by the property's appraised value). A ratio of less than 60 percent is viewed as high quality, similar to an A-bond rating.
- Major tenant-lease rollovers. The timing of lease rollovers has a significant impact on the loan's quality. For example, if a large percentage of an office build-

ing's leases are renewable during the loan term or near the loan's maturity, the property's cash flows are sensitive to market conditions because the new rentals will reflect current market conditions. This feature implies a lower-quality loan and a higher-risk premium for investors. For example, during the commercial real estate depression of 1988 to 1990 in the Northeast, office vacancies rose dramatically, rental rates dropped, and tenants often benefited by lower lease rentals or opted not to re-lease. Many institutional investors learned that modest risk premiums (25 basis points) received for accepting lower-quality loans did not compensate for the loan interest and principal losses that occurred as property values declined (i.e., tenant lease rollovers, rents resetting to lower market levels).

- Regional tenant occupancy. An occupancy rate of greater than 90 percent is viewed as a high-quality factor for most commercial real estate loans, while lower occupancy rates imply lower-quality loans.
- Regional lease-absorption rates, new construction, and rental rate trends. Those supply and demand factors provide a leading indicator of the geographical region's health. For example, if new office building construction does not exist and available office space is being readily leased at increasing rates, this is indicative of a high-growth market in which property values should be increasing. This was representative of many U.S. real estate markets during the 1990s.
- Major tenant dark. Although the tenant is locked into a long-term lease and is paying rent, the tenant vacates the property because maintaining its business at the site may be uneconomical. This generally has an adverse cash flow impact on other tenants renting the property. For example, assume that one has a loan secured by a shopping center and a major tenant that draws customers to the shopping center vacates the property but continues to make lease payments. Because of the reduction in sales revenues as the traffic in the shopping center falls off, other tenants are adversely affected. Thus, they may not renew their leases or may ask for a rent reduction because their cash flows are unfavorably impacted by the reduction of traffic in the shopping center.
- Economic health of the property's geographical region and sector. The economic strength or weakness in the property's region or sector (i.e., a shopping center versus an office building) affects the quality of a loan. For example, the real estate depression in the Southwest during the 1980s was largely caused by the collapse of oil prices and an economy that was not diversified. The office sector first reacted to this downturn as economic growth trends were reversed and office building vacancy rates skyrocketed. However, as the Southwest's population decreased, apartment and retail sectors also declined. This trend reversed in the 1990s as the economic health of the region improved with a more diversified economic base.
- Borrower's financial strength. This may impact the property's value, since a borrower in financial distress may divert money from the property where it should be spent for maintenance and tenant improvements. However, a financially strong borrower does not necessarily equate to a borrower being more

likely to stay with a property that is failing, since most commercial real estate loans are nonrecourse. Recall that nonrecourse means that the investor has legal recourse only to the collateral, rather than to the borrower personally.

The overall importance of these factors in determining the quality of a loan is affected by an analyst's judgment of the loan's characteristics. For example, a loan could be secured by an office building that is in a marketplace where employment growth is negative, office vacancies are increasing, and rental rates are plummeting. However, the loan still could be rated high quality if the major tenant is financially secure (a *credit tenant*) and locked into a long-term lease. Therefore, the debt service coverage and loan-to-value ratio will be favorable in spite of adverse market conditions. In contrast, an office building loan could be in a rapid growth market yet be classified as having low quality. This could be caused by the long-term nature of its lease terms, which may include below-market rates, or the property having certain physical characteristics that reduce its value (i.e., an obsolete design that does not accommodate computer networks or changing office configurations).

Exhibit 3-13 illustrates a mortgage data summary sheet that may be maintained for each mortgage in support of its quality rating. The information contained in a completed form is used to establish an asset-quality-rating database. The data can be updated quarterly on an exception basis and completely updated on an annual basis.

VALUING A WHOLE COMMERCIAL MORTGAGE LOAN

The pricing of this asset will be illustrated with a hypothetical $50 million, first mortgage loan on RMT Company's office building. An investment report similar to the private-placement investment report was written when the loan was made and included:

- Summary of transaction
- Loan rate, maturity, amortization, and other terms
- Hurdle investment return, as a yield spread over comparable-term Treasuries and public corporate bonds
- Loan-to-value ratio, debt service coverage, internal loan quality rating, etc.
- Description of the borrower (e.g., loan-repayment track record and net worth)
- Borrower's use of the loan proceeds
- Assessment of marketplace (absorption rate, vacancy rate, exposure to key employers)
- Key strengths of transaction
- Key risks of transaction
- Description of secured property, including square footage, age, and condition

Exhibit 3-13 Mortgage Summary Data Form.

Loan Number: _____ Investor: _____ Correspondent: _____

Reviewer: _____ Review Date: _____

Borrower: _____

Street: _____

City: _____ County: _____ ST: _____ Zip: _____

CM Principal: $ _____ Maturity: _____ Balloon: $ _____

Rate: _____ % Payment: $ _____

Property Type: _____ Apart./Retail/Office/Indust./Mixed/Hotel/Other

NRA: _____ sf/units Land: _____ Acres

Mortgage Type(s) ___ First ___ Second ___ Leasehold ___ Recourse

___ Superior: $ _____ ___ Subordinate: $ _____

Delinquency History: _____ Yes or No

Explain: _____

Position of Subject in Market

Relative to Competition –

Physical Condition: _____ Superior, Comparable, Not as Good or Poor

Location: _____ Superior, Comparable, Not as Good or Poor

Quality of Tenancy: _____ Superior, Comparable, Not as Good or Poor

Does Subject Represent Best Use of Land: _____ Yes or No

Explain: _____

Market Characteristics

Market Area: _____ Market Strength: _____

Size: _____ of/units Absorption: _____ sf/units

New Construction: _____ sf/units

Occupancy Subject: _____ % Market: _____ % Break Even: _____ %

Rent Subject Average: $ _____ /sf Effective:$ _____ /sf Break Even: $ _____ /sf

Market Trend: _____

Borrower Information

Borrower 1: _____

Borrower 2: _____

Borrower 3: _____

Borrower 4: _____

Borrower 5: _____

Reputation: _____ Excellent, Good, Fair, Poor or Unknown

Space Occupied by Borrower or Related Party: _____ sf/units

Financial Capacity: _____ Equity in Subject: $ _____

Prop. Mgr.: _____

Reputation: _____ Excellent, Good, Fair, Poor or Unknown

Local: ____ Yes or No

Economic Summary

Orig. Appraised Value: $ _____   Loan/Value (19x1): _____ %

NOI: $ _____   Market CAP Rate: _____ %

Value: $ _____   Debt Coverage: _____

Total Leverage: $ _____   /sf Overall Debt Coverage: _____

Replacement Cost: $ _____   Land Value: $ _____

Liquidation Value: $ _____   Loan Value (19x2): $ _____

NOI: $ _____

	(19X2)	%	(19X3)	%
Vacancy History: (19X1): _____ %		Space Turning		Market Rent
		19X1: _____ %		$ _____ /sf
Another Turnover: _____		19X2: _____ %		$ _____ /sf
		19X3: _____ %		$ _____ /sf

Inflation Rate   (1.5%)   (3.0%)   (5.0%)

Present Value: Discount @ _____ % $ _____ $ _____ $ _____

Escrow/Holdback Funds Outstanding: $ _____

- Description of tenants, lease terms, and exposure to lease rollovers
- Description of covenants, such as borrower agreeing to:
  - Grant periodic site inspection
  - Provide periodic property financial information (i.e., property rent rolls, net operating income, etc.)
  - Maintain capital improvement reserve fund
  - Provide certificate of insurance at specified property dollar values
  - Make timely property tax payments and notify lender of dates and amounts paid
  - Agree to not take out second mortgages

The hypothetical RMT office building loan that will now be valued, as of October 1, 1998, has the characteristics depicted in Exhibit 3-14.

Value of Loan at October 1, 1998

Assume that at October 1, 1998, the loan is in good standing with an internal quality credit rating of A. The market yield for this credit rating and term is 6.40

Exhibit 3-14   RMT First Mortgage Office Building Loan.

Loan carrying amount	$50 million
Loan security (nonrecourse as to borrower)	First lien on property
Loan-to-value ratio	65 percent
Debt service coverage	1.35 times
Loan maturity	10/1/08
Coupon rate	9.15 percent
Date loan made	10/1/92
Spread over comparable-term Treasuries at issuance	250 basis points
Periodic monthly interest payments	$381,250
Amortization	None
Internal quality rating	A
Major tenant lease expiration	10/1/15
Key loan covenants	• Prohibition on any additional debt
	• Make-whole provision of Treasury rate plus 50 basis points
	• Tenant capital improvement reserve
	• Periodic leasing and property financial information provided to lender
	• Annual lender site inspection

Exhibit 3-15 RMT Office Building Loan, Matures 10/1/2008, Percent Yield to Maturity = 6.40, Valued at 10/1/98.

Principal Balance	Coupon Rate	Monthly Cash Flow— Interest	Present Value of Interest Annuity	Maturity Cash Flow	Present Value of Principal Cash Flow	RMT Loan Fair Value
50,000,000	9.15	381,250	33,733,106	50,000,000	26,420,005	60,153,111

percent, as shown in Exhibit 2-12. The loan's current book value is $50 million, and its fair value is $60,153,111, as calculated in Exhibit 3-15.

The keystrokes on an HP12C calculator used to calculate the present values provided in Exhibit 3-15 are:

Present value of annuity of $381,250 for 120 periods, discounted at a monthly rate of .533 percent: 381,250[PMT], 120[n], .533[i], [PV] = $33,733,106

Present value of $50 million received at October 1, 1999, discounted at a monthly rate of .533 percent: 50,000,000[FV], 120[n], .533[i], [PV] = $26,420,005.

Thus, the fair value of the loan at October 1, 1998, is:

$$\$60,153,111 = \$33,733,106 + \$26,420,005$$

The $10,153,111 gain ($60,153,111 fair value less the $50,000,000 book value) resulted from the positive impact of a decrease in the risk-free rate from 6.65 percent (9.15 percent less 250 basis points) to 4.43 percent and the narrowing of sector spreads (and other spread charges) over Treasuries by 53 basis points (from 250 basis points to 197 basis points).

Although this process appears relatively easy, amortizing loans involves a more complicated calculation. Entities could efficiently price entire portfolios similar to this portfolio by using software such as BondCalc Corporation's software, discussed earlier and illustrated in Appendix D at the end of this chapter. Information that would have to be inputted:

- The Treasury yield curve, corresponding to each loan's average life
- The yield spread over Treasuries corresponding to each loan's quality rating and sector (office versus apartments)
- An electronic portfolio data file, detailing each loan's characteristics, such as cash flows (including coupon payments), maturity, and principal amortization.

MONETARY DEFAULT SCENARIOS

Assume that the RMT loan became a problem loan because a major tenant defaulted on its lease and vacated the property. The loan valuation process would now focus on determining the investment's expected cash flows, assessing the level of risk associated with the investment, and deciding on the optimum strategy to maximize the investor's recovery of principal and interest. To illustrate this process, we will analyze three common situations: (1) a loan restructuring, (2) a foreclosure, and (3) a negotiated discounted payoff.

Loan Restructuring

Assume that the borrower is acting in good faith and taking steps to correct the property's temporary cash flow problem. The problem was caused by a major tenant that went bankrupt; however, the property remains economically viable. The borrower is now awaiting the investor's approval for a loan modification prior to entering into a lease with a replacement tenant. The borrower estimates incurring $4 million of tenant improvement costs and cash flow shortfalls because it will take four months before the new tenant moves in and starts paying rent. Therefore, the borrower has requested a four-month suspension of interest payments and the addition of deferred interest to the loan balance. The borrower will pay for the improvements personally and through property cash flows that otherwise would be used to pay the four months of interest beginning with the October 1, 1998, payment due on that date ($1,525,000 = 4 × $381,250).

In this case, the investor should agree to work with the borrower because the borrower is acting in good faith and is providing its own funds to cover a portion of the tenant improvement costs. Since the loan will become restructured and not pay interest for four months, the investor assesses that the loan quality has dropped to a B rating. The discount rate for a B-rated loan is approximately 12 percent, as reflected in Exhibit 2-12, for a public B-1-quality bond. The fair value of the loan using this 12 percent discount rate is then calculated at $41,476,741, as indicated in Exhibit 3-16.

The calculation consists of two parts, a present value of an annuity of interest payments and a present value of a balloon-principal payment:

The present value of the interest payments is calculated on an HP12C as 116[n]; 1[i]; 393,012[PMT]; [PV]. Annuity interest payments of $26,909,627 are then measured at a present value back four months: 4[n]; 1[i]; 26,909,627[FV]; [PV], to arrive at $25,859,623. The present value of the $51,542,531 principal payment to be received at October 1, 2008, is $15,617,118, calculated as 51,542,531[FV]; 1[i]; 120[n], [PV]. Valuation software such as BondCalc Corporation's software can be used for those calculations.

Loan Foreclosure

Assume that the lender has decided that the most prudent course of action is to foreclose on the property because, due to many issues, the borrower has given up on the property. For example, the property has other large vacancies, it requires

Exhibit 3-16 Price of RMT Restructured Loan, 12 Percent Yield to Maturity, Calculated at 10/1/99, Loan Matures 10/1/2008.

Balance	Coupon Rate	Coupon Interest	Present Value Interest Annuity at 12.0%	Present Value of Principal at Maturity
50,000,000	0.0915	0	0	0
50,381,250	0.0915	0	0	0
50,765,407	0.0915	0	0	0
51,152,493	0.0915	0	0	0
51,542,531	0.0915	0	0	0
51,542,531	0.0915	393,012	25,859,623	15,617,118
Present value of total cash flows				41,476,741

significant tenant improvements and leasing costs, and the borrower no longer has any equity interest in the office building.

Based on this situation, the loan's fair value may be calculated using the following method, which estimates the value of the office building. This calculation is done because the office building typically will be sold after the investor acquires the title to the property.

Capitalization of Current Net Operating Income

This method assumes that NOI is stabilized at current levels. It is a simple formula to apply, since it uses the actual NOI to arrive at a value. The formula for calculating fair value is as follows:

Real Estate Fair Value = NOI/Market Capitalization Rate

NOI is calculated as the property's gross income less cash operating expenses. It does not include depreciation, capital improvements, and debt service charges. The market capitalization rate is the variable that is more difficult to estimate. It may be estimated as the reciprocal of the price-to-earnings ratio that similar properties are trading for in the market, which is calculated by dividing NOI by the sales price of the property (no deduction for sales commissions). For example, assume a similar quality office building in the same market was just sold for $20 million, and its current NOI was $2 million. This means that an appropriate capitalization rate would be 10 percent. Assuming that the RMT office building's NOI is $3 million, the estimated fair value of the building would be $30 million ($3 million/.10). Valuing the loan also would require determining the loan's legal and other collection costs and the time period it will take actually to gain control of and sell the property. Assuming $100,000 in collection costs, $1 million in sales costs, and six months for this sale to occur, the loan's fair value would be the present value of the $28,900,000 ($30 million less $1.1 million), which is the net realizable value to be received in six months. This amount may be discounted at a higher rate, for example, 12 percent (or a periodic monthly interest rate of 1 percent), to arrive at a $27,225,107 fair value. This is calculated on an HP12C calculator as 28,900,000[FV], 1[i], 6[n], PV. Note that due to the increased risk, a higher discount rate may be used. However, the market tends to trade those types of problem loans at a discount reflective of using higher discount rates.

Advantages and Disadvantages of the Capitalization of NOI Approach

Although this formula is simple to apply, it may be difficult to obtain comparable transactions for determining the capitalization rate. It also does not consider the possibility that future cash flows may be different from past cash flows and that the same cash flows may not be received perpetually (e.g., increased NOI caused by improving markets and active property management and vice versa). Therefore, the following valuation approach may be used.

Discounting Cash Flows for a Finite Period

This discounted cash flow approach estimates a value by discounting the property's estimated yearly NOI and estimated property sales price at the end of a specified period. A key aspect of this approach is the ability to estimate the components of NOI. For example, the rent roll must be estimated based on the existing leases in place, expected changes in market conditions, forecasts of tenant retentions as leases expire, and forecasts of new leasing volume and rates. Although expenses such as taxes, property management fees, and insurance are relatively easy to estimate, capital improvements and repairs present more of a challenge, since those may depend on new tenant demands. After determining the NOI, one also must estimate when the property will be sold and at what price. Holding periods may vary depending on the investor's expectation of the point in which the NOI has stabilized and the property value has been maximized. In the RMT office building example, one may assume that capital improvements made in years 1 and 2 will cause rents to increase and stabilize at $6 million per year, with future adjustments for inflation (provided in leases). Therefore, one may assume the property will be sold at the end of the fourth year. The property value at this point is estimated as a capitalization of the fourth year NOI of $4,331,379.

The discount rate used in those calculations is determined by reference to other comparably risky investments. In the case of the RMT office building loan, the property value is determined as shown in Exhibit 3-17.

Using an HP12C calculator, the property value of $30,572,151 is calculated as 12[i], 0[g] [Cfo], 2,000,000[CHS], [g] [CFj], 212,000[g] [CFj], 3,372,480[g] [CFj],

Exhibit 3-17 RMT Office Building Loan, Discounted Cash Flow Approach.

	Year 1	Year 2	Year 3	Year 4
Gross Rental Income	4,550,000	5,000,000	5,500,000	6,000,000
Cash Outflows				
Taxes	600,000	624,000	648,960	674,918
Property management	200,000	208,000	216,320	224,973
Insurance	150,000	156,000	162,240	168,730
Repairs/maintenance	600,000	800,000	800,000	500,000
Capital improvements	5,000,000	3,000,000	300,000	100,000
Total Cash Outflow	6,550,000	4,788,000	2,127,520	1,668,621
Property Sale				42,541,238
($4,431,379 NOI/.10 Cap				
less 4% sales expenses)				
Net Cash Flow	−2,000,000	212,000	3,372,480	46,872,617
Present value at 12%				
discount rate	30,572,151			

46,872,617[CFj], [f] [NPV]. This property value then would be measured at present value to give effect to discount for the six-month period required to gain control of the property. This amounts to $28,800,349, calculated as 30,572,151[FV], 1[i], 6[n], [PV]. As can be seen, this approach produces a different amount from the method discussed earlier and is very sensitive to changing cash flow estimates and the residual (i.e., expected net sales price) estimated for the property.

Comparable-Sales Valuation Method

Another method that may be used to determine the collateral's price uses recent sales prices of comparable properties with adjustments to reflect differences between the referenced property sold and the collateral. A common example of when comparable sales prices of real estate sold are used to arrive at a fair value is when valuing apartments or condominium units. A price reference such as recent sales at $40,000 per unit of comparable quality and square footage units may be referenced. It is more difficult to obtain comparable quotes for office buildings, since they are not as homogenous as apartments. However, the recent sales prices of reasonably comparable office buildings may be adjusted for property differences such as occupancy, maintenance costs, environmental issues, or other differences to arrive at a fair value. For example, assume that an A-quality office building in the same market as the RMT office building was recently sold at a price of $200 per square foot. However, this property was 70 percent leased, while the RMT building requires $10 million of tenant improvements to reach this occupancy. The RMT office building would then be valued at $30 million, calculated as $40 million (200,000 square feet times $200) less $10 million of tenant improvements. This amount then would be discounted to reflect sales commissions, the time necessary to sell the property, and risks of realizing the value to arrive at the nonperforming loan's fair value, when using the discounted cash flow valuation method.

Negotiated Discounted Payoff Approach

Under certain circumstances, a borrower will offer to repay the loan at a discounted amount. A lender may choose this alternative based on an analysis of many factors, including the assessment of the property's fair value (using the above methods), the lender's cash flow needs, alternative investment returns, financial statement presentation issues (i.e., the negative impact of owning non-earning loans or foreclosed real estate), and the costs of foreclosing the property. In certain circumstances, state bankruptcy laws may delay foreclosure and drive collection costs up. Also, a borrower may be in a better position to maximize the property's value if he or she maintains the property. For example, the borrower may have a tenant who wants to lease this property. Furthermore, if the lender foreclosed the property, the borrower may place this tenant in another one of the borrower's properties, thus causing more vacancy at this property. In those circumstances, an offer by the borrower for a discounted payoff in the range of values in line with values estimated with the above valuation methods would make economic sense to the lender. However, if the lender has a better plan for leasing the property and generating higher returns, it probably would not make economic sense.

Other Pricing Issues

Similar to the private-placement investment process, the quality and track record of the lender's management team and its system of internal controls are very important. They are important because fair values estimated with data provided by management are only as reliable as the financial information used in the valuations. Therefore, a number of asset information management controls should be in place:

- Annual site inspection and appraisals should be performed.
- Market sector and geographical region's economic health should be assessed periodically. (For example, the office market may be weakening due to over-building, yet the retail and apartment sectors remain healthy because those sectors were not overbuilt.)

- Periodic (and at least annual) property financial information should be provided to the lender or servicing agent, including the property's NOI, rent roll, and completed property improvements.
- A reporting system that requires borrowers and servicing agents (if any) to notify the lender if any material events occur that affect the property's value or operations should exist.

NOTES

1. For a complete explanation of the OAS model and other option-pricing models, refer to Bennett W. Golub and Leo M. Tilman, *Risk Management—Approaches for Fixed Income Markets* (New York: John Wiley & Sons, Inc., 2000).

2. For a detailed explanation of private-placement covenants, refer to the *Financial Covenants Reference Manual,* at *users.aol.com/covenants/.* The manual was developed by the joint efforts of various law firms and private-placement departments.

Bloomberg—
Yield to Call Data

Yields to Call – YTC <GO>

```
Page                                              DG04 Corp  YTC

              YIELDS TO CALL                    Page 1 of  1
AMC ENTERTAINMNT  AEN9 ½ 03/15/09  92.5452/ 92.7952 (10.70 /66) BGN  MATRIX
    Settlement Date      9/25/1998           Price  92.79524
    Yield To Maturity    3/15/2009 @REDM 100         10.657
    Yield to Custom      3/15/2009 @REDM 100         10.657 CNV Duration
    Yield to Next Call    3/15/2002 @REDM 104-24      13.275 & Risk Calc
    Yield To Refunding    3/15/2002 @REDM 104-24      13.275
    Yield to Worst Call  3/15/2009 @REDM 100         10.657

                               Treas    Treas    Adjusted  Risk
    Date      Price      Yield  Curve    Spread   Duration  Factor
    3/15/02   104.7500   13.275 4.598    8.677    2.829     2.633
    3/15/03   103.5600   12.260 4.567    7.692    3.497     3.254
    3/15/04   102.3750   11.637 4.575    7.063    4.100     3.816
    3/15/05   101.1900   11.224 4.609    6.615    4.645     4.322
    3/15/06   100.0000   10.935 4.644    6.291    5.136     4.779
    3/15/09   100.0000   10.657 4.737    5.921    6.350     5.909




Copyright 1998 BLOOMBERG L.P.  Frankfurt:69-920410  Hong Kong:2-2977-6000  London:171-330-7500  New York:212-318-2000
Princeton:609-279-3000    Singapore:226-3000    Sydney:2-9777-8666    Tokyo:3-3201-8900    Sao Paulo:11-3048-4500
                                                                      I557-367-0 22-Sep-98  9:49:42
```

Bloomberg's Yields to Call application helps users to understand the price and yield relationship for a bond at each possible redemption date. It also provides the bond's spread to a benchmark for each of these yields, as well as the relevant risk measures.

BENEFITS: *YTC helps users to anticipate what yields to expect given their redemption assumptions for a bond. It provides insight into the range of possible yield scenarios, so that users can better gauge the value of the securities they are buying, selling, and analyzing.*

Source: © 2001 Bloomberg L.P. All rights reserved. Reprinted with permission. Visit *www. Bloomberg.com.*

Salespeople: **YTC** allows salespeople to become the "go-to person" for their buyside clients. It helps them to fully inform their customers of the range of possible yields they can expect based on their interest rate assumptions.

Portfolio Managers: **YTC** helps portfolio managers to anticipate the possible yields on a bond based on their redemption assumptions in order to make fully informed buy and sell decisions that will help them to meet their portfolio's objectives.

Traders: **YTC** helps traders to view all the redemption scenarios of a bond in one place in order to ensure they are pricing the bond to worst call.

INTERPRETATION:
The **YTC** screen is divided into two main sections. The top half calculates yields for predetermined call dates for the bond. This section helps users to anticipate the best and worst case scenario for holding this bond. In this example, the yield to maturity on the AMC Entertainment bond is 10.657, which matches the yield to worst. In this case the yield to maturity is also the worst case yield scenario.

```
  Page                                              DG04 Corp   YTC
                    YIELDS  TO  CALL               Page 1 of  1
  AMC ENTERTAINMNT   AEN9 '₂ 03/15/09  92.5452/ 92.7952 (10.70 /66) BGN   MATRIX
           Settlement Date       9/25/1998         Price  92.79524
           Yield To Maturity    3/15/2009 @REDM  100       10.657
           Yield to Custom      3/15/2009 @REDM  100       10.657 INV Duration
           Yield to Next Call   3/15/2002 @REDM  104-24    13.275 & Risk Calc
           Yield To Refunding   3/15/2002 @REDM  104-24    13.275
           Yield to Worst Call  3/15/2009 @REDM  100       10.657

                                 Treas    Treas   Adjusted  Risk
          Date    Price    Yield Curve   Spread   Duration  Factor
          3/15/02  104.7500 13.275 4.598  8.677     2.829    2.633
          3/15/03  103.5600 12.260 4.567  7.692     3.497    3.254
          3/15/04  102.3750 11.637 4.575  7.063     4.100    3.816
          3/15/05  101.1900 11.224 4.609  6.615     4.645    4.322
          3/15/06  100.0000 10.935 4.644  6.291     5.136    4.779
          3/15/09  100.0000 10.657 4.737  5.921     6.350    5.909




  Copyright 1998 BLOOMBERG L.P.  Frankfurt:69-920410  Hong Kong:2-2977-6000  London:171-330-7500  New York:212-318-2000
  Princeton:609-279-3000    Singapore:226-3000    Sydney:2-9777-8666    Tokyo:3-3201-8900    Sao Paulo:11-3048-4500
                                                                        I557-367-0 22-Sep-98  9:49:42
```

*The settlement date and current price of the bond can be customized to fit the user's
assumptions. Notice below, that if the price of the bond were to rise to a price of 101, it
would now trade to a worst call of 3/15/06, with a yield of 9.310.*

```
3                                                        DG04 Corp   YTC
                     YIELDS  TO  CALL                      Page 1 of  1
AMC ENTERTAINMNT  AEN9 ½ 03/15/09  92.8106/ 93.0606 (10.65 /61) BGN  MATRIX
        Settlement Date      9/25/1998            Price  101.0000
        Yield To Maturity    3/15/2009  @REDM  100        9.347
        Yield to Custom      3/15/2009  @REDM  100        9.347 CNV Duration
        Yield to Next Call   3/15/2002  @REDM  104-24    10.320 & Risk Calc
        Yield To Refunding   3/15/2002  @REDM  104-24    10.320
        Yield to Worst Call  3/15/2006  @REDM  100        9.310

                                       Treas    Treas    Adjusted  Risk
           Date     Price     Yield    Curve    Spread   Duration  Factor
          3/15/02  104.7500  10.320    4.558    5.762     2.890    2.927
          3/15/03  103.5600   9.869    4.523    5.346     3.572    3.617
          3/15/04  102.3750   9.599    4.529    5.071     4.192    4.245
          3/15/05  101.1900   9.427    4.563    4.864     4.756    4.816
          3/15/06  100.0000   9.310    4.597    4.713     5.268    5.334
          3/15/09  100.0000   9.347    4.691    4.656     6.551    6.634



Copyright 1998 BLOOMBERG L.P.  Frankfurt:69-920410  Hong Kong:2-2977-6000  London:171-330-7500  New York:212-318-2000
Princeton:609-279-3000      Singapore:226-3000     Sydney:2-9777-8666     Tokyo:3-3201-8900    Sao Paulo:11-3048-4500
                                                                          I557-367-0 22-Sep-98 11:48:33
```

*All of the yellow and white highlighted fields can be changed so that users can calculate
prices based on their yield assumptions for each of the redemption scenarios. The Yield
to Custom field allows users to input their own redemption date and price to determine
the yield they will receive if they hold the bond to an expected date.*

The bottom section lists each of the possible call dates for the bond, with their corresponding price and yield given that the bond is redeemed at each of those dates. In this example, we can see that the AMC Entertainment bond may be called each year from 2002 through 2006, and then again in 2009. For instance, if the bond is called in 2004, it will be priced at 102 3/8, and a yield of 11.637.

```
Page                                                   DG04 Corp   YTC
                   YIELDS  TO  CALL                    Page 1 of  1
AMC ENTERTAINMNT   AEN9 ½ 03/15/09  92.5452/ 92.7952 (10.70 /66) BGN  MATRIX
        Settlement Date      9/25/1998             Price  92.79524
        Yield To Maturity    3/15/2009  @REDM  100         10.657
        Yield to Custom      3/15/2009  @REDM  100         10.657 CNV Duration
        Yield to Next Call   3/15/2002  @REDM  104-24      13.275 & Risk Calc
        Yield To Refunding   3/15/2002  @REDM  104-24      13.275
        Yield to Worst Call  3/15/2009  @REDM  100         10.657

                                    Treas    Treas   Adjusted  Risk
        Date      Price     Yield   Curve    Spread  Duration  Factor
        3/15/02   104.7500  13.275  4.598    8.677   2.829     2.633
        3/15/03   103.5600  12.260  4.567    7.692   3.497     3.254
        3/15/04   102.3750  11.637  4.575    7.063   4.100     3.816
        3/15/05   101.1900  11.224  4.609    6.615   4.645     4.322
        3/15/06   100.0000  10.935  4.644    6.291   5.136     4.779
        3/15/09   100.0000  10.657  4.737    5.921   6.350     5.909




Copyright 1998 BLOOMBERG L.P.  Frankfurt:69-920410  Hong Kong:2-2977-6000  London:171-330-7500  New York:212-318-2000
Princeton:609-279-3000      Singapore:226-3000    Sydney:2-9777-8666    Tokyo:3-3201-8900    Sao Paulo:11-3048-4500
                                                                    I557-367-0 22-Sep-98  9:49:42
```

To the right of these prices and yields, the corresponding yield for that point on the Treasury curve is listed, as well as the spread in basis points. Finally the last two columns on the right provide risk measures on the bond. These columns list the Adjusted Duration and Risk Factor for the bond given each of the redemption dates, prices, and yields. In the above example of a call date of 2004, the Treasury curve at that interpolated point yields 4.575, which is 7.063 points below the yield of the AMC bond. Based on the price and yield of this bond at this 2004 call date, its adjusted duration would be 4.1 and it would have a risk factor of 3.816. This bottom section provides users with key information that will help them to predict the behavior of the bond, given different redemption scenarios.

SUMMARY:
YTC *helps users to anticipate what yields to expect given their redemption assumptions for a bond. It provides insight into the range of possible yield scenarios, so that users can better gauge the value of the securities they are buying, selling, and analyzing.*

WHERE THE DATA COMES FROM:
The structure and terms of the bond, including the call schedule, are fed into **YTC** *from the description of the bond. The price of the security is filtered into this screen based on the customer's choice of pricing source that he/she set up on* **PCS**. *Bloomberg has a vast number of pricing sources that provide executable, indicative and composite prices.*

RELATED FUNCTIONS: *YA, YAS, YT*

Selected Portions
of BondCalc® Brochures

BONDCALC®

It handles *all* types of fixed income securities with after tax, leveraging, and multi-currency capabilities. Includes extensive support for private placements, commercial mortgages, bank loans, high yield securities, municipals, emerging market debt, convertibles, serial issues, and other corporate securities. Portfolio calculations based on all underlying cash flows and are not weighted averages.

BondCalc® Values Securities and Portfolios Using: OAS (arbitrage-free binomial tree), option-free yield, yield-to-worst and static spread discounting (off theoretical spot curve). Matrix pricing leads to total return, projected total return, and performance attribution. Uses either implied forward yield curve or 2-dimensional interest rate forecasts to value make-whole calls, bond for bond swaps, and horizon analysis work-outs. Manages trader's book with daily marking-to-market, cost of funds charge, and month-to-date P&L or manages short-term portfolios with daily marking to accreted value. Handles hedging and liabilities. Analyzes bond refundings. Equity portion of convertibles are valued over a range of stock growth rates using artificial intelligence techniques.

Output includes: 1. results returned to the screen, 2. 100 preset analytical graphs and reports, 3. a portfolio report and graph writer with over 200 columns to choose from, and 4. a single-security report writer with over 50 statistics for each call date. All output is publication quality, and can be easily exported to spreadsheets. Supports import of descriptive data via comprehensive file format.

BondCalc® Corporation
492 First Street
Brooklyn, New York 11215
718.499.9900
Fax 718.499.2018

Matrix Pricing

Choice of pricing to: (1) Option Free Yield. BondCalc® iteratively solves for price that gives this yield. (2) Lowest matrix priced call date. Includes full worst/worst logic (that is, sinkers doubled and issue called). (3) Maturity. (4) Static spread either to worst or to term. Yield curve and matrices can be in term, average life or duration space. Has optional noncurrent coupon adjustment which can be either multiplicative or additive. Distribution of portfolio by rating can be analyzed with either clustered horizontal bar chart or pie chart. Spread matrix distribution has pie char. Prints a report and clones the portfolio inserting the matrix derived prices. Prices in cloned portfolio can then be adjusted and used to run all other portfolio reports in the system. Does not matrix price if the portfolio has a price for that security already input. Maintains a database of an unlimited number of spread matrices. Can also have spread sector differentials for up to 48 market sectors. Cleanly handles after-tax pricing of issues with tax preferences, e.g. ESOP bonds. Performance attribution can be calculated if portfolios for beginning and end transactions are available. Has comprehensive import format for getting data from databases and accounting systems. Matrix pricing can be optionally done as of a future date. A projected total return can then be calculated to this horizon. BondCalc® can also calculate Performance Return and Attribution.

Issues/Securities

Each bond or security is stored in an appropriate format when it is first entered into the database. Different Input Screens are used for different securities. Many securities may fit under more than one input screen. The following are short explanations of the Bonds/Securities that are handled by BondCalc®.

Simple Bonds/MTNs

This is for bonds with simple sinking funds. Also Securities floating off an Index, with an Increasing Rate, and with the Coupon Rate offset from the Maturity Date.

PIK Securities

Paid-In-Kind Securities allow the issuer the option of paying the interest or dividend with more of the same Securities. They are usually preferred issues. There is an extra report to show sensitivity to the date when it switches from PIKing to paying.

Zeros/Zero-Pays/DIBs

The Zero-Coupon screen. Also Zero-Pays, Deferred Coupon Bonds and Treasury Strips.

Sinking Funds: Level Amount/Preferred Stock

This format is intended for Sinking Fund Preferred. As a preferred has no stated maturity, it is usually defined in term of its sinking fund. If the issue also has a "doubling-up" option the program will calculate yields under such a scenario.

Sinking Funds: Varied/Bundled Serial Bonds/Level Pay, etc.

The most comprehensive input screen for a sinking fund issue with mandatory pro rata S.F. Also can be used for public issue if selling at a premium and a large block is held. By selecting an option, each sinking fund can become the maturity amount of a bond in a serial issue. Can also handle serial zeros calculating a composite accretion curve. Handles all private placement level-payment commercial mortgages. Has options for handling: Sinking Funds offset from coupon date, Negative Amortization Bonds and compound interest, all received with principle redemption.

Sinking Funds: Redeem at Amortized Value

Those bonds are issued at a discount and have S.F. that are redeemed at the OID accretion curve value. This feature gives the bonds a relatively low duration and lack of volatility. If S.F. are not entered, it will default to all S.F., including maturity, being the same. Merrill Lynch did some originations of this structure in 1985.

Pass-through Mortgages

Handles all pass-through mortgages. Has options for a Balloon, a Graduated Payment and an Initial Interest-Only Period. Defaults to 30/360 day counting. User sets payment frequency. Can also handle Title 11 and SBA loans.

Money Market Instruments/GICs

Covers all Money Market issues that pay all interest at maturity, e.g. Discount and Interest Bearing issues.

Perpetual Annuities

Those are included for Preferreds, UK Bonds and the educational value. (At this time perpetuities are in beta testing.)

Lyons and Other Convertibles

This is a comprehensive screen that can cover many variants. Included is conversion information to analyze the conversions for a range in per annum stock prices. (Refer to page 8 for more.)

Free Form Cash Flow Input

Allows for custom creation of any unusual security, such as might be received in a restructuring. One has columns for date, principal amount and interest/dividends. An entered price will be multiplied against the remaining balance in the principal column. The easiest way to build an initial set of cash flows it to use the cloning facility on a single security report menu.

Swaps

Here the user can do a side-by-side comparison of two or more issues (up to 12 total on both sides.) Any type of security can be compared to any other. Results, including yields, statistics and a breakeven rate after a rollover, are displayed to the screen. Reports are available to understand the underlying cash flows. Includes financial statement impact of swap.

Compare/Batch Portfolio

This section allows the comparison of portfolios against other portfolios. Output includes a convexity graph. It also can group together Portfolios for concurrent processing.

Return on Portfolio/Attribution

BondCalc® can calculate the return over a specified time period. All that are needed are a beginning and ending portfolio, and entries in a ticket database. Attribution, using multiple matrix pricings, has categories for: Coupon, Change in Yield Curve, Change in Spread Matrix, Change in Market Sector Differential, Change in Rating and Change in Exchange Rate.

File Importing Utilities

BondCalc® can import: (1) Security descriptive information from other databases, (2) Portfolios, and (3) Security prices.

Yield Curve Scenarios

One can have a database of yield curves, current market and projected. The theoretical Zero Spot Curve and the Implied Forward Yield Curve are calculated. Those Curves are usable throughout BondCalc® for pricing, Horizon/Workout Analysis and Make-whole pricing. Output consists of a 3-D surface plot (implied or forecasted), a comparison line graph, scatter plot and others. One has a choice of six input screens. Yield curves can always be directly accessed with a "hot" key.

Calculation Routines

The pop-up calculator menu can be called on by a hot key and includes the following functions:

Black-Scholes
Convertible Payback
Rate/Compounding Basis Changer
Bond Calculator/Backsolver
Pub 1212 OID Tax Calcs & Report
FX Cross Rates Matrix
IRR Calculator—Date Driven
Combined Short-Term Issue & Bond
Currency Equivalencies
Delayed Delivery Bonds
Warrant Pricing Models

Output—On Screen

For a single security, a swap and portfolio one sees a page of results displayed on the screen. The single security section includes: a call/put date matrix of yields (pretax and after tax) and prices, additional information on money market issues, accrued interest, make-whole call information, average life, YTM without S.F. calculation of sinking fund issues, modified duration, convexity and the current accreted price if issued at a discount. If horizon information is input, the screen will display the horizon date, horizon price and yield, reinvestment rate(s) and total return. A sinking fund issue can also be priced using a yield for each sinking fund principal (input or off a yield curve). The Security Report Writer (with 60 columns to choose from) can be used to create a custom display, and with horizontal scrolling, all columns can be seen on the screen.

The swap section displays two columns with: maturity date, initial price/ basis, yield to maturity, swap horizon yield and price/basis, yield to workout, modified duration, convexity, accrued interest, market value, future value and effective yield. If the maturity dates of each side are different the following rollover breakeven information will also be displayed: reinvestment rate(s) until the rollover date, future value at maturity, effective yield and the breakeven rate.

The Portfolio section displays yields and statistics to maturities, to worsts, to next calls and to first par calls. Monetary amounts are shown.

Report Writers Feed Into Graphic Writer

BondCalc® has numerous analytical graphs which are derived from most of the 210 columns of data available from the Portfolio Report Writer. Some other graphs are convexity, portfolio distributions (horizontal bar charts of modified duration, coupon, average life and maturity), vertical bar chart of future cash flows (with control over time increment and ending date), pie charts breaking down the portfolio into rating, classification or input schemas, and a yield/duration scatter plot.

Portfolio and Security Reports

BondCalc® prints cash flows (amortization schedules) to either the call dates or maturity date with extensive footnote explanations. Pretax and after tax versions are available. A sensitivity report shows yields to call for a range of prices (basically a convexity graph in numerical form). The statistical report is a formatted version of the single security on-screen results (discussed above). There is a make-whole call premium report that shows the return for a range of future treasury yields. A report pricing a sinking fund or serial issue off the Treasury yield curve is available. In the Portfolio section a Statistics Report is available that calculates the averages (including "to-worst" numbers) using all portfolio cash flows. Listings of the portfolio holdings are producible using a fully custom Report Writer with 210 columns to choose from. A report lists all the portfolio cash flows due so the accounting department can check funds received. A report calculates the price effects on a portfolio after a projected yield curve change. The reports in the Swap Section include various cash flow reports to analyze results. All reports (and graph numbers) can be easily imported by Lotus 1-2-3 or Excel.

USES FOR BONDCALC®

S.F. Desk & Private Placement Trading

BondCalc® can handle any sinking fund or serial bond structure using discounted cash flow techniques. Compare true DCF prices with formula price shortcuts used by some analytic vendors. One can price off-Treasury yield curve, handle ESOP debt, calculate make-whole call premiums.

Purchasers of Private Placements

Understand the valuation characteristics of holdings. Calculate all commercial mortgages. Matrix price portfolio.

Emerging Market Debt Trading

Price, analyze and compare all issues. BondCalc® can handle floating rates, increasing rate, or any custom coupon schedule. Sinking funds can be more frequent than coupons.

High Yield Trading

Correctly price, analyze and compare all esoteric issues. Price bank loans that have been margined.

Mortgage-backed Securities

Pass-through, commercial mortgages, Title 11, SBA's and graduated payment mortgages.

High Net Worth Individuals/Financial Planners

Manage portfolios. Help with investment decisions. Analyze swap opportunities. Evaluate relative worth of investments.

Portfolio Managers

Compare effects of changes in market conditions on different portfolios of fixed income securities. Analyze portfolio composition. Produce custom reports. Performance measurement/total return is available.

Fixed Income and High Yield Research

Compare changes in market conditions on different types of securities. Compare price arbitrage between two securities. Store your own price histories and graph yields.

Foreign Currency Bonds

Given exchange rates and projected appreciation or depreciation rates, Bond-Calc® will calculate the return converted back to the base currency. Payment frequencies can be based on a multiple of a week. It handles all currencies.

Convertible Bonds

BondCalc® handles every regular, sinking fund and puttable zero-coupon convert. BondCalc® graphically values the equity of the convert. For a range of annual stock growth rates the program will use artificial intelligence to determine when the issue ends, (either by maturity, voluntary conversion, forced conversion or put). Any converted stock is sold to return the principal, and a zero spot present value and modified IRR are calculated.

Municipal Bonds

BondCalc® can do after-tax comparisons of investment alternatives and easily handle serial issues with varying coupon rates. Traders can base their decisions on pretax yields off of high grade index or after tax off Treasuries. Can handle super sinkers.

Debt Origination Function/Corporate
Finance/Financial Engineering

Prepare after-tax analysis of premium debt refundings. Compare costs of financing alternatives under different interest rate scenarios. Use reports and graphs to explain structure. Has excellent bundling capabilities. Create new securities.

MTN Trading

The MTN community has some issues with stepped rates in addition to their usual fixed coupon dates with a varying maturity date.

Private Placement Origination

BondCalc® can combine bonds to simulate a multi-tranche takedown. A short term interim financing can be combined with a bond to get the total financing cost.

Institutional Sales

BondCalc® has a term sheet and many reports that help sell bonds.

Educational

BondCalc® extensive footnoting and help screens make for an excellent hands-on tutorial on all types of corporate fixed income securities. All calculations are explained.

Mortgage-Backed and Asset-Backed Securities

INTRODUCTION

Chapter 4 discusses the characteristics and pricing of mortgage-backed and asset-backed securities. The term "mortgage-backed securities" generally refers to two categories of investments: mortgage-pass-through certificates and collateralized mortgage obligations (CMOs). Both investment types represent securitization transactions in which pools of mortgages serve as the collateral for securities that are issued to investors. Mortgage-pass-through certificates receive a pro rata allocation of all the principal and interest (net of servicing fees) generated by the loans in the securitization. In contrast, CMOs, also termed pay-through securities, may receive a stated coupon payment that can be subject to allocations of the pool's principal, interest, or both, as specified in the trust agreement. The pool collateral commonly comprises conforming (federally guaranteed principal and interest) single-family residential mortgage loans. The market also has evolved to include asset-backed securities, which are securities collateralized by loans, commercial mortgages, receivables, bonds, and other collateral.

Many mortgage-backed securities are publicly traded (SEC and exchange registered) and, therefore, have available market prices. To illustrate the characteristics of mortgage-pass-through certificates and CMOs, a hypothetical securitization of residential mortgages in both a mortgage-pass-through certificate and a CMO will be explained. The concepts illustrated in that hypothetical example will be used to explain actual publicly traded mortgage-backed securities. Next, certain analytical tools commonly used by analysts will be demonstrated. Finally, those concepts will be applied to private investments that do not have publicly available market values.

To understand how those securities are valued, one must understand the investment characteristics and terminology used by investment analysts. Although analysts price those investments by measuring at present value an expected series of cash flows using a risk-adjusted discount rate, mortgage-backed securities differ from the fixed-income investments discussed in Chapter 3 because they have significant cash flow uncertainty. This uncertainty is due to the nature of the collateral supporting the investment (e.g., 30-year residential loans that are subject to unscheduled principal repayments). Analysts recognize this aspect of those investments and, therefore, use various models to estimate what are termed "unscheduled prepayments." Therefore, mortgage-backed security investments are purchased with an estimated yield and average life in mind based on assumptions concerning anticipated prepayments, in addition to other risks related to the quality of the security. An important aspect in understanding and pricing those investments is to be aware that the investor is never certain what the actual yield or average life on the investment will be. However, the investor hopes that the actual yield and life for the investment will be close to the estimates made at the time of purchase. Keep this concept in mind as those investment types are explained.

EVOLUTION OF THE MORTGAGE-BACKED SECURITIES MARKET

The first securitization was sponsored by the Government National Mortgage Association (GNMA) and issued in the early 1970s, consisting of residential mortgages, or GNMA securities. In a GNMA security, the amount and timing of mortgage principal and interest are guaranteed by the U.S. government. Therefore, from a credit-quality standpoint, GNMA securities are considered to be AAA quality, since they do not have default risk even though they are not rated. This security type evolved to include other types of assets that were used as collateral, such as conventional residential mortgages (not guaranteed), credit card receivables, consumer loans, leases, private-placement bonds, and commercial mortgages.

Other entities that were not federally sponsored began issuing mortgage-backed securities that were backed by residential mortgages during the late 1970s. As the mortgage-backed security market evolved, cash flows became allocated to different classes or tranches to suit investor risk and return profiles. In various securitization forms, the investor is purchasing a trust participation certificate. The trust participation certificate identifies the securitization's cash flows or tranches that are allocated to the investor. Various types of tranches are available, such as a sequential-pay tranche, in which principal repayments in excess of contractual amounts (also referred to as prepayments or unscheduled principal) are sequentially allocated to tranches (beginning with the senior tranche). Under the sequential allocation process, when the senior tranche is paid off, the next level tranche will (in sequence) receive the unscheduled principal prepayments. A sequential mortgage-backed security is illustrated later in the chapter.

By the 1990s, structured note transactions evolved to include asset-backed securities (which are collateralized with assets other than single-family residential mortgages), such as:

- Collateral debt obligations. These may involve pools of private-placement bonds and, therefore, credit risk. Potentially, higher returns exist.

- Commercial mortgage-backed securities. These involve pools of commercial mortgages and also present credit risk and the potential for higher returns.

Key factors affecting the riskiness and pricing of government mortgage-backed and asset-backed investments (securitizations) include:

- The quality of the underlying assets. For example, federally insured single-family residential loans are indicative of high quality (e.g., AAA-rated securities); used-car loans are indicative of lower quality and higher risk.
- The quality of the loan servicer. For example, a well-capitalized and established servicer with a strong performance history is indicative of a high-quality servicer; a new, thinly capitalized, less-experienced servicer is indicative of a lower-quality and higher-risk servicer. This aspect is most important when the securitized collateral involves higher-risk assets, such as used-car loans. In that case, the servicer's ability to manage delinquent loans and minimize credit-related losses may be critical to the investor realizing targeted returns. It is expensive and disruptive when the investor must replace the servicer due to poor performance. For example, consider replacing a servicer that is handling a securitization collateralized by used-auto loans. Obtaining and transferring the loan files and then beginning to sort out the status of delinquent loans is cumbersome and time-consuming. Furthermore, while this process takes place, delinquent loans remain unresolved.
- The loan's prepayment risk related to the asset's embedded option to prepay the loans. Prepayment options increase risk. For example, single-family residential loans, which are prepayable, reduce an investor's potential returns on investments, since they may be repaid early.
- Tranche attributes that prioritize cash flows, such as credit support features or lock-out provisions. Certain tranches (discussed in the section entitled "Collateralized Mortgage Obligations" that follows) are somewhat protected from credit losses because junior tranches are allocated credit losses first.
- Lock-out provisions that assign prepayments to specific tranches, thus sheltering or locking out prepayments from other tranches. The lockout is effective as long as the assigned tranches have not been completely paid out.
- Financial guarantees or insurance providing some level of protection for those investments involving credit losses. For example, a trust may purchase an insurance policy that reimburses the trust for credit losses up to 5 percent of the mortgage's balances.

The rest of the chapter provides an overview and examples of both simple and more complex securitizations. However, readers interested in the more complex transactions may refer to the Standard & Poor's *Structured Finance* publication that is issued monthly. For example, the April 2000 publication covers global structured financial transactions.

MORTGAGE-BACKED SECURITIES

Mortgage-backed securities are created through a sale of securities backed by assets, such as single-family residential home loans, a tax-exempt trust, or other form of a bankruptcy-remote special-purpose entity (vehicle). The sale is performed for the benefit of the owners of the assets. The owners of the trust hold pass-through certificates, which entitle them to principal and interest cash flows from the underlying assets. An investor's cash flows vary based on the performance of the assets. Specifically, unscheduled principal payments may cause a shorter investment life and less interest income to be earned. For example, the principle may be repaid at a later date when interest rates have fallen, forcing the investor to reinvest at lower rates of return. The following example illustrates those concepts.

ACE Portfolio Manager

For purposes of illustrating mortgage-backed security concepts, the following example, which is unrealistically simple, will enable one to focus on key concepts. Assume that the ACE portfolio manager has $4 million to invest for a client and that the client's cash flow requirements are met by investing in the High Roller Real Estate Mortgage Income Conduit (called a REMIC, which is a type of mortgage-pass-through certificate). Assume that the client requires the cash flows provided from this investment (explained below) to satisfy obligations in connection with financial products sold to customers. This investment also will provide the client with a greater return than investing in Treasuries; however, it involves the assumption of prepayment and credit risks. The High Roller REMIC comprises 16, $250,000, single family, 7 percent coupon, 15-year, fully amortizing mortgages. The government does not guarantee the mortgages' principal and interest payments because the loan amounts exceed the limit for conforming government mortgages. Assume that each mortgage is identical and has the contractual cash flows illustrated in Exhibit 4-1. Notice how the $35,953 monthly mortgage payments are allocated between interest and principal as time passes. Early in the investment's term, the payments consist of mostly interest; however, as time passes, the payments are increasingly allocated to principal.

   Exhibit 4-2 illustrates the combined contractual cash flows of the 16 identical residential mortgages held in the REMIC without consideration of unscheduled prepayments. In practice, securitizations often comprise mortgages with similar characteristics, such as mortgage portfolios with similar weighted-average coupons and similar credit quality.

   ACE recognizes that residential mortgage borrowers have a contractual right to prepay the balance at any time during the term of the loan. Therefore, ACE realizes that the contractual principal cash flows, shown in Exhibit 4-2, require an adjustment for this prepayment risk. ACE projects the prepayment assumptions that are shown in Exhibit 4-3. ACE also recognizes that the mortgages have

Exhibit 4-1   High Roller REMIC, Cash Flow Schedule for $250,000 7 Percent Residential Mortgage, Mortgage Terms of 15 years, Fully Amortizing Mortgages.

Period	Principal Balance	Monthly Payment	Interest	Principal
0				
1	250,000.00	2,247.06	1,458.25	788.81
2	249,211.19	2,247.06	1,453.65	793.41
3	248,417.78	2,247.06	1,449.02	798.04
4	247,619.74	2,247.06	1,444.37	802.69
5	246,817.05	2,247.06	1,439.68	807.38
6	246,009.67	2,247.06	1,434.97	812.09
7	245,197.58	2,247.06	1,430.24	816.82
8	244,380.76	2,247.06	1,425.47	821.59
9	243,559.17	2,247.06	1,420.68	826.38
10	242,732.80	2,247.06	1,415.86	831.20
11	241,901.60	2,247.06	1,411.01	836.05
12	241,065.55	2,247.06	1,406.14	840.92
13	240,224.62	2,247.06	1,401.23	845.83
14	239,378.79	2,247.06	1,396.30	850.76
15	238,528.03	2,247.06	1,391.33	855.73
16	237,672.30	2,247.06	1,386.34	860.72
17	236,811.59	2,247.06	1,381.32	865.74
18	235,945.85	2,247.06	1,376.27	870.79
19	235,075.06	2,247.06	1,371.19	875.87
20	234,199.19	2,247.06	1,366.08	880.98
21	233,318.22	2,247.06	1,360.95	886.11
22	232,432.10	2,247.06	1,355.78	891.28
23	231,540.82	2,247.06	1,350.58	896.48
24	230,644.34	2,247.06	1,345.35	901.71
25	229,742.62	2,247.06	1,340.09	906.97
26	228,835.65	2,247.06	1,334.80	912.26
27	227,923.39	2,247.06	1,329.48	917.58
28	227,005.81	2,247.06	1,324.12	922.94
29	226,082.87	2,247.06	1,318.74	928.32
30	225,154.56	2,247.06	1,313.33	933.73
31	224,220.82	2,247.06	1,307.88	939.18
32	223,281.64	2,247.06	1,302.40	944.66
33	222,336.98	2,247.06	1,296.89	950.17
34	221,386.82	2,247.06	1,291.35	955.71
35	220,431.10	2,247.06	1,285.77	961.29
36	219,469.82	2,247.06	1,280.17	966.89
37	218,502.93	2,247.06	1,274.53	972.53

(continued)

Exhibit 4-1   (*continued*)

Period	Principal Balance	Monthly Payment	Interest	Principal
38	217,530.39	2,247.06	1,268.85	978.21
39	216,552.19	2,247.06	1,263.15	983.91
40	215,568.28	2,247.06	1,257.41	989.65
41	214,578.63	2,247.06	1,251.64	995.42
42	213,583.20	2,247.06	1,245.83	1,001.23
43	212,581.98	2,247.06	1,239.99	1,007.07
44	211,574.91	2,247.06	1,234.12	1,012.94
45	210,561.96	2,247.06	1,228.21	1,018.85
46	209,543.11	2,247.06	1,222.26	1,024.80
47	208,518.32	2,247.06	1,216.29	1,030.77
48	207,487.54	2,247.06	1,210.27	1,036.79
49	206,450.76	2,247.06	1,204.23	1,042.83
50	205,407.92	2,247.06	1,198.14	1,048.92
51	204,359.01	2,247.06	1,192.03	1,055.03
52	203,303.98	2,247.06	1,185.87	1,061.19
53	202,242.79	2,247.06	1,179.68	1,067.38
54	201,175.41	2,247.06	1,173.46	1,073.60
55	200,101.81	2,247.06	1,167.19	1,079.87
56	199,021.94	2,247.06	1,160.89	1,086.17
57	197,935.77	2,247.06	1,154.56	1,092.50
58	196,843.27	2,247.06	1,148.19	1,098.87
59	195,744.40	2,247.06	1,141.78	1,105.28
60	194,639.12	2,247.06	1,135.33	1,111.73
61	193,527.39	2,247.06	1,128.85	1,118.21
62	192,409.17	2,247.06	1,122.32	1,124.74
63	191,284.44	2,247.06	1,115.76	1,131.30
64	190,153.14	2,247.06	1,109.16	1,137.90
65	189,015.24	2,247.06	1,102.53	1,144.53
66	187,870.71	2,247.06	1,095.85	1,151.21
67	186,719.50	2,247.06	1,089.13	1,157.93
68	185,561.57	2,247.06	1,082.38	1,164.68
69	184,396.89	2,247.06	1,075.59	1,171.47
70	183,225.42	2,247.06	1,068.75	1,178.31
71	182,047.11	2,247.06	1,061.88	1,185.18
72	180,861.93	2,247.06	1,054.97	1,192.09
73	179,669.84	2,247.06	1,048.01	1,199.05
74	178,470.80	2,247.06	1,041.02	1,206.04
75	177,264.76	2,247.06	1,033.99	1,213.07
76	176,051.68	2,247.06	1,026.91	1,220.15

Exhibit 4-1   *(continued)*

Period	Principal Balance	Monthly Payment	Interest	Principal
77	174,831.53	2,247.06	1,019.79	1,227.27
78	173,604.26	2,247.06	1,012.63	1,234.43
79	172,369.84	2,247.06	1,005.43	1,241.63
80	171,128.21	2,247.06	998.19	1,248.87
81	169,879.34	2,247.06	990.91	1,256.15
82	168,623.19	2,247.06	983.58	1,263.48
83	167,359.71	2,247.06	976.21	1,270.85
84	166,088.86	2,247.06	968.80	1,278.26
85	164,810.59	2,247.06	961.34	1,285.72
86	163,524.87	2,247.06	953.84	1,293.22
87	162,231.65	2,247.06	946.30	1,300.76
88	160,930.89	2,247.06	938.71	1,308.35
89	159,622.54	2,247.06	931.08	1,315.98
90	158,306.56	2,247.06	923.40	1,323.66
91	156,982.90	2,247.06	915.68	1,331.38
92	155,651.52	2,247.06	907.92	1,339.14
93	154,312.38	2,247.06	900.10	1,346.96
94	152,965.42	2,247.06	892.25	1,354.81
95	151,610.61	2,247.06	884.34	1,362.72
96	150,247.89	2,247.06	876.40	1,370.66
97	148,877.23	2,247.06	868.40	1,378.66
98	147,498.57	2,247.06	860.36	1,386.70
99	146,111.87	2,247.06	852.27	1,394.79
100	144,717.08	2,247.06	844.13	1,402.93
101	143,314.15	2,247.06	835.95	1,411.11
102	141,903.05	2,247.06	827.72	1,419.34
103	140,483.71	2,247.06	819.44	1,427.62
104	139,056.09	2,247.06	811.11	1,435.95
105	137,620.14	2,247.06	802.74	1,444.32
106	136,175.82	2,247.06	794.31	1,452.75
107	134,723.07	2,247.06	785.84	1,461.22
108	133,261.85	2,247.06	777.32	1,469.74
109	131,792.11	2,247.06	768.74	1,478.32
110	130,313.79	2,247.06	760.12	1,486.94
111	128,826.85	2,247.06	751.45	1,495.61
112	127,331.24	2,247.06	742.72	1,504.34
113	125,826.90	2,247.06	733.95	1,513.11
114	124,313.79	2,247.06	725.12	1,521.94

(continued)

Exhibit 4-1   (*continued*)

Period	Principal Balance	Monthly Payment	Interest	Principal
115	122,791.85	2,247.06	716.24	1,530.82
116	121,261.04	2,247.06	707.32	1,539.74
117	119,721.29	2,247.06	698.33	1,548.73
118	118,172.57	2,247.06	689.30	1,557.76
119	116,614.81	2,247.06	680.21	1,566.85
120	115,047.96	2,247.06	671.07	1,575.99
121	113,471.98	2,247.06	661.88	1,585.18
122	111,886.80	2,247.06	652.64	1,594.42
123	110,292.38	2,247.06	643.34	1,603.72
124	108,688.65	2,247.06	633.98	1,613.08
125	107,075.57	2,247.06	624.57	1,622.49
126	105,453.08	2,247.06	615.11	1,631.95
127	103,821.13	2,247.06	605.59	1,641.47
128	102,179.66	2,247.06	596.01	1,651.05
129	100,528.61	2,247.06	586.38	1,660.68
130	98,867.94	2,247.06	576.70	1,670.36
131	97,197.57	2,247.06	566.95	1,680.11
132	95,517.47	2,247.06	557.15	1,689.91
133	93,827.56	2,247.06	547.30	1,699.76
134	92,127.80	2,247.06	537.38	1,709.68
135	90,418.12	2,247.06	527.41	1,719.65
136	88,698.47	2,247.06	517.38	1,729.68
137	86,968.79	2,247.06	507.29	1,739.77
138	85,229.02	2,247.06	497.14	1,749.92
139	83,479.10	2,247.06	486.93	1,760.13
140	81,718.97	2,247.06	476.67	1,770.39
141	79,948.58	2,247.06	466.34	1,780.72
142	78,167.86	2,247.06	455.95	1,791.11
143	76,376.75	2,247.06	445.51	1,801.55
144	74,575.20	2,247.06	435.00	1,812.06
145	72,763.13	2,247.06	424.43	1,822.63
146	70,940.50	2,247.06	413.80	1,833.26
147	69,107.24	2,247.06	403.10	1,843.96
148	67,263.28	2,247.06	392.35	1,854.71
149	65,408.56	2,247.06	381.53	1,865.53
150	63,543.03	2,247.06	370.65	1,876.41
151	61,666.62	2,247.06	359.70	1,887.36
152	59,779.26	2,247.06	348.69	1,898.37

Exhibit 4-1   (*continued*)

Period	Principal Balance	Monthly Payment	Interest	Principal
153	57,880.89	2,247.06	337.62	1,909.44
154	55,971.45	2,247.06	326.48	1,920.58
155	54,050.87	2,247.06	315.28	1,931.78
156	52,119.09	2,247.06	304.01	1,943.05
157	50,176.04	2,247.06	292.68	1,954.38
158	48,221.66	2,247.06	281.28	1,965.78
159	46,255.88	2,247.06	269.81	1,977.25
160	44,278.63	2,247.06	258.28	1,988.78
161	42,289.85	2,247.06	246.68	2,000.38
162	40,289.46	2,247.06	235.01	2,012.05
163	38,277.41	2,247.06	223.27	2,023.79
164	36,253.62	2,247.06	211.47	2,035.59
165	34,218.03	2,247.06	199.59	2,047.47
166	32,170.56	2,247.06	187.65	2,059.41
167	30,111.15	2,247.06	175.64	2,071.42
168	28,039.73	2,247.06	163.56	2,083.50
169	25,956.23	2,247.06	151.40	2,095.66
170	23,860.57	2,247.06	139.18	2,107.88
171	21,752.69	2,247.06	126.88	2,120.18
172	19,632.51	2,247.06	114.52	2,132.54
173	17,499.97	2,247.06	102.08	2,144.98
174	15,354.99	2,247.06	89.57	2,157.49
175	13,197.49	2,247.06	76.98	2,170.08
176	11,027.41	2,247.06	64.32	2,182.74
177	8,844.68	2,247.06	51.59	2,195.47
178	6,649.21	2,247.06	38.78	2,208.28
179	4,440.93	2,247.06	25.90	2,221.16
180	2,219.78	2,247.06	12.95	2,234.11
			154,456.46	250,014.34

Exhibit 4-2　High Roller REMIC, Cash Flow Schedule for $4,000,000 7 Percent Mortgage Pool, Mortgage Terms of 15 Years, Fully Amortizing Pool Comprising 16, $250,000 Jumbo Residential Mortgages (P and I Not Government Guaranteed), Assumes No Defaults or Unscheduled Principal Payments.

Period	Principal Balance	Sch. Monthly Payment	Interest	Principal	Servicing Fee	Net Cash Flow to Investor
0						
1	4,000,000	35,953	23,333	12,620	667	35,286
2	3,987,380	35,953	23,260	12,693	665	35,288
3	3,974,687	35,953	23,186	12,768	662	35,291
4	3,961,919	35,953	23,111	12,842	660	35,293
5	3,949,077	35,953	23,036	12,917	658	35,295
6	3,936,160	35,953	22,961	12,992	656	35,297
7	3,923,168	35,953	22,885	13,068	654	35,299
8	3,910,100	35,953	22,809	13,144	652	35,301
9	3,896,956	35,953	22,732	13,221	649	35,304
10	3,883,735	35,953	22,655	13,298	647	35,306
11	3,870,437	35,953	22,577	13,376	645	35,308
12	3,857,061	35,953	22,499	13,454	643	35,310
13	3,843,607	35,953	22,421	13,532	641	35,312
14	3,830,075	35,953	22,342	13,611	638	35,315
15	3,816,464	35,953	22,263	13,690	636	35,317
16	3,802,774	35,953	22,183	13,770	634	35,319
17	3,789,003	35,953	22,102	13,851	632	35,322
18	3,775,153	35,953	22,022	13,931	629	35,324
19	3,761,221	35,953	21,940	14,013	627	35,326
20	3,747,208	35,953	21,859	14,094	625	35,329
21	3,733,114	35,953	21,776	14,177	622	35,331
22	3,718,937	35,953	21,694	14,259	620	35,333
23	3,704,678	35,953	21,610	14,343	617	35,336
24	3,690,335	35,953	21,527	14,426	615	35,338
25	3,675,909	35,953	21,443	14,510	613	35,340
26	3,661,399	35,953	21,358	14,595	610	35,343
27	3,646,804	35,953	21,273	14,680	608	35,345
28	3,632,124	35,953	21,187	14,766	605	35,348
29	3,617,358	35,953	21,101	14,852	603	35,350
30	3,602,506	35,953	21,014	14,939	600	35,353
31	3,587,567	35,953	20,927	15,026	598	35,355
32	3,572,542	35,953	20,840	15,113	595	35,358
33	3,557,428	35,953	20,752	15,202	593	35,360

Exhibit 4-2 (*continued*)

Period	Principal Balance	Sch. Monthly Payment	Interest	Principal	Servicing Fee	Net Cash Flow to Investor
34	3,542,227	35,953	20,663	15,290	590	35,363
35	3,526,936	35,953	20,574	15,379	588	35,365
36	3,511,557	35,953	20,484	15,469	585	35,368
37	3,496,088	35,953	20,394	15,559	583	35,370
38	3,480,529	35,953	20,303	15,650	580	35,373
39	3,464,879	35,953	20,212	15,741	577	35,376
40	3,449,137	35,953	20,120	15,833	575	35,378
41	3,433,304	35,953	20,027	15,926	572	35,381
42	3,417,378	35,953	19,935	16,018	570	35,383
43	3,401,360	35,953	19,841	16,112	567	35,386
44	3,385,248	35,953	19,747	16,206	564	35,389
45	3,369,042	35,953	19,653	16,300	562	35,392
46	3,352,742	35,953	19,558	16,396	559	35,394
47	3,336,346	35,953	19,462	16,491	556	35,397
48	3,319,855	35,953	19,366	16,587	553	35,400
49	3,303,268	35,953	19,269	16,684	551	35,403
50	3,286,584	35,953	19,172	16,781	548	35,405
51	3,269,802	35,953	19,074	16,879	545	35,408
52	3,252,923	35,953	18,975	16,978	542	35,411
53	3,235,945	35,953	18,876	17,077	539	35,414
54	3,218,868	35,953	18,777	17,176	536	35,417
55	3,201,692	35,953	18,676	17,277	534	35,419
56	3,184,415	35,953	18,576	17,377	531	35,422
57	3,167,038	35,953	18,474	17,479	528	35,425
58	3,149,559	35,953	18,372	17,581	525	35,428
59	3,131,978	35,953	18,270	17,683	522	35,431
60	3,114,295	35,953	18,167	17,786	519	35,434
61	3,096,509	35,953	18,063	17,890	516	35,437
62	3,078,618	35,953	17,959	17,995	513	35,440
63	3,060,624	35,953	17,854	18,100	510	35,443
64	3,042,524	35,953	17,748	18,205	507	35,446
65	3,024,319	35,953	17,642	18,311	504	35,449
66	3,006,008	35,953	17,535	18,418	501	35,452
67	2,987,590	35,953	17,428	18,526	498	35,455
68	2,969,064	35,953	17,319	18,634	495	35,458
69	2,950,431	35,953	17,211	18,742	492	35,461
70	2,931,688	35,953	17,101	18,852	489	35,464

(continued)

Exhibit 4-2 (*continued*)

Period	Principal Balance	Sch. Monthly Payment	Interest	Principal	Servicing Fee	Net Cash Flow to Investor
71	2,912,837	35,953	16,991	18,962	485	35,468
72	2,893,875	35,953	16,881	19,072	482	35,471
73	2,874,803	35,953	16,770	19,183	479	35,474
74	2,855,619	35,953	16,658	19,295	476	35,477
75	2,836,324	35,953	16,545	19,408	473	35,480
76	2,816,916	35,953	16,432	19,521	469	35,484
77	2,797,395	35,953	16,318	19,635	466	35,487
78	2,777,760	35,953	16,204	19,750	463	35,490
79	2,758,010	35,953	16,088	19,865	460	35,493
80	2,738,146	35,953	15,972	19,981	456	35,497
81	2,718,165	35,953	15,856	20,097	453	35,500
82	2,698,068	35,953	15,739	20,214	450	35,503
83	2,677,853	35,953	15,621	20,332	446	35,507
84	2,657,521	35,953	15,502	20,451	443	35,510
85	2,637,070	35,953	15,383	20,570	440	35,514
86	2,616,500	35,953	15,263	20,690	436	35,517
87	2,595,810	35,953	15,142	20,811	433	35,520
88	2,574,999	35,953	15,021	20,932	429	35,524
89	2,554,066	35,953	14,899	21,054	426	35,527
90	2,533,012	35,953	14,776	21,177	422	35,531
91	2,511,835	35,953	14,652	21,301	419	35,534
92	2,490,534	35,953	14,528	21,425	415	35,538
93	2,469,109	35,953	14,403	21,550	412	35,542
94	2,447,559	35,953	14,277	21,676	408	35,545
95	2,425,883	35,953	14,151	21,802	404	35,549
96	2,404,081	35,953	14,024	21,929	401	35,552
97	2,382,152	35,953	13,896	22,057	397	35,556
98	2,360,094	35,953	13,767	22,186	393	35,560
99	2,337,908	35,953	13,638	22,315	390	35,563
100	2,315,593	35,953	13,508	22,446	386	35,567
101	2,293,148	35,953	13,377	22,576	382	35,571
102	2,270,571	35,953	13,245	22,708	378	35,575
103	2,247,863	35,953	13,112	22,841	375	35,578
104	2,225,022	35,953	12,979	22,974	371	35,582
105	2,202,049	35,953	12,845	23,108	367	35,586
106	2,178,941	35,953	12,710	23,243	363	35,590
107	2,155,698	35,953	12,575	23,378	359	35,594
108	2,132,320	35,953	12,438	23,515	355	35,598

Exhibit 4-2 (*continued*)

Period	Principal Balance	Sch. Monthly Payment	Interest	Principal	Servicing Fee	Net Cash Flow to Investor
109	2,108,805	35,953	12,301	23,652	351	35,602
110	2,085,153	35,953	12,163	23,790	348	35,606
111	2,061,364	35,953	12,025	23,929	344	35,609
112	2,037,435	35,953	11,885	24,068	340	35,613
113	2,013,367	35,953	11,745	24,208	336	35,617
114	1,989,159	35,953	11,603	24,350	332	35,622
115	1,964,809	35,953	11,461	24,492	327	35,626
116	1,940,317	35,953	11,318	24,635	323	35,630
117	1,915,683	35,953	11,175	24,778	319	35,634
118	1,890,904	35,953	11,030	24,923	315	35,638
119	1,865,981	35,953	10,885	25,068	311	35,642
120	1,840,913	35,953	10,739	25,214	307	35,646
121	1,815,699	35,953	10,592	25,362	303	35,650
122	1,790,337	35,953	10,444	25,509	298	35,655
123	1,764,828	35,953	10,295	25,658	294	35,659
124	1,739,169	35,953	10,145	25,808	290	35,663
125	1,713,361	35,953	9,995	25,959	286	35,667
126	1,687,403	35,953	9,843	26,110	281	35,672
127	1,661,293	35,953	9,691	26,262	277	35,676
128	1,635,031	35,953	9,538	26,415	273	35,681
129	1,608,615	35,953	9,384	26,570	268	35,685
130	1,582,046	35,953	9,229	26,725	264	35,689
131	1,555,321	35,953	9,073	26,880	259	35,694
132	1,528,441	35,953	8,916	27,037	255	35,698
133	1,501,404	35,953	8,758	27,195	250	35,703
134	1,474,209	35,953	8,600	27,354	246	35,707
135	1,446,855	35,953	8,440	27,513	241	35,712
136	1,419,342	35,953	8,279	27,674	237	35,717
137	1,391,669	35,953	8,118	27,835	232	35,721
138	1,363,833	35,953	7,956	27,997	227	35,726
139	1,335,836	35,953	7,792	28,161	223	35,730
140	1,307,675	35,953	7,628	28,325	218	35,735
141	1,279,350	35,953	7,463	28,490	213	35,740
142	1,250,860	35,953	7,297	28,656	208	35,745
143	1,222,204	35,953	7,129	28,824	204	35,749
144	1,193,380	35,953	6,961	28,992	199	35,754
145	1,164,388	35,953	6,792	29,161	194	35,759

(*continued*)

Exhibit 4-2   (*continued*)

Period	Principal Balance	Sch. Monthly Payment	Interest	Principal	Servicing Fee	Net Cash Flow to Investor
146	1,135,228	35,953	6,622	29,331	189	35,764
147	1,105,897	35,953	6,451	29,502	184	35,769
148	1,076,395	35,953	6,279	29,674	179	35,774
149	1,046,720	35,953	6,106	29,847	174	35,779
150	1,016,873	35,953	5,932	30,021	169	35,784
151	986,852	35,953	5,757	30,196	164	35,789
152	956,655	35,953	5,580	30,373	159	35,794
153	926,283	35,953	5,403	30,550	154	35,799
154	895,733	35,953	5,225	30,728	149	35,804
155	865,005	35,953	5,046	30,907	144	35,809
156	834,098	35,953	4,866	31,088	139	35,814
157	803,010	35,953	4,684	31,269	134	35,819
158	771,741	35,953	4,502	31,451	129	35,824
159	740,290	35,953	4,318	31,635	123	35,830
160	708,656	35,953	4,134	31,819	118	35,835
161	676,836	35,953	3,948	32,005	113	35,840
162	644,831	35,953	3,761	32,192	107	35,846
163	612,640	35,953	3,574	32,379	102	35,851
164	580,260	35,953	3,385	32,568	97	35,856
165	547,692	35,953	3,195	32,758	91	35,862
166	514,934	35,953	3,004	32,949	86	35,867
167	481,985	35,953	2,812	33,141	80	35,873
168	448,843	35,953	2,618	33,335	75	35,878
169	415,508	35,953	2,424	33,529	69	35,884
170	381,979	35,953	2,228	33,725	64	35,889
171	348,254	35,953	2,031	33,922	58	35,895
172	314,333	35,953	1,834	34,119	52	35,901
173	280,213	35,953	1,635	34,318	47	35,906
174	245,895	35,953	1,434	34,519	41	35,912
175	211,376	35,953	1,233	34,720	35	35,918
176	176,656	35,953	1,030	34,923	29	35,924
177	141,733	35,953	827	35,126	24	35,929
178	106,607	35,953	622	35,331	18	35,935
179	71,276	35,953	416	35,537	12	35,941
180	35,739	35,953	208	35,745	6	35,947

default risk, since the U.S. government does not provide a guarantee. ACE will therefore adjust the discount rate (or spread over comparable-term Treasuries) to compensate for this risk. Industry practice reflects the default risk in the discount rate rather than adjusting the estimated cash flows to their certainty equivalent (i.e., credit risk-free cash flows). All of this information will be used in Exhibit 4-4 to illustrate how this investment is priced.

Exhibit 4-3   High Roller REMIC, Prepayment and Default Assumptions.

Code Reference	Description of Event
Pdiv	Prepayment at par due to divorce
Pmove	Prepayment at par due to job relocation
PI	Prepayment at par due to interest rate decline
Pmoveup	Prepayment at par due to moving to larger house
Pdeath	Prepayment at par due to borrower death

Pricing the High Roller Mortgage-Pass-Through

Assuming that a publicly available market price is not available for this security, pricing would be accomplished by discounting the best estimate of the expected future cash flows (discussed earlier and in Exhibit 4-3), using a yield to maturity of a security with comparable credit quality and average life. This yield could be estimated by reference to publicly traded securities. Notice in Exhibit 4-4 that the cash flows are discounted at a rate of 6.50 percent. At the time of pricing this investment, the 6.50 percent rate was sufficient to compensate investors for credit and other risks.

The last column of Exhibit 4-4 shows that this security would be priced at $4,056,074, given the above assumptions and also assuming the entire pool was purchased. A summary of the concepts related to the mortgage-pass-through certificates illustrated in this example include:

- Residential mortgages are the collateral backing the issuance of the mortgage-backed securities sold to investors. The securities are referred to as mortgage-pass-through certificates.
- The investor in a mortgage-pass-through certificate receives a pro rata share of the interest and principal generated by the mortgage collateral.
- The sales of mortgage-backed security investments provide market liquidity to mortgage issuers and are an important investment source for institutional investors.

Exhibit 4-4 High Roller, REMIC Cash Flow Schedule for $4,000,000 7 Percent Mortgage Pool, Mortgage Terms of 15 Years, Fully Amortizing Pool Comprising 16, $250,000 Jumbo Residential Mortgages (P and I Not Government Guaranteed), Effect of Unscheduled Principal Repayments as Projected in Exhibit 4-2.

Period	Principal Balance	Scheduled Monthly Payment	Interest	Principal	Servicing Fee	Unscheduled Prepayments at Par	Net Cash Flow to Investor	Present Value at 6.50% YTM
0	4,000,000						-4,000,000	
1	4,000,000	35,953	23,333	12,620	667		35,286	35,096
2	3,987,380	35,953	23,260	12,693	665		35,288	34,909
3	3,974,687	35,953	23,186	12,768	662		35,291	34,723
4	3,961,919	35,953	23,111	12,842	660		35,293	34,538
5	3,949,077	35,953	23,036	12,917	658		35,295	34,354
6	3,936,160	35,953	22,961	12,992	656		35,297	34,171
7	3,923,168	35,953	22,885	13,068	654		35,299	33,989
8	3,910,100	35,953	22,809	13,144	652		35,301	33,808
9	3,896,956	35,953	22,732	13,221	649		35,304	33,628
10	3,883,735	35,953	22,655	13,298	647		35,306	33,449
11	3,870,437	35,953	22,577	13,376	645		35,308	33,271
12	3,857,061	35,953	22,499	13,454	643	240,225	275,535	258,239
13	3,603,382	33,706	21,020	12,686	601		33,105	30,860
14	3,590,696	33,706	20,946	12,760	598		33,108	30,696
15	3,577,936	33,706	20,871	12,835	596		33,110	30,532
16	3,565,101	33,706	20,796	12,910	594		33,112	30,370
17	3,552,191	33,706	20,721	12,985	592		33,114	30,208

18	3,539,206	33,706	20,645	590	235,075	268,191	243,339
19	3,291,070	31,459	19,198	549		30,910	27,895
20	3,278,809	31,459	19,126	546		30,912	27,747
21	3,266,476	31,459	19,054	544		30,915	27,599
22	3,254,072	31,459	18,982	542		30,917	27,452
23	3,241,595	31,459	18,909	540		30,919	27,306
24	3,229,045	31,459	18,836	538	229,743	260,663	228,966
25	2,986,680	29,212	17,422	498		28,714	25,086
26	2,974,890	29,212	17,353	496		28,716	24,953
27	2,963,031	29,212	17,284	494		28,718	24,820
28	2,951,104	29,212	17,215	492		28,720	24,688
29	2,939,107	29,212	17,145	490		28,722	24,557
30	2,927,039	29,212	17,074	488	224,221	252,945	215,099
31	2,690,681	26,965	15,696	448		26,516	22,428
32	2,679,412	26,965	15,630	447		26,518	22,308
33	2,668,077	26,965	15,564	445		26,520	22,190
34	2,656,676	26,965	15,497	443		26,522	22,072
35	2,645,208	26,965	15,430	441		26,524	21,954
36	2,633,673	26,965	15,363	439		26,526	21,838
37	2,622,072	26,965	15,295	437		26,528	21,722
38	2,610,402	26,965	15,227	435		26,530	21,606
39	2,598,665	26,965	15,159	433		26,532	21,491
40	2,586,859	26,965	15,090	431		26,534	21,377
41	2,574,984	26,965	15,021	429		26,536	21,263
42	2,563,039	26,965	14,951	427		26,538	21,151
43	2,551,026	26,965	14,881	425		26,540	21,038

(continued)

Exhibit 4-4 (continued)

Period	Principal Balance	Scheduled Monthly Payment	Interest	Principal	Servicing Fee	Unscheduled Prepayments at Par	Net Cash Flow to Investor	Present Value at 6.50% YTM
44	2,538,942	26,965	14,810	12,154	423		26,542	20,926
45	2,526,787	26,965	14,740	12,225	421		26,544	20,815
46	2,514,562	26,965	14,668	12,297	419		26,546	20,705
47	2,502,265	26,965	14,596	12,368	417		26,548	20,595
48	2,489,897	26,965	14,524	12,441	415	206,451	233,001	179,779
49	2,271,006	24,718	13,247	11,470	379		24,339	18,679
50	2,259,535	24,718	13,181	11,537	377		24,341	18,579
51	2,247,998	24,718	13,113	11,605	375		24,343	18,481
52	2,236,394	24,718	13,046	11,672	373		24,345	18,383
53	2,224,721	24,718	12,977	11,740	371		24,347	18,285
54	2,212,981	24,718	12,909	11,809	369		24,349	18,188
55	2,201,172	24,718	12,840	11,878	367		24,351	18,091
56	2,189,295	24,718	12,771	11,947	365		24,353	17,995
57	2,177,348	24,718	12,701	12,017	363		24,355	17,900
58	2,165,331	24,718	12,631	12,087	361		24,357	17,805
59	2,153,244	24,718	12,561	12,157	359		24,359	17,710
60	2,141,087	24,718	12,490	12,228	357	193,527	217,888	157,565
61	1,935,332	22,471	11,289	11,181	323		22,148	15,930
62	1,924,150	22,471	11,224	11,247	321		22,150	15,846
63	1,912,904	22,471	11,159	11,312	319		22,152	15,762
64	1,901,592	22,471	11,093	11,378	317		22,154	15,678
65	1,890,213	22,471	11,026	11,445	315		22,156	15,595

66	1,878,769	22,471	10,959	11,511	313	22,158	15,512
67	1,867,258	22,471	10,892	11,578	311	22,159	15,430
68	1,855,679	22,471	10,825	11,646	309	22,161	15,348
69	1,844,033	22,471	10,757	11,714	307	22,163	15,267
70	1,832,319	22,471	10,688	11,782	305	22,165	15,186
71	1,820,537	22,471	10,620	11,851	303	22,167	15,105
72	1,808,686	22,471	10,551	11,920	301	22,169	15,025
73	1,796,766	22,471	10,481	11,990	299	22,171	14,946
74	1,784,776	22,471	10,411	12,060	297	22,173	14,866
75	1,772,717	22,471	10,341	12,130	295	22,175	14,788
76	1,760,587	22,471	10,270	12,201	293	22,177	14,709
77	1,748,386	22,471	10,199	12,272	291	22,179	14,631
78	1,736,114	22,471	10,127	12,343	289	22,181	14,554
79	1,723,771	22,471	10,055	12,415	287	22,183	14,477
80	1,711,356	22,471	9,983	12,488	285	22,185	14,400
81	1,698,868	22,471	9,910	12,561	283	22,188	14,324
82	1,686,307	22,471	9,837	12,634	281	22,190	14,248
83	1,673,673	22,471	9,763	12,708	279	22,192	14,173
84	1,660,965	22,471	9,689	12,782	277	22,194	14,098
85	1,648,184	22,471	9,614	12,856	275	22,196	14,023
86	1,635,327	22,471	9,539	12,931	273	22,198	13,949
87	1,622,396	22,471	9,464	13,007	270	22,200	13,875
88	1,609,389	22,471	9,388	13,083	268	22,202	13,802
89	1,596,307	22,471	9,312	13,159	266	22,205	13,729
90	1,583,148	22,471	9,235	13,236	264	22,207	13,656
91	1,569,912	22,471	9,158	13,313	262	22,209	13,584

(continued)

Exhibit 4-4 (continued)

Period	Principal Balance	Scheduled Monthly Payment	Interest	Principal	Servicing Fee	Unscheduled Prepayments at Par	Net Cash Flow to Investor	Present Value at 6.50% YTM
92	1,556,599	22,471	9,080	13,391	259		22,211	13,512
93	1,543,208	22,471	9,002	13,469	257		22,213	13,441
94	1,529,740	22,471	8,923	13,547	255		22,216	13,370
95	1,516,192	22,471	8,844	13,626	253		22,218	13,299
96	1,502,566	22,471	8,765	13,706	250		22,220	13,229
97	1,488,860	22,471	8,685	13,786	248		22,223	13,159
98	1,475,075	22,471	8,605	13,866	246		22,225	13,089
99	1,461,208	22,471	8,524	13,947	244		22,227	13,020
100	1,447,261	22,471	8,442	14,028	241		22,229	12,951
101	1,433,233	22,471	8,360	14,110	239		22,232	12,883
102	1,419,123	22,471	8,278	14,193	237		22,234	12,815
103	1,404,930	22,471	8,195	14,275	234		22,237	12,747
104	1,390,655	22,471	8,112	14,359	232		22,239	12,680
105	1,376,296	22,471	8,028	14,442	229		22,241	12,613
106	1,361,854	22,471	7,944	14,527	227		22,244	12,546
107	1,347,327	22,471	7,859	14,611	225		22,246	12,480
108	1,332,716	22,471	7,774	14,697	222		22,249	12,414
109	1,318,019	22,471	7,688	14,782	220		22,251	12,348
110	1,303,237	22,471	7,602	14,869	217		22,253	12,283
111	1,288,369	22,471	7,515	14,955	215		22,256	12,218
112	1,273,413	22,471	7,428	15,042	212		22,258	12,154
113	1,258,371	22,471	7,340	15,130	210		22,261	12,090

114	1,243,241	22,471	7,252	15,219	207		22,263	12,026
115	1,228,022	22,471	7,163	15,307	205		22,266	11,963
116	1,212,715	22,471	7,074	15,397	202		22,269	11,900
117	1,197,318	22,471	6,984	15,486	200		22,271	11,837
118	1,181,832	22,471	6,894	15,577	197		22,274	11,774
119	1,166,255	22,471	6,803	15,668	194		22,276	11,712
120	1,150,588	22,471	6,712	15,759	192		22,279	11,651
121	1,134,829	22,471	6,620	15,851	189		22,282	11,589
122	1,118,978	22,471	6,527	15,943	186		22,284	11,528
123	1,103,034	22,471	6,434	16,036	184		22,287	11,467
124	1,086,998	22,471	6,341	16,130	181		22,290	11,407
125	1,070,868	22,471	6,247	16,224	178		22,292	11,347
126	1,054,644	22,471	6,152	16,319	176		22,295	11,287
127	1,038,325	22,471	6,057	16,414	173		22,298	11,228
128	1,021,912	22,471	5,961	16,510	170		22,300	11,169
129	1,005,402	22,471	5,865	16,606	168		22,303	11,110
130	988,796	22,471	5,768	16,703	165	97,198	119,503	59,207
131	874,896	20,224	5,104	15,120	146		20,078	9,894
132	859,776	20,224	5,015	15,208	143		20,080	9,842
133	844,567	20,224	4,927	15,297	141		20,083	9,790
134	829,270	20,224	4,837	15,386	138		20,085	9,738
135	813,884	20,224	4,748	15,476	136		20,088	9,687
136	798,408	20,224	4,657	15,566	133		20,091	9,636
137	782,842	20,224	4,567	15,657	130		20,093	9,586
138	767,185	20,224	4,475	15,748	128		20,096	9,535
139	751,436	20,224	4,383	15,840	125		20,098	9,485

(continued)

Exhibit 4-4 (*continued*)

Period	Principal Balance	Scheduled Monthly Payment	Interest	Principal	Servicing Fee	Unscheduled Prepayments at Par	Net Cash Flow to Investor	Present Value at 6.50% YTM
140	735,596	20,224	4,291	15,933	123		20,101	9,435
141	719,663	20,224	4,198	16,026	120		20,104	9,386
142	703,638	20,224	4,105	16,119	117		20,106	9,336
143	687,519	20,224	4,011	16,213	115		20,109	9,287
144	671,305	20,224	3,916	16,308	112	654,998	675,110	310,112

Present Value of Expected Cash Flows (discounted at 6.50% YTM)   4,056,074

- Interest rate declines may reduce the expected life of an outstanding issue of this type of investment because homeowners will prepay their existing loans and refinance the mortgages at lower rates.
- Other factors, such as homeowner moves, divorces, and deaths, also impact prepayment rates.
- When the mortgage loans are not federally insured, there is a probability that mortgage defaults will occur. Default risk is factored into the pricing by adjusting the spread over Treasuries for a risk premium that is built into the discount rate used to measure the present value of the expected cash flows.

Over the life of the security, pricing would be accomplished by performing the following steps:

- Estimating prepayments
- Determining the estimated average life (prepayment levels)
- Estimating or obtaining a comparable market yield corresponding to the security's average life and credit quality that then will be used to discount the security's estimated future cash flows
- Discounting the estimated cash flows using an estimated or comparable yield to arrive at the present value of the security's future cash flows
- Summing the total of the present values to arrive at the fair value

A discussion of CMOs in which mortgages are used as collateral for the securities follows.

COLLATERALIZED MORTGAGE OBLIGATIONS

Collateralized mortgage obligations (CMOs) are created by separating the cash flows of a pool of mortgage loans into tranches. Tranches represent contractual rights to specific cash flows, or slices of the entire pool of loans that are being allocated. The investments therefore can be tailored to satisfy investor's return requirements, time horizon, and risk parameters. These CMOs are also referred to as pay-through securities, because the investor may receive a scheduled interest payment per the terms of the note.

For example, a tranche may have a stated par amount and coupon payment, which is in contrast to a pass-through certificate investment, where the holder receives a pro rata distribution of the entire principal and interest generated by the collateral. A CMO investor may obtain a higher yield than from investing in Treasury bonds but a somewhat lower yield than alternate mortgage-backed securities in exchange for more or less predictable cash flows. For example, ACE (the portfolio manager assumed in the previous example) has three clients that require different risk and return profiles for their investments:

- Client 1 requires a $3 million investment and is willing to accept prepayment risk but does not want to accept a high level of credit-loss exposure. The client expects interest rates to remain stable and therefore is not concerned with prepayments.
- Client 2 requires a $500,000 investment and wants to minimize prepayment risk. However, the client is willing to accept credit risk in return for a higher yield.
- Client 3 requires a $400,000 investment and is willing to accept high credit risk. The client wants a high-risk, high-potential return investment.

To demonstrate how the mortgage investment pool may be broken into different tranches to satisfy each of those investors' needs, the following example illustrates an A-1 senior tranche, a B-1 subordinate tranche, and an equity tranche. ACE identified an identical pool of mortgages that were modeled in the previous High Roller REMIC example. These mortgages will serve as collateral for and be modeled into the following investments.

Class A-1 Senior Tranche

The Class A-1 senior tranche bears coupon interest at 5.50 percent and was issued at a $3 million par value. This security is assigned all unscheduled principal prepayments. However, all credit-related losses are first assigned to the equity and Class B-1 subordinate tranches. This tranche has a 15-year contractual life and is fully amortizing, although as would be expected, unscheduled principal repayments (prepayments) will shorten its term. Its cash flow and risk profile fit the needs of Client 1; therefore, the tranche is purchased for this client. Exhibit 4-5 illustrates the estimated cash flows and pricing for this tranche. Note that the fair value of $2,969,760 was calculated in the last column by discounting the expected cash flows at a 5.75 percent yield to maturity (an assumed market yield).

Class B-1 Subordinate Tranche

The Class B-1 subordinate tranche bears coupon interest at 6.40 percent and was issued at a $500,000 par value. This security is not entitled to receive unscheduled principal repayments until the Class A-1 senior tranche is paid off in full. All credit-related losses are first assigned to the equity tranche and then to this Class B-1 subordinate tranche. This tranche has a 15-year contractual life and will be fully amortized. Its cash flow and risk profile fit the needs of Client 2; therefore, the tranche is purchased for this client. Exhibit 4-6 illustrates the estimated cash flows and pricing for this tranche. Note that the price of $496,591 was calculated in the last column by discounting the expected cash flows at a 6.50 percent yield to maturity (an assumed market yield).

Exhibit 4-5 Cash Flow Schedule and Pricing, High Roller Senior A-1 Tranche, $3 Million par Value, 5.50 Percent Coupon, 15 Years, Fully Amortizing, Participation Agreement Allocates All Unscheduled Principal to Senior Tranche, until Completely Repaid.

Period	Principal Balance	Scheduled Monthly Payment	Unscheduled Principal Repayments	Interest	Principal	Net Cash Flow to Investor	Present Value at 5.75% YTM
0	3,000,000					-3,000,000	
1	3,000,000	24,513		13,750	10,763	24,513	24,396
2	2,989,238	24,513		13,701	10,812	24,513	24,279
3	2,978,426	24,513		13,651	10,861	24,513	24,163
4	2,967,564	24,513		13,601	10,911	24,513	24,048
5	2,956,653	24,513		13,551	10,961	24,513	23,934
6	2,945,692	24,513		13,501	11,011	24,513	23,819
7	2,934,681	24,513		13,451	11,062	24,513	23,706
8	2,923,619	24,513		13,400	11,113	24,513	23,593
9	2,912,506	24,513		13,349	11,164	24,513	23,480
10	2,901,343	24,513		13,298	11,215	24,513	23,368
11	2,890,128	24,513		13,246	11,266	24,513	23,257
12	2,878,862	24,513	240,225	13,195	11,318	264,738	249,979
13	2,627,319	23,308		12,042	11,266	23,308	21,904
14	2,616,053	23,308		11,990	11,318	23,308	21,799
15	2,604,735	23,308		11,938	11,370	23,308	21,695
16	2,593,366	23,308		11,886	11,422	23,308	21,592
17	2,581,944	23,308		11,834	11,474	23,308	21,489
18	2,570,470	23,308	235,075	11,781	11,527	258,383	237,080
19	2,323,868	21,250		10,651	10,599	21,250	19,405
20	2,313,269	21,250		10,602	10,648	21,250	19,312
21	2,302,622	21,250		10,554	10,696	21,250	19,220
22	2,291,925	21,250		10,505	10,745	21,250	19,129
23	2,281,180	21,250		10,455	10,795	21,250	19,038
24	2,270,385	21,250	229,743	10,406	10,844	250,993	223,788
25	2,029,798	19,187		9,303	9,884	19,187	17,026
26	2,019,915	19,187		9,258	9,929	19,187	16,945
27	2,009,985	19,187		9,212	9,975	19,187	16,864
28	2,000,011	19,187		9,167	10,020	19,187	16,783
29	1,989,991	19,187		9,121	10,066	19,187	16,703
30	1,979,924	19,187	224,221	9,075	10,112	243,408	210,889
31	1,745,591	17,117		8,001	9,116	17,117	14,759
32	1,736,475	17,117		7,959	9,158	17,117	14,689

(continued)

Exhibit 4-5   (*continued*)

Period	Principal Balance	Scheduled Monthly Payment	Unscheduled Principal Repayments	Interest	Principal	Net Cash Flow to Investor	Present Value at 5.75% YTM
33	1,727,317	17,117		7,917	9,200	17,117	14,619
34	1,718,116	17,117		7,875	9,242	17,117	14,549
35	1,708,874	17,117		7,832	9,285	17,117	14,480
36	1,699,589	17,117		7,790	9,327	17,117	14,411
37	1,690,262	17,117		7,747	9,370	17,117	14,342
38	1,680,892	17,117		7,704	9,413	17,117	14,274
39	1,671,479	17,117		7,661	9,456	17,117	14,206
40	1,662,023	17,117		7,618	9,499	17,117	14,138
41	1,652,524	17,117		7,574	9,543	17,117	14,071
42	1,642,981	17,117		7,530	9,587	17,117	14,003
43	1,633,394	17,117		7,486	9,631	17,117	13,937
44	1,623,764	17,117		7,442	9,675	17,117	13,870
45	1,614,089	17,117		7,398	9,719	17,117	13,804
46	1,604,370	17,117		7,353	9,764	17,117	13,738
47	1,594,606	17,117		7,309	9,808	17,117	13,673
48	1,584,798	17,117	206,451	7,264	9,853	223,568	177,730
49	1,368,493	15,030		6,272	8,758	15,030	11,891
50	1,359,736	15,030		6,232	8,798	15,030	11,835
51	1,350,938	15,030		6,192	8,838	15,030	11,778
52	1,342,100	15,030		6,151	8,879	15,030	11,722
53	1,333,221	15,030		6,111	8,919	15,030	11,666
54	1,324,302	15,030		6,070	8,960	15,030	11,611
55	1,315,341	15,030		6,029	9,001	15,030	11,555
56	1,306,340	15,030		5,987	9,043	15,030	11,500
57	1,297,297	15,030		5,946	9,084	15,030	11,445
58	1,288,213	15,030		5,904	9,126	15,030	11,391
59	1,279,088	15,030		5,862	9,168	15,030	11,336
60	1,269,920	15,030	193,527	5,820	9,210	208,557	156,554
61	1,067,184	12,931		4,891	8,040	12,931	9,660
62	1,059,144	12,931		4,854	8,077	12,931	9,614
63	1,051,067	12,931		4,817	8,114	12,931	9,568
64	1,042,954	12,931		4,780	8,151	12,931	9,523
65	1,034,803	12,931		4,743	8,188	12,931	9,477
66	1,026,615	12,931		4,705	8,226	12,931	9,432
67	1,018,389	12,931		4,668	8,263	12,931	9,387
68	1,010,126	12,931		4,630	8,301	12,931	9,342
69	1,001,824	12,931		4,592	8,339	12,931	9,298
70	993,485	12,931		4,553	8,378	12,931	9,254

Exhibit 4-5 *(continued)*

Period	Principal Balance	Scheduled Monthly Payment	Unscheduled Principal Repayments	Interest	Principal	Net Cash Flow to Investor	Present Value at 5.75% YTM
71	985,107	12,931		4,515	8,416	12,931	9,209
72	976,692	12,931		4,477	8,454	12,931	9,166
73	968,237	12,931		4,438	8,493	12,931	9,122
74	959,744	12,931		4,399	8,532	12,931	9,078
75	951,212	12,931		4,360	8,571	12,931	9,035
76	942,640	12,931		4,320	8,611	12,931	8,992
77	934,030	12,931		4,281	8,650	12,931	8,949
78	925,380	12,931		4,241	8,690	12,931	8,906
79	916,690	12,931		4,201	8,730	12,931	8,864
80	907,961	12,931		4,161	8,770	12,931	8,822
81	899,191	12,931		4,121	8,810	12,931	8,780
82	890,381	12,931		4,081	8,850	12,931	8,738
83	881,531	12,931		4,040	8,891	12,931	8,696
84	872,641	12,931		4,000	8,931	12,931	8,655
85	863,709	12,931		3,959	8,972	12,931	8,613
86	854,737	12,931		3,918	9,013	12,931	8,572
87	845,723	12,931		3,876	9,055	12,931	8,531
88	836,669	12,931		3,835	9,096	12,931	8,491
89	827,572	12,931		3,793	9,138	12,931	8,450
90	818,434	12,931		3,751	9,180	12,931	8,410
91	809,255	12,931		3,709	9,222	12,931	8,370
92	800,033	12,931		3,667	9,264	12,931	8,330
93	790,768	12,931		3,624	9,307	12,931	8,290
94	781,462	12,931		3,582	9,349	12,931	8,251
95	772,113	12,931		3,539	9,392	12,931	8,211
96	762,720	12,931		3,496	9,435	12,931	8,172
97	753,285	12,931		3,453	9,478	12,931	8,133
98	743,807	12,931		3,409	9,522	12,931	8,094
99	734,285	12,931		3,365	9,566	12,931	8,056
100	724,719	12,931		3,322	9,609	12,931	8,017
101	715,110	12,931		3,278	9,653	12,931	7,979
102	705,457	12,931		3,233	9,698	12,931	7,941
103	695,759	12,931		3,189	9,742	12,931	7,903
104	686,017	12,931		3,144	9,787	12,931	7,865
105	676,230	12,931		3,099	9,832	12,931	7,828
106	666,398	12,931		3,054	9,877	12,931	7,791
107	656,522	12,931		3,009	9,922	12,931	7,753

(continued)

Exhibit 4-5   (*continued*)

Period	Principal Balance	Scheduled Monthly Payment	Unscheduled Principal Repayments	Interest	Principal	Net Cash Flow to Investor	Present Value at 5.75% YTM
108	646,600	12,931		2,964	9,967	12,931	7,717
109	636,632	12,931		2,918	10,013	12,931	7,680
110	626,619	12,931		2,872	10,059	12,931	7,643
111	616,560	12,931		2,826	10,105	12,931	7,607
112	606,455	12,931		2,780	10,151	12,931	7,570
113	596,304	12,931		2,733	10,198	12,931	7,534
114	586,106	12,931		2,686	10,245	12,931	7,498
115	575,861	12,931		2,639	10,292	12,931	7,463
116	565,570	12,931		2,592	10,339	12,931	7,427
117	555,231	12,931		2,545	10,386	12,931	7,392
118	544,845	12,931		2,497	10,434	12,931	7,356
119	534,411	12,931		2,449	10,482	12,931	7,321
120	523,929	12,931		2,401	10,530	12,931	7,286
121	513,399	12,931		2,353	10,578	12,931	7,252
122	502,822	12,931		2,305	10,626	12,931	7,217
123	492,195	12,931		2,256	10,675	12,931	7,183
124	481,520	12,931		2,207	10,724	12,931	7,148
125	470,796	12,931		2,158	10,773	12,931	7,114
126	460,023	12,931		2,108	10,823	12,931	7,080
127	449,200	12,931		2,059	10,872	12,931	7,047
128	438,328	12,931		2,009	10,922	12,931	7,013
129	427,406	12,931		1,959	10,972	12,931	6,980
130	416,434	12,931	97,198	1,909	11,022	110,129	59,159
131	308,214	10,757		1,413	9,344	10,757	5,751
132	298,869	10,757		1,370	9,387	10,757	5,723
133	289,482	10,757		1,327	9,430	10,757	5,696
134	280,052	10,757		1,284	9,473	10,757	5,669
135	270,579	10,757		1,240	9,517	10,757	5,642
136	261,062	10,757		1,197	9,560	10,757	5,615
137	251,501	10,757		1,153	9,604	10,757	5,588
138	241,897	10,757		1,109	9,648	10,757	5,562
139	232,249	10,757		1,064	9,693	10,757	5,535
140	222,556	10,757		1,020	9,737	10,757	5,509
141	212,819	10,757		975	9,782	10,757	5,482
142	203,038	10,757		931	9,826	10,757	5,456
143	193,211	10,757		886	9,871	10,757	5,430
144	183,340	10,757	173,423	840	9,917	184,180	92,533

Present Value of Expected Cash Flows (discounted at 5.75% YTM)   2,969,760

Exhibit 4-6 Cash Flow Schedule and Pricing, High Roller Subordinate B-1 Tranche, $500,000 par Value, 6.40 Percent Coupon, 15 Years, Fully Amortizing, Participation Agreement Allocates All Unscheduled Principal to Senior Tranche, until Completely Repaid.

Period	Principal Balance	Scheduled Monthly Payment	Interest	Principal	Net Cash Flow to Investor	Present Value at 6.50% YTM
0	500,000				-500,000	
1	500,000	4,328	2,667	1,661	4,328	4,305
2	498,339	4,328	2,658	1,670	4,328	4,282
3	496,668	4,328	2,649	1,679	4,328	4,259
4	494,989	4,328	2,640	1,688	4,328	4,236
5	493,301	4,328	2,631	1,697	4,328	4,213
6	491,604	4,328	2,622	1,706	4,328	4,190
7	489,898	4,328	2,613	1,715	4,328	4,167
8	488,182	4,328	2,604	1,724	4,328	4,145
9	486,458	4,328	2,594	1,734	4,328	4,123
10	484,724	4,328	2,585	1,743	4,328	4,100
11	482,981	4,328	2,576	1,752	4,328	4,078
12	481,229	4,328	2,567	1,762	4,328	4,056
13	479,467	4,328	2,557	1,771	4,328	4,035
14	477,697	4,328	2,548	1,780	4,328	4,013
15	475,916	4,328	2,538	1,790	4,328	3,991
16	474,126	4,328	2,529	1,799	4,328	3,970
17	472,327	4,328	2,519	1,809	4,328	3,948
18	470,518	4,328	2,509	1,819	4,328	3,927
19	468,699	4,328	2,500	1,828	4,328	3,906
20	466,871	4,328	2,490	1,838	4,328	3,885
21	465,033	4,328	2,480	1,848	4,328	3,864
22	463,185	4,328	2,470	1,858	4,328	3,843
23	461,327	4,328	2,460	1,868	4,328	3,822
24	459,459	4,328	2,450	1,878	4,328	3,802
25	457,582	4,328	2,440	1,888	4,328	3,781
26	455,694	4,328	2,430	1,898	4,328	3,761
27	453,796	4,328	2,420	1,908	4,328	3,741
28	451,888	4,328	2,410	1,918	4,328	3,721
29	449,970	4,328	2,400	1,928	4,328	3,701
30	448,042	4,328	2,390	1,939	4,328	3,681
31	446,104	4,328	2,379	1,949	4,328	3,661
32	444,155	4,328	2,369	1,959	4,328	3,641
33	442,195	4,328	2,358	1,970	4,328	3,621
34	440,226	4,328	2,348	1,980	4,328	3,602

(continued)

Exhibit 4-6 *(continued)*

Period	Principal Balance	Scheduled Monthly Payment	Interest	Principal	Net Cash Flow to Investor	Present Value at 6.50% YTM
35	438,245	4,328	2,337	1,991	4,328	3,582
36	436,255	4,328	2,327	2,001	4,328	3,563
37	434,253	4,328	2,316	2,012	4,328	3,544
38	432,241	4,328	2,305	2,023	4,328	3,525
39	430,218	4,328	2,294	2,034	4,328	3,506
40	428,185	4,328	2,284	2,044	4,328	3,487
41	426,140	4,328	2,273	2,055	4,328	3,468
42	424,085	4,328	2,262	2,066	4,328	3,450
43	422,019	4,328	2,251	2,077	4,328	3,431
44	419,941	4,328	2,240	2,088	4,328	3,412
45	417,853	4,328	2,229	2,100	4,328	3,394
46	415,753	4,328	2,217	2,111	4,328	3,376
47	413,643	4,328	2,206	2,122	4,328	3,358
48	411,521	4,328	2,195	2,133	4,328	3,340
49	409,387	4,328	2,183	2,145	4,328	3,322
50	407,242	4,328	2,172	2,156	4,328	3,304
51	405,086	4,328	2,160	2,168	4,328	3,286
52	402,919	4,328	2,149	2,179	4,328	3,268
53	400,740	4,328	2,137	2,191	4,328	3,251
54	398,549	4,328	2,126	2,203	4,328	3,233
55	396,346	4,328	2,114	2,214	4,328	3,216
56	394,132	4,328	2,102	2,226	4,328	3,198
57	391,906	4,328	2,090	2,238	4,328	3,181
58	389,668	4,328	2,078	2,250	4,328	3,164
59	387,418	4,328	2,066	2,262	4,328	3,147
60	385,156	4,328	2,054	2,274	4,328	3,130
61	382,882	4,328	2,042	2,286	4,328	3,113
62	380,596	4,328	2,030	2,298	4,328	3,096
63	378,298	4,328	2,018	2,311	4,328	3,080
64	375,987	4,328	2,005	2,323	4,328	3,063
65	373,665	4,328	1,993	2,335	4,328	3,047
66	371,329	4,328	1,980	2,348	4,328	3,030
67	368,982	4,328	1,968	2,360	4,328	3,014
68	366,622	4,328	1,955	2,373	4,328	2,998
69	364,249	4,328	1,943	2,385	4,328	2,981
70	361,863	4,328	1,930	2,398	4,328	2,965
71	359,465	4,328	1,917	2,411	4,328	2,949
72	357,054	4,328	1,904	2,424	4,328	2,933

Exhibit 4-6 (*continued*)

Period	Principal Balance	Scheduled Monthly Payment	Interest	Principal	Net Cash Flow to Investor	Present Value at 6.50% YTM
73	354,630	4,328	1,891	2,437	4,328	2,918
74	352,194	4,328	1,878	2,450	4,328	2,902
75	349,744	4,328	1,865	2,463	4,328	2,886
76	347,281	4,328	1,852	2,476	4,328	2,871
77	344,805	4,328	1,839	2,489	4,328	2,855
78	342,316	4,328	1,826	2,502	4,328	2,840
79	339,814	4,328	1,812	2,516	4,328	2,825
80	337,298	4,328	1,799	2,529	4,328	2,809
81	334,769	4,328	1,785	2,543	4,328	2,794
82	332,226	4,328	1,772	2,556	4,328	2,779
83	329,670	4,328	1,758	2,570	4,328	2,764
84	327,100	4,328	1,745	2,584	4,328	2,749
85	324,516	4,328	1,731	2,597	4,328	2,735
86	321,919	4,328	1,717	2,611	4,328	2,720
87	319,308	4,328	1,703	2,625	4,328	2,705
88	316,683	4,328	1,689	2,639	4,328	2,691
89	314,044	4,328	1,675	2,653	4,328	2,676
90	311,390	4,328	1,661	2,667	4,328	2,662
91	308,723	4,328	1,647	2,682	4,328	2,647
92	306,041	4,328	1,632	2,696	4,328	2,633
93	303,346	4,328	1,618	2,710	4,328	2,619
94	300,635	4,328	1,603	2,725	4,328	2,605
95	297,911	4,328	1,589	2,739	4,328	2,591
96	295,171	4,328	1,574	2,754	4,328	2,577
97	292,417	4,328	1,560	2,769	4,328	2,563
98	289,649	4,328	1,545	2,783	4,328	2,549
99	286,866	4,328	1,530	2,798	4,328	2,535
100	284,067	4,328	1,515	2,813	4,328	2,522
101	281,254	4,328	1,500	2,828	4,328	2,508
102	278,426	4,328	1,485	2,843	4,328	2,495
103	275,583	4,328	1,470	2,858	4,328	2,481
104	272,725	4,328	1,455	2,874	4,328	2,468
105	269,851	4,328	1,439	2,889	4,328	2,454
106	266,962	4,328	1,424	2,904	4,328	2,441
107	264,058	4,328	1,408	2,920	4,328	2,428
108	261,138	4,328	1,393	2,935	4,328	2,415
109	258,203	4,328	1,377	2,951	4,328	2,402

(*continued*)

Exhibit 4-6   (*continued*)

Period	Principal Balance	Scheduled Monthly Payment	Interest	Principal	Net Cash Flow to Investor	Present Value at 6.50% YTM
110	255,252	4,328	1,361	2,967	4,328	2,389
111	252,285	4,328	1,346	2,983	4,328	2,376
112	249,303	4,328	1,330	2,998	4,328	2,363
113	246,304	4,328	1,314	3,014	4,328	2,351
114	243,290	4,328	1,298	3,031	4,328	2,338
115	240,259	4,328	1,281	3,047	4,328	2,325
116	237,212	4,328	1,265	3,063	4,328	2,313
117	234,149	4,328	1,249	3,079	4,328	2,300
118	231,070	4,328	1,232	3,096	4,328	2,288
119	227,974	4,328	1,216	3,112	4,328	2,276
120	224,862	4,328	1,199	3,129	4,328	2,263
121	221,733	4,328	1,183	3,146	4,328	2,251
122	218,588	4,328	1,166	3,162	4,328	2,239
123	215,425	4,328	1,149	3,179	4,328	2,227
124	212,246	4,328	1,132	3,196	4,328	2,215
125	209,050	4,328	1,115	3,213	4,328	2,203
126	205,837	4,328	1,098	3,230	4,328	2,191
127	202,607	4,328	1,081	3,248	4,328	2,179
128	199,359	4,328	1,063	3,265	4,328	2,168
129	196,094	4,328	1,046	3,282	4,328	2,156
130	192,812	4,328	1,028	3,300	4,328	2,144
131	189,512	4,328	1,011	3,317	4,328	2,133
132	186,195	4,328	993	3,335	4,328	2,121
133	182,860	4,328	975	3,353	4,328	2,110
134	179,507	4,328	957	3,371	4,328	2,099
135	176,136	4,328	939	3,389	4,328	2,087
136	172,748	4,328	921	3,407	4,328	2,076
137	169,341	4,328	903	3,425	4,328	2,065
138	165,916	4,328	885	3,443	4,328	2,054
139	162,473	4,328	867	3,462	4,328	2,043
140	159,011	4,328	848	3,480	4,328	2,032
141	155,531	4,328	829	3,499	4,328	2,021
142	152,032	4,328	811	3,517	4,328	2,010
143	148,515	4,328	792	3,536	4,328	1,999
144	144,979	4,328	773	144,206	144,979	66,599

Present Value of Expected Cash Flows (discounted at 6.50% YTM)   496,591

Equity Tranche

The equity tranche serves as a level of default protection to the Class A-1 senior and Class B-1 subordinate tranches, since it bears a first loss position on credit losses. Exhibit 4-7 illustrates the estimated cash flows and pricing for this tranche. Note that the price of $411,623 was calculated in the last column by discounting the expected cash flows at a 15 percent yield to maturity (an assumed market yield). This discount rate compensates the investor for the high level of credit risk.

A summary of the concepts related to the CMO security illustrated in this example include:

- As with a mortgage-pass-through certificate previously illustrated, residential mortgage loans represent the collateral backing that the securities issued. However, the investor receives cash flows as specified in the trust-participation agreement. For example, investors in the A-1 senior tranche, B-1 subordinate tranche, and equity tranche have different rights to the cash flows and are exposed to different levels of risk and return.
- Different tranches can provide varying types of risk protection. For example, in this illustration, the B-1 tranche receives prepayment protection because the A-1 tranche is first allotted all of the unscheduled prepayments. The B-1 tranche receives default protection because default losses are first allocated to the equity tranche. The A-1 tranche is also protected from defaults because default losses are first allocated to the equity and B-1 tranches.
- The expected return increases with the level of risk assumed. For example, the equity investor expects a 15 percent return in this example. However, to obtain this return, the investor assumes a higher level of default risk.

Mortgage-pass-through investments and CMOs are more complex than those provided in the hypothetical illustrations discussed earlier. It is common practice to structure these types of investments with a senior tranche that is rated by a public rating agency (e.g., Moody's, S&P, or Duff & Phelps) and unrated subordinate tranches that have higher risks and higher expected returns. One also would expect to receive monthly, unscheduled principal repayments and to see sophisticated models being used to estimate those amounts. For example, market conventions have been developed to provide an estimate of the security's principal prepayment rate. This statistic is applied to the outstanding balance of the mortgage principal to estimate prepayments. This is termed a "PSA" because it is an index originally developed by the Public Security Administration (PSA) that measures principal prepayment speeds in mortgages. For example, a mortgage pool assigned a 100 PSA may indicate that 6 percent of the pool's mortgage principal balance will prepay each year (assuming the pool has aged a certain number of months). This statistic also is adjusted to determine a monthly prepayment rate

Exhibit 4-7 High Roller REMIC CMO, Cash Flow Available for Equity Tranche and Equity Pricing, Assumes Cash Flows as Projected to A-1 and B-1 Tranches.

Period	Principal Balance	Scheduled Monthly Payment	Interest	Principal	Servicing Fee	Unscheduled Prepayments at Par	Net Cash Flow Available	Cash Flow Allocated to A-1 Tranche	Cash Flow Allocated to B-1 Tranche	Cash Flow Allocated to Equity	Present Value at 15% YTM
0	4,000,000									-411,623	
1	4,000,000	35,953	21,668	14,285	667		35,286	24,513	4,328	6,446	6,366
2	3,985,715	35,953	21,668	14,285	664		35,289	24,513	4,328	6,448	6,290
3	3,971,430	35,953	21,591	14,362	662		35,291	24,513	4,328	6,451	6,215
4	3,957,067	35,953	21,513	14,440	660		35,294	24,513	4,328	6,453	6,140
5	3,942,628	35,953	21,435	14,518	657		35,296	24,513	4,328	6,455	6,067
6	3,928,110	35,953	21,357	14,596	655		35,298	24,513	4,328	6,458	5,994
7	3,913,514	35,953	21,279	14,674	652		35,301	24,513	4,328	6,460	5,922
8	3,898,840	35,953	21,200	14,754	650		35,303	24,513	4,328	6,463	5,851
9	3,884,086	35,953	21,120	14,833	647		35,306	24,513	4,328	6,465	5,781
10	3,869,253	35,953	21,040	14,913	645		35,308	24,513	4,328	6,468	5,712
11	3,854,340	35,953	20,960	14,993	642		35,311	24,513	4,328	6,470	5,644
12	3,839,347	35,953	20,879	15,074	640	240,225	275,538	264,738	4,328	6,473	5,576
13	3,584,048	33,706	20,798	12,908	597		33,109	23,308	4,328	5,473	4,656
14	3,571,139	33,706	19,415	14,291	595		33,111	23,308	4,328	5,475	4,601
15	3,556,848	33,706	19,345	14,361	593		33,113	23,308	4,328	5,477	4,546
16	3,542,487	33,706	19,267	14,439	590		33,116	23,308	4,328	5,479	4,492
17	3,528,049	33,706	19,190	14,516	588		33,118	23,308	4,328	5,482	4,438
18	3,513,532	33,706	19,111	14,595	586	235,075	268,195	258,383	4,328	5,484	4,385
19	3,263,863	31,459	19,033	12,426	544		30,915	21,250	4,328	5,337	4,215
20	3,251,436	31,459	17,680	13,779	542		30,917	21,250	4,328	5,339	4,164

Period	Principal Balance	Scheduled Monthly Payment	Interest	Principal	Servicing Fee	Unscheduled Prepayments at Par	Net Cash Flow Available	Cash Flow Allocated to A-1 Tranche	Cash Flow Allocated to B-1 Tranche	Cash Flow Allocated to Equity	Present Value at 15% YTM
21	3,237,658	31,459	17,613	13,846	540		30,919	21,250	4,328	5,341	4,115
22	3,223,812	31,459	17,538	13,921	537		30,922	21,250	4,328	5,344	4,066
23	3,209,891	31,459	17,463	13,996	535		30,924	21,250	4,328	5,346	4,017
24	3,195,896	31,459	17,388	14,071	533	229,743	260,669	250,993	4,328	5,348	3,969
25	2,952,082	29,212	17,312	11,900	492		28,720	19,187	4,328	5,205	3,815
26	2,940,183	29,212	15,991	13,220	490		28,722	19,187	4,328	5,207	3,770
27	2,926,962	29,212	15,927	13,285	488		28,724	19,187	4,328	5,209	3,725
28	2,913,677	29,212	15,855	13,357	486		28,726	19,187	4,328	5,211	3,680
29	2,900,321	29,212	15,783	13,428	483		28,728	19,187	4,328	5,213	3,636
30	2,886,892	29,212	15,711	13,501	481	224,221	252,952	243,408	4,328	5,215	3,593
31	2,649,171	26,965	15,638	11,327	442		26,523	17,117	4,328	5,078	3,455
32	2,637,844	26,965	14,351	12,614	440		26,525	17,117	4,328	5,080	3,414
33	2,625,230	26,965	14,289	12,676	438		26,527	17,117	4,328	5,082	3,373
34	2,612,554	26,965	14,221	12,744	435		26,529	17,117	4,328	5,084	3,333
35	2,599,810	26,965	14,152	12,813	433		26,532	17,117	4,328	5,086	3,293
36	2,586,998	26,965	14,083	12,882	431		26,534	17,117	4,328	5,089	3,254
37	2,574,116	26,965	14,014	12,951	429		26,536	17,117	4,328	5,091	3,215
38	2,561,165	26,965	13,944	13,021	427		26,538	17,117	4,328	5,093	3,177
39	2,548,144	26,965	13,874	13,091	425		26,540	17,117	4,328	5,095	3,139
40	2,535,053	26,965	13,803	13,162	423		26,542	17,117	4,328	5,097	3,101
41	2,521,892	26,965	13,732	13,232	420		26,545	17,117	4,328	5,099	3,064

(continued)

Exhibit 4-7 *(continued)*

Period	Principal Balance	Scheduled Monthly Payment	Interest	Principal	Servicing Fee	Unscheduled Prepayments at Par	Net Cash Flow Available	Cash Flow Allocated to A-1 Tranche	Cash Flow Allocated to B-1 Tranche	Cash Flow Allocated to Equity	Present Value at 15% YTM
42	2,508,659	26,965	13,661	13,304	418		26,547	17,117	4,328	5,102	3,028
43	2,495,355	26,965	13,589	13,375	416		26,549	17,117	4,328	5,104	2,992
44	2,481,980	26,965	13,517	13,447	414		26,551	17,117	4,328	5,106	2,956
45	2,468,532	26,965	13,445	13,520	411		26,553	17,117	4,328	5,108	2,921
46	2,455,013	26,965	13,372	13,593	409		26,556	17,117	4,328	5,111	2,886
47	2,441,420	26,965	13,299	13,666	407		26,558	17,117	4,328	5,113	2,852
48	2,427,754	26,965	13,225	13,740	405	206,451	233,011	223,568	4,328	5,115	2,818
49	2,207,563	24,718	13,151	11,567	368		24,350	15,030	4,328	4,992	2,716
50	2,195,997	24,718	11,958	12,759	366		24,352	15,030	4,328	4,994	2,683
51	2,183,237	24,718	11,896	12,822	364		24,354	15,030	4,328	4,996	2,651
52	2,170,415	24,718	11,827	12,891	362		24,356	15,030	4,328	4,998	2,620
53	2,157,524	24,718	11,757	12,961	360		24,358	15,030	4,328	5,000	2,588
54	2,144,563	24,718	11,687	13,030	357		24,360	15,030	4,328	5,002	2,558
55	2,131,533	24,718	11,617	13,101	355		24,363	15,030	4,328	5,004	2,527
56	2,118,432	24,718	11,547	13,171	353		24,365	15,030	4,328	5,007	2,497
57	2,105,261	24,718	11,476	13,242	351		24,367	15,030	4,328	5,009	2,467
58	2,092,019	24,718	11,404	13,314	349		24,369	15,030	4,328	5,011	2,438
59	2,078,705	24,718	11,332	13,385	346		24,371	15,030	4,328	5,013	2,409
60	2,065,320	24,718	11,260	13,457	344	193,527	217,901	208,557	4,328	5,016	2,380
61	1,858,335	22,471	11,188	11,283	310		22,161	12,931	4,328	4,902	2,298
62	1,847,052	22,471	10,067	12,404	308		22,163	12,931	4,328	4,904	2,270
63	1,834,648	22,471	10,005	12,465	306		22,165	12,931	4,328	4,906	2,243

Period	Principal Balance	Scheduled Monthly Payment	Interest	Principal	Servicing Fee	Unscheduled Prepayments at Par	Net Cash Flow Available	Cash Flow Allocated to A-1 Tranche	Cash Flow Allocated to B-1 Tranche	Cash Flow Allocated to Equity	Present Value at 15% YTM
64	1,822,183	22,471	9,938	12,532	304		22,167	12,931	4,328	4,908	2,216
65	1,809,651	22,471	9,871	12,600	302		22,169	12,931	4,328	4,910	2,190
66	1,797,051	22,471	9,803	12,668	300		22,171	12,931	4,328	4,912	2,164
67	1,784,383	22,471	9,735	12,736	297		22,173	12,931	4,328	4,914	2,138
68	1,771,647	22,471	9,666	12,805	295		22,175	12,931	4,328	4,916	2,112
69	1,758,842	22,471	9,597	12,874	293		22,178	12,931	4,328	4,918	2,087
70	1,745,968	22,471	9,528	12,943	291		22,180	12,931	4,328	4,921	2,062
71	1,733,025	22,471	9,458	13,013	289		22,182	12,931	4,328	4,923	2,038
72	1,720,013	22,471	9,388	13,083	287		22,184	12,931	4,328	4,925	2,014
73	1,706,930	22,471	9,317	13,153	284		22,186	12,931	4,328	4,927	1,990
74	1,693,776	22,471	9,246	13,224	282		22,188	12,931	4,328	4,929	1,966
75	1,680,552	22,471	9,175	13,296	280		22,191	12,931	4,328	4,932	1,942
76	1,667,257	22,471	9,104	13,367	278		22,193	12,931	4,328	4,934	1,919
77	1,653,889	22,471	9,032	13,439	276		22,195	12,931	4,328	4,936	1,897
78	1,640,450	22,471	8,959	13,512	273		22,197	12,931	4,328	4,938	1,874
79	1,626,939	22,471	8,886	13,584	271		22,200	12,931	4,328	4,940	1,852
80	1,613,354	22,471	8,813	13,658	269		22,202	12,931	4,328	4,943	1,830
81	1,599,697	22,471	8,740	13,731	267		22,204	12,931	4,328	4,945	1,808
82	1,585,966	22,471	8,666	13,805	264		22,206	12,931	4,328	4,947	1,786
83	1,572,160	22,471	8,591	13,880	262		22,209	12,931	4,328	4,950	1,765
84	1,558,281	22,471	8,516	13,954	260		22,211	12,931	4,328	4,952	1,744

(continued)

Exhibit 4-7 (continued)

Period	Principal Balance	Scheduled Monthly Payment	Interest	Principal	Servicing Fee	Unscheduled Prepayments at Par	Net Cash Flow Available	Cash Flow Allocated to A-1 Tranche	Cash Flow Allocated to B-1 Tranche	Cash Flow Allocated to Equity	Present Value at 15% YTM
85	1,544,327	22,471	8,441	14,029	257		22,213	12,931	4,328	4,954	1,723
86	1,530,297	22,471	8,366	14,105	255		22,216	12,931	4,328	4,957	1,703
87	1,516,192	22,471	8,290	14,181	253		22,218	12,931	4,328	4,959	1,683
88	1,502,011	22,471	8,213	14,257	250		22,220	12,931	4,328	4,961	1,663
89	1,487,753	22,471	8,136	14,334	248		22,223	12,931	4,328	4,964	1,643
90	1,473,419	22,471	8,059	14,412	246		22,225	12,931	4,328	4,966	1,624
91	1,459,008	22,471	7,982	14,489	243		22,228	12,931	4,328	4,968	1,604
92	1,444,518	22,471	7,903	14,567	241		22,230	12,931	4,328	4,971	1,585
93	1,429,951	22,471	7,825	14,646	238		22,232	12,931	4,328	4,973	1,566
94	1,415,305	22,471	7,746	14,725	236		22,235	12,931	4,328	4,976	1,548
95	1,400,581	22,471	7,667	14,804	233		22,237	12,931	4,328	4,978	1,529
96	1,385,777	22,471	7,587	14,884	231		22,240	12,931	4,328	4,981	1,511
97	1,370,893	22,471	7,507	14,964	228		22,242	12,931	4,328	4,983	1,493
98	1,355,929	22,471	7,426	15,045	226		22,245	12,931	4,328	4,986	1,476
99	1,340,884	22,471	7,345	15,126	223		22,247	12,931	4,328	4,988	1,458
100	1,325,759	22,471	7,264	15,207	221		22,250	12,931	4,328	4,991	1,441
101	1,310,552	22,471	7,182	15,289	218		22,252	12,931	4,328	4,993	1,424
102	1,295,263	22,471	7,099	15,371	216		22,255	12,931	4,328	4,996	1,407
103	1,279,891	22,471	7,016	15,454	213		22,257	12,931	4,328	4,998	1,390
104	1,264,437	22,471	6,933	15,538	211		22,260	12,931	4,328	5,001	1,374
105	1,248,899	22,471	6,849	15,621	208		22,263	12,931	4,328	5,003	1,358
106	1,233,278	22,471	6,765	15,705	206		22,265	12,931	4,328	5,006	1,342

Period	Principal Balance	Scheduled Monthly Payment	Interest	Principal	Servicing Fee	Unscheduled Prepayments at Par	Net Cash Flow Available	Cash Flow Allocated to A-1 Tranche	Cash Flow Allocated to B-1 Tranche	Cash Flow Allocated to Equity	Present Value at 15% YTM
107	1,217,573	22,471	6,681	15,790	203		22,268	12,931	4,328	5,009	1,326
108	1,201,783	22,471	6,596	15,875	200		22,270	12,931	4,328	5,011	1,310
109	1,185,908	22,471	6,510	15,961	198		22,273	12,931	4,328	5,014	1,295
110	1,169,947	22,471	6,424	16,047	195		22,276	12,931	4,328	5,017	1,279
111	1,153,900	22,471	6,338	16,133	192		22,278	12,931	4,328	5,019	1,264
112	1,137,767	22,471	6,251	16,220	190		22,281	12,931	4,328	5,022	1,249
113	1,121,547	22,471	6,163	16,307	187		22,284	12,931	4,328	5,025	1,234
114	1,105,240	22,471	6,075	16,395	184		22,286	12,931	4,328	5,027	1,220
115	1,088,844	22,471	5,987	16,484	181		22,289	12,931	4,328	5,030	1,205
116	1,072,361	22,471	5,898	16,572	179		22,292	12,931	4,328	5,033	1,191
117	1,055,788	22,471	5,809	16,662	176		22,295	12,931	4,328	5,036	1,177
118	1,039,127	22,471	5,719	16,751	173		22,298	12,931	4,328	5,038	1,163
119	1,022,375	22,471	5,629	16,842	170		22,300	12,931	4,328	5,041	1,150
120	1,005,533	22,471	5,538	16,932	168		22,303	12,931	4,328	5,044	1,136
121	988,601	22,471	5,447	17,024	165		22,306	12,931	4,328	5,047	1,123
122	971,577	22,471	5,355	17,115	162		22,309	12,931	4,328	5,050	1,109
123	954,462	22,471	5,263	17,208	159		22,312	12,931	4,328	5,053	1,096
124	937,254	22,471	5,170	17,300	156		22,314	12,931	4,328	5,055	1,083
125	919,954	22,471	5,077	17,394	153		22,317	12,931	4,328	5,058	1,071
126	902,560	22,471	4,983	17,487	150		22,320	12,931	4,328	5,061	1,058
127	885,073	22,471	4,889	17,582	148		22,323	12,931	4,328	5,064	1,046

(continued)

Exhibit 4-7 (continued)

Period	Principal Balance	Scheduled Monthly Payment	Interest	Principal	Servicing Fee	Unscheduled Prepayments at Par	Net Cash Flow Available	Cash Flow Allocated to A-1 Tranche	Cash Flow Allocated to B-1 Tranche	Cash Flow Allocated to Equity	Present Value at 15% YTM
128	867,491	22,471	4,794	17,676	145		22,326	12,931	4,328	5,067	1,033
129	849,815	22,471	4,699	17,771	142		22,329	12,931	4,328	5,070	1,021
130	832,044	22,471	4,603	17,867	139	97,198	119,530	110,129	4,328	5,072	1,009
131	716,979	20,224	4,507	15,716	119		20,104	10,757	4,328	5,019	986
132	701,262	20,224	3,884	16,340	117		20,107	10,757	4,328	5,022	974
133	684,923	20,224	3,799	16,425	114		20,109	10,757	4,328	5,024	963
134	668,498	20,224	3,710	16,513	111		20,112	10,757	4,328	5,027	951
135	651,984	20,224	3,621	16,602	109		20,115	10,757	4,328	5,030	940
136	635,382	20,224	3,532	16,692	106		20,118	10,757	4,328	5,033	929
137	618,690	20,224	3,442	16,782	103		20,121	10,757	4,328	5,035	918
138	601,908	20,224	3,351	16,872	100		20,123	10,757	4,328	5,038	907
139	585,036	20,224	3,261	16,963	98		20,126	10,757	4,328	5,041	897
140	568,073	20,224	3,169	17,055	95		20,129	10,757	4,328	5,044	886
141	551,018	20,224	3,077	17,146	92		20,132	10,757	4,328	5,047	876
142	533,872	20,224	2,985	17,239	89		20,135	10,757	4,328	5,050	865
143	516,633	20,224	2,892	17,332	86		20,138	10,757	4,328	5,052	855
144	499,302	20,224	2,799	17,425	83	654,998	675,139	184,180	144,979	345,979	57,832

Present Value of Expected Cash Flows (discounted at 15% YTM)   411,623

that is used in cash flow models. Another common term used to describe the cash flow characteristics of a security is the "window." This window indicates the estimated period during which principal cash flows are expected to be received, before the entire balance is paid. Models that incorporate data statistics, such as window and PSA, provide investors with the information necessary to achieve their investment goals. Those models specifically allow an investor to identify investments that meet their goals with respect to these items:

- Achieve a yield spread over Treasuries that fairly compensates the investor for risk. Therefore, investors buying those types of investments believe that their pricing models allow them to manage prepayment risk and achieve the target rate of return.
- Match the duration of their assets and liabilities, a process referred to as "immunization." When a portfolio's asset duration equals the duration of its liabilities, interest rate changes should not materially result in a net gain or loss due to changes in the prices of assets and liabilities. When investing in mortgage-backed securities, prepayments that were higher than expected may make estimates of duration unreliable. Hence, the immunization process may be flawed. Furthermore, during periods of declining interest rates, the cash flows resulting from prepayments generally are reinvested at lower rates (assuming similar term and quality investments). At the same time, the cash flows on liabilities that are not refinanced remain at the higher rates. This mismatch results in a net loss because cash inflows are lower than cash outflows. For example, insurance companies experienced this problem during the 1990s when they sold fixed-rate guaranteed investment contracts (GIC contracts) and funded this liability by various strategies including mortgage-backed securities, CMOs, and commercial real estate loans. (In a GIC contract, the policyholder pays premiums and is entitled to a fixed periodic return plus the return of premiums at the end of the contract period.)

These goals are important to recognize as we analyze the more complicated aspects of mortgage-backed security investments. For example, there are numerous types of tranches; two types are:

- A planned amortization class (PAC) CMO (PAC CMO) allocates cash flows based on specific investor needs. An investor requiring very predictable cash flows may buy PACs; for example, the investor described earlier, who required principal cash flows in years 4 through 6. The participation agreement therefore would allocate prepayments and contractual principal repayments to other tranches until this time period occurs. The PAC CMO class has some protective cash flow priorities over other tranches and therefore is less affected by interest rate movements. In contrast, the other tranches will have greater cash flow variability and earn a higher risk premium in the form of a higher yield. However, the PAC protection may not be absolute when interest rates change drastically. An illustration of an actual PAC CMO will be given later in this discussion. The main concept that must be understood here is that a trust participation certificate can be structured to carve up the mortgage cash flows into different tranches to suit investors' needs.

- Accrual CMOs (also referred to as *Zs*) are the last tranches to receive principal repayments before the equity tranche. The accrual tranche cash flows will be volatile. Therefore, this investment requires a higher risk premium in the form of a higher potential yield. An investor with a long time horizon and a larger risk tolerance may consider this a viable investment.

A review of several actual public mortgage-backed securities follows to show how various analytical tools available in the marketplace are used to analyze their characteristics.

American Business Financial Services Inc. Collateralized Loan Obligation

American Business Financial Services Inc. originates various types of commercial and residential loans and at times securitizes groups of loans.[1] This company provided the following hypothetical case to illustrate the pricing of a reserve-fund tranche valued at $2,352,775.90. In this case, the collateral of $6,848,786.99 comprises 98 amortizing commercial loans with an average balance of $70,000. The cash flows from the loans are used to satisfy the requirements of two tranches:

1. A-1 Senior tranche, 6.545 percent coupon, $6,813,856 par value. (The example is modeled assuming that the A-1 tranche is sold for $6,813,856 at issuance.)
2. Reserve-fund tranche, with a $2,352,775.90 present value (price) at issuance.

This case provides realistic transaction characteristics and a private investment pricing methodology. The pricing is accomplished using BondCalc software and the company's pricing assumptions. Exhibit 4-8 presents the characteristics of securitization.

Exhibit 4-9 comprises 27 pages. It begins with a summary sheet that shows that the A-1 tranche was sold for $6,813,856.21 and that the estimated price of the reserve fund tranche at issuance is $2,352,775.90. Key points of the exhibit include:

- Page 154 provides a summary sheet. The transaction was priced on February 28, 1999. The class A tranche was issued at par at $6,813,856.21 with a 6.545 percent coupon. Note that the collateral balance of $6,848,786.77 is earning an average coupon of 16.049703 percent. This coupon spread between class A (6.545 percent) and the collateral (16.049703 percent) provides the cash flow for expenses and the $2,352,775.90 reserve fund.

Exhibit 4-8   Hypothetical CMO Characteristics.

Collateral par value	$6,848,786.77
Average life	5.342 years
Loan contractual terms	13.836 years
Duration	4.225
Average size of loans comprising collateral	$70,000
Weighted-average loan coupon rate	16.049703 fixed rate
Call features in loans	Borrowers may prepay without penalty
A-1 (senior) tranche coupon rate	6.545 percent
A-1 tranche cash flow priority	All unscheduled principal payments are allocated to the A-1 tranche until it is repaid. After the A-1 tranche is repaid, unscheduled principal payments are allocated to the reserve fund tranche.
A-1 public rating	This is a hypothetical transaction; however, an actual transaction would be AAA-rated by Moody's or S&P.
Surety fee *wraps* the deal (This fee buys insurance to reimburse for credit losses up to 5 percent of the initial collateral par value, amounting to $342,000 of losses.)	19 bps Collateral is based on each year's collateral principal balance.
Credit-related loan loss allocation	All credit-related loan losses are first covered by insurance up to $342,000, then allocated to the reserve tranche.
Discount rate used to compute the present value of the reserve tranche estimated cash flows to calculate its price at the issuance date	11 percent. This rate compensates the investor for default risks associated with the reserve tranche.
Servicing fee	50 bps
Trustee fee	2.5 bps
CPR (an annualized rate of unscheduled principal repayments)	3 to 13
Overcollateralization requirement (This refers to limiting equity-holder cash flow distributions until a level of cash is built up in equity as a cushion to protect the note holders.)	5 percent
Clean-up call (This provides the issuer the right to call the A-1 tranche when the balance is reduced to 10 percent of the original par value. At this level, it may be more cost effective for the issuer to pay off the investors and avoid the servicing costs related to the remaining balance.)	10 percent

Exhibit 4-9   S10B10299 Securitization Summary

						Term	
			Semiannual	Avg Life	Mod.		
Class	Size	Rate	IPR	Years	Duration	1st Pay	Maturity
A1	99.490%	6.545%	6.637%	5.342	4.225	0.086	13.836

Settlement Date (PV's time zero): 2/28/99

Proceeds

Security's Proceeds - Class A	$ 6,813,856.21
Less Reserve Fund	—
Less Deal Expenses	—
Net Proceeds	$ 6,813,856.21

Accounting Summary

Book Value	$ 6,848,786.77
Cash Proceeds	6,813,856.21
PV of Reserve Fund	2,352,775.90
Accounting Gain on Sale - No reserves	2,352,775.90
Gain as a Percent of Book	34.353178%

Other

Book Value	$ 6,848,786.77
Term	235
Average Coupon - Weighted by Par	16.049703%
Average Coupon - Weighted by Par X Duration	16.052084%
Servicing Fee	0.500000%
Trustee Fee	0.025000%
Surety Fee	0.190000%
Net Interest Rate	15.527084%
Securitization Rate	6.545000%
CPR	3-13%
Proceeds	$6,848,786.77
Gain on Sale	34.353178%
PV of Reserve Fund	$2,352,775.90
Reserve Fund Size	$0.00
Reserve Fund % of Book	0%
Earnings on RF Balance	0%
RF Discount Rate (Semi-annual)	11%
Overcolleralization Requirement	5%
Unpaid Balance RF Cap	0%
Clean-Up Call	10%
Annual Loss Rate	0%
Annual Defaults	0%

PV = $2,352,776
Average Lives = 5.342

(A)	(B)	(C)	(D)	(E)	(F)	(G)	(H)	(I)	(J)	(K)	(L)	(M)	(N)	(O)
				Total						A - Senior				
Period Ending	Period	Balance	Scheduled Principal	Scheduled Interest	Unsch Principal	Balloons	Total Cash Flow	Balance	Pct	Scheduled Principal	Scheduled Interest	Excess Interest	Balloons/ Unsch Prin	Total Cash Flow
4/01/99	1.03	6,848,787	7,184	72,093	17,344	-	96,621	6,813,856	100.00%	7,184	37,164	30,854	17,344	92,546
5/01/99	2.03	6,824,259	9,114	91,273	17,277	-	117,663	6,758,474	100.00	9,114	36,862	50,356	17,277	113,608
6/01/99	3.03	6,797,868	9,212	90,921	17,210	-	117,342	6,681,728	100.00	9,212	36,443	50,445	17,210	113,310
7/01/99	4.03	6,771,447	9,311	90,568	17,142	-	117,021	6,604,862	100.00	9,311	36,024	50,535	17,142	113,012
8/01/99	5.03	6,744,994	9,411	90,214	17,075	-	116,700	6,527,873	100.00	9,411	35,604	50,626	17,075	112,716
9/01/99	6.03	6,718,508	9,512	89,860	17,008	-	116,380	6,450,762	100.00	9,512	35,184	50,716	17,008	112,419
10/01/99	7.03	6,691,988	9,615	89,506	16,940	-	116,061	6,373,526	100.00	9,615	34,762	50,807	16,940	112,124
11/01/99	8.03	6,665,434	9,718	89,151	16,873	-	115,742	6,298,164	100.00	9,718	34,340	-	16,873	60,931
12/01/99	9.03	6,638,843	9,823	88,796	16,805	-	115,424	6,269,574	100.00	9,823	34,195	-	16,805	60,823
1/01/00	10.03	6,612,215	9,928	88,440	16,737	-	115,105	6,242,946	100.00	9,928	34,050	-	16,737	60,715
2/01/00	11.03	6,585,550	10,035	88,084	16,669	-	114,789	6,216,281	100.00	10,035	33,905	-	16,669	60,609
3/01/00	12.03	6,558,846	10,143	87,728	33,680	-	131,551	6,189,577	100.00	10,143	33,759	-	33,680	77,582
4/01/00	13.03	6,515,023	10,225	87,142	33,454	-	130,822	6,145,753	100.00	10,225	33,520	-	33,454	77,200
5/01/00	14.03	6,471,343	10,308	86,558	33,229	-	130,096	6,102,074	100.00	10,308	33,282	-	33,229	76,819
6/01/00	15.03	6,427,805	10,392	85,976	33,005	-	129,373	6,058,536	100.00	10,392	33,044	-	33,005	76,441
7/01/00	16.03	6,384,408	10,477	85,396	32,781	-	128,654	6,015,139	100.00	10,477	32,808	-	32,781	76,065
8/01/00	17.03	6,341,150	10,562	84,818	32,558	-	127,938	5,971,881	100.00	10,562	32,572	-	32,558	75,692
9/01/00	18.03	6,298,031	10,647	84,242	32,336	-	127,225	5,928,761	100.00	10,647	32,336	-	32,336	75,320

(continued)

Exhibit 4-9 *(continued)*

PV = $2,352,776
Average Lives = 5.342

					Total					A - Senior				
(A)	(B)	(C)	(D)	(E)	(F)	(G)	(H)	(I)	(J)	(K)	(L)	(M)	(N)	(O)
Period Ending	Period	Balance	Scheduled Principal	Scheduled Interest	Unsch Principal	Balloons	Total Cash Flow	Balance	Pct	Scheduled Principal	Scheduled Interest	Excess Interest	Balloons/ Unsch Prin	Total Cash Flow
10/01/00	19.03	6,255,047	10,734	83,667	32,115	-	126,516	5,885,778	100.00	10,734	32,102	-	32,115	74,950
11/01/00	20.03	6,212,199	10,821	83,095	31,894	-	125,809	5,842,930	100.00	10,821	31,868	-	31,894	74,583
12/01/00	21.03	6,169,484	10,909	82,524	31,674	-	125,106	5,800,215	100.00	10,909	31,635	-	31,674	74,218
1/01/01	22.03	6,126,902	10,997	81,955	31,454	-	124,406	5,757,633	100.00	10,997	31,403	-	31,454	73,855
2/01/01	23.03	6,084,450	11,087	81,387	31,235	-	123,709	5,715,181	100.00	11,087	31,172	-	31,235	73,494
3/01/01	24.03	6,042,128	11,177	80,822	69,586	-	161,584	5,672,859	100.00	11,177	30,941	-	69,586	111,703
4/01/01	25.03	5,961,366	11,195	79,742	68,654	-	159,591	5,592,097	100.00	11,195	30,500	-	68,654	110,349
5/01/01	26.03	5,881,518	11,213	78,674	67,732	-	157,620	5,512,248	100.00	11,213	30,065	-	67,732	109,010
6/01/01	27.03	5,802,572	11,232	77,619	66,821	-	155,672	5,433,303	100.00	11,232	29,634	-	66,821	107,687
7/01/01	28.03	5,724,520	11,250	76,575	65,920	-	153,746	5,355,251	100.00	11,250	29,208	-	65,920	106,379
8/01/01	29.03	5,647,349	11,268	75,544	65,030	-	151,842	5,278,080	100.00	11,268	28,788	-	65,030	105,086
9/01/01	30.03	5,571,051	11,287	74,524	64,149	-	149,959	5,201,782	100.00	11,287	28,371	-	64,149	103,807
10/01/01	31.03	5,495,615	11,305	73,515	63,278	-	148,099	5,126,346	100.00	11,305	27,960	-	63,278	102,544
11/01/01	32.03	5,421,032	11,324	72,518	62,418	-	146,259	5,051,763	100.00	11,324	27,553	-	62,418	101,295
12/01/01	33.03	5,347,290	11,342	71,532	61,567	-	144,441	4,978,021	100.00	11,342	27,151	-	61,567	100,060
1/01/02	34.03	5,274,381	11,375	70,557	60,726	-	142,657	4,905,112	100.00	11,375	26,753	-	60,725	98,853
2/01/02	35.03	5,202,281	11,040	69,593	59,897	-	140,530	4,833,012	100.00	11,040	26,360	-	59,897	97,297
3/01/02	36.03	5,131,344	11,058	68,645	59,078	-	138,781	4,762,075	100.00	11,058	25,973	-	59,078	96,110

PV = $2,352,776
Average Lives = 5.342

(A)	(B)	(C)	(D)	(E)	(F)	(G)	(H)	(I)	(J)	(K)	(L)	(M)	(N)	(O)
		Total						A - Senior						
Period Ending	Period	Balance	Scheduled Principal	Scheduled Interest	Unsch Principal	Balloons	Total Cash Flow	Balance	Pct	Scheduled Principal	Scheduled Interest	Excess Interest	Balloons/ Unsch Prin	Total Cash Flow
4/01/02	37.03	5,061,207	11,077	67,707	58,269	-	137,052	4,691,938	100.00	11,077	25,591	-	58,269	94,936
5/01/02	38.03	4,991,861	11,095	66,780	57,469	-	135,343	4,622,592	100.00	11,095	25,212	-	57,469	93,776
6/01/02	39.03	4,923,298	11,113	65,863	56,677	-	133,653	4,554,029	100.00	11,113	24,838	-	56,677	92,629
7/01/02	40.03	4,855,508	11,131	64,957	55,895	-	131,983	4,486,239	100.00	11,131	24,469	-	55,895	91,495
8/01/02	41.03	4,788,482	11,149	64,061	55,121	-	130,331	4,419,213	100.00	11,149	24,103	-	55,121	90,374
9/01/02	42.03	4,722,211	11,168	63,174	54,356	-	128,699	4,352,942	100.00	11,168	23,742	-	54,356	89,266
10/01/02	43.03	4,656,687	11,186	62,298	53,600	-	127,085	4,287,418	100.00	11,186	23,384	-	53,600	88,170
11/01/02	44.03	4,591,901	11,204	61,432	52,852	-	125,489	4,222,632	100.00	11,204	23,031	-	52,852	87,088
12/01/02	45.03	4,527,844	11,223	60,576	52,113	-	123,912	4,158,575	100.00	11,223	22,682	-	52,113	86,017
1/01/03	46.03	4,464,508	11,241	59,729	51,382	-	122,352	4,095,239	100.00	11,241	22,336	-	51,382	84,959
2/01/03	47.03	4,401,885	11,259	58,892	50,659	-	120,811	4,032,616	100.00	11,259	21,995	-	50,659	83,913
3/01/03	48.03	4,339,966	11,278	58,054	49,945	-	119,287	3,970,697	100.00	11,278	21,657	-	49,945	82,880
4/01/03	49.03	4,278,744	11,296	57,245	49,238	-	117,780	3,909,474	100.00	11,296	21,323	-	49,238	81,857
5/01/03	50.03	4,218,209	11,315	56,436	48,540	-	116,290	3,848,940	100.00	11,315	20,993	-	48,540	80,847
6/01/03	51.03	4,158,355	11,333	55,636	47,849	-	114,818	3,789,085	100.00	11,333	20,666	-	47,849	79,848
7/01/03	52.03	4,099,172	11,352	54,844	47,166	-	113,362	3,729,903	100.00	11,352	20,344	-	47,166	78,861
8/01/03	53.03	4,040,655	11,371	54,062	46,490	-	111,923	3,671,386	100.00	11,371	20,024	-	46,490	77,885
9/01/03	54.03	3,982,794	11,389	53,288	45,822	-	110,500	3,613,525	100.00	11,389	19,709	-	45,822	76,920

(continued)

Exhibit 4-9 (continued)

PV = $2,352,776
Average Lives = 5.342

(A)	(B)	(C)	(D)	(E)	(F)	(G)	(H)	(I)	(J)	(K)	(L)	(M)	(N)	(O)
			Total							A - Senior				
Period Ending	Period	Balance	Scheduled Principal	Scheduled Interest	Unsch Principal	Balloons	Total Cash Flow	Balance	Pct	Scheduled Principal	Scheduled Interest	Excess Interest	Balloons/ Unsch Prin	Total Cash Flow
10/01/03	55.03	3,925,582	11,408	52,524	45,155	622	109,708	3,556,313	100.00	11,408	19,397	-	45,777	76,582
11/01/03	56.03	3,868,397	11,251	51,759	44,504	-	107,514	3,499,128	100.00	11,251	19,085	-	44,504	74,840
12/01/03	57.03	3,812,642	11,269	51,014	43,861	-	106,143	3,443,373	100.00	11,269	18,781	-	43,861	73,911
1/01/04	58.03	3,757,513	11,288	50,276	42,333	77,209	181,107	3,388,244	100.00	11,288	18,480	-	119,543	149,310
2/01/04	59.03	3,626,682	11,054	48,531	41,619	8,571	109,774	3,257,413	100.00	11,054	17,766	-	50,189	79,010
3/01/04	60.03	3,565,439	11,043	47,712	40,565	38,629	137,949	3,196,170	100.00	11,043	17,432	-	79,194	107,669
4/01/04	61.03	3,475,202	10,731	46,499	39,904	6,033	103,167	3,105,933	100.00	10,731	16,940	-	45,937	73,608
5/01/04	62.03	3,418,534	10,537	45,741	39,322	-	95,600	3,049,265	100.00	10,537	16,631	-	39,322	66,490
6/01/04	63.03	3,368,676	10,554	45,075	38,746	-	94,375	2,999,406	100.00	10,554	16,359	-	38,746	65,659
7/01/04	64.03	3,319,375	10,571	44,415	38,177	-	93,164	2,950,106	100.00	10,571	16,090	-	38,177	64,839
8/01/04	65.03	3,270,627	10,589	43,764	37,615	-	91,967	2,901,358	100.00	10,589	15,824	-	37,615	64,028
9/01/04	66.03	3,222,424	10,606	43,119	37,058	-	90,783	2,853,155	100.00	10,606	15,562	-	37,058	63,226
10/01/04	67.03	3,174,760	10,623	42,482	36,508	-	89,613	2,805,490	100.00	10,623	15,302	-	36,508	62,433
11/01/04	68.03	3,127,628	10,641	41,852	35,964	-	88,457	2,758,359	100.00	10,641	15,045	-	35,964	61,649
12/01/04	69.03	3,081,023	10,658	41,229	35,426	-	87,313	2,711,754	100.00	10,658	14,790	-	35,426	60,875
1/01/05	70.03	3,034,939	10,676	40,612	34,894	-	86,182	2,665,670	100.00	10,676	14,539	-	34,894	60,109
2/01/05	71.03	2,989,369	10,693	40,003	34,368	-	85,065	2,620,100	100.00	10,693	14,290	-	34,368	59,352
3/01/05	72.03	2,944,308	10,711	39,401	33,848	-	83,960	2,575,039	100.00	10,711	14,045	-	33,848	58,604

PV = $2,352.776
Average Lives = 5.342

(A)	(B)	(C)	(D)	(E)	(F)	(G)	(H)	(I)	(J)	(K)	(L)	(M)	(N)	(O)
		Total							A - Senior					
Period Ending	Period	Balance	Scheduled Principal	Scheduled Interest	Unsch Principal	Balloons	Total Cash Flow	Balance	Pct	Scheduled Principal	Scheduled Interest	Excess Interest	Balloons/ Unsch Prin	Total Cash Flow
4/01/05	73.03	2,899,749	10,728	38,805	33,334	-	82,867	2,530,480	100.00	10,728	13,802	-	33,334	57,864
5/01/05	74.03	2,855,687	10,746	38,216	32,825	-	81,787	2,486,418	100.00	10,746	13,561	-	32,825	57,132
6/01/05	75.03	2,812,116	10,764	37,633	32,322	-	80,719	2,442,847	100.00	10,764	13,324	-	32,322	56,409
7/01/05	76.03	2,769,030	10,781	37,057	31,825	-	79,663	2,399,761	100.00	10,781	13,089	-	31,825	55,695
8/01/05	77.03	2,726,424	10,799	36,488	31,333	-	78,620	2,357,155	100.00	10,799	12,856	-	31,333	54,988
9/01/05	78.03	2,684,292	10,817	35,924	30,847	-	77,588	2,315,023	100.00	10,817	12,627	-	30,847	54,290
10/01/05	79.03	2,642,628	10,834	35,367	30,366	-	76,567	2,273,359	100.00	10,834	12,399	-	30,366	53,599
11/01/05	80.03	2,601,428	10,852	34,816	29,890	-	75,559	2,232,159	100.00	10,852	12,175	-	29,890	52,917
12/01/05	81.03	2,560,686	10,870	34,272	29,420	-	74,562	2,191,417	100.00	10,870	11,952	-	29,420	52,242
1/01/06	82.03	2,520,396	10,868	33,733	28,955	-	73,576	2,151,127	100.00	10,888	11,733	-	28,955	51,575
2/01/06	83.03	2,480,553	10,906	33,200	28,495	-	72,601	2,111,284	100.00	10,906	11,515	-	28,495	50,916
3/01/06	84.03	2,441,153	10,923	32,673	28,040	-	71,637	2,071,884	100.00	10,923	11,300	-	28,040	50,264
4/01/06	85.03	2,402,189	10,941	32,152	27,590	-	70,684	2,032,920	100.00	10,941	11,088	-	27,590	49,620
5/01/06	86.03	2,363,657	10,783	31,637	27,148	-	69,568	1,994,388	100.00	10,783	10,878	-	27,148	48,808
6/01/06	87.03	2,325,727	10,800	31,130	26,710	-	68,640	1,956,458	100.00	10,800	10,671	-	26,710	48,181
7/01/06	88.03	2,288,217	10,818	30,629	26,277	-	67,723	1,918,948	100.00	10,818	10,466	-	26,277	47,561
8/01/06	89.03	2,251,122	10,836	30,133	25,849	-	66,817	1,881,853	100.00	10,836	10,264	-	25,849	46,948
9/01/06	90.03	2,214,438	10,854	29,642	25,425	-	65,921	1,845,169	100.00	10,854	10,064	-	25,425	46,343

(continued)

159

Exhibit 4-9 *(continued)*

PV = $2,352,776
Average Lives = 5.342

		Total								A - Senior				
(A)	(B)	(C)	(D)	(E)	(F)	(G)	(H)	(I)	(J)	(K)	(L)	(M)	(N)	(O)
Period Ending	Period	Balance	Scheduled Principal	Scheduled Interest	Unsch Principal	Balloons	Total Cash Flow	Balance	Pct	Scheduled Principal	Scheduled Interest	Excess Interest	Balloons/ Unsch Prin	Total Cash Flow
10/01/06	91.03	2,178,159	10,871	29,157	25,006	-	65,035	1,808,890	100.00	10,871	9,866	-	23,006	45,744
11/01/06	92.03	2,142,281	10,889	28,677	24,592	-	64,159	1,773,012	100.00	10,889	9,670	-	24,592	45,152
12/01/06	93.03	2,106,800	10,907	28,203	24,183	-	63,293	1,737,531	100.00	10,907	9,477	-	24,183	44,566
1/01/07	94.03	2,071,710	10,925	27,734	23,778	-	62,436	1,702,441	100.00	10,925	9,285	-	23,778	43,988
2/01/07	95.03	2,037,008	10,943	27,270	23,377	-	61,590	1,667,739	100.00	10,943	9,096	-	23,377	43,416
3/01/07	96.03	2,002,688	10,961	26,811	22,981	-	60,753	1,633,419	100.00	10,961	8,909	-	22,981	42,850
4/01/07	97.03	1,968,747	10,979	26,357	22,589	-	59,925	1,599,478	100.00	10,979	8,724	-	22,589	42,292
5/01/07	98.03	1,935,179	10,997	25,908	22,201	-	59,107	1,565,910	100.00	10,997	8,541	-	22,201	41,739
6/01/07	99.03	1,901,981	11,015	25,465	21,818	-	58,298	1,532,712	100.00	11,015	8,360	-	21,818	41,193
7/01/07	100.03	1,869,148	11,033	25,026	21,439	-	57,498	1,499,879	100.00	11,033	8,181	-	21,439	40,653
8/01/07	101.03	1,836,676	11,051	24,591	21,064	-	56,707	1,467,407	100.00	11,051	8,003	-	21,064	40,119
9/01/07	102.03	1,804,560	11,069	24,162	20,693	-	55,925	1,435,291	100.00	11,069	7,828	-	20,693	39,591
10/01/07	103.03	1,772,798	11,087	23,737	20,327	-	55,152	1,403,529	100.00	11,087	7,655	-	20,327	39,069
11/01/07	104.03	1,741,384	11,106	23,317	19,964	-	54,387	1,372,115	100.00	11,106	7,484	-	19,964	38,553
12/01/07	105.03	1,710,314	11,124	22,902	19,605	-	53,631	1,341,045	100.00	11,124	7,314	-	19,605	38,043
1/01/08	106.03	1,679,585	11,142	22,491	19,251	-	52,884	1,310,316	100.00	11,142	7,147	-	19,251	37,539
2/01/08	107.03	1,649,192	11,160	22,085	18,900	-	52,145	1,279,923	100.00	11,160	6,981	-	18,900	37,041
3/01/08	108.03	1,619,132	11,179	21,683	18,553	-	51,414	1,249,863	100.00	11,179	6,817	-	18,553	36,548

PV = $2,352.776
Average Lives = 5.342

					Total					A - Senior					
(A)	(B)	(C)	(D)	(E)	(F)	(G)	(H)	(I)	(J)	(K)	(L)	(M)	(N)	(O)
Period Ending	Period	Balance	Scheduled Principal	Scheduled Interest	Unsch Principal	Balloons	Total Cash Flow	Balance	Pct	Scheduled Principal	Scheduled Interest	Excess Interest	Balloons/ Unsch Prin	Total Cash Flow
4/01/08	109.03	1,589,401	11,197	21,285	18,209	-	50,692	1,220,132	100.00	11,197	6,655	-	18,209	36,061
5/01/08	110.03	1,559,995	11,215	20,892	17,870	-	49,978	1,190,725	100.00	11,215	6,494	-	17,870	35,580
6/01/08	111.03	1,530,909	11,234	20,503	17,534	-	49,271	1,161,640	100.00	11,234	6,336	-	17,534	35,104
7/01/08	112.03	1,502,141	11,252	20,119	17,202	-	48,573	1,132,872	100.00	11,252	6,179	-	17,202	34,633
8/01/08	113.03	1,473,687	11,271	19,738	16,873	-	47,882	1,104,418	100.00	11,271	6,024	-	16,873	34,168
9/01/08	114.03	1,445,543	11,289	19,362	16,549	-	47,200	1,076,274	100.00	11,289	5,870	-	16,549	33,708
10/01/08	115.03	1,417,705	11,308	18,990	16,227	-	46,525	1,048,436	100.00	11,308	5,718	-	16,227	33,253
11/01/08	116.03	1,390,171	11,326	18,622	15,909	-	45,857	1,020,902	100.00	11,326	5,568	-	15,909	32,804
12/01/08	117.03	1,362,935	11,345	18,258	15,595	-	45,197	993,666	100.00	11,345	5,420	-	15,595	32,359
1/01/09	118.03	1,335,996	11,363	17,897	15,284	-	44,545	966,727	100.00	11,363	5,273	-	15,284	31,920
2/01/09	119.03	1,309,348	11,561	17,541	14,694	24,268	68,064	940,079	100.00	11,561	5,127	-	38,962	55,650
3/01/09	120.03	1,258,825	9,764	16,867	14,255	13,600	54,486	889,556	100.00	9,764	4,852	-	27,855	42,471
4/01/09	121.03	1,221,206	9,620	16,364	13,897	7,163	47,043	851,937	100.00	9,620	4,647	-	21,059	35,326
5/01/09	122.03	1,190,528	9,435	15,954	13,628	-	39,017	821,258	100.00	9,435	4,479	-	13,628	27,542
6/01/09	123.03	1,167,465	9,451	15,646	13,361	-	38,458	798,196	100.00	9,451	4,353	-	13,361	27,165
7/01/09	124.03	1,144,653	9,466	15,341	13,098	-	37,905	775,384	100.00	9,466	4,229	-	13,098	26,793
8/01/09	125.03	1,122,089	9,482	15,039	12,837	-	37,358	752,820	100.00	9,482	4,106	-	12,837	26,425
9/01/09	126.03	1,099,770	9,497	14,741	12,580	-	36,817	730,501	100.00	9,497	3,984	-	12,580	26,061
10/01/09	127.03	1,077,693	9,513	14,445	12,325	-	36,283	708,424	100.00	9,513	3,864	-	12,325	25,701

(continued)

161

Exhibit 4-9 *(continued)*

PV = $2,352,776
Average Lives = 5.342

(A)	(B)	(C)	(D)	(E)	(F)	(G)	(H)	(I)	(J)	(K)	(L)	(M)	(N)	(O)
						Total						A - Senior		
Period Ending	Period	Balance	Scheduled Principal	Scheduled Interest	Unsch Principal	Balloons	Total Cash Flow	Balance	Pct	Scheduled Principal	Scheduled Interest	Excess Interest	Balloons/ Unsch Prin	Total Cash Flow
11/01/09	128.03	1,055,856	9,528	14,153	12,073	-	35,754	686,586	100.00	9,528	3,745	-	12,073	25,346
12/01/09	129.03	1,034,255	9,544	13,864	11,823	-	35,232	664,985	100.00	9,544	3,627	-	11,823	24,994
1/01/10	130.03	1,012,887	9,560	13,579	11,576	-	34,715	643,618	100.00	9,560	3,510	-	11,576	24,647
2/01/10	131.03	991,751	9,576	13,295	11,332	-	34,204	622,482	100.00	9,576	3,395	-	11,332	24,303
3/01/10	132.03	970,843	9,591	13,016	11,091	-	33,699	601,574	100.00	9,591	3,281	-	11,091	23,963
4/01/10	133.03	950,161	9,607	12,740	10,852	-	33,199	580,892	100.00	9,607	3,168	-	10,852	23,627
5/01/10	134.03	929,702	9,623	12,466	10,616	-	32,705	560,432	100.00	9,623	3,057	-	10,616	23,295
6/01/10	135.03	909,463	9,639	12,195	10,382	-	32,216	540,194	100.00	9,639	2,946	-	10,382	22,967
7/01/10	136.03	889,442	9,654	11,928	10,151	-	31,733	520,173	100.00	9,654	2,837	-	10,151	22,643
8/01/10	137.03	859,636	9,670	11,663	9,922	-	31,255	500,367	100.00	9,670	2,729	-	9,922	22,322
9/01/10	138.03	850,044	9,686	11,401	9,696	-	30,783	480,775	100.00	9,686	2,622	-	9,696	22,005
10/01/10	139.03	830,661	9,702	11,142	9,472	-	30,316	461,392	100.00	9,702	2,517	-	9,472	21,691
11/01/10	140.03	811,487	9,718	10,885	9,251	-	29,854	442,218	100.00	9,718	2,412	-	9,251	21,381
12/01/10	141.03	792,518	9,734	10,631	9,032	-	29,397	423,249	100.00	9,734	2,308	-	9,032	21,074
1/01/11	142.03	773,752	9,750	10,380	8,815	-	28,946	404,483	100.00	9,750	2,206	-	8,815	20,771
2/01/11	143.03	755,187	9,766	10,132	8,601	-	28,499	385,918	100.00	9,766	2,105	-	8,601	20,472
3/01/11	144.03	736,820	9,782	9,886	8,389	-	28,057	367,551	100.00	9,782	2,005	-	8,389	20,175
4/01/11	145.03	718,650	9,798	9,643	8,179	-	27,620	349,381	100.00	9,798	1,906	-	8,179	19,883

PV = $2,352,776
Average Lives = 5.342

(A)	(B)	(C)	(D)	(E)	(F)	(G)	(H)	(I)	(J)	(K)	(L)	(M)	(N)	(O)
											A - Senior			
Period Ending	Period	Balance	Scheduled Principal	Scheduled Interest	Unsch Principal	Balloons	Total Cash Flow	Balance	Pct	Scheduled Principal	Scheduled Interest	Excess Interest	Balloons/ Unsch Prin	Total Cash Flow
5/01/11	146.03	700,673	9,814	9,403	7,971	-	27,188	331,404	100.00	9,814	1,808	-	7,971	19,593
6/01/11	147.03	682,887	9,830	9,165	7,766	-	26,761	313,618	100.00	9,830	1,711	-	7,766	19,307
7/01/11	148.03	665,291	9,847	8,930	7,563	-	26,339	296,022	100.00	9,847	1,738	-	7,563	19,147
8/01/11	149.03	647,882	9,863	8,697	7,362	-	25,921	278,613	100.00	9,863	1,636	-	7,362	18,860
9/01/11	150.03	630,658	9,879	8,467	7,163	-	25,508	261,389	100.00	9,879	1,535	-	7,163	18,576
10/01/11	151.03	613,616	9,895	8,239	6,966	-	25,100	244,347	100.00	9,895	1,435	-	6,966	18,295
11/01/11	152.03	596,755	9,911	8,013	6,771	-	24,696	227,486	100.00	9,911	1,336	-	6,771	18,018
12/01/11	153.03	580,073	9,928	7,790	6,578	-	24,296	210,804	100.00	9,928	1,238	-	6,578	17,744
1/01/12	154.03	563,567	9,944	7,569	6,388	-	23,901	194,298	100.00	9,944	1,141	-	6,388	17,472
2/01/12	155.03	547,235	9,960	7,351	6,199	-	23,511	177,966	100.00	9,960	1,045	-	6,199	17,204
3/01/12	156.03	531,075	9,977	7,135	6,012	-	23,124	161,806	100.00	9,977	950	-	6,012	16,939
4/01/12	157.03	515,086	9,993	6,921	5,828	-	22,742	145,817	100.00	9,993	856	-	5,828	16,677
5/01/12	158.03	499,265	10,010	6,709	5,645	-	22,364	129,996	100.00	10,010	763	-	5,645	16,418
6/01/12	159.03	483,611	10,026	6,500	5,464	-	21,990	114,341	100.00	10,026	671	-	5,464	16,162
7/01/12	160.03	468,120	10,043	6,293	5,285	-	21,621	98,851	100.00	10,043	580	-	5,285	15,908
8/01/12	161.03	452,792	10,059	6,088	5,108	-	21,255	83,523	100.00	10,059	490	-	5,108	15,658
9/01/12	162.03	437,625	10,076	5,885	4,933	-	20,894	68,356	100.00	10,076	401	-	4,933	15,410
10/01/12	163.03	422,616	10,092	5,684	4,760	-	20,536	53,347	100.00	10,092	313	-	4,760	15,165

(continued)

163

Exhibit 4-9 *(continued)*

PV = $2,352,776
Average Lives = 5.342

		Total						A - Senior						
(A)	(B)	(C)	(D)	(E)	(F)	(G)	(H)	(I)	(J)	(K)	(L)	(M)	(N)	(O)
Period Ending	Period	Balance	Scheduled Principal	Scheduled Interest	Unsch Principal	Balloons	Total Cash Flow	Balance	Pct	Scheduled Principal	Scheduled Interest	Excess Interest	Balloons/ Unsch Prin	Total Cash Flow
11/01/12	164.03	407,765	10,109	5,486	4,588	-	20,183	38,495	100.00	10,109	226	-	4,588	14,923
12/01/12	165.03	393,068	10,125	5,289	4,418	-	19,833	23,799	100.00	10,125	140	-	4,418	14,683
1/01/13	166.03	378,524	10,142	5,095	4,250	-	19,487	9,255	100.00	9,255	54	-	-	9,309
2/01/13	167.03	364,132	10,159	4,902	4,084	-	19,145	-	-	-	-	-	-	-
3/01/13	168.03	349,889	10,062	4,712	3,921	-	18,695	-	-	-	-	-	-	-
4/01/13	169.03	335,906	9,966	4,525	3,761	-	18,252	-	-	-	-	-	-	-
5/01/13	170.03	322,179	9,982	4,341	3,602	-	17,926	-	-	-	-	-	-	-
6/01/13	171.03	308,595	9,999	4,160	3,445	-	17,604	-	-	-	-	-	-	-
7/01/13	172.03	295,151	10,015	3,980	3,290	-	17,285	-	-	-	-	-	-	-
8/01/13	173.03	281,845	10,032	3,802	3,136	-	16,970	-	-	-	-	-	-	-
9/01/13	174.03	268,677	10,048	3,626	2,984	-	16,658	-	-	-	-	-	-	-
10/01/13	175.03	255,645	10,065	3,451	2,834	-	16,350	-	-	-	-	-	-	-
11/01/13	176.03	242,747	10,081	3,279	2,685	-	16,045	-	-	-	-	-	-	-
12/01/13	177.03	229,981	9,776	3,108	2,541	-	15,424	-	-	-	-	-	-	-
1/01/14	178.03	217,664	9,078	2,943	2,060	30,062	44,142	-	-	-	-	-	-	-
2/01/14	179.03	176,465	8,385	2,394	1,939	-	12,718	-	-	-	-	-	-	-
3/01/14	180.03	166,141	6,252	2,256	662	102,535	111,705	-	-	-	-	-	-	-
4/01/14	181.03	56,692	2,365	755	108	44,926	48,155	-	-	-	-	-	-	-

PV = $2,352,776
Average Lives = 5.342

(A)	(B)	(C)	(D)	(E)	(F)	(G)	(H)	(I)	(J)	(K)	(L)	(M)	(N)	(O)
					Total						A - Senior			
Period Ending	Period	Balance	Scheduled Principal	Scheduled Interest	Unsch Principal	Balloons	Total Cash Flow	Balance	Pct	Scheduled Principal	Scheduled Interest	Excess Interest	Balloons/ Unsch Prin	Total Cash Flow
5/01/14	182.03	9,292	120	124	106	-	350	-	-	-	-	-	-	-
6/01/14	183.03	9,067	120	121	103	-	344	-	-	-	-	-	-	-
7/01/14	184.03	8,843	120	118	101	-	339	-	-	-	-	-	-	-
8/01/14	185.03	8,622	121	115	98	-	334	-	-	-	-	-	-	-
9/01/14	186.03	8,403	121	112	96	-	328	-	-	-	-	-	-	-
10/01/14	187.03	8,187	121	109	93	-	323	-	-	-	-	-	-	-
11/01/14	188.03	7,973	121	106	91	-	318	-	-	-	-	-	-	-
12/01/14	189.03	7,761	121	103	88	-	313	-	-	-	-	-	-	-
1/01/15	190.03	7,552	122	101	86	-	308	-	-	-	-	-	-	-
2/01/15	191.03	7,345	122	98	83	-	303	-	-	-	-	-	-	-
3/01/15	192.03	7,140	122	95	81	-	298	-	-	-	-	-	-	-
4/01/15	193.03	6,937	122	92	79	-	293	-	-	-	-	-	-	-
5/01/15	194.03	6,736	122	90	76	-	288	-	-	-	-	-	-	-
6/01/15	195.03	6,537	123	87	74	-	284	-	-	-	-	-	-	-
7/01/15	196.03	6,341	123	84	72	-	279	-	-	-	-	-	-	-
8/01/15	197.03	6,146	123	82	69	-	274	-	-	-	-	-	-	-
9/01/15	198.03	5,954	123	79	67	-	270	-	-	-	-	-	-	-
10/01/15	199.03	5,763	123	77	65	-	265	-	-	-	-	-	-	-

(continued)

Exhibit 4-9 *(continued)*

PV = $2,352,776
Average Lives = 5.342

(A)	(B)	(C)	(D)	(E)	(F)	(G)	(H)	(I)	(J)	(K)	(L)	(M)	(N)	(O)
			Total							A - Senior				
Period Ending	Period	Balance	Scheduled Principal	Scheduled Interest	Unsch Principal	Balloons	Total Cash Flow	Balance	Pct	Scheduled Principal	Scheduled Interest	Excess Interest	Balloons/ Unsch Prin	Total Cash Flow
11/01/15	200.03	5,575	124	74	63	-	261	-	-	-	-	-	-	-
12/01/15	201.03	5,388	124	72	61	-	256	-	-	-	-	-	-	-
1/01/16	202.03	5,204	124	69	59	-	252	-	-	-	-	-	-	-
2/01/16	203.03	5,021	124	67	57	-	248	-	-	-	-	-	-	-
3/01/16	204.03	4,841	124	65	54	-	243	-	-	-	-	-	-	-
4/01/16	205.03	4,662	125	62	52	-	239	-	-	-	-	-	-	-
5/01/16	206.03	4,485	125	60	50	-	235	-	-	-	-	-	-	-
6/01/16	207.03	4,310	125	57	48	-	231	-	-	-	-	-	-	-
7/01/16	208.03	4,137	125	55	46	-	227	-	-	-	-	-	-	-
8/01/16	209.03	3,965	125	53	44	-	223	-	-	-	-	-	-	-
9/01/16	210.03	3,795	126	51	42	-	219	-	-	-	-	-	-	-
10/01/16	211.03	3,628	126	48	40	-	215	-	-	-	-	-	-	-
11/01/16	212.03	3,461	126	46	38	-	211	-	-	-	-	-	-	-
12/01/16	213.03	3,297	126	44	37	-	207	-	-	-	-	-	-	-
1/01/17	214.03	3,134	126	42	35	-	203	-	-	-	-	-	-	-
2/01/17	215.03	2,973	127	40	33	-	199	-	-	-	-	-	-	-
3/01/17	216.03	2,814	127	37	31	-	195	-	-	-	-	-	-	-
4/01/17	217.03	2,656	127	35	29	-	192	-	-	-	-	-	-	-

PV = $2,352,776
Average Lives = 5.342

			Total						A - Senior					
(A)	(B)	(C)	(D)	(E)	(F)	(G)	(H)	(I)	(J)	(K)	(L)	(M)	(N)	(O)
Period Ending	Period	Balance	Scheduled Principal	Scheduled Interest	Unsch Principal	Balloons	Total Cash Flow	Balance	Pct	Scheduled Principal	Scheduled Interest	Excess Interest	Balloons/ Unsch Prin	Total Cash Flow
5/01/17	218.03	2,500	127	33	27	-	188	-	-	-	-	-	-	-
6/01/17	219.03	2,345	127	31	26	-	184	-	-	-	-	-	-	-
7/01/17	220.03	2,192	128	29	24	-	181	-	-	-	-	-	-	-
8/01/17	221.03	2,040	128	27	22	-	177	-	-	-	-	-	-	-
9/01/17	222.03	1,890	128	25	20	-	174	-	-	-	-	-	-	-
10/01/17	223.03	1,742	128	23	19	-	170	-	-	-	-	-	-	-
11/01/17	224.03	1,595	128	21	17	-	167	-	-	-	-	-	-	-
12/01/17	225.03	1,450	129	19	15	-	163	-	-	-	-	-	-	-
1/01/18	226.03	1,306	129	17	14	-	160	-	-	-	-	-	-	-
2/01/18	227.03	1,163	129	16	12	-	157	-	-	-	-	-	-	-
3/01/18	228.03	1,022	129	14	10	-	153	-	-	-	-	-	-	-
4/01/18	229.03	883	130	12	9	-	150	-	-	-	-	-	-	-
5/01/18	230.03	744	130	10	7	-	147	-	-	-	-	-	-	-
6/01/18	231.03	608	130	8	6	-	144	-	-	-	-	-	-	-
7/01/18	232.03	472	130	6	4	-	140	-	-	-	-	-	-	-
8/01/18	233.03	338	130	5	2	-	137	-	-	-	-	-	-	-
9/01/18	234.03	205	131	3	1	-	134	-	-	-	-	-	-	-

(continued)

167

Exhibit 4-9 *(continued)*

PV = $2,352,776
Average Lives = 5.342

			Total						A - Senior					
(A)	(B)	(C)	(D)	(E)	(F)	(G)	(H)	(I)	(J)	(K)	(L)	(M)	(N)	(O)
Period Ending	Period	Balance	Scheduled Principal	Scheduled Interest	Unsch Principal	Balloons	Total Cash Flow	Balance	Pct	Scheduled Principal	Scheduled Interest	Excess Interest	Balloons/ Unsch Prin	Total Cash Flow
10/01/18	235.03	74	74	1	-	-	75	-	-	-	-	-	-	-
			1,893,702	6,680,013	4,601,467	353,618	13,528,800			1,749,840	2,382,469	334,339	4,729,677	9,196,326

Column Notes:
(A) Any intraperiod cash flows are assumed to be on period ending dates.
(B) Monthly periods from settlement date.
(C) Balance outstanding on which interest is paid. Clean-up call was not exercised and the rate to Class A holders increased by 0.5% when the balance fell below 10%.
(D) Fully amortizes over 19.586 years.
(E) Interest is paid at a weighted gross rate of 16.052%.
(F) Unscheduled principal prepayments assumed at a CPR of 3-13%.
(G) Any principal redemption on the final date that is in excess of the scheduled level amount.
(H) The sum of Columns (D), (E), (F) and (G).
(I) The balance of the senior piece. It is the prior balance less Columns (K), (M) and (N).
(J) There is no subordinated piece.
(K) Column (D) times Column (J).
(L) Column (I) times 6.545%.
(M) Excess interest is Column (H) less the sum of Columns (K), (L), and (N), and Page 2 Column (H). It is given to the senior piece until overcolleralization of 5% is reached (see Page 2 Column (C)). It then becomes cash to the reserve fund (see Page 2 Column (I)).
(N) The senior piece is being given 100% of the unscheduled principal in Column (F) and balloons in Column (G).
(O) The sum of Columns (K), (L), (M) and (N).

(A)	(B)	(C)	(D)	(E)	(F)	(G)	(H)	(I)	(J)	(K)	(L)	(M)	(N)
				Fees					Reserve				Present
Period Ending	Period	Over Coll	Cumulative Excess	Servicing	Trustee	Surety	Total	Cash In	Fund Balance	Reinvest Income	Cash Out	Losses	Value of Servicing Fee
4/01/99	1.03	0.51%	30,854	2,854	143	1,079	4,075	-	-	-	-	-	2,827
5/01/99	2.03	0.96	81,209	2,843	142	1,070	4,056	-	-	-	-	-	2,792
6/01/99	3.03	1.71	131,655	2,832	142	1,058	4,032	-	-	-	-	-	2,757
7/01/99	4.03	2.46	182,190	2,821	141	1,046	4,008	-	-	-	-	-	2,722
8/01/99	5.03	3.22	232,816	2,810	141	1,034	3,985	-	-	-	-	-	2,687
9/01/99	6.03	3.99	283,532	2,799	140	1,021	3,961	-	-	-	-	-	2,653
10/01/99	7.03	4.76	334,339	2,788	139	1,009	3,937	-	-	-	-	-	2,619
11/01/99	8.03	5.54	334,339	2,777	139	997	3,913	50,898	-	-	50,898	-	2,585
12/01/99	9.03	5.56	334,339	2,766	138	993	3,897	50,704	50,898	-	50,704	-	2,552
1/01/00	10.03	5.58	334,339	2,755	138	988	3,881	50,509	50,704	-	50,509	-	2,519
2/01/00	11.03	5.61	334,339	2,744	137	984	3,865	50,314	50,509	-	50,314	-	2,487
3/01/00	12.03	5.63	334,339	2,733	137	980	3,850	50,119	50,314	-	50,119	-	2,455
4/01/00	13.03	5.67	334,339	2,715	136	973	3,823	49,798	50,119	-	49,798	-	2,417
5/01/00	14.03	5.71	334,339	2,696	135	966	3,797	49,479	49,798	-	49,479	-	2,379
6/01/00	15.03	5.74	334,339	2,678	134	959	3,771	49,160	49,479	-	49,160	-	2,342
7/01/00	16.03	5.78	334,339	2,660	133	952	3,746	48,843	49,160	-	48,843	-	2,306
8/01/00	17.03	5.82	334,339	2,642	132	946	3,720	48,527	48,843	-	48,527	-	2,270
9/01/00	18.03	5.86	334,339	2,624	131	939	3,694	48,211	48,527	-	48,211	-	2,234
10/01/00	19.03	5.90	334,339	2,606	130	932	3,668	47,897	48,211	-	47,897	-	2,199
11/01/00	20.03	5.94	334,339	2,588	129	925	3,643	47,583	47,897	-	47,583	-	2,165
12/01/00	21.03	5.99	334,339	2,571	129	918	3,618	47,271	47,583	-	47,271	-	2,131

(continued)

Exhibit 4-9 *(continued)*

(A)	(B)	(C)	(D)	(E)	(F)	(G)	(H)	(I)	(J)	(K)	(L)	(M)	(N)
				Fees					Reserve				Present
Period Ending	Period	Over Coll	Cumulative Excess	Servicing	Trustee	Surety	Total	Cash In	Fund Balance	Reinvest Income	Cash Out	Losses	Value of Servicing Fee
1/01/01	22.03	6.03	334,339	2,553	128	912	3,592	46,959	47,271	-	46,959	-	2,097
2/01/01	23.03	6.07	334,339	2,535	127	905	3,567	46,649	46,959	-	46,649	-	2,064
3/01/01	24.03	6.11	334,339	2,518	126	898	3,542	46,339	46,649	-	46,339	-	2,032
4/01/01	25.03	6.19	334,339	2,484	124	885	3,494	45,748	46,339	-	45,748	-	1,987
5/01/01	26.03	6.28	334,339	2,451	123	873	3,446	45,164	45,748	-	45,164	-	1,943
6/01/01	27.03	6.36	334,339	2,418	121	860	3,399	44,586	45,164	-	44,586	-	1,900
7/01/01	28.03	6.45	334,339	2,385	119	848	3,352	44,015	44,586	-	44,015	-	1,857
8/01/01	29.03	6.54	334,339	2,353	118	836	3,306	43,450	44,015	-	43,450	-	1,816
9/01/01	30.03	6.63	334,339	2,321	116	824	3,261	42,891	43,450	-	42,891	-	1,776
10/01/01	31.03	6.72	334,339	2,290	114	812	3,216	42,339	42,891	-	42,339	-	1,736
11/01/01	32.03	6.81	334,339	2,259	113	800	3,172	41,793	42,339	-	41,793	-	1,697
12/01/01	33.03	6.91	334,339	2,228	111	788	3,128	41,253	41,793	-	41,253	-	1,659
1/01/02	34.03	7.00	334,339	2,198	110	777	3,084	40,720	41,253	-	40,720	-	1,622
2/01/02	35.03	7.10	334,339	2,168	108	765	3,041	40,192	40,720	-	40,192	-	1,586
3/01/02	36.03	7.20	334,339	2,138	107	754	2,999	39,673	40,192	-	39,673	-	1,550
4/01/02	37.03	7.30	334,339	2,109	105	743	2,957	39,159	39,673	-	39,159	-	1,515
5/01/02	38.03	7.40	334,339	2,080	104	732	2,916	38,651	39,159	-	38,651	-	1,481
6/01/02	39.03	7.50	334,339	2,051	103	721	2,875	38,150	38,651	-	38,150	-	1,448
7/01/02	40.03	7.61	334,339	2,023	101	710	2,835	37,653	38,150	-	37,653	-	1,415
8/01/02	41.03	7.71	334,339	1,995	100	700	2,795	37,163	37,653	-	37,163	-	1,383
9/01/02	42.03	7.82	334,339	1,968	98	689	2,755	36,678	37,163	-	36,678	-	1,352

(A) Period Ending	(B) Period	(C) Over Coll	(D) Cumulative Excess	(E) Servicing	(F) Trustee	(G) Surety	(H) Total	(I) Cash In	(J) Fund Balance	(K) Reinvest Income	(L) Cash Out	(M) Losses	(N) Present Value of Servicing Fee
				Fees					**Reserve**				
10/01/02	43.03	7.93	334,339	1,940	97	679	2,716	36,198	36,678	–	36,198	–	1,322
11/01/02	44.03	8.04	334,339	1,913	96	669	2,678	35,724	36,198	–	35,724	–	1,292
12/01/02	45.03	8.16	334,339	1,887	94	658	2,639	35,255	35,724	–	35,255	–	1,262
1/01/03	46.03	8.27	334,339	1,860	93	648	2,602	34,791	35,255	–	34,791	–	1,234
2/01/03	47.03	8.39	334,339	1,834	92	638	2,564	34,333	34,791	–	34,333	–	1,205
3/01/03	48.03	8.51	334,339	1,808	90	629	2,527	33,880	34,333	–	33,880	–	1,178
4/01/03	49.03	8.63	334,339	1,783	89	619	2,491	33,431	33,880	–	33,431	–	1,151
5/01/03	50.03	8.75	334,339	1,758	88	609	2,455	32,988	33,431	–	32,988	–	1,125
6/01/03	51.03	8.88	334,339	1,733	87	600	2,419	32,550	32,988	–	32,550	–	1,099
7/01/03	52.03	9.01	334,339	1,708	85	591	2,384	32,117	32,550	–	32,117	–	1,074
8/01/03	53.03	9.14	334,339	1,684	84	581	2,349	31,689	32,117	–	31,689	–	1,049
9/01/03	54.03	9.27	334,339	1,659	83	572	2,315	31,265	31,689	–	31,265	–	1,025
10/01/03	55.03	9.41	334,339	1,636	82	563	2,281	30,846	31,265	–	30,846	–	1,001
11/01/03	56.03	9.55	334,339	1,612	81	554	2,246	30,428	30,846	–	30,428	–	978
12/01/03	57.03	9.69	334,339	1,589	79	545	2,213	30,020	30,428	–	30,020	–	955
1/01/04	58.03	9.83	334,339	1,566	78	536	2,180	29,616	30,020	–	29,616	–	933
2/01/04	59.03	10.18	334,339	1,511	76	516	2,102	28,662	29,616	–	28,662	–	892
3/01/04	60.03	10.36	334,339	1,486	74	506	2,066	28,214	28,662	–	28,214	–	869
4/01/04	61.03	10.63	334,339	1,448	72	492	2,012	27,546	28,214	–	27,546	–	840
5/01/04	62.03	10.80	334,339	1,424	71	483	1,978	27,132	27,546	–	27,132	–	819
6/01/04	63.03	10.96	334,339	1,404	70	475	1,949	26,767	27,132	–	26,767	–	800

(continued)

171

Exhibit 4-9 *(continued)*

(A)	(B)	(C)	(D)	(E)	(F)	(G)	(H)	(I)	(J)	(K)	(L)	(M)	(N)
				Fees					Reserve				Present
Period Ending	Period	Over Coll	Cumulative Excess	Servicing	Trustee	Surety	Total	Cash In	Fund Balance	Reinvest Income	Cash Out	Losses	Value of Servicing Fee
7/01/04	64.03	11.12	334,339	1,383	69	467	1,919	26,406	26,767	-	26,406	-	781
8/01/04	65.03	11.29	334,339	1,363	68	459	1,890	26,049	26,406	-	26,049	-	763
9/01/04	66.03	11.46	334,339	1,343	67	452	1,862	25,696	26,049	-	25,696	-	745
10/01/04	67.03	11.63	334,339	1,323	66	444	1,833	25,347	25,696	-	25,347	-	727
11/01/04	68.03	11.81	334,339	1,303	65	437	1,805	25,002	25,347	-	25,002	-	710
12/01/04	69.03	11.99	334,339	1,284	64	429	1,777	24,661	25,002	-	24,661	-	693
1/01/05	70.03	12.17	334,339	1,265	63	422	1,750	24,324	24,661	-	24,324	-	677
2/01/05	71.03	12.35	334,339	1,246	62	415	1,723	23,990	24,324	-	23,990	-	661
3/01/05	72.03	12.54	334,339	1,227	61	408	1,696	23,660	23,990	-	23,660	-	645
4/01/05	73.03	12.73	334,339	1,208	60	401	1,669	23,334	23,660	-	23,334	-	630
5/01/05	74.03	12.93	334,339	1,190	59	394	1,643	23,011	23,334	-	23,011	-	615
6/01/05	75.03	13.13	334,339	1,172	59	387	1,617	22,692	23,011	-	22,692	-	600
7/01/05	76.03	13.34	334,339	1,154	58	380	1,591	22,377	22,692	-	22,377	-	585
8/01/05	77.03	13.54	334,339	1,136	57	373	1,566	22,065	22,377	-	22,065	-	571
9/01/05	78.03	13.76	334,339	1,118	56	367	1,541	21,757	22,065	-	21,757	-	557
10/01/05	79.03	13.97	334,339	1,101	55	360	1,516	21,452	21,757	-	21,452	-	544
11/01/05	80.03	14.19	334,339	1,084	54	353	1,492	21,150	21,452	-	21,150	-	531
12/01/05	81.03	14.42	334,339	1,067	53	347	1,467	20,852	21,150	-	20,852	-	518
1/01/06	82.03	14.65	334,339	1,050	53	341	1,443	20,557	20,852	-	20,557	-	505
2/01/06	83.03	14.89	334,339	1,034	52	334	1,420	20,265	20,557	-	20,265	-	493
3/01/06	84.03	15.13	334,339	1,017	51	328	1,396	19,977	20,265	-	19,977	-	481

| (A) | (B) | (C) | (D) | Fees | | | | Reserve | | | | (M) | (N) |
Period Ending	Period	Over Coll	Cumulative Excess	(E) Servicing	(F) Trustee	(G) Surety	(H) Total	(I) Cash In	(J) Fund Balance	(K) Reinvest Income	(L) Cash Out	Losses	Present Value of Servicing Fee
4/01/06	85.03	15.37	334,339	1,001	50	322	1,373	19,692	19,977	-	19,692	-	469
5/01/06	86.03	15.62	334,339	985	49	316	1,350	19,410	19,692	-	19,410	-	457
6/01/06	87.03	15.88	334,339	969	48	310	1,327	19,132	19,410	-	19,132	-	446
7/01/06	88.03	16.14	334,339	953	48	304	1,305	18,857	19,132	-	18,857	-	435
8/01/06	89.03	16.40	334,339	938	47	298	1,283	18,586	18,857	-	18,586	-	424
9/01/06	90.03	16.68	334,339	923	46	292	1,261	18,317	18,586	-	18,317	-	413
10/01/06	91.03	16.95	334,339	908	45	286	1,239	18,052	18,317	-	18,052	-	403
11/01/06	92.03	17.24	334,339	893	45	281	1,218	17,789	18,052	-	17,789	-	393
12/01/06	93.03	17.53	334,339	878	44	275	1,197	17,529	17,789	-	17,529	-	383
1/01/07	94.03	17.82	334,339	863	43	270	1,176	17,273	17,529	-	17,273	-	373
2/01/07	95.03	18.13	334,339	849	42	264	1,155	17,019	17,273	-	17,019	-	363
3/01/07	96.03	18.44	334,339	834	42	259	1,135	16,767	17,019	-	16,767	-	354
4/01/07	97.03	18.76	334,339	820	41	253	1,115	16,519	16,767	-	16,519	-	345
5/01/07	98.03	19.08	334,339	806	40	248	1,095	16,273	16,519	-	16,273	-	336
6/01/07	99.03	19.41	334,339	792	40	243	1,075	16,030	16,273	-	16,030	-	327
7/01/07	100.03	19.76	334,339	779	39	237	1,056	15,790	16,030	-	15,790	-	319
8/01/07	101.03	20.11	334,339	765	38	232	1,036	15,552	15,790	-	15,552	-	311
9/01/07	102.03	20.46	334,339	752	38	227	1,017	15,317	15,552	-	15,317	-	303
10/01/07	103.03	20.83	334,339	739	37	222	998	15,085	15,317	-	15,085	-	295
11/01/07	104.03	21.21	334,339	726	36	217	979	14,855	15,085	-	14,855	-	287
12/01/07	105.03	21.59	334,339	713	36	212	961	14,627	14,855	-	14,627	-	279

(continued)

Exhibit 4-9 (continued)

(A) Period Ending	(B) Period	(C) Over Coll	(D) Cumulative Excess	(E) Servicing	(F) Trustee	(G) Surety	(H) Total	(I) Cash In	(J) Fund Balance	(K) Reinvest Income	(L) Cash Out	(M) Losses	(N) Present Value of Servicing Fee
				Fees					Reserve				
1/01/08	106.03	21.99	334,339	700	35	207	942	14,402	14,627	–	14,402	–	272
2/01/08	107.03	22.39	334,339	687	34	203	924	14,180	14,402	–	14,180	–	264
3/01/08	108.03	22.81	334,339	675	34	198	906	13,960	14,180	–	13,960	–	257
4/01/08	109.03	23.23	334,339	662	33	193	889	13,742	13,960	–	13,742	–	250
5/01/08	110.03	23.67	334,339	650	32	189	871	13,527	13,742	–	13,527	–	243
6/01/08	111.03	24.12	334,339	638	32	184	854	13,314	13,527	–	13,314	–	237
7/01/08	112.03	24.58	334,339	626	31	179	837	13,103	13,314	–	13,103	–	230
8/01/08	113.03	25.06	334,339	614	31	175	820	12,895	13,103	–	12,895	–	224
9/01/08	114.03	25.55	334,339	602	30	170	803	12,689	12,895	–	12,689	–	218
10/01/08	115.03	26.05	334,339	591	30	166	786	12,485	12,689	–	12,485	–	212
11/01/08	116.03	26.56	334,339	579	29	162	770	12,284	12,485	–	12,284	–	206
12/01/08	117.03	27.09	334,339	568	28	157	754	12,084	12,284	–	12,084	–	200
1/01/09	118.03	27.64	334,339	557	28	153	738	11,887	12,084	–	11,887	–	194
2/01/09	119.03	28.20	334,339	546	27	149	722	11,692	11,887	–	11,692	–	189
3/01/09	120.03	29.33	334,339	525	26	141	692	11,323	11,692	–	11,323	–	180
4/01/09	121.03	30.24	334,339	509	25	135	669	11,049	11,323	–	11,049	–	173
5/01/09	122.03	31.02	334,339	496	25	130	651	10,824	11,049	–	10,824	–	167
6/01/09	123.03	31.63	334,339	486	24	126	637	10,655	10,824	–	10,655	–	162
7/01/09	124.03	32.26	334,339	477	24	123	624	10,488	10,655	–	10,488	–	158
8/01/09	125.03	32.91	334,339	468	23	119	610	10,323	10,488	–	10,323	–	153
9/01/09	126.03	33.58	334,339	458	23	116	597	10,160	10,323	–	10,160	–	149

(A) Period Ending	(B) Period	(C) Over Coll	(D) Cumulative Excess	(E) Servicing	(F) Trustee	(G) Surety	(H) Total	(I) Cash In	(J) Fund Balance	(K) Reinvest Income	(L) Cash Out	(M) Losses	(N) Present Value of Servicing Fee
				Fees				Reserve					
10/01/09	127.03	34.26	334,339	449	22	112	584	9,998	10,160	–	9,998	–	145
11/01/09	128.03	34.97	334,339	440	22	109	571	9,838	9,998	–	9,838	–	140
12/01/09	129.03	35.70	334,339	431	22	105	558	9,680	9,838	–	9,680	–	136
1/01/10	130.03	36.46	334,339	422	21	102	545	9,523	9,680	–	9,523	–	132
2/01/10	131.03	37.23	334,339	413	21	99	532	9,368	9,523	–	9,368	–	128
3/01/10	132.03	38.04	334,339	405	20	95	520	9,215	9,368	–	9,215	–	125
4/01/10	133.03	38.86	334,339	396	20	92	508	9,064	9,215	–	9,064	–	121
5/01/10	134.03	39.72	334,339	387	19	89	495	8,914	9,064	–	8,914	–	117
6/01/10	135.03	40.60	334,339	379	19	86	483	8,766	8,914	–	8,766	–	114
7/01/10	136.03	41.52	334,339	371	19	82	471	8,619	8,766	–	8,619	–	110
8/01/10	137.03	42.46	334,339	362	18	79	460	8,474	8,619	–	8,474	–	107
9/01/10	138.03	43.44	334,339	354	18	76	448	8,330	8,474	–	8,330	–	103
10/01/10	139.03	44.45	334,339	346	17	73	436	8,189	8,330	–	8,189	–	100
11/01/10	140.03	45.51	334,339	338	17	70	425	8,048	8,189	–	8,048	–	97
12/01/10	141.03	46.59	334,339	330	17	67	414	7,909	8,048	–	7,909	–	94
1/01/11	142.03	47.72	334,339	322	16	64	403	7,772	7,909	–	7,772	–	91
2/01/11	143.03	48.90	334,339	315	16	61	391	7,636	7,772	–	7,636	–	88
3/01/11	144.03	50.12	334,339	307	15	58	381	7,501	7,636	–	7,501	–	85
4/01/11	145.03	51.38	334,339	299	15	55	370	7,368	7,501	–	7,368	–	82
5/01/11	146.03	52.70	334,339	292	15	52	359	7,236	7,368	–	7,236	–	79
6/01/11	147.03	54.07	334,339	285	14	50	348	7,106	7,236	–	7,106	–	77

(continued)

Exhibit 4-9 *(continued)*

| (A) | (B) | (C) | (D) | Fees | | | | Reserve | | | | | (N) |
Period Ending	Period	Over Coll	Cumulative Excess	(E) Servicing	(F) Trustee	(G) Surety	(H) Total	(I) Cash In	(J) Fund Balance	(K) Reinvest Income	(L) Cash Out	(M) Losses	Present Value of Servicing Fee
7/01/11	148.03	55.50	334,339	277	14	47	338	6,854	7,106	-	6,854	-	74
8/01/11	149.03	57.00	334,339	270	13	44	328	6,734	6,854	-	6,734	-	71
9/01/11	150.03	58.55	334,339	263	13	41	317	6,615	6,734	-	6,615	-	69
10/01/11	151.03	60.18	334,339	256	13	39	307	6,497	6,615	-	6,497	-	66
11/01/11	152.03	61.88	334,339	249	12	36	297	6,381	6,497	-	6,381	-	64
12/01/11	153.03	63.66	334,339	242	12	33	287	6,265	6,381	-	6,265	-	62
1/01/12	154.03	65.52	334,339	235	12	31	277	6,151	6,265	-	6,151	-	59
2/01/12	155.03	67.48	334,339	228	11	28	268	6,039	6,151	-	6,039	-	57
3/01/12	156.03	69.53	334,339	221	11	26	258	5,927	6,039	-	5,927	-	55
4/01/12	157.03	71.69	334,339	215	11	23	248	5,817	5,927	-	5,817	-	53
5/01/12	158.03	73.96	334,339	208	10	21	239	5,707	5,817	-	5,707	-	51
6/01/12	159.03	76.36	334,339	202	10	18	230	5,599	5,707	-	5,599	-	49
7/01/12	160.03	78.88	334,339	195	10	16	220	5,492	5,599	-	5,492	-	47
8/01/12	161.03	81.55	334,339	189	9	13	211	5,386	5,492	-	5,386	-	45
9/01/12	162.03	84.38	334,339	182	9	11	202	5,282	5,386	-	5,282	-	43
10/01/12	163.03	87.38	334,339	176	9	8	193	5,178	5,282	-	5,178	-	41
11/01/12	164.03	90.56	334,339	170	8	6	184	5,075	5,178	-	5,075	-	39
12/01/12	165.03	93.95	334,339	164	8	4	176	4,974	5,075	-	4,974	-	38
1/01/13	166.03	97.56	334,339	158	8	1	167	10,011	4,974	-	10,011	-	36
2/01/13	167.03	100.00	334,339	152	8	-	159	18,986	10,011	-	18,986	-	34
3/01/13	168.03	100.00	334,339	146	7	-	153	18,542	18,986	-	18,542	-	33

(A)	(B)	(C)	(D)	(E)	(F)	(G)	(H)	(I)	(J)	(K)	(L)	(M)	(N)
				Fees				Reserve					Present
Period Ending	Period	Over Coll	Cumulative Excess	Servicing	Trustee	Surety	Total	Cash In	Fund Balance	Reinvest Income	Cash Out	Losses	Value of Servicing Fee
4/01/13	169.03	100.00	334,339	140	7	–	147	18,105	18,542	–	18,105	–	31
5/01/13	170.03	100.00	334,339	134	7	–	141	17,785	18,105	–	17,785	–	29
6/01/13	171.03	100.00	334,339	129	6	–	135	17,469	17,785	–	17,469	–	28
7/01/13	172.03	100.00	334,339	123	6	–	129	17,156	17,469	–	17,156	–	26
8/01/13	173.03	100.00	334,339	117	6	–	123	16,846	17,156	–	16,846	–	25
9/01/13	174.03	100.00	334,339	112	6	–	118	16,541	16,846	–	16,541	–	24
10/01/13	175.03	100.00	334,339	107	5	–	112	16,238	16,541	–	16,238	–	22
11/01/13	176.03	100.00	334,339	101	5	–	106	15,939	16,238	–	15,939	–	21
12/01/13	177.03	100.00	334,339	96	5	–	101	15,324	15,939	–	15,324	–	20
1/01/14	178.03	100.00	334,339	91	5	–	95	44,047	15,324	–	44,047	–	19
2/01/14	179.03	100.00	334,339	74	4	–	77	12,641	44,047	–	12,641	–	15
3/01/14	180.03	100.00	334,339	69	3	–	73	111,632	12,641	–	111,632	–	14
4/01/14	181.03	100.00	334,339	24	1	–	25	48,130	111,632	–	48,130	–	5
5/01/14	182.03	100.00	334,339	4	–	–	4	346	48,130	–	346	–	1
6/01/14	183.03	100.00	334,339	4	–	–	4	340	346	–	340	–	1
7/01/14	184.03	100.00	334,339	4	–	–	4	335	340	–	335	–	1
8/01/14	185.03	100.00	334,339	4	–	–	4	330	335	–	330	–	1
9/01/14	186.03	100.00	334,339	4	–	–	4	325	330	–	325	–	1
10/01/14	187.03	100.00	334,339	3	–	–	4	320	325	–	320	–	1
11/01/14	188.03	100.00	334,339	3	–	–	3	315	320	–	315	–	1
12/01/14	189.03	100.00	334,339	3	–	–	3	310	315	–	310	–	1

(continued)

177

Exhibit 4-9 *(continued)*

(A)	(B)	(C)	(D)	(E)	(F)	(G)	(H)	(I)	(J)	(K)	(L)	(M)	(N)
				Fees				Reserve					Present
Period		Over	Cumulative					Cash	Fund	Reinvest	Cash		Value of
Ending	Period	Coll	Excess	Servicing	Trustee	Surety	Total	In	Balance	Income	Out	Losses	Servicing Fee
1/01/15	190.03	100.00	334,339	3	-	-	3	305	310	-	305	-	1
2/01/15	191.03	100.00	334,339	3	-	-	3	300	305	-	300	-	1
3/01/15	192.03	100.00	334,339	3	-	-	3	295	300	-	295	-	1
4/01/15	193.03	100.00	334,339	3	-	-	3	290	295	-	290	-	1
5/01/15	194.03	100.00	334,339	3	-	-	3	285	290	-	285	-	-
6/01/15	195.03	100.00	334,339	3	-	-	3	281	285	-	281	-	-
7/01/15	196.03	100.00	334,339	3	-	-	3	276	281	-	276	-	-
8/01/15	197.03	100.00	334,339	3	-	-	3	272	276	-	272	-	-
9/01/15	198.03	100.00	334,339	3	-	-	3	267	272	-	267	-	-
10/01/15	199.03	100.00	334,339	2	-	-	3	263	267	-	263	-	-
11/01/15	200.03	100.00	334,339	2	-	-	2	258	263	-	258	-	-
12/01/15	201.03	100.00	334,339	2	-	-	2	254	258	-	254	-	-
1/01/16	202.03	100.00	334,339	2	-	-	2	250	254	-	250	-	-
2/01/16	203.03	100.00	334,339	2	-	-	2	245	250	-	245	-	-
3/01/16	204.03	100.00	334,339	2	-	-	2	241	245	-	241	-	-
4/01/16	205.03	100.00	334,339	2	-	-	2	237	241	-	237	-	-
5/01/16	206.03	100.00	334,339	2	-	-	2	233	237	-	233	-	-
6/01/16	207.03	100.00	334,339	2	-	-	2	229	233	-	229	-	-
7/01/16	208.03	100.00	334,339	2	-	-	2	225	229	-	225	-	-
8/01/16	209.03	100.00	334,339	2	-	-	2	221	225	-	221	-	-
9/01/16	210.03	100.00	334,339	2	-	-	2	217	221	-	217	-	-

(A)	(B)	(C)	(D)	(E)	(F)	(G)	(H)	(I)	(J)	(K)	(L)	(M)	(N)
				Fees					Reserve				Present Value of
Period Ending	Period	Over Coll	Cumulative Excess	Servicing	Trustee	Surety	Total	Cash In	Fund Balance	Reinvest Income	Cash Out	Losses	Servicing Fee
10/01/16	211.03	100.00	334,339	2	-	-	2	213	217	-	213	-	-
11/01/16	212.03	100.00	334,339	1	-	-	2	209	213	-	209	-	-
12/01/16	213.03	100.00	334,339	1	-	-	1	205	209	-	205	-	-
1/01/17	214.03	100.00	334,339	1	-	-	1	202	205	-	202	-	-
2/01/17	215.03	100.00	334,339	1	-	-	1	198	202	-	198	-	-
3/01/17	216.03	100.00	334,339	1	-	-	1	194	198	-	194	-	-
4/01/17	217.03	100.00	334,339	1	-	-	1	190	194	-	190	-	-
5/01/17	218.03	100.00	334,339	1	-	-	1	187	190	-	187	-	-
6/01/17	219.03	100.00	334,339	1	-	-	1	183	187	-	183	-	-
7/01/17	220.03	100.00	334,339	1	-	-	1	180	183	-	180	-	-
8/01/17	221.03	100.00	334,339	1	-	-	1	176	180	-	176	-	-
9/01/17	222.03	100.00	334,339	1	-	-	1	173	176	-	173	-	-
10/01/17	223.03	100.00	334,339	1	-	-	1	169	173	-	169	-	-
11/01/17	224.03	100.00	334,339	1	-	-	1	166	169	-	166	-	-
12/01/17	225.03	100.00	334,339	1	-	-	1	163	166	-	163	-	-
1/01/18	226.03	100.00	334,339	1	-	-	1	159	163	-	159	-	-
2/01/18	227.03	100.00	334,339	-	-	-	1	156	159	-	156	-	-
3/01/18	228.03	100.00	334,339	-	-	-	-	153	156	-	153	-	-
4/01/18	229.03	100.00	334,339	-	-	-	-	150	153	-	150	-	-
5/01/18	230.03	100.00	334,339	-	-	-	-	146	150	-	146	-	-
6/01/18	231.03	100.00	334,339	-	-	-	-	143	146	-	143	-	-

(continued)

Exhibit 4-9 *(continued)*

(A)	(B)	(C)	(D)	(E)	(F)	(G)	(H)	(I)	(J)	(K)	(L)	(M)	(N)
				Fees					Reserve				Present
Period Ending	Period	Over Coll	Cumulative Excess	Servicing	Trustee	Surety	Total	Cash In	Fund Balance	Reinvest Income	Cash Out	Losses	Value of Servicing Fee
7/01/18	232.03	100.00	334,339	-	-	-	-	140	143	-	140	-	-
8/01/18	233.03	100.00	334,339	-	-	-	-	137	140	-	137	-	-
9/01/18	234.03	100.00	334,339	-	-	-	-	134	137	-	134	-	-
10/01/18	235.03	100.00	334,339	-	-	-	-	75	134	-	75	-	-
				208,585	10,429	69,129	288,143	4,044,331		-	4,044,331	-	138,845

Column Notes:

(C) Overcollateralization is the current principal from Page 1 Column (C) less the sum of senior principal on Page 1 Column (I), all divided by the current principal.

(D) This is the cumulative sum of Page 1 Column (M).

(E) Servicing fee is 0.5% of principal balance in Page 1 Column (C).

(F) Trustee fee is 0.025% of principal balance in Page 1 Column (C).

(G) Surety fee is 0.19% of senior balance in Page 1 Column (I).

(H) The sum of Columns (E), (F), and (G).

(I) This is the cash flow left. It is Page 1 Column (H) less the sum of Page 1 Column (O), and Page 2 Column (H).

(J) The reserve fund balance is initially 0% of the opening balance on Page 1 Column (C). After overcollateralization requirement is met, the balance is the "excess interest" coming in.

(K) Column (J) times a reinvestment rate of 0% (monthly compounding).

(L) Cash out is reinvestment income from Column (K) plus prior month balance, after overcollateralization requirement is met. This is the column used for the present value (using a discount rate of 11%).

(N) Present value of Column (E) using a discount rate of 11%.

Reprinted with permission.

- Pages 155 to 168 detail the cash flows projected to the class A tranche. The cash flows begin on April 1, 1999, and the projections estimate that the A tranche will be repaid by January 1, 2013.
- Page 168 summarizes how the columns are calculated. Note that the class A-1 tranche earns a 6.545 percent coupon rate (column L) and is allocated all scheduled and unscheduled principal repayments, until repaid.
- Pages 169 to 180 detail the cash flows as projected to the reserve fund tranche. The cash flows are projected to begin on November 1, 1999. Column L shows the cash flows projected to be distributed to the investor of the reserve fund. Note that the fees in columns E to G must be paid prior to the reserve fund investors receiving the cash flow.
- Page 180 summarizes how the columns are calculated. Note that the reserve fund does not begin receiving principal cash flows until the class A tranche is repaid, and in contrast to the class A tranche, it does not earn a stated coupon rate.
- All unscheduled principal cash flows are allocated to the A-1 tranche until it is repaid at the estimated date of January 1, 2013.
- The fair value of the reserve-fund tranche was derived using an 11 percent discount rate. This rate compensates the investor for default-related losses above the insurance limits and prepayment risks. The insurance will cover the first 5 percent of losses ($342,000).

BLOOMBERG MEDIAN PREPAYMENTS

A common investment analysis and pricing tool used by investment analysts is the *Bloomberg Median Prepayments* application. It is used in estimating publicly issued mortgage-backed security cash flows and determining prices for those investments. It also may be used as a reference for obtaining input when pricing private securitizations. Note that many other prepayment models are available, and some of those are proprietary to Wall Street firms. Therefore, analysts must understand that those types of tools exist, how to interpret the data they produce, and the limitations of the output.

Exhibits 4-10 through 4-13 are reproduced from *Bloomberg* to compare and contrast the estimated cash flow attributes and fair values for several mortgage-pass-through investments and a CMO. This type of information summarizes certain data that could be obtained by reading the investment's prospectus or trust participation agreement. Although the exhibits look complicated, they can be deciphered if one first thinks about the information needed to value a mortgage-backed security. For example, one must ask the questions provided below and then look to *Bloomberg* for the answers. (Note that the numbers presented in the answers to the following questions correspond to the cross-references in the Exhibit 4-10 *Bloomberg Median Prepayments* screen.)

Question 1: Is the investment in Exhibit 4-10 a mortgage-pass through (in which the investor receives a pro rata distribution of a mortgage pool's total principal and interest cash flows) or a CMO (in which the investor purchases a tranche and the trust participation certificates allocate specific cash flows to several tranches)? What is the identifying label for the specific investment?

Bloomberg Reference 1

FNCL[2] 7, 7%, Generic: FNMA. This notation identifies the pool of mortgages as 7 percent, Federal National Mortgage Association (FNMA) guaranteed mortgages. This is a pass-through security, which means that each investor receives a pro rata share of the entire pool's principal and interest. This is not a CMO. (Pro rata distribution means no tranches exist.) However, an actual PAC CMO will be discussed below.

Question 2: How "seasoned" are the mortgages? Are they new issues as opposed to being outstanding for a period of time?

Bloomberg Reference 2

FNCL 7 A. This identifies a new issuance; the "A" comes from "TBA," as in to-be-announced securities.

Question 3: What is the weighted-average coupon of the mortgages in the pool?

Bloomberg Reference 3

7.640 (352) 8. This shows that the weighted-average coupon (WAC) of the pool of mortgages is 7.640 years. The higher the WAC, the greater the loan's sensitivity to prepayments, since borrowers will have a greater economic incentive to refinance than borrow with lower rate mortgages. This is illustrated later in the chapter, as the estimated PSA of an FNMA 8 (Exhibit 4-11) is compared with the PSA in the FNMA 7 (Exhibit 4-10).

Question 4: What is the expected average life of the investment, assuming no shift in the Treasury bond yield curve? This is often referred to as a "0 bp," or a zero-basis-point shift in the yield curve.

Exhibit 4-10 Bloomberg Median Prepayments for FNMA 7.

(13)

FNCL 7 Mtge YT   DG65Msg:W. LAWRENCE

M Bloomberg   66   (3)   **F N C L   7 (1.)**   7%   ADV:<PAGE>
MEDIAN PREPAYMENTS <GO>   Generic:**FNMA**   Vectors
                                                                        99 <Go>
FNCL 7 A (2)   7.640 (352) 8 WAC (WAM) CAGE

1mo	639P	28.9	next pay 1/25/99 (monthly) Age 0 8
3mo	486	21.8	rcd date 12/31/98 (24 Delay) (4)WAM 29 4
6mo	405	19.0	accrual 12/ 1/98-12/31/98 WAC 7.640
12mo	316	16.0	
Life	216	10.2	

12/10/98   **Y I E L D   T A B L E**   (5)
B.Median: +300bp 126 +200bp 140 +100bp 159 0bp 279 -100bp 859 -200bp 1119 -300bp 1216
Vary   1   **126** PSA   **140** PSA   **159** PSA   **279** PSA   **859** PSA   **1119** PSA   **1216** PSA
PRICE   32

(6)   (7.)
102-3   6.694   6.676   6.652   [6.493]   5.725   5.387   5.260

AvgLife	9.98	9.38	8.65	5.68 (8.)	2.08	1.63	1.51
Mod Dur	6.27	6.00	5.68	4.20 (9.)	1.86	1.49	1.39
YEARWindow	0.2-29.4m	0.2-29.4m	0.2-29.4m	0.2-29.4m	0.2-22.9m	0.2-15.7m	0.2-13.7
Spread I	+197/AL	+198/AL	+199/AL	+196/AL (10.)	+120/AL	+87/AL	+74/AL

(13)

(12)
NOV98 OCT SEP AUG JUL JUN MAY APR MAR FEB JAN DEC97   (11.)Treasury Curve - BGN 14:04
- 639 414 388 377 328 300 322 368 325 173 176p   3mo 6mo -1- -2- -5- -10- -30-
- 28.9 18.4 17.1 16.7 14.6 13.5 14.6 16.8 14.7 7.8 8.0c   4.52 4.59 4.51 4.53 4.50 4.72 5.07

Parity Px 99.535   Format# 1-YT   5y**98-29+** 10y**100-7**

Copyright 1998 BLOOMBERG L.P.   Frankfurt:69-920410 Hong Kong:2-977-6000 London:171-330-7500 New York:212-318-2000
Princeton:609-279-3000   Singapore:226-3000   Sydney:2-9777-8686   Tokyo:3-3201-8900   Sao Paulo:11-3048-4500
                                                                    G134-206-1 30-Nov-98 14:05:33

<HELP> for explanation, <MENU> for similar functions.   DG65Msg:W. LAWRENCE

(14) **Bloomberg** D E A L E R   P R E P A Y M E N T   F O R E C A S T S Pg 1 of 2
CHO

For: **FNCL 7.00** T FNMA Conv. 30Yr   7.00%   as of:**11/30/98**
                 TBA

Firm	OBP PSA	WAM Yr Mo	WAC	-300	-200	-100	-50	+0	+50	+100	+200	+300
FBC	267	28 6	7.64	1125	1053	749	499	267	182	149	121	114
DLJ	261	29 10	7.45	1875	1813	1398	553	261	147	127	104	95
UBS			n/a for this ticker/coupon/age									
PW	317	29 5	7.47	1620	1444	1082	744	317	209	160	140	126
BS			n/a for this ticker/coupon/age									
PRU	309	29 10	7.75	1216	1119	790	541	309	231	186	140	124
ML	272	27 8	7.70	1213	1103	859	422	272	209	171	147	140
LB	311	28 9	7.64	1040	892	679	504	311	197	159	141	127
SAL	279	29 9	7.50	1736	1604	1216	659	279	182	147	134	126

Avg	288		1404	1290	968	560	288	194	157	132	122

(15)
MED	279	**M Bloomberg** MEDIAN PREPAYMENTS	1216	1119	859	541	279	197	159	140	126

Copyright 1998 BLOOMBERG L.P.   Frankfurt:69-920410 Hong Kong:2-977-6000 London:171-330-7500 New York:212-318-2000
Princeton:609-279-3000   Singapore:226-3000   Sydney:2-9777-8686   Tokyo:3-3201-8900   Sao Paulo:11-3048-4500
                                                                    G134-206-1 30-Nov-98 14:06:00

Bloomberg Reference 4

Age 0:8; WAM 29:4; WAC 7.640. This refers to the mortgage loan attributes. The mortgages are 8 months old, have a weighted-average maturity of 29 years and 4 months, and have a weighted-average yield of 7.640 percent.

Question 5: What is the security's sensitivity to prepayments?

A security's sensitivity to prepayments is generally expressed as a prepayment speed, or PSA. The PSA represents a numerical prepayment benchmark. The PSA measure is specific to the pool's total assets and is not impacted by any tranche allocations. It represents a numerical percentage of the outstanding pool's principal that is expected to be repaid (excluding contractually specified prepayments) on an annual basis over the entire life of the pool. For example, a seasoned pool of mortgages that is over 30 months old and assigned a PSA of 100 would be expected to have unscheduled principal prepayments at the rate of 6 percent of the outstanding principal each year. A PSA of 200 means that each year, 12 percent (2 times the 6 percent) of the outstanding principal is expected to prepay. A PSA of 50 would indicate that 3 percent (1/2 of the 100 PSA rate of 6 percent) of the outstanding principal is expected to prepay each year, and so on. This is derived from a constant prepayment rate (CPR) that indicates an annualized rate of unscheduled prepayments and a single monthly mortality (SMM) that estimates the monthly unscheduled prepayments. Important aspects of those measures are:

- When mortgage-backed securities are purchased, investors refer to the securities as having expected prepayment speeds in terms of a PSA or CPR measure. Those are only estimates, and, historically, prepayment models have not been reliable at forecasting prepayments when interest rates are volatile.
- A PSA of 100 equates to an annual prepayment rate or CPR of 6 percent.
- The PSA assumes that new mortgages have a lower prepayment rate during the first 30 months, and this is not factored into the CPR. Assuming the mortgages in a pool are at least 30 months old, a 6 percent CPR is equal to an SMM of .005143, calculated as:

$$\text{SMM} = 1 - (1 - .06)^{1/12}$$

For mortgages outstanding less than 30 months, a CPR of .2 percent for the first month is assumed, and this increases by .2 percent each month until month 30, when the CPR is assumed at a constant 6 percent rate. (This equates to a 100 PSA.)

Bloomberg Reference 5

YIELD TABLE 0 bp 279 PSA. This estimate indicates that if the yield curve does not shift, prepayments will be at an annual rate of 16.74 percent (6 percent times

2.79), after the mortgages reach 30 months of seasoning. If the yield curve shifts, PSAs are modeled to change. For example, if the yield curve decreases 100 basis points (to –100 basis points), the PSA increases to 859 (or 8.59 × 100); if the yield curve increases 100 basis points, the PSA decreases to 159.

Question 6: What is the security's price (fair value) assuming a zero-basis-point shift in the yield curve, at the expected investment yield?

Bloomberg Reference 6

102.3. This estimated bond price is based on a yield with a 196-basis-point spread over Treasuries and cash flows determined using the 279 PSA. (Keep in mind that we are computing the present value of the expected cash flows at a market yield to maturity to arrive at the price.) Market supply and demand factors may influence this price. For example, certain coupon streams may be in favor, on any given day, due to investor preferences and needs. During September and October 1998, liquidity and sector spreads widened in response to global flight-to-quality investments and a prepayment wave occurred (due to interest rate declines to record lows). For example, Kenneth L. Hackel of Merrill Lynch cited the following technical factors affecting mortgage-backed securities during this time period:

- Large expected supply of 30-year, 6.0 percent, and 6.50 percent pass-throughs due to the refinancing wave
- Modest agency CMO issuance because of poor market conditions
- Reduced demand from highly leveraged investors due to increased borrowing costs and turbulent market conditions
- Reduced liquidity due to a decline in investor demand for spread products
- Large supply of certain products, such as commercial-mortgage-backed securities (CMBS) and home-equity loans (HELs).

Question 7: What is the estimated expected yield on the investment, which was used to discount the expected cash flows?

Bloomberg Reference 7

6.493. This represents the market's required yield-to-maturity calculated as 196 basis points over Treasuries. Also, remember the illustrations in Exhibits 1-4 and 1-5, which illustrated how yields change as the timing of the cash flows change. Therefore, when analyzing mortgage-backed investments, remember that the yield is only an estimated yield because cash flows vary based on unscheduled prepayments.

Question 8: What is the security's average life?

Bloomberg Reference 8

AvgLife 5.68. This life assumes no shift in the yield curve and a predicted prepayment speed of 279 PSA. Note that as the yield curve shifts upward 100 basis points, the predicted PSA drops to 159, the yield increases to 6.652, and the average life increases to 8.65 years. This is the result of lower expected prepayments. Alternatively, as the yield curve decreases 100 basis points, the PSA drastically increases to 859, the yield decreases to 5.725, and average life decreases to 2.08 years.

Question 9: What is the investment's modified duration?

Bloomberg Reference 9

Mod Dur 4.20. This refers to the bond's price sensitivity to interest rate changes. For each 100-basis-point change in interest rates, the estimated bond price will change 4.20 percent. However, as discussed in the glossary, duration generally is relevant only for modest changes in interest rates. As the yield curve decreases 100 basis points, the modified duration decreases to 1.86 due to the effect of higher expected prepayments.

Question 10: What is the investment's estimated-yield spread over Treasuries?

Bloomberg Reference 10

Spread +196/AL. This is the calculated market spread over Treasuries for a given price, based on the average model predicted cash flows, at a PSA estimate of 279. This spread, when added to the Treasury rate (i.e., interpolated from the Treasury curve described in item 11), produces a yield of 6.493 percent. The yield, shown in item 7, also can be calculated using the spread (196) plus the interpolated Treasury yield (4.533), corresponding to the 5.68 average life, as shown in item 8.

Question 11: What is the Treasury yield at the date of this analysis?

Bloomberg Reference 11

Treasury Curve, 5 @ 4.50; 10 @ 4.72. These rates refer to the Treasury yields for five-year and 10-year maturities.

Question 12: What are the actual PSA and CPR for FNCL 7 securities?

Bloomberg Reference 12

Oct 98; 639; 28.9. Those statistics describe the actual October PSA and CPR. These historical data are generally a poor predictor of what will occur in the future.

Question 13: What is the time period or window during which the principal cash flows are forecasted?

Bloomberg Reference 13

0.2 – 29.4m. At a zero-basis-point shift in the yield curve, the estimated window is between 2 months (.2) to 29 years, 4 months (29.4m). As rates increase (the PSA speed decreases), the window remains the same. However, as rates decrease (the PSA speed increases), the window decreases to an estimated 13 years 7 months (at an estimated PSA of 1216).

Question 14: How have investment firms modeled prepayment sensitivity, and what prepayment speeds have been estimated for the specific investments, assuming different interest rate levels?

Bloomberg Reference 14

An industry practice is to model prepayment expectations over ranges of between 100- to 300-basis-point increases and decreases in interest rates.

Reference 14 is the dealer prepayment forecast. This shows the prepayment estimates that seven dealers have modeled pertaining to this investment. Notice that Reference 15 shows the average of the seven dealer models. For example, at a zero-basis-point shift in the yield curve, the median PSA is 279. Will the FNCL 7 trade at a price of 102.3 on the date this average was computed (as shown in Reference 6)? Not exactly; however, this information provides investors with a good indication of the investment's value and will likely pay a price in this range.

Mortgage-Pass-Through Certificate with a Higher Weighted-Average Coupon

An FNMA 8 is similar in form to an FNMA 7 because it is a pass-through investment collateralized by 30-year conventional, government-guaranteed residential mortgages. However, the weighted-average coupon (WAC) is higher than that of an FNMA 7, 8.470 percent versus 7.640 percent. Exhibit 4-11 enables one to compare and contrast those two similar investments. Based on the higher WAC, it would be expected that the FNMA 8 is more sensitive to declining interest rates. Consider the following questions that an investor may want to address when evaluating which investment is more suitable for a given portfolio. (Numerical cross-references to the numbers provided in the following answers to the questions are provided in Exhibit 4-11.)

Question 1: Assuming a zero-basis-point shift in the yield curve, what is the security's estimated PSA and average life?

Bloomberg Reference 1

Due to the higher WAC, the pool is estimated to have a PSA of 511 and a 2.86 average life at a zero-basis-point change in the yield curve. This is in contrast to the 279 PSA and 5.68 average life of the FNMA 7 (Exhibit 4-10).

Question 2: How do the estimated yields change in response to shifts in the yield curve?

Bloomberg Reference 2

As rates decrease, expected yields decrease because the prepayments will be accelerated. For example, the FNMA 8 expected yield, at a −300-basis-point shift in the yield curve, drops to 4.485 in contrast to the smaller drop in yield to 5.260 for the FNMA 7. However, as rates increase, the FNMA 8 expected yield rises to 7.395 at a +300-basis-point shift, in contrast to a smaller increase in yield to 6.694 for the FNMA 7.

Question 3: Why may an investor select the FNMA 8 over the FNMA 7 as an investment choice?

Answer: To the extent that the investor anticipates that interest rate increases are likely, the higher WAC of the FNMA 8 may provide a higher yield as prepayments decrease in response to rising rates. To the extent an investor anticipates that interest rates are likely to decrease, the FNMA 7 provides a more favorable yield.

Exhibit 4-11   Bloomberg Median Prepayments for FNMA 8.

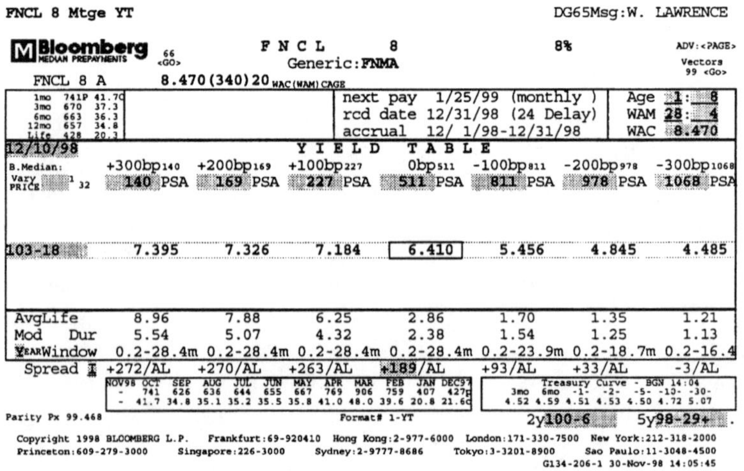

Analysis of a Collateralized Mortgage Obligation Planned Amortization Class

In contrast to the above mortgage-pass-through securities that receive a pro rata distribution of the total mortgage collateral cash flows, Exhibit 4-12 details a PAC collateralized mortgage obligation that receives cash flows governed by the trust agreement (CMO tranching contractual parameters). The mortgage collateral is held in a REMIC. A PAC is a type of tranche that has very predictable cash flows, assuming that interest rates remain in a certain range. Therefore, an investor requiring more predictable cash flows may consider certain types of CMO investments preferable to mortgage-pass-through securities. This would be true, for example, if it is assumed that the investor requires all principal cash flows to be repaid during the years 4 through 6.

The following questions should be addressed when evaluating which investment is more suitable for a given portfolio. (Numerical cross-references to the numbers in the following answers to questions are provided in Exhibit 4-12.)

Question 1: What is the window of expected cash flows over various yield curves?

Bloomberg Reference 1

The expected window of principal cash flows is from 4 years and 3 months to 6 years and 6 months, based on yield curves ranging from a zero shift to a +300-basis-point increase. Note how this is significantly different from the FNMA 7 and FNMA 8 expected principal cash flows that extended to over 28 years, assuming similar shifts in the yield curve. However, as the yield curve decreases, the PAC CMO's principal cash flows decrease to a one- to two-year range.

Question 2: Is the expected PAC yield lower than the FNMA 7 and FNMA 8?

Bloomberg Reference 2

The PAC expected yield is lower than the pass-through securities—6.121 percent versus approximately 6.4 percent. This lower yield represents the cost of having more predictable (less risky) cash flows. The cash flows are discounted at a lower spread over Treasuries—161 (Reference 3) versus 189 to 196 basis points.

Exhibit 4-13 details the prepayment attributes of some of the REMIC tranches. For example, tranche PE relates to the PAC shown in Exhibit 4-12. Notice that the window of principal cash flows is estimated as being between March 2003 and December 2004, assuming prepayment speeds stay within a specified range of between 96 and 255 PSA (Reference 1). Certain tranches represent higher-risk investments, and, therefore, the predictability of cash flows is not modeled; this can be seen as the tranches labeled no band or not labeled.

Exhibit 4-12   Bloomberg Median Prepayments for CMO.

```
 100-20  Price supplied by Merrill Lynch                    DG65Msg:W. LAWRENCE
Note:  Projections start with 12/18/1998 payment.
   Net Bid/Offer Price          F N R    1 9 9 8 - 2 4    P E      6.25% 11/18/21   ADV:<PAGE>
   Merrill Lynch  66                                               [  96  255 11/98]  NO Notes
              <GO> 31359TPW2   CMO:PAC(11)                                          88 <Go>
     FNCL 7 N        7.615(340)16 MAC(WAM)CAGE NOV98
NOV 1mo 1048P 34.7d  4/30/98: 278,460,000 │next pay 1/18/99 (monthly ) │30/360 Cashflows
'98 3mo  797  24.4  11/18/98: 278,460,000 │rcd date 12/31/98 (17 Delay)│created 11/18/98
     6mo  680  18.7  factor 1.000000000000 │accrual  12/ 1/98-12/31/98 │1stPro: 12/18/98
    12mo   -    -                                                       │Collat: 8803 Pools
    Life  658  17.4
12/ 3/98              Y I E L D    T A B L E
B.Median    +300bp124  +200bp135  +100bp154   0bp281  -100bp828  -200bp1313 -300bp1468
Vary      1 32   124 PSA   135 PSA   154 PSA   275 PSA  830 PSA   1315 PSA   1470 PSA
PRICE

          CLASS: CUR GEO DIST (Nov98): CA 17.5% TX 5.4% MI 5.3% FL 4.7% IL 4.1% OTHER 63.1%

(2) 100-20      6.126      6.126      6.126      6.121     5.771      5.426      5.291


    AvgLife     5.40       5.40       5.40       5.24      1.77       1.07       0.93
(1) Mod  Dur    4.47       4.47       4.47       4.36      1.64       1.01       0.88
(3) YEARWindow 4.3-6.6    4.3-6.6    4.3-6.6    4.3-6.1   1.6-2.0    1.0-1.2    0.8-1.0
    Spread I   +161/AL    +161/AL    +161/AL    +161/AL   +125/AL    +91/AL     +78/AL
              NOV98 OCT  SEP  AUG  JUL  JUN MAY98                Treasury Curve - BGN 14:04
NON-CALLABLE  1048  675  581  591  458  462  463p        3mo  6mo  -1-  -2-  -5- -10- -30-
              34.7 20.6 16.6 15.7 11.2 10.4  9.5c        4.52 4.59 4.51 4.53 4.50 4.72 5.07
Parity Px 99.706                          Format# 1-YT   5y98-29+  10y100-7
Copyright 1998 BLOOMBERG L.P.  Frankfurt:69-920410  Hong Kong:2-977-6000  London:171-330-7500  New York:212-318-2000
Princeton:609-279-3000     Singapore:226-3000    Sydney:2-9777-8686   Tokyo:3-3201-8900   Sao Paulo:11-3048-4500
                                                                    G134-206-1 30-Nov-98 14:05:23
```

Source: © 2001 Bloomberg L.P. All rights reserved. Reprinted with permission. Visit *www. Bloomberg.com.*

Exhibit 4-13   REMIC Structure View.

```
SPA                                                        DG65 Mtge   S P A

Bloomberg      F N R   1 9 9 8 - 2 4  Group- 1: 30YR/7.0/FNMA/g1    Pg 1 of 2
CMO            275 PSA  S T R U C T U R E   V I E W    0<Page>   View: 1/99- 4/28
                                                        Monthly
Class C Curr  Cpn  Type      WAL  PSA Band  Window     .=Int P=P+I a=Accrue N=Notional
PA 149,870  6.00  PAC(11)    .9   78-621   1/99- 5/00 PPP
PB 119,949  6.00  PAC(11)   1.9   87-428   5/00- 3/01 ..PPP
PC 163,423  6.00  PAC(11)   2.9   89-328   3/01- 5/02 ....PPPP
PD 109,503  6.25  PAC(11)   3.9   90-294   5/02- 3/03 .......PPP
PE 278,460  6.25  PAC(11)   5.2   96-255   3/03-12/04 ........PPPP
PK 103,459  7.00  IO,NTL,PAC 1.9  96-255   1/99-12/04 NNXNNNNNNNNNN
PG 811,190  7.00  PAC(11)  10.8  113-175  12/04- 4/28 ...........PPPPPPPPPPPPPPPPPPPPPPPPPPPPPPPPPPPPPPPPPPPPPPPPPP
A   67,085  7.00  PAC(22)   2.8  No Band   1/99-12/03 PPPPPPPPPPP
FA  44,239  6.02  FLT,DLY,S+ 1.1           1/99- 5/01 PPPPPP
SA   9,480 11.58  INV,DLY,S+ 1.1           1/99- 5/01 PPPPPP
B   29,993  6.50  PAC(22)   2.7  No Band   1/99-12/03 PPPPPPPPPPP
FB  18,867  6.02  FLT,DLY,S+ 1.0           1/99-12/00 PPPPP
SB   4,043 11.58  INV,DLY,S+ 1.0           1/99-12/00 PPPPP
CA  48,659  7.00  PAC(22)   2.7  No Band   1/99-12/03 PPPPPPPPPPP
C  159,840  6.50  PAC(22)   2.7  No Band   1/99-12/03 PPPPPPPPPP
FC  96,910  6.02  FLT,DLY,S+ 1.2           1/99- 7/01 PPPPPP
SC  20,766 11.58  INV,DLY,S+ 1.2           1/99- 7/01 PPPPPP
FE     865  5.82  FLT,DLY,SUP  -           Paid Off by JAN 1999
SE     185 12.51  INV,DLY,SUP  -           Paid Off by JAN 1999
FH   9,774  6.07  FLT,DLY,S+  .7           1/99- 4/00 PPP
SH   1,354 12.85  INV,DLY,S+  .7           1/99- 4/00 PPP
SJ     391 10.00  INV,DLY,S+  .7           1/99- 4/00 PPP
FG  28,409  6.17  FLT,DLY,S+ 1.2           1/99- 7/01 PPPPP
SG   5,000 12.81  INV,DLY,S+ 1.2           1/99- 7/01 PPPPP
FK  25,000  6.17  FLT,DLY,S+ 1.2           1/99- 7/01 PPPPP
ST   2,630 12.81  INV,DLY,S+ 1.2           1/99- 7/01 PPPPP
Copyright 1998 BLOOMBERG L.P.  Frankfurt:69-920410  Hong Kong:2-977-6000  London:171-330-7500  New York:212-318-2000
Princeton:609-279-3000     Singapore:226-3000    Sydney:2-9777-8686   Tokyo:3-3201-8900   Sao Paulo:11-3048-4500
                                                                    G134-206-1 30-Nov-98 14:17:58
```

Source: © 2001 Bloomberg L.P. All rights reserved. Reprinted with permission. Visit *www. Bloomberg.com.*

STRIPPED SECURITIES

Other common but high-risk tranches are interest-only (I/O) and principal-only (P/O) CMOs. These also are referred to as *stripped securities* because the interest cash flows are stripped from the underlying mortgage-pool cash flows to then make up interest-only and principal-only securities. Although both CMO types are highly sensitive to interest rate movements, each is impacted differently by such changes. Please note some of the characteristics of these securities.

Interest-only Tranches

The I/O does not have a true principal amount but rather a *notional amount* that is the reference point from which interest is calculated. The I/O purchaser is buying the right to a stream of interest and has no claim to any principal. Interest-only tranches are priced based on the present value of cash flows discounted at a yield to maturity. The I/O cash flows are highly sensitive to interest rate changes and the cash flow patterns of the entire mortgage pool. If interest rates drop and prepayments speed up, the I/O will receive less interest because the principal is outstanding for a shorter period of time. The I/O loses value when prepayments exceed forecasted levels. Buyers therefore acquire I/Os when they expect that interest rates will rise and the average life of the mortgages will extend, since the principal remains outstanding longer than forecasted at the time the investment was acquired, thus generating more interest. Alternatively, if an investor expected interest rates to decrease and prepayments to speed up, an I/O investment would not be a viable strategy.

Principal-only Tranches

Alternatively, P/Os receive an allocation of principal only and no right to interest cash flows. Principal-only tranches are also priced based on expectations of interest rate levels and expected cash flow patterns of the entire mortgage pool. Therefore, as interest rates increase and a CMO's average life increases beyond the expected level in the pricing, it takes a longer time to recover the principal and the P/O value decreases. Buyers of P/Os are expecting rates to drop and loans to prepay. Since P/Os are purchased at a deep discount and receive par as the mortgages pay out, the sooner the principal is repaid, the sooner this gain will be earned (the difference between the discounted cost and par).

Forecasting how I/Os and P/Os will perform as rates change is extremely complex and risky because prepayments are difficult to determine; for example, interest rates may fall yet prepayments do not speed up because an economic downturn occurs. The downturn causes house prices to drop, and borrowers cannot refinance since their loan-to-value ratio is too high. This occurred in the early 1990s as certain investment analysts correctly forecasted that interest rates would decrease and, therefore, bought P/Os. Rates did decrease; however, prepayments did not speed up because of an economic downturn and the drop in house prices.

Alternatively, at other times in the 1990s, interest rates dropped more quickly than expected, causing greater than expected prepayments and large losses in I/O investments because the initial investment (and interest) was not returned.

PRIVATE-PLACEMENT ASSET-BACKED SECURITIES

The following discussion explains asset-backed securities and the types of private transactions that may be seen in the marketplace. Because computer models are needed to model the cash flows, detailed pricings will not be illustrated. However, there will be a focus on the characteristics of these investments that impact their valuations. The key aspect of these investment types is that they may assume credit risk, in addition to interest rate risk, and earn a higher yield than comparable public investments because of the added management costs and risks assumed. In response to those costs and uncertainties, the investments often have features to minimize risks that include:

• Credit support is given. It protects certain tranches from credit losses through the participation agreement's allocating first credit losses to junior tranches. This protection is limited, since credit losses in excess of the junior-level tranche balances will reduce the senior tranche's cash flows.
• Credit insurance is acquired to insure a certain amount of loan losses.
• Contractual loan provisions, known as *lock-out periods,* prohibit unscheduled principal repayments during an initial loan period, such as the first five years of the loan. This tends to reduce prepayment risk.

The following summarizes the key aspects of private asset-backed investments.

Benefits to issuers of Private-Asset-Backed Investments may include[3]

1. Lower cost of funding
   a. Provides higher credit rating than issuer could obtain directly
   b. Provides access to capital markets not otherwise open
2. Removal of assets from balance sheet, which results in:
   a. Lower capital requirements for banks
   b. More lending flexibility for industrial and financial companies
3. Predictable and favorable tax consequences
   a. REMIC for mortgages to avoid double taxation (trust structure)
   b. Nonmortgage receivables structured as debt to avoid double taxation

4. A variety of possible assets available for collateral include:
    a. Home-related:
        (1) Conventional mortgage
        (2) Home-equity loans
        (3) Manufactured-housing loans
    b. Other consumer loans:
        (1) Auto loans
        (2) Boat and recreational vehicle loans
        (3) Student loans
        (4) Time-share loans
    c. Receivables:
        (1) Telephone receivables
        (2) Credit card receivables
        (3) Oil and gas receivables
        (4) Healthcare receivables
        (5) Insurance premium finance receivables
        (6) Trade receivables
    d. Other:
        (1) Below investment-grade bonds (the type of CMO where bonds are collateralized is called a collateralized bond obligation, or "CBO")
        (2) Commercial paper
        (3) Equipment loans
        (4) Commercial mortgage
        (5) Small-ticket leases
        (6) Franchise loans
5. Increased funding sources are provided from:
    a. Insurance companies
    b. Pension plans
    c. Mutual funds

Benefits to Asset-Backed Security Purchasers include

1. High credit-quality investments due to:
    a. Ownership of senior tranches (usually rated Aa or Aaa)
    b. Robust structure to withstand severe recession or bankruptcy
2. Attractive spreads
    a. Senior tranches that frequently provide returns of 50 to 100 basis points over comparably rated, unstructured debt

    b. Subordinate tranches greater than 100 basis points

3. Reduced prepayment risk

    a. PAC bonds for mortgages

    b. Lower interest rate sensitivity for most nonmortgage securitized transactions

4. Flexible maturities

    a. Revolving fund

    b. Senior/subordinate

    Valuing private-placement structured notes is complicated by the nature of the transaction, types of collateral involved, and the differences in the collateral within each transaction. For example, a pool made up of equipment lease receivables does not exhibit the homogenous characteristics that a pool of single-family residential mortgages originated within the GNMA guidelines would have. Publicly available information, such as the *Bloomberg Median Prepayments* data, may not be available. (At times the transaction may be available on *Bloomberg,* since this enhances the note's salability.) Investment analysts therefore require sufficient knowledge in order to structure and identify investment opportunities that compensate the lender for the risk taken. As a result, the marketplace demands a higher risk premium to compensate for the lack of information, increased investment analytical and management costs, and credit risk.

    Based on those factors, ratings grids generally are not used, and analysts rely on evaluations of the asset quality and characteristics, the servicer's track record, and credit support features.

Illustrations of Private Asset-Backed Transactions

The following transactions illustrate why valuing private asset-backed transactions is more complex than valuing pass-through certificates and public CMOs. Review the transactions to identify the added risks, methods of managing risks, and cash flow characteristics concepts that are important to the pricing process.

Re-Real Estate Mortgage Income Conduit (RE-REMIC)— Collateralized Mortgage Obligation (CMO)

During 1992, a bank sold $3.6 billion of par-value, 9.3 percent, 30-year jumbo residential mortgages to a REMIC.[4] Key terminology used to describe aspects of this transaction include:

- A REMIC (real estate mortgage investment conduit) is a trust or conduit that flows through the cash flows of the collateral to the owners of the trust. An important aspect of REMICs is that they are not subject to federal income tax.

- This transaction is labeled a "re-remic" because the B-tranche of the original REMIC is transferred to another REMIC in which it serves as collateral for new tranches issued.
- Jumbo mortgages are residential loans with balances in excess of a dollar limit and, due to dollar size restrictions, do not conform to federally insured mortgage guidelines.

The residential loans in the REMIC had an average 9.3 percent coupon rate (recall that this is a 1992 investment and rates were higher than in the late 1990s), and the associated underlying home loan-to-value ratios were 65 percent. The servicing agent (responsible for collecting principal and interest, monitoring the residential loans, and preparing investor reports) was experienced and well capitalized (financially strong). The REMIC issued two classes of securities:

1. *Class-A tranche with a par value of $3.4 billion.* The A tranche was protected from credit losses because the B tranche was allocated first losses, while the A tranche was allocated all principal prepayments until it was fully paid off. The A tranche had a 7.5 percent coupon rate.
2. *Class-B tranche with a par value of $200 million.* This represented approximately 6 percent of the total REMIC assets. This $200 million level met rating agency requirements to support the A-tranche credit rating of AAA (since it absorbs the first credit losses). The B tranche had an estimated 8 percent coupon rate, computed based on the weighted average of the mortgage-pass-through rates paid (less the servicer fees). The cash flows and yield on the investment therefore would vary based on mortgage-prepayment levels. For example, some of the mortgages had rates up to 13 percent and were likely to prepay.

Why the RE-REMIC Structure?

A key aspect of this transaction is that to facilitate the sale of the B tranche (one investment), the bank sold the B tranche to a newly created REMIC. The REMIC then used the B tranche as collateral for the sale of new tranches (with different principal amounts). Therefore, the original B-tranche salability was enhanced because investors could choose from 12 different tranches with the varying risk and return attributes. The B-tranche cash flows were allocated (by the trust participation agreement) to an equity tranche (B-12), and 11 tranches, B-1 through B-11. Characteristics of those tranches are:

- Prepayments were first allocated to the B-1 tranche and then sequentially to the remaining tranches after the B-1 tranche was paid off.
- Unscheduled repayments were first allocated to the B-1 tranche and upon its repayment to each next tranche.

- The B-12 equity tranche was assigned the risk of first-credit losses; however, the B-12 tranche received the cash flows after the B-1 through B-11 tranches were repaid.
- To the extent that the equity tranche was eliminated through credit loss allocations, losses then were allocated to tranche B-11 until its principal balance was reduced to zero and then to each tranche, in descending order.
- The higher-level tranches (e.g., B-8 through B-11) earned a higher yield to compensate the investor for the higher credit risk.

Characteristics of the Class B-1 Tranche

At issuance in 1992, the B-2 tranche was purchased to yield an estimated 8 percent and at an expected estimated average life of 9.5 years. It had an internal rating of BBB quality, and its par value was $64 million. Its characteristics included some protection from credit losses, since the B-3 through B-12 tranches had a first-loss position up to their face amount. Tranche B-2 also received some protection from prepayments because the A tranche was allocated all prepayments until the time was completely repaid ($3.4 billion).

Impact of Interest Rate Declines

As of the end of the year 1998, the A-1, B-1, and B-2 tranches had been completely repaid due to mortgage prepayments that were not forecasted when the 1992 investment was acquired. The 300-basis-point decrease in interest rates between 1992 and 1998 caused the investment to have a significantly shorter than expected 9.5-year average life. Therefore, although the investor did not experience credit losses allocable to those tranches, the allocation of prepayments to the A tranche did not provide the level of prepayment protection that was expected. If the investor purchased the tranche at a discount, this would have provided some prepayment risk protection because an early repayment at par would result in a gain (in the amount of the unamortized discount).

This example illustrates a key concept—credit and interest rate risks can be minimized but not eliminated through tranche selection. During the 1990s, many asset-backed transactions experienced a shortening of their expected average lives. The financial impact of this is as obvious as credit losses, since the effect relates to reinvestment of the proceeds at lower rates.

What Steps Would Be Taken to Value the B-2 Tranche If the Par Value Was $5 Million at October 1, 1998?

To illustrate the steps of asset-backed valuations, assume that a $5 million balance of the investment was outstanding at October 1, 1998. The three steps required to estimate the B-1 tranche's fair value are:

1. Identify the quality rating. Since the A tranche was repaid, the loans outstanding in the trust would be well-seasoned and the B-2 tranche would have a higher credit rating than at issue. An A-1 credit rating may have been justifiable because the B-2 tranche would now be in a senior position and supported by other tranches (that are in a first-loss position).

2. Determine the loan prepayment speeds by reference to MBS prepayment models or by reviewing the PSAs of similar transactions. Assume, for purposes of this example and simplicity, that a 500 PSA would be applicable. This means that each month the unscheduled principal repayments would be estimated at 2.5 percent of the beginning of the month's balance (6 percent times 5 divided by 12 months). Software, such as BondCalc, can be used to generate those expected cash flows, provided each mortgage's amortization schedule is input.

3. Discount the expected principal and interest cash at the market-discount rate to arrive at a fair value. Assume that A-1-rated public corporate bonds corresponding to this term were priced at 180 basis points over Treasuries and that the applicable discount rate for this investment is 210 basis points over Treasuries. Assuming that the Treasury rate is 4.30 percent, the discount rate would be 6.40 percent.

Based on those assumptions, the fair value would reflect a modest gain over the $5 million book value because the underlying mortgages are at a higher coupon rate than the discount rate. The gain would be expected to be modest because the mortgages would be expected to prepay based on the interest rate levels.

Connecticut Mutual Collateralized Mortgage Obligation

In the early 1990s, the National Association of Insurance Commissioners (NAIC) expanded bond-quality rating categories from three to six. One result of this expansion was that certain private-placement bonds that had been classified as investment grade dropped into the non–investment-grade category. This created a marketing problem, since the public and rating agencies may have viewed this as indicative of a higher-risk portfolio. Additionally, Connecticut Mutual wanted to restructure its portfolio by buying longer-term investment-grade securities. However, it could not effectively sell the private-placement investments, in part due to the new NAIC rules. The company therefore sold $372 million of non–investment-grade private-placement investments to an independently owned trust. This transaction was the first private-placement CBO, and, from the issuer's perspective, was a highly successful transaction. The transaction is shown in Exhibit 4-14.

Briefly, the following steps occurred:

• A bankruptcy-remote special-purpose trust was created and a trustee and investment banker was appointed.

Exhibit 4-14   Connecticut Mutual Transaction.

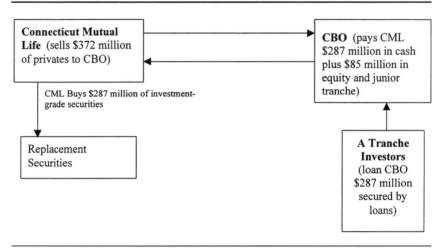

Source: *Investment Dealers Digest* (January 13, 1992).

- Identification and valuation of the investments were to be sold into the bankruptcy-remote special-purpose trust. An appraisal was performed on the approximately $372 million of loans using the rating grids and processes discussed in Chapter 2. Rating agencies, external auditors, and buyers of the senior AAA-rated tranche reviewed those valuations as part of their due diligence review. The loans were all performing (not delinquent), fixed rate, and call-protected with make-whole provisions. (Refer to the "Private Placement" section for a discussion of make-whole provisions.)

- Credit support features were determined so as to obtain an AAA rating for the senior tranche (A tranche). Based on historical loan performance and projected credit losses, it was determined that $85 million of combined equity and junior tranches were required to support the AAA rating for the senior tranche. Connecticut Mutual maintained its servicing of the loans.

- The loans were sold by the insurance company to the trust at fair value, in consideration of cash of $287 million and $85 million in equity and a junior (non-rated) tranche.

- The trust sold the senior tranche (approximately $287 million) to other institutions in a private-placement transaction. The senior tranche received all principal repayments before the junior tranches and therefore had a coupon lower than the average rate on the loans supporting the transaction. The senior tranche was not entitled to any prepayment penalties resulting from make-whole or call provisions.

The net effect of this transaction was that the insurance company retained the risks and rewards of those loans through ownership of the equity and high-yielding C tranche, without the negative impact of the $372 million of non–investment-grade bonds. The $287 million of proceeds were invested in investment-grade, fixed-income, call-protected bonds. Due to business changes and rates dropping, the majority of the loans were prepaid. This caused the investors in the A tranche to receive their principal back in a shorter average life than expected and face reinvestment at lower rates, while the equity and C tranches benefited from zero-credit losses in addition to the equity receiving all the prepayment and call-related fees. The equity portion of the return on investment was therefore significant.

Valuation Aspects of Collateralized Mortgage Obligation Tranches and Equity during the Investment Term

Important aspects of valuing those tranches during the investment term are by identifying the changes occurring since issuance—most important of which are credit risk, interest rate risk, and the overall economic forecast. For example, as the A tranche pays down, its expected cash flows reflect higher prepayment speeds. This would be reflected in limited price appreciation, in spite of the rate decline. Credit quality would be upgraded since the loans did not experience defaults and were repaid sooner than expected. The equity value would reflect an increasing value because of the significant early-loan payoffs, the lack of defaults or losses, and the receipt of prepayment and call-related fees. The junior tranche also would reflect an upgrade in quality due to the loan payoffs and favorable loan performance, although the cash flows would be impacted by faster prepayments.

The above senior tranches were sold as private placements; however, later CBOs (or collateralized debt obligations) evolved to be public security transactions.

Structured Finance Cross-Border Receivables

Structured finance cross-border receivables[5] are another type of private-placement asset-backed investment that present different valuation issues. Those transactions involve an entity securitizing its future accounts receivable through a sale of future account receivables to a trust. The trust issues debt (that investors buy) that was secured by the rights to the future flows of receivables. The receivables are generated in a below-investment-grade host country (e.g., from a Brazilian commodity producer) but are paid for by purchasers who are from investment-grade countries. The purchasers pay the accounts receivable with dollars sent to a U.S.-based trust account. The trustee deducts the required debt service and any reserve amounts and sends the balance on to the host country. This process substantially reduces the sovereign risk, allowing those transactions to be rated higher than those of the host country. The earliest of those types of transactions were made by Telmex during the late 1980s. Cash flow characteristics were estimated based on a 60-year history of payments by AT&T® to Telmex in Mexico. The investments have evolved to include rights to receivables generated from the export of eucalyptus pulp, propane gas, and oil in countries such as Brazil, Venezuela, and Argentina.

Those transactions have a number of common features that are key to making them an attractive investment:

- There is a history of stable dollar-based cash flows despite country volatility.
- The producer-servicer is a major player in its industry and would be investment grade if not constrained by a sovereign ceiling (i.e., the non–investment-grade-quality rating of certain countries).
- There are strong economic incentives for both the company and the country to continue to support the business.
- There is a legally sound and stable trust structure.
- The transactions provide credit enhancement that will withstand significant stress.

From an investor's perspective, those transactions provide several significant advantages:

- They provide significantly wider spreads for a given quality rating than is available in the general private-placement market.
- Fewer investors are experienced in this area, allowing greater latitude in negotiations concerning structure, covenants, and spreads.
- The transactions provide an opportunity to become familiar with many of the better companies in the emerging market countries that may facilitate future direct investments.

For additional information concerning these types of securitizations, refer to Standard and Poor's *Securitization in Latin America 1999,* a special report issued by the monthly publication *Structured Finance.*

Export Receivable Illustration

A typical deal involves a foreign-based commodity producer securitizing future U.S.-dollar-paid accounts receivable. The commodity producer establishes a U.S. trust that is assigned future receivables from the sale of its commodities to certain customers. Those customers are investment-grade Western European (members of the Organization for Economic Cooperation and Development [OECD]) entities and are directed to pay the trust in U.S. dollars in satisfaction of their payables to the commodity producer. The investor lends money to the trust and is secured by the trust's future receivables. In a typical transaction, the investor buys the investment at a deep discount (original issue discount [OID]) and therefore is protected from interest rate declines (similar to the previous I/O discussion, since repayment is at par).

Structured finance cross-border receivable investment risks include:

- Credit risk related to the performance of future export receivables. The customers must remain in business and not default on their accounts payable to the trust.
- Commodity risk related to a possible collapse or oversupply of the commodity, such as oil. For example, the note typically will have set sinking-fund payments that can be impacted by both credit or commodity risks.
- Foreign-currency risk. This exists only to the extent that the currency collapses and causes the commodity producer to slow or stop production when export sales are insufficient to support the repayment schedule to the trust.
- Sovereign risk. This exists only if the commodity producer's country nationalizes the industry.

In pricing those types of investments, the focus is therefore on the credit quality of the customers, the economic outlook for the commodity and the producer's country, and the market spreads for similar quality transactions to determine the required spread over the Treasury-risk premium. The discounted cash flow method is similar to pricing the debt of the commodity purchaser with an adjustment to the purchaser's risk premium for the market spreads attributable to cross-border receivables.

CONCLUDING REMARKS

At this point, the range and characteristics of mortgage-backed securities and how this marketplace has evolved to include asset-backed securities should be clear. With an understanding one can apply the pricing concepts covered in earlier chapters. For additional information on mortgage-backed securities, refer to the Salomon Smith Barney Fixed-Income Research Report, *Guide to Mortgage-Backed Securities.*

NOTES

1. This case was provided by Anna M. Bucceroni, senior vice president, Asset Securitization, American Business Financial Services Inc.
2. FNCL is a type of bond offered by Fannie Mae.
3. This case was provided by Kenneth D. Andersen, former Private Placement Department head at Connecticut Mutual Insurance Company, and Norman Thetford of MBIA Insurance Corporation.
4. Theodore W. Kappler, an asset-backed analyst, assisted with the following discussion of the re-REMIC.
5. Information provided by Norman A. Thetford of MBIA Insurance Corporation.

Chapter 5

Privately Held Equity

INTRODUCTION

Chapters 5 and 6 explain private and public equity pricing methodologies, respectively. Public stock quotes are available on the Internet or published in the *Wall Street Journal;* however, private-equity pricings are not. This chapter provides a conceptual valuation framework with examples of valuations of private equities that are also applicable to public stocks. Two common equity-pricing models are illustrated—an earnings multiple model and a discounted cash flow model. Chapter 6 reinforces the earnings multiple and discounted cash flow pricing concepts with an illustration of an actual investment analyst's pricing of a publicly traded common stock. Before explaining equity-pricing techniques, the relatively imprecise nature of equity pricings as compared to pricing investment-grade, fixed-income securities must be emphasized. For example, a private-placement or commercial mortgage investment pricing, as explained in Chapter 3, will generally reflect a close approximation of the actual price that the investments can be sold for in the marketplace. Their associated cash flows are contractual and also somewhat insulated by capital in the form of stockholders' equity or a borrower's equity in the real estate or other assets. In contrast, common stock equity does not have contractually specified cash flows or an equity cushion to protect its value. Therefore, equity pricings can change quickly and dramatically in response to changes in market conditions, company-specific factors, and investor requirements and preferences. The valuations illustrated in this chapter, although using what appear to be precise equations, are models that produce approximate values that may not always be reflective of prices that investors are willing to pay. Furthermore, the purpose of this book is to familiarize accountants with pricing methods commonly used by investment analysts rather than to provide a complete guide to prepare investment valuations. Therefore, this chapter provides an understanding of the key components of equity valuation models used by investment analysts.

EQUITY VOLATILITY

The market statistics presented in the two research charts provided in Exhibits 5-1 and 5-2, available on the *Yahoo Finance* website (at *http://finance.yahoo.com*), illustrate stock price volatility and other valuation data for PriceLine.com and Boeing companies. The volatility in the prices of those equities is presented here to illustrate that equity valuation techniques may be more of an art than a precise science and are impacted by changes in the economy and changes in a specific company's financial condition.

PriceLine.com

PriceLine.com is an Internet commerce company that enables consumers to use the Internet to "name their price" to obtain leisure airline tickets (and other items). The company began business in April 1998 and went public in April 1999. During its first year of operation, stock options were granted at an exercise price that was determined to be the current market value. The information provided by PriceLine.com in its S-1 registration form that it filed with the SEC indicated that 23,449,219 options were issued in 1998, at a weighted-average price of $0.93. The S-1 also indicated that at the initial public offering (IPO) date of March 30, 1999, PriceLine.com sold 10 million shares at $16 per share. However, the shares began publicly trading on March 31, 1999, at an opening price of $81 per share. The price volatility that day was significant, as 13 million shares were traded, with a low for the day of $69, a high of $85, and a closing price of $69. Exhibit 5-1 illustrates the price volatility as the stock rose to a high of $165 per share then falling to $1.125 per share. At the March 31, 1999, IPO date, investors were willing to pay those prices in spite of operating losses that are common in start-up Internet service companies (due to the initial large fixed costs). However, investors refocused on a fundamental pricing methodology, driven by earnings or free cash flows, that will be discussed in this chapter. Investors were also reacting to the U.S. Federal Reserve actions that increased interest rates throughout 2000 and to an expected economic slowdown.

Boeing

In contrast, Boeing is an established aircraft producer that is in what many analysts consider to be a mature industry. The price of Boeing's stock over a two-year period ended December 2000 ranged from $29 to $70 per share as shown in Exhibit 5-2. Airline production problems, order cancellations related to the Asian economy, and restructuring charges caused Boeing's stock price to drop sharply in 1998 because investors were responding to Boeing's lower earnings and free cash flows. During 1999 and 2000, the company improved its earnings and free cash flows, and investors expected these favorable trends to continue.

Review the two-year charts in Exhibits 5-3 and 5-4 illustrating Boeing's and PriceLine's share-price changes relative to the Dow Jones Industrial average. Note the following aspects:

• PriceLine.com significantly underperformed the Dow Jones Industrial average.
• Boeing significantly outperformed the Dow Jones Industrial average during the same period.

Exhibit 5-1   PriceLine.com Stock Prices.

Wednesday, January 17 2001 5:09pm ET - U.S. Markets Closed.

PRICELINE.COM (NasdaqNM:PCLN) - More Info: News, Msgs, Profile, Research, Insider, Options				
Last Trade 4:00PM · 3 $^{11}/_{32}$	Change -$^5/_{32}$ (-4.46%)		Prev Cls 3 $^1/_2$	Volume 7,940,700	Div Date N/A
Day's Range 3 $^1/_8$ - 4 $^5/_{32}$	Bid 3 $^3/_{16}$	Ask 3 $^7/_{32}$	Open 4 $^9/_{64}$	Avg Vol 3,373,318	Ex-Div N/A
52-week Range 1 $^1/_{16}$ - 104 $^1/_4$	Earn/Shr -7.26	P/E N/A	Mkt Cap 563.5M	Div/Shr N/A	Yield N/A

```
Priceline.Com Inc
as of 12-Jan-2001
 200
 100
  50


   1
       Apr99   Jul99   Oct99   Jan00   Apr00   Jul00   Oct00   Jan01
50000
40000
30000
20000
10000
    0
Copyright 2001 Yahoo! Inc.      Volume (1000's)     http://finance.yahoo.com/
                            Splits: none
```

| 1d | 5d | 3m | 1y | **2y**   Other: historical quotes | small chart |
| **Basic** | Moving Avg | Compare ☐   ☐ S&P ☐ Nasdaq ☐ Dow Compare |
| PCLN vs. |

Source: Available at *http://biz.yahoo.com/p/p/pcln.html.*

- The changes in PriceLine.com's and Boeing's share prices can be attributed to investors demanding existing earnings and forecasted growth in earnings and free cash flows.

The equity-pricing methodologies are illustrated next.

PRICING EQUITY ISSUES

Pricing equity securities is not an easy task because of the difficulties incurred in estimating the magnitude and timing of the related uncertain cash flows. For example, PriceLine.com's expected future cash flows, which include its future expected earnings, may be impacted by changing capital expenditures (generally larger for the start-up stage entities), changing consumer demands, changing technology, and changing competition. Furthermore, significantly different valu-

Exhibit 5-2   Boeing Company's Stock Prices.

Wednesday, January 17 2001 5:06pm ET - U.S. Markets Closed.

BOEING CO (NYSE:BA) - More Info: News , Msgs , Profile , Research , Insider , Options

Last Trade 4:01PM · **58** $^3/_4$	Change -2 $^1/_4$ (-3.69%)	Prev Cls 61	Volume 6,591,900	Div Date Mar 2
Day's Range 58 $^5/_{16}$ - 62 $^5/_8$	Bid N/A	Ask N/A	Open 62 $^7/_{16}$	Avg Vol 3,854,545	Ex-Div Feb 7
52-week Range 32 - 70 $^{15}/_{16}$	Earn/Shr 2.44	P/E 25.00	Mkt Cap 52.196B	Div/Shr 0.68	Yield 1.11

Splits: 13-Sep-77 [2:1], 16-Apr-79 [3:2], 15-Apr-80 [3:2], 10-Jun-85 [3:2], 12-Jun-89 [3:2], 11-Jun-90 [3:2], 9-Jun-97 [2:1]

1d | 5d | 3m | 1y | **2y** | 5y | max   Other: historical quotes | small chart

Basic | Moving Avg | Compare BA vs.   ⌐ S&P ⌐ Nasdaq ⌐ Dow   Compare

ation techniques often are used, depending on the type of entity being considered. For example, some analysts may favor discounted cash flow valuation models for industrial companies, while other analysts may favor earnings or revenue price multiple valuation models for technology companies. Another significant complexity involved in valuing privately held common stock, even after an enterprise value is determined using a model, is the degree of control over the entity that one or more investors may have as well as certain debt covenant provisions. For example, an investor having a controlling interest in a private company will command a higher price per share than an investor holding a minority interest in the same company because the controlling shareholder can influence the overall direction and, hence, cash flows of the company.

Exhibit 5-3   Boeing Company's Prices Relative to the Dow Jones Industrial Average.

Wednesday, January 17 2001 5:08pm ET - U.S. Markets Closed.

BOEING CO (NYSE:BA) - More Info: News , Msgs , Profile , Research , Insider , Options						
Last Trade 4:01PM · **58** $^3/_4$	Change -2 $^1/_4$ (-3.69%)		Prev Cls 61	Volume 6,591,900	Div Date Mar 2	
Day's Range 58 $^5/_{16}$ - 62 $^5/_8$	Bid N/A	Ask N/A	Open 62 $^7/_{16}$	Avg Vol 3,854,545	Ex-Div Feb 7	
52-week Range 32 - 70 $^{15}/_{16}$	Earn/Shr 2.44	P/E 25.00	Mkt Cap 52.196B	Div/Shr 0.68	Yield 1.11	

The Boeing Co

Copyright 2000 Yahoo! Inc.   http://finance.yahoo.com/

1d | 5d | 3m | 1y | 2y | 5y | max   Other: historical quotes | small chart

Basic | Moving Avg | Compare BA vs.   ▢ S&P ▢ Nasdaq ☑ Dow   Compare

COMMON EQUITY PRICING MODELS USED BY INVESTMENT ANALYSTS

The two most common entity-valuation methods include:

1. An enterprise valuation based on a price multiple. With this method, a current measure of performance or a single forecast of performance is converted into a price through the application of some type of price multiple. For example, a firm's value can be estimated by applying a ratio of enterprise value to a forecast of earnings before deducting interest, income taxes, depreciation, and amortization (EBITDA). Other commonly used price multiples include price-to-earnings, price-to-book, and price-to-sales ratios.

Exhibit 5-4   Priceline.com's Stock Prices Relative to the Dow Jones Industrial Average.

Wednesday, January 17 2001 5:10pm ET - U.S. Markets Closed.

PRICELINE.COM (NasdaqNM:PCLN) - More Info: News , Msgs , Profile , Research , Insider , Options

Last Trade 4:00PM · 3 $^{11}/_{32}$	Change $^{-5}/_{32}$ (-4.46%)		Prev Cls 3 $^{1}/_{2}$	Volume 7,940,700	Div Date N/A
Day's Range 3 $^{1}/_{8}$ - 4 $^{5}/_{32}$	Bid 3 $^{3}/_{16}$	Ask 3 $^{3}/_{8}$	Open 4 $^{9}/_{64}$	Avg Vol 3,373,318	Ex-Div N/A
52-week Range 1 $^{1}/_{16}$ - 104 $^{1}/_{4}$	Earn/Shr -7.26	P/E N/A	Mkt Cap 563.5M	Div/Shr N/A	Yield N/A

Priceline.Com Inc

1d | 5d | 3m | 1y | 2y   Other: historical quotes | small chart

Basic | Moving Avg | **Compare** ⌐   ⌐ S&P ⌐ Nasdaq ☑ Dow _Compare_
                              PCLN vs.

---

2. An enterprise value based on a discounted cash flow (DCF) model. This approach involves the estimation of the present value of an enterprise's future expected free cash flows. The unlevered free cash flows, which are typically used, comprise EBITDA minus income taxes, capital expenditures required to maintain a certain level of productive capacity, and required changes in working capital. The estimated free cash flows over a specified period and an estimated terminal value of the enterprise at the end of that period then are discounted at an estimated, risk-adjusted cost of capital to arrive at an estimate of the enterprise's total market value.

ActionSportsCo, a hypothetical company, will be used to illustrate those common valuation approaches. It is assumed that ActionSportsCo manufactures and distributes golf clubs and tennis rackets.

PRICE-MULTIPLE EQUITY PRICING MODELS

One formulation of a price-multiple model is based on the ratio of a firm's enterprise value to its EBITDA. The ratio is expressed as:

$$\text{Price multiple} = \frac{\text{Enterprise value}}{\text{EBITDA}}$$

Therefore, an estimate of the value of an entity may be expressed as:

$$\text{Enterprise value} = \text{EBITDA} \times \text{Price multiple}$$

EBITDA comprises the enterprise's reported GAAP net income with interest, the entire tax provision, depreciation, and amortization expenses added back. Although no accounting rules govern the proper calculation of EBITDA, analysts find this to be a useful measure. In a valuation of a specific private company, the entity's current EBITDA would be known by the analyst and next year's EBITDA would be estimated. An enterprise value to EBITDA multiple must be either estimated using the entity's forecasted future earnings and/or cash flows or obtained from comparable publicly traded entities, in order to calculate the enterprise value of entity. Obtaining the comparable price-earning multiples can be difficult. Often market multiples are generally known in practice for different types of entities. However, none of these may exactly match the company being valued. For example, assume that a market price-earnings multiple of 16 times EBITDA is appropriate for public golf and tennis racket manufacturers. This price multiple then may be adjusted for the fact that ActionSportsCo is a less-liquid private company or for other factors, such as the perceived quality of its earnings and its estimated growth rate.

Assume adjustments were made to reflect the fact that ActionSportsCo is a private, less-liquid company than the public companies in its industry (a downward adjustment) and has higher-quality earnings (an upward adjustment) to arrive at a price-earnings multiple of 17 times EBITDA. A price-earnings multiple of 17 to value a forecast of its earnings, which would have to be estimated, would then be used. Exhibit 5-5 illustrates a methodology for calculating ActionSportsCo's EBITDA.

ActionSportsCo's enterprise value is then estimated to be $34,000,000 (17 times $2,000,000). The per-share value of ActionSportsCo common stock can then be calculated, assuming that it has $7.5 million of debt (assumed equal to the fair value) and 1 million shares of common stock outstanding:

Enterprise value	$34,000,000
Less fair value of debt	– (7,500,000)
Fair value attributable to equity	$26,500,000

Exhibit 5-5   ActionSportsCo Estimated 2001 EBITDA.

Sales	50,000,000
Cost of goods sold	38,000,000
Gross margin	**13,000,000**
Selling, general and administrative expenses	10,000,000
Interest	450,000
Depreciation and amortization	500,000
Operating income	**2,050,000**
Income taxes	512,500
GAAP net income	**1,537,500**
Plus interest	450,000
Plus income taxes	512,500
Plus depreciation and amortization	500,000
EBITDA	**2,000,000**

The $26,500,000 million fair value attributable to the equity is then divided by 1 million common shares, to arrive at a fair value per share of $26.50. Several points related to this illustration should be emphasized:

- Because debt is often privately traded, determining its fair value may require some of the additional steps explained in Chapter 3.
- This example assumed a simple capital structure in which multiple classes of common stock and convertible debt did not exist. In practice, complex capital structures will be present at times and will increase the complexity of valuation calculations. For example, stock options outstanding would effectively increase the number of shares outstanding.

DISCOUNTED CASH FLOW APPROACH EQUITY PRICING MODEL

While the discounted cash flow (DCF) techniques used to value fixed-income securities can be applied to the valuation of common stocks, three features of equity make the DCF valuations of common stock values more difficult.

1. There exists a high degree of uncertainty associated with the entity's future expected cash flows. Bond interest payments are contractual obligations, and preferred-stock dividends are usually fixed. Therefore, those cash flows can be forecasted with more confidence than the estimation of common stocks' earnings, dividends, and capital gains (or losses).

2. Unlike interest and preferred stock dividends, common stocks' earnings, dividends, and market prices generally are expected to grow, not remain constant, so annuity formulas cannot be used unless certain simplifying assumptions are made. If those simplifications cannot be made, complex conceptual models may have to be developed to value equity securities.

3. An investor's required rate of return, or cost of capital, used to measure present value future cash flows is difficult to estimate because it depends on the term structure of interest rates, the riskiness of the equity investment, and other factors.

Multiperiod Discounted Cash Flow Analysis

Three basic DCF models may be used to estimate the value of equity:

1. The discounted free cash flow enterprise valuation model. This model will be fully explained because it is most widely used.

2. The discounted dividend valuation model. This model values a common stock based on the present value of a stream of future dividend cash flows and an assumed sale of the stock at some point in the future. Because this model is used in limited circumstances—for example, companies that pay a stable dividend—it will not be explained here.

3. The discounted abnormal earnings model. This model values the firm's equity as the sum of its book value and the discounted future abnormal earnings. Future abnormal earnings are defined as forecasted earnings plus the earnings required by investors. Because this model's use is limited in practice, it will not be covered in this chapter.

In practice, analysts generally use a multiple-stage, DCF enterprise model. This model takes into account an entity's future amounts of free cash flows with different growth rates over certain periods of time. For example, it is common that an entity will experience a period of high growth rates in its future free cash flows for a period of years, followed by a period of constant or normal free cash flow growth as the firm matures. This model is also referred to as a multiple-stage DCF.

The multiple-stage DCF model requires forecasts of the cash flows that will be available to all providers of capital, both debt and equity holders, over the forecasted time interval, and then discounts those cash flows by the weighted-average cost of capital, as defined below, to arrive at a total enterprise value. The market value of debt (as well as preferred stock, if any) then is deducted from the estimated enterprise value to arrive at the value attributable to equity shareholders. This amount is then divided by the number of common shares outstanding to arrive at a per-share value.

Steps in Estimating Enterprise Value Using the Discounted Cash Flow Method

Estimating the Free Cash Flows over a Finite or Abnormal Growth Period
Unlevered free cash flows are composed primarily of an entity's operating cash flows and are generally equal to its cash sales minus cash operating expenses and minus taxes paid. Capital expenditures necessary to replace assets worn out during operations and net additions to working capital also are deducted in order to arrive at the amount of free cash flows for the period that may be reinvested to promote real growth. Expenses such as depreciation and amortization are operating costs, which reduce profits but do not use cash. Thus, they are noncash expenses. Because those types of noncash expenses reduce the amount of taxes to be paid currently without requiring a cash outlay, they actually increase the after-tax cash flows that will be available to the firm and are included in the estimates of free cash flows. Free cash flows can be calculated in the following manner. (This is the same method used to estimate the cash flows to value publicly traded equity shares, presented in Chapter 6.)

> *GAAP net income* (refer to Exhibit 5-5)
> Plus depreciation and amortization
> Plus interest expense
> Plus the total tax provision (current and deferred)
> *EBITDA*
> Less income tax paid
> Less capital expenditures
> > Plus or minus net deductions or increases to working capital
> Equals free cash flows[1]

Note that unlevered free cash flows are being calculated before deducting interest on debt.

Analysts generally will begin a free cash flow DCF by evaluating the entity's growth stage, in order to determine a forecast period over which free cash flows will be estimated. An entity's growth opportunities and its position in its economic life cycle impact the magnitude and timing of its future free cash flows. For example:

- A start-up-type entity generally requires significant capital expenditures for product development, organizing systems, and training staff. This investment will pay off, it is hoped, as profits eventually increase and future capital improvement requirements diminish. Therefore, this type of entity's free cash flows initially will be minimal or even negative.
- A high-growth entity experiences rates of return on its investments that exceed its required rate of return by a significant amount, and this generates high operating

profit margins. Therefore, high-growth-stage entities would not be expected to pay dividends during this period of strong growth because earnings would be reinvested into the business in which they are earning a high rate of return.

• A mature constant or declining growth entity is characterized by a stabilized or declining growth rate in free cash flows because the return on investment is equal to or less than the entity's required rate of return. As a result, those entities would be expected to distribute all or large amounts of their earnings as dividends.

Based on the changing cash flow patterns that entities experience as they move from the start-up stage to high growth and the mature stages in their economic life cycle, investment analysts use multiple-stage DCF cash flow models that reflect different growth rates and changing levels of estimated cash flows to estimate enterprise value. A company may be able to realize rates of return on invested capital (r) that significantly exceed its cost of capital (R) for several years. However, competition eventually will drive rates of return on new capital investments down to the required rate of return. When this occurs, real growth in earnings decreases and free cash flows grow at a relatively low, constant, perpetual rate that is normal for the competitive nature of the industry. This means that an approximation procedure to estimate the present value of the cash flows can be used when this phenomenon is expected to occur. Investment analysts first will estimate an entity's cash flows over an abnormal growth rate period and then estimate a *terminal value* of the firm at the point when growth is stabilized at a perpetual rate. This period may be estimated from five to 10 years in the future, depending on the analyst's expectations and preferences.

Estimating an entity's free cash flows may be accomplished by projecting financial results based on management's plans, adjusted for analysts' assumptions in view of the entity's growth stage. Analysts generally will use the most recent reported financial statements and an analysis of the entity's future earnings growth potential to estimate its cash flows for the forecast period. Important variables in this process include the rate of return on invested capital, the growth rate of EBITDA, the level of capital improvements, dividend distributions, debt repayments, and additions to working capital. In grasping DCF valuation concepts, it is critical to recognize that free cash flows may be volatile. It is therefore difficult to estimate both the magnitude and timing of the free cash flows and terminal value to be calculated in the model. Recall the statistics shown earlier for PriceLine.com and Boeing. PriceLine.com's stock price volatility probably was attributable to factors such as investors' changing pricing methodologies and diminished expectations about profitability and free cash flows. Boeing's stock price volatility was linked to changing expectations about profitability and free cash flows, resulting from production problems, restructuring charges, and cancellations of new orders, followed by improved results and forecasts.

Estimating the Weighted-Average Cost of Capital
Another important variable used in DCF valuation models is the cost of capital
or discount rate. The following procedures are used to estimate the weighted-
average cost of capital, which is used to discount both the entity's free cash flows
and terminal value estimated over the forecast period of the valuation analysis.

The estimated weighted-average cost of capital can be calculated by using
the formula:

$$R = R_e\left(\frac{E}{D+E}\right) + R_d\left(\frac{D}{D+E}\right)$$

Where:
- R = the required rate of return or weighted-average cost of capital
- R_e = the required rate of return on equity capital
- R_d = the after tax, required rate of return on debt capital
- E = the fair value of the outstanding equity in the entity's capital structure
- D = the fair value of the outstanding debt capital
- $E/(D+E)$ and $D/(D+E)$ = the entity's optimal proportions of equity and debt
  financing

For example, assume ActionSportsCo's optimal capital structure (which
determines the optimal proportions of debt and equity financing it should use) is
50 percent debt, with an after-tax cost of 6 percent, and 50 percent equity, with a
cost of 15 percent. The 15 percent rate is an assumed rate based on the return
required by ActionSportsCo's investors for bearing the risk associated with the
firm. The ActionSportsCo weighted-average cost of capital therefore would be
10.5 percent (calculated as .50(.06) + .50(.15)). In practice, for public companies,
weighting should be based on the market values of the company's debt and
equity. However, with private companies, the weights for the cost of capital calculations are difficult to calculate because market values of both debt and equity
are not available. Therefore, they must be estimated. Note that analysts also may
review historical rates of return that investors required as a starting point for
determining the discount rate. Such historical required rates of return may not
be indicative of future required rates because inflation, risk factors, and interest
rate levels change over time. For example, in 1999, long-term interest-bearing,
investment-grade investments provided investors with relatively modest returns
approximating a range of from 6 to 8 percent. During the 1980s and early 1990s,
investors generally required much higher rates of return.

Although the cost of debt is readily determinable from the current rates
charged by lenders (calculated on an after-tax basis by multiplying the interest rate
cost times one minus the entity's effective tax rate), the required rate of return that
investors charge for equity is more difficult to obtain. One method of determining
the required rate of return on equity is to estimate the components of a discounted
cash flow model for the same or a similar public company. Because the current

price of the stock is known, and future cash flows may be estimated, an analyst can solve for the unknown discount rate. This process is illustrated in Chapter 6.

Factors impacting an entity's discount rate include:

- The company's industry and its competitive position in the industry
- The stock, given the company's stage in its economic life cycle
- The company's business and financial risks
- The company's historical financial performance and forecasts of future earnings and free cash flows

Another theoretical technique commonly used by analysts to estimate an entity's required rate of return is to compute the sum of a risk-free rate plus a risk premium (which is based on the security's beta coefficient and the market's price of risk). This is referred to as the capital asset pricing model (or CAPM), which is used to estimate the discount rate. In this model, the risk premium is a function of the entity's beta coefficient, which is a measure of its nondiversifiable market risk. For example, assume that the return on U.S. Treasuries (the risk-free rate) is 5 percent, the risk premium for the market risk is 6 percent (associated with a beta of 1), and the beta coefficient of an investment is estimated to be 1.5 (meaning that the company is viewed as 1.5 times as risky as the market portfolio). The required rate of return would then be 14 percent, calculated as 5 percent plus 1.5 times the 6 percent market risk premium.

Estimating the Terminal (or Residual) Value of the Firm

The next step in the valuation process requires that the entity's terminal value at the end of its abnormal (or variable) growth-rate period be estimated. The terminal value generally is estimated at the theoretical point when the growth in free cash flows has stabilized to a relatively normal constant rate. At this point, competitive factors have reduced the entity's return on investment to its required rate of return. The return on investment, however, should include a normal profit margin necessary for the firm to stay in business in the long run. Therefore, free cash flows are expected to continue to grow at a long-term sustainable growth rate, which is less than the required rate of return. The terminal value of the firm at the beginning of the constant-growth period may be calculated by various methods depending on the analyst's preferences. The following points are provided to identify and explain key aspects of this calculation.

Terminal Value Formula

Once the analyst has obtained an estimate of the present value of an entity's cash flows over the abnormal growth period, he or she then must estimate the present value of the entity's terminal value to obtain an estimate of its total fair value. The terminal value of an entity at the end of its estimated abnormal growth period is often determined using this formula:

$$\text{Terminal value at period T} = \frac{\text{Estimated free cash flows in period T}+1}{R-G}$$

Where:
- Period T+1 = the period following the end of the forecasted abnormal growth rate period, T
- R = the required rate of return, estimated as the weighted-average cost of debt and equity capital
- G = the constant perpetual growth rate in cash flows beginning in T+1

Some analysts may use free cash flows, as discussed earlier, while others may use operating earnings or net operating profit after taxes (NOPAT) as the numerator, depending on preferences. Furthermore, analysts often use different methodologies to estimate the constant growth rate in free cash flows expected after time T. Once this normal or constant growth rate is obtained, it is multiplied times the estimated cash flows in Period T to arrive at the estimated cash flows in Period T+1.

Calculation of the Free Cash Flows

The lower the required rate of return R, or the higher the perpetual growth rate, G in the terminal value formula, the larger the terminal value. Conversely, the higher the R or the lower the G, the lower will be the estimated terminal value. For example, assuming that G = 0, that free cash flows, estimated for T+1, are $5 million, and that a 12 percent weighted-average cost of capital applies; the terminal value would be $41,666,667:

$$\text{Terminal value} = \frac{5,000,000}{.12} = \$41,666,667$$

Estimating the expected growth rate in cash flows is very difficult because of the high degree of uncertainty involved. Analysts use several different approaches. However, conceptually, the growth rate can be considered to be a function of the rate of return that an entity can earn on its invested capital and its reinvestment rate. If a firm uses only equity financing, then its growth rate may be estimated as:

$$\text{Growth rate} = r(1-k)$$

Where:
- r = the entity's rate of return on invested capital
- K = dividend pay-out ratio, so that (1-k) equals its retention or reinvestment rate

Therefore, if it is assumed that r equals 16 percent and that the K equals 50 percent, the expected growth rate is estimated at 8 percent (.16(1 − .5)). Assuming free cash flows of $5 million in period T+1, a 12 percent weighted-average cost of capital, a 16 percent return on invested capital, and a 50 percent pay-out ratio, the terminal value would be $125,000,000:

$$\text{Terminal value} = \frac{5,000,000}{[.12 - .16(1 - .50)]} = \frac{5,000,000}{.12 - .08} = \$125,000,000$$

Other methods are used to calculate the terminal value but are similar to the one presented above. Chapter 6 illustrates a method used by certain analysts at Bear Stearns. The key point is that a plethora of techniques is used in practice to estimate the discount rate, growth rate, and other economic variables used in the valuation estimate. Therefore, this process is more of an art than a precise science.

Discounting the Terminal Value and the Free Cash Flows in the Super-Growth Period

The required rate of return (R), estimated as the weighted-average cost of capital, is used to discount the free cash flows experienced during the abnormal growth years and the entity's terminal value that is estimated at the beginning of the constant growth period, to arrive at the enterprise's total fair value. This is demonstrated in Exhibits 5-6 through 5-8.

Reducing the Estimated Total Enterprise Value by the Value of the Debt to Arrive at a Fair Value of the Equity

Once an estimate of the entity's total enterprise value is obtained, the enterprise value is reduced by the fair value of outstanding debt. This procedure produces an estimate of the fair value of the entity's outstanding equity. The fair value of the equity then can be divided by the number of outstanding shares of common stock to arrive at the value per share. (This assumes that no other classes of equity exist.)

ActionSportsCo's Discounted Cash Flow Enterprise Valuation

The steps just described in the discounted cash flow discussion will now be combined to estimate the value of ActionSportsCo.

Exhibit 5-6 provides estimates of ActionSportsCo's free cash flows over a five-year period, based on assumed financial projections. It is assumed here that ActionSportsCo's free cash flows will initially be growing at an abnormally high rate because its ability to earn a superior rate of return on investment, until it reaches a theoretically stabilized (sustainable) growth rate level in the year 2006. Thus, after the year 2005, the entity will be forced to earn normal returns on investment and experience constant rates of growth in free cash flows because of competition. Since real growth would have virtually ceased because investments made by the entity would only earn a rate of return required by investors, capital expenditures would be reduced, as assumed in Exhibit 5-6. Exhibits 5-6 and 5-7 provide the estimates of free cash flow inputs for ActionSportsCo's equity pricing.

Assume in Exhibit 5-7 that ActionSportsCo's free cash flow growth rate is 1 percent after the forecasted super growth period. This constant flat growth rate

Exhibit 5-6   Estimation of ActionSportsCo Free Cash Flows during the Abnormal Growth Period (T).

	Estimated				
	2001	2002	2003	2004	2005
EBITDA	**2,000,000**	**2,500,000**	**3,250,000**	**4,387,500**	**5,703,750**
Less total income tax provision	-11,250	-101,250	-191,250	-366,000	-557,925
Less capital improvements and net additions to working capital	-1,000,000	-1,000,000	-1,000,000	-1,000,000	-750,000
Unlevered free cash flow	**988,750**	**1,398,750**	**2,058,750**	**3,021,500**	**4,395,825**

Exhibit 5-7   Estimation of ActionSportsCo's Free Cash Flows in Period T+1.

Estimated free cash flow in year 2005	4,395,825
Estimated growth rate in free cash flows at 1 percent	1.01
Estimated free cash flow in year 2006	4,439,783

assumption can be made only after analyzing the competitive and economic factors related to ActionSportsCo's sporting goods products.

Terminal Value Calculation

Assume that ActionSportsCo's weighted-average cost of capital is 10.5 percent, as calculated earlier. The terminal value at the beginning of year T+1 = 2006 is calculated as:

$$\text{Terminal value} = \frac{4,439,783}{.105 - .01} = \$46,734,557$$

Where:
- $\$4,439,783$ = the free cash flow in the first year of the constant growth period T+1 = 2006
- $.105$ = the weighted-average cost of capital
- $.01$ = the assumed constant perpetual growth rate in free cash flows starting in period T+1

Discounting the Terminal Value and the Free Cash Flows during the Abnormal Growth Periods

Exhibit 5-8 illustrates how to discount the free cash flows and terminal value estimated above, using the company's weighted-average cost of capital of 10.5 percent.

Exhibit 5-8   ActionSportsCo's Enterprise Fair Value.

	2001	2002	2003	2004	2005
Unlevered free cash flows	988,750	1,398,750	2,058,750	3,021,500	4,395,825
Terminal value					46,734,558
Total cash flows	988,750	1,398,750	2,058,750	3,021,500	51,130,383
Net present value at					
10.5% discount rate	894,796	1,145,554	1,525,867	2,026,625	31,036,167
Enterprise fair value					36,629,009

Reducing the Estimated Total Enterprise Value by the Fair Value of the Debt to Arrive at a Fair Value of the Equity

Based on a $36,629,009 enterprise value and assuming that $7,500,000 equals the current fair value of the entity's debt, the fair value attributable to the equity holders is $29,129,009. Assuming that only one class of equity exists and that this is in the form of 1 million shares of voting common stock, fair value per share is $29.13 ($32,429,009/1 million).

Before moving to other valuation considerations, it is important to stress that the values obtained using equity valuation models may be significantly different from those experienced in the market, especially in the short run. This is because changing investors' expectations may result in drastically different prices from those estimated with the models explained in this chapter. However, over the long term, the marketplace may tend to price equity securities in the ranges estimated with the fundamental models explained herein. At the other extreme, if the market believes that an entity will not be able to produce free cash flows in the future (e.g., because of bankruptcy), investors may be willing to pay only a price based on an estimated liquidation value of the entity's net assets (which can be quite small). For example, Applied Magnetics Corporation (APM) was a publicly traded stock whose price decreased from $60 a share to become worthless in the year 2000. This occurred because it was unable to meet new technological requirements for its major product, personal computer magnetic disk-drive heads.

The fact that changes in economic variables and investors' requirements also have significant impacts on stock valuations is illustrated by the significant technology stock selloff that occurred in March and April 2000. During this time, the shares of many technology companies were down by 40 to 50 percent in less than a month.

Impact of Controlling and Minority Interests

Private entities are generally not owned by large groups of shareholders but, rather, owned by a controlling shareholder and minority shareholders. This complicates the valuation process because each share of stock may not have the same fair value. For example, a majority shareholder is in the position to influence the entity's cash flows by determining or influencing salaries, expanding or contracting the business, or taking other actions, such as merging the entity with another company. A majority-owned block of shares in an entity may trade at a significant premium (such as 30 percent) above the value estimated with a traditional valuation technique. In contrast, a minority shareholder may not be able to influence the business or even obtain timely information about the company's financial results. Therefore, a minority shareholder's stock may be discounted by a certain percentage, depending on the situation. The key point is that when reviewing investment valuations of privately owned common stock, control premiums or discounts may be significant.

Private-equity investments are often joint ventures or start-up situations that create additional valuation issues. The following section discusses those complicating factors and provides a conceptual foundation for better understanding the factors that may affect their values.

BASIC FRAMEWORK OF PRIVATE-EQUITY INVESTING

Private-equity investments are generally high-risk, high-return type investments. Therefore, investors require an in-depth understanding of the business in which the entity operates in order to be successful in this type of investing. The type of business will vary from closely held operating companies providing existing products and services to venture capital projects formed to create a product. Also, the type of the investment will vary and may be in the form of a direct common stock investment, a preferred stock investment with or without detachable warrants, or a loan with nondetachable warrants. Consideration also should be given to the nature of the product or service produced by the entity. For example, the value of an Internet service provider company may be based on the estimated value of its current stream of service fees or on the basis of a DCF model in which the free cash flows are assumed to grow as the large initial capital investments pay off in later years. A company's stage in its growth life cycle significantly impacts the level of risk and the type of valuation model to be used. An entity currently generating earnings, such as the example of ActionSportsCo, may be valued differently from an entity in an early, unprofitable stage of its product development. Free cash flow and earnings multiple-valuation methods are often used to value private-equity investments, although analysts may favor one type of valuation method over another for certain industries. For example, technology companies often are valued based on earnings multiples rather than on free cash flows. Due to the nature of private investing, the following aspects must be completely understood prior to considering the valuation method that may be used in those circumstances.

Risk Nature of Private Investing

Private companies with growing operating earnings and favorable future economic prospects are the least risky types of private investments. One type of investment in this area may be in the form of preferred stock with detachable warrants issued by a company with a good earnings history. For example, a portion of ActionSportsCo's equity could be preferred stock with detachable warrants. The preferred stock would most likely pay a dividend, usually fixed. In contrast, at the high end of the risk spectrum are venture capital investments that are in the product research and development stage, with no prior profitable earnings history. Venture capital investments are characterized by a high rate of failure but with large returns for the ventures that succeed. In a typical deal, the investors provide the capital and the joint-venture partners provide the expertise in developing the product. The extent of risks involved depends on the nature and expected time span of the venture. For example, a biotech start-up venture that is estimated to have a three-year investment horizon would probably entail these risks:

- A competing product may enter the market prior to the product's development. Note that sometimes it may be difficult to determine if there really is a lead over competitors in developing a product.
- The product development costs may exceed estimates.
- The regulatory approval process may take longer than expected and patent costs may be higher than expected.
- Venture partners may fail to honor cash contribution commitments.
- The venture may fail to develop the product.
- The market share for the product may be smaller than expected.
- Product sales may be unfavorably impacted by cyclical factors.
- The expected production costs and profit margins may not meet expectations.

These risks impact the estimates of cash flows and their timing. Therefore, the required rate of return used to discount those cash flows in arriving at an enterprise value is high, and it is typical to seek rates exceeding 50 percent on these types of investments.

Quality of Management

The integrity, track record, and ability of the management team to deliver as indicated in forecasted operating plans are key to the success of any type of private (or public) enterprise. The ability to maintain a competent management team over the life of the investment is also important.

Exit Strategy

Private capital shares cannot be sold readily, since they are not traded on an exchange. Therefore, at the inception of the investment, the investor should have a strategy for cashing out of the investment. In the case of a venture capital investment, that strategy typically would be an expected sale of the stock to a company that requires the product or service. For example, a venture to develop a new type of drug likely would entail a plan to conclude with a successful Food and Drug Administration (FDA) approval and sale of the venture stock to a large pharmaceutical company. The exit strategy also may include operating the venture and building critical mass to permit an IPO. An exit strategy for an operating (as opposed to a development-stage venture that is not currently producing a product) company also may take the sale or IPO approach. The key point is that those investments are illiquid and will require time and planning to realize profits through a sale.

Financial Projections

The venture management team must have the ability to forecast realistic cash flow projections and meet those projections. A key projection involves an estimate of future cash flows used to determine the terminal value of the venture at the end of an investment period, typically three to five years. For example, a biotech product venture may be expected to sell at 20 to 30 times EBITDA when profitable operations eventually evolve from the development stage. A big challenge facing an investment analyst is determining comparable market multiples for such ventures because data on entities with similar products may not be available. In any event, the reliability of market multiples for similar products and the likelihood of management delivering on plans must be carefully evaluated.

Obtaining Relevant Economic Information

Private companies do not have SEC oversight; therefore, it is important that shareholders have access to reliable and timely financial and operating information when valuing the investment. An important aspect of this type of investing is to become an insider through such steps as obtaining the right to be on the board of directors or to attend the board meetings. In this manner, the investor obtains board mailings, attends monthly board meetings, and actively participates in operational decisions. Thus, the investor becomes an insider and has complete information about the investment.

Control and Covenants

Investors generally require covenants that protect their investment. A key aspect of this process is making sure that relevant covenants are negotiated at the inception of the investment. Covenants vary by the type of deal; for example, an equity kicker included as part of a loan differs from a convertible preferred stock investment or a debt issue with a detachable warrant investment. An equity kicker or warrant investment likely would require audited financial statements, limit intercompany transactions, prohibit or limit additional debt issuances, and prohibit a change of control or sale without investor approval and compensation. A direct equity investment, such as preferred convertible stock, may include seats on the board of directors for the investor in the event of a default. (This cannot be obtained in debt-related investments due to lender liability issues.)

Specific Characteristics of Private-Equity Investments

The following examples provide important characteristics specific to certain types of private-equity investments and explain key items that accountants, who may review related valuations, should understand. Private-equity investments are diverse and high risk. These examples will, it is hoped, begin to provide readers with insight into asking the right questions when reviewing such investments. Examples of fair value estimations in those situations will not be presented because such calculations may be confusing or may provide a false impression that the estimates are reliable. Instead, three simple types of private investments and a number of other investment-related issues are discussed.

Investment 1: A Minority Interest in a Voting Common Stock Investment in a Start-up Venture

An institutional investor made an initial $1.5 million common stock investment in a start-up venture to organize a foreign-bond management firm. The venture's purpose is to organize and operate a foreign-bond management firm that attracts pension funds and other institutional investor clients. The exit strategy is that after the third year, a critical mass of assets under management will be achieved and the firm will be sold to an investment firm. The initial investment involves four investors that are each providing $1.5 million in the form of seed capital to get the firm organized and into operation. The investors are each financial institutions and also have promised to provide the firm with $150 million of funds for the firm to invest.

The anticipated initial funds under management's control are targeted at $1 billion, comprising $600 million (4 times $150 million) of funds from the partners and $400 million of outside funds that have been identified, based on discussions with potential clients. The initial $600 million of funds under management, provided by the partners, is estimated to provide a fee base to cover fixed operating costs plus a performance track record for the new firm. Each investor has a minority voting interest and holds a seat on the board of directors. At the end of the first year, each investor has made a capital contribution of $1.5 million, and the firm has rented office space, staffed the organization with highly qualified professionals, and is operational. However, only two partners have been able to honor a total of $300 million of funds for the entity to manage. The other two partners were unable to provide the promised funds of $300 million due to changes in business circumstances and have informed the firm that they cannot honor their commitments to provide seed money. The firm therefore must seek additional clients, since it requires $600 million of assets under management's control in order to break even. Also, the firm is in need of additional seed money to maintain operating deficits expected in the second year.

Question: What key factors must be determined in valuing the $1.5 million investment of one of the active partners (who committed $150 million of funds to be managed)?

Answer: Key valuation factors include:
- The financial projections for the entity (e.g., have other clients provided funds to be managed and when will they be available?)
- The ability of the active partners to channel additional funds for the entity to manage
- The active partners' investment committees' permission to increase or maintain their capital contributions
- The prospects for funding additional investors
- The fund manager's performance, relative to comparisons of total return on assets under control of peer groups
- The common valuation methodologies for money management firms (e.g., a multiple of yearly fees and a multiple of recent sales of comparable firms)
- The partners' and fund managers' reputations, which are important to the likelihood of attracting additional partners and clients for the venture
- The competitive environment for money managers and the level of critical mass for funds needed by management for this organization to be viable; the time it will take for a critical mass of assets under management to be accumulated and the portion of those investment funds required in the short term

If the firm has a good reputation, has achieved competitive returns on assets under management's control, and has attracted significant outside funds, the investor may estimate a positive value for the investment and continue to contribute capital. The actual results of first year's operations and forecasted financial projections will form a basis for the valuation process. Other key factors would include the valuation of yearly fees.

If additional funds under management were not obtained or were unlikely to be obtained in the near term, the critical mass of assets needed by management would not be achieved and operating losses would continue for an undetermined period of time. Therefore, the analyst may value this investment at close to zero, unless some very favorable developments were under way (specifically, obtaining new capital from other investors and clients).

Investment 2: A Preferred Stock Investment in an Operating Entity

An institutional investor made a $20 million loan in the form of a preferred stock investment to an industrial firm. The investment earns a market rate of interest and has these characteristics:

- The investment earns a cumulative, preferred dividend, payable on a semiannual basis. This means that the dividend must be satisfied before the common shareholders are entitled to equity distributions.
- The investor requires restrictive covenants to restrict new loans, changes of control, asset sales, intercompany transactions, and related-party transactions.
- The investor requires that the entity maintain a minimum net worth level, provide quarterly financial statements, and provide audited annual financial statements.
- The investor has covenant protection that in the event of a nonmonetary or monetary default; the investor immediately has the right to convert the preferred stock into the sole voting common stock of the entity.

Assume that deteriorating conditions in the economy have caused the entity to breach the covenant requiring that a minimum net worth be maintained.

Question: What are the key considerations in valuing the $20 million preferred stock investment?

Answer: The investor's covenant to gain control of all the voting stock (and, therefore, seize control of the company by replacing the board of directors) is key to the valuation. The investor can require management to submit and follow through on a plan to either remedy the covenant default or raise funds to repay the investment in the near future. For example, the company could identify and sell off certain assets to repay the investor. If management refused to take appropriate action, the investor could oust them. Therefore, management generally will take all steps necessary to keep the investor from seizing control of the company and will plan to address that problem immediately. Often the covenant default is triggered at a point in which the company is financially able to resolve the problem. One alternative, assuming that the company is viable and its management team is trustworthy, would be for the investor to stay in the deal but require additional common stock and a higher rate of return on the preferred stock. A discounted cash flow valuation could be used to value the investment's restructured cash flows, using a higher discount rate to adjust for the added risk.

If the investor required a less-complete covenant protection package than that just discussed, the value of the investment may be significantly less. Consider the impact of not restricting related-party transactions and intercompany loans, or of not being able to control a company through the conversion of preferred stock to voting common stock. The company's management could consume the firm's assets and let the value of the investment erode, leaving the investor powerless to recover his or her investment. An investor in this situation may have no viable exit strategy as the assets of the company are expended in what may be unsuccessful efforts. The free cash flow estimates would be reduced by large expected capital expenditures and diminished margins. In addition, the risk to the entity will increase because of the uncertain cash flows resulting from the to-be-developed technology.

Investment 3: A Loan with an Equity Kicker to an Operating Entity

An institutional investor made a $15 million par, 10-year, fixed-rate, nonamortizing loan to a manufacturing company. The interest rate was set slightly below market because, as part of the loan, the borrower agreed to provide the investor with the right to purchase 10 percent of the common stock of the company for $10,000. The plant assets of the company secured the loan. The standard loan covenants included:

- Standard representations and warranties
- Restrictive covenants to prohibit new loans, changes of control, material asset sales, intercompany transactions, and related-party transactions
- Minimum net worth levels maintained by the entity, and quarterly and annual audited financial statements provided

However, assume that the investor did not have the right to attend company board meetings. When the loan was close to its maturity, the borrower was delinquent but offered to repay the loan at par. The investor welcomed the payoff and released the borrower's collateral; however, the investor subsequently determined that the borrower had sold the entity's entire plant and equipment concurrent with the loan payoff. Because this action constituted a breach of the loan covenants, the investor is seeking to recover the fair value of the 10 percent equity kicker. Assume that the only asset remaining in the company is a $50 million intercompany loan and that the company's net worth is $50 million. Also assume that over the course of the investment, the investor waived the right to receive audited financial statements and agreed to waive the covenant prohibiting intercompany transactions.

Question: What are some of the key valuation issues in this investment?

Answer: The best indicator of value for this investment is the willingness of the investor and borrower to negotiate a settlement. Clearly, this situation involves improper actions by both parties. The borrower breached the covenant requiring that it notify the investor about the sale of assets; the investor waived key covenants and appeared to be disinterested in the equity-kicker investment.

Other aspects of this valuation are the litigation costs and risks of not prevailing if this matter is brought to court. A value of 10 percent of the company's net worth is probably overly optimistic. A near-term payment of 25 to 50 percent of this value without costly litigation is probably realistic.

ACCOUNTANT'S REVIEW OF PRIVATE-EQUITY VALUATIONS

Readers now may be wondering how accountants can evaluate the reasonableness of private-equity valuations. Here we summarize some of the steps accountants may follow in reviewing the reasonableness of private-equity valuations.

Discounted Cash Flow Valuations

The key components of the valuation are the estimated free cash flows and the discount rate. Accountants performing a review of an investment's pricing are expected to conduct various reasonableness checks.

Free Cash Flows

Probably the most important reasonableness check is determining how the free cash flows are estimated and if and how the free cash flow assumptions changed from the last valuation. Alternatively, if the free cash flows have not changed from the last valuation, one must determine whether this is realistic given the industry, economy, and pace of business changes. Also, one must assess the analyst's track record for prior valuations and examine the prior valuations to determine the nature of the changing assumptions and if prior estimates of valuation variables were validated through time. For example, have the estimated capital expenditures and EBITDA levels used in prior valuations actually occurred? Other important factors include:

- Do the assumptions appear reasonable, given an assessment of the firm's position in its industry life cycle? Is the firm still in the high-growth stage, or is it in a mature or even declining stage? For example, in evaluating a producer of personal computer components, if the product has become a commodity available from other sources, the industry may be maturing and a constant normal industry growth rather than high growth in free cash flows would be expected. Also, a possible decreasing margin may occur, even though expanded sales volume provides a positive net growth rate in free cash flows.
- Is the industry consolidating due to decreased product demand? A firm may be commanding a larger market share in what could be a declining market; for example, the firm is one of the surviving producers of horseshoe nails.
- Do the gross margins seem attainable, or may competitors enter the industry, driving prices and margins down? Do patents or other barriers limit competition? A good example of this is Pfizer's Viagra drug patent. The stock of Pfizer rallied in 1998 as the FDA approved Viagra and Pfizer began selling it.

- Is product obsolescence a significant factor? In evaluating a high-tech company, product obsolescence is a key risk factor because the product's life is so short. Further compounding this risk is the volatility of the product's demand. For example, a firm may produce what is acknowledged to be the best personal computer modem; however, its sales are drastically reduced because of slowing personal computer sales and high inventory stockpiles. This occurred in the fall of 1998, as Asia's economic problems surfaced and demand from this sector declined.
- Are the estimates of capital expenditures realistic? In evaluating the capital expenditures for an Internet service provider, assume that the early years of the DCF model show significant capital expenditures while the later years show much lower capital expenditures. Is it reasonable to assume that technological and marketplace changes will not require ongoing large capital expenditures?
- Do potential industry or labor developments exist that may require adjustments to the free cash flow estimates? In evaluating a subcontractor (whose main customer is Boeing), did the free cash flow estimates consider the Boeing labor contract negotiations scheduled for August 1999, which may have impacted the firm's value? (This factor is also relevant to determining the risk-premium portion of the discount rate.)

Discount Rate

As previously discussed in this chapter, the discount rate comprises the weighted-average cost of the firm's debt and equity financing. The debt cost is readily determinable by reference to the firm's loan agreements. However, the firm's cost of equity capital cannot be directly linked to a verifiable source. One method used in practice to estimate the cost of equity capital is to use the current price and expected cash flows of a comparable but publicly traded firm and solve for its cost of capital using the DCF model. The resulting cost of equity then may be adjusted for other factors unique to the firm. Although this process may be somewhat more imprecise when applied to a private entity, since it is not completely comparable to a public entity, it does provide a reasonableness test. For example, if a public personal computer hardware firm had an estimated cost of equity capital of 22 percent, what factors justify a private firm in the same industry to use a lower or higher rate?

Price-Multiple Models

Compare the price multiples to similar public companies and assess if differences are reasonable. For example, if a public Internet service provider's stock is trading at a certain multiple of service revenue, is it reasonable for a private Internet service provider firm to be valued at a higher multiple? In the valuation of an industrial firm using a multiple of EBITDA, comparing and understanding the differences in EBITDA price multiples of similar public firms could be performed.

CONCLUDING REMARKS

Chapter 6 illustrates an investment research report provided by Bear Stearns, analyzing the Fox Entertainment Group, Inc. The report was included to illustrate the above valuation processes used in practice for publicly traded firms. It highlights the importance of the estimates of cash flows, competitive position, risks, and financial projections used in a valuation model.

NOTE

1. May also deduct noncash income, such as a joint venture's undistributed income accounted for under the equity method.

Public Equity Pricing

INTRODUCTION

This chapter shows how the discounted cash flow (DCF) and price-multiple pricing methods are used in an actual Bear Stearns investment research report entitled "Fox Rocks" (portions of which are reprinted as Appendix E at the end of this chapter).[1] This report is not provided here to recommend Fox stock as a buy or sell; rather, it illustrates how the DCF model is used to combine market information with the analyst's assumptions and projections to arrive at an independent estimate of fair value. A key aspect of this process is to solve for the market discount rate (R), or cost of capital, used by the market to compute the present value of the estimated future cash flows of Fox Entertainment Group, Inc. Recall that Chapter 5 described how to estimate the costs of equity and debt capital, which are used to calculate a weighted-average cost of equity capital appropriate for a specific company. Analysts use information readily available in the market to estimate the cost of capital.

The "Fox Rocks" report provides an excellent summary of the stock pricing process. Bear Stearns focuses on a fundamental equity analysis, which also entails an analysis of the company's profitability, financial condition, and market position. However, technical analysis, which involves charting and reviewing market trends to determine undervalued and overvalued securities that should be bought or sold short, will not be covered.

"FOX ROCKS" VALUATION ILLUSTRATION

Consider the following key valuation assumptions and estimates that analysts would expect to make (and that accountants should understand), based on the concepts discussed in Chapter 5:

- An evaluation and projection of the company's industry and company competitive position
- An indication of the company's stage in its operating life cycle and sales growth prospects

- A determination of the company's risk and growth potential integrated into the determination of the discount rate (R), expected future cash flow growth rates (g), and free cash flow estimates
- An analysis of the company's historical financial performance and an estimate of its weighted-average cost of capital

Company Description and Financial and Investment Summary

Bear Stearns has conducted a financial analysis of Fox Entertainment Group, Inc., and is recommending that the stock be purchased based on the expected growth in its future cash flows combined with its current market value (considered to be undervalued by Bear Sterns). Their 12-month estimated target price is $30, or a gain of approximately 30 percent over the current price of $21 5/16. The share appreciation is attributed to cash flow growth expected as a result of the company's vertical integration efforts. The report presents this price-related information:

- Fox is one of the industry's leading vertically integrated entertainment companies (page 2 of the report). The synergies of its production and worldwide distribution platforms permit the retention of its film and programming divisions' strong economic value.
- The historical performance of the entity's EBITDA and net income is shown on page 2 of the report. Note the positive trends in EBITDA and profit margins.
- The vertical integration of the manufacturing and distribution of films and television shows divisions are expected to add $1.3 billion to the valuation, or $2 per share (page 4).
- The benefits of assured distribution of the Fox Television Network will not be felt fully until fiscal year 2002, at which time it is expected that the company's EBITDA will grow 37 percent from the off-network syndication of high-profile television properties. Those syndication sales should produce a compound annual growth rate of 15.1 percent in EBITDA during 1998 to 2004. Perhaps more important, the off-network sales should produce better than a 46 percent compound annual growth rate in free cash flows for the same period.
- The Company Description/Organization Chart shows the three major business groupings (pages 6–8 of the report):
  - Feature Film and Television Production and Distribution. This accounted for revenues of $3.9 billion and EBITDA of $292 million during 1998.
  - Television Broadcasting. This accounted for revenues of $3.1 billion and EBITDA of $727 million in 1998.
  - Cable Network Programming. This accounted for revenues of $72 million and a $96 million loss in EBITDA during 1998.
- The Fox Entertainment Group, Inc., is 18.6 percent publicly held (Class A shares) and 81.4 percent held by News Corp (Class B shares). The Class B shares have 97.8 percent of the voting shares.

DISCOUNTED CASH FLOW MODEL

Page 9 of the report explains that a DCF model is the primary valuation approach because it better reflects the company's underlying economics. A price-to-EBITDA analysis was not used because it would misrepresent the studio's underlying economics. Analysts did not use a price-EBITDA multiple valuation approach because they felt that a multiple of 1999 EBITDA would understate the value by focusing on near-term earnings and cash flow estimates, to the detriment of better, longer-term projections of these amounts. The DCF valuation model captures both the short-term and long-term projected cash flows of an entity and is the appropriate method to be used in these circumstances. For example, the terminal (or residual) value estimated at the end of the 5-year investment horizon, accounts for over 60 percent of the value of Fox Entertainment Group, Inc.

Page 9 summarizes how Bear Stearns applied the mechanics of the DCF model to value the stock:

1. Future expected cash flows were estimated over a 5-year, variable growth rate period (1998 to 2003) and the constant growth rate period (beyond 2003) used to estimate the terminal value cash flow.

2. The cash flow estimates and the current market price per share were inserted into the DCF model. The DCF model then is used to solve for the market discount rate (or the market's estimated weighted-average cost of capital of 11.9 percent) that equates the operating cash flow projections and the terminal value of the enterprise to the current share price. Note that this report uses the term "residual value" for what we have defined as "terminal value" in the DCF model. Also note that the discount rate is calculated as a weighted-average cost of capital.

3. The discount rate was separated into its component parts—the cost of debt (which was estimated) and the cost of equity capital (which was derived from the formula for the weighted cost of capital). The derived cost of equity then is evaluated relative to the cost of debt by comparing the yield spread currently used by the market to the historical yield spreads between equity and fixed-income returns (an average of 550 basis points during 1980 to 1997) to evaluate whether it adequately reflected Fox Entertainment Group's risk to equity holders. It was decided that the current equity yield spread was too high and should be reduced (page 16 of the "Fox Rocks" report).

4. The cost of equity was adjusted from 15.0 to 14.0 percent, which is considered to be a fair required rate of return, given the perception of risk in the marketplace. This yields a new discount rate of 11.2 percent (calculated as the weighted-average costs of debt and equity, see Exhibit 10).

5. The revised estimate of the discount rate was then used to calculate the present value of the entity's future cash flows, including the terminal value in the DCF model to produce an estimated current share price of $30 (Exhibit 11 on page 19 of the report).

Additional Observations of the Discounted Cash Flow Valuation Approach Used

The DCF model first was used to compute the market's estimate of the weighted average cost of capital of 11.9 percent (Exhibits 7 and 8). As a starting point, review Exhibit 7 (page 15 of the report) and focus on these inputs:

- Estimated unlevered free cash flows for the years 1998 to 2003 ranged from $497 to $888. Note that the free cash flows of $888 in 2003 were used to determine the terminal value of the enterprise at the end of 2003.
- The enterprise's terminal value was estimated at $17,016 in the initial valuation analysis, based on a cost of capital of 11.9 percent. Note that the discount rate of 11.9 percent discounted the cash flows used in the valuation model to the current price per share of 23\frac{1}{8}$. The discount rate of 11.9 percent was used to discount the cash flows and to calculate the internal or excess growth rate.
- The perpetual growth rate (g) in cash flows beginning in the year 2003, which was used to estimate the terminal value, is estimated as the excess of the implied rate of return on invested capital over the cost of capital. Note that this method of estimating (g), which is different from the traditional method discussed in Chapter 5, highlights the diversity used in practice.
- The implied perpetual return on invested capital (r) was estimated to be 18.7 percent. This rate less the required rate of return determined the excess return or internal growth rate of 6.7 percent (18.7 percent less 11.9 percent [rounding error of .1 percent]).

Assuming that the appropriate weighted average cost of capital (R) was equal to 11.9 percent, also assume that the marketplace factored all the available information into the DCF model when arriving at the current 23\frac{1}{8}$ share price. Therefore, in order to forecast a higher targeted price, some of the estimated variables in the DCF model must change. The "Fox Rocks" report identified that the 15.0 percent historical cost of equity capital was too high and therefore produced an overvalued average weighted average cost of capital (discount rate) of 11.9 percent (see Exhibit 8). This is discussed below.

Running Fox through the Discounted Cash Flow Model

Estimating the Free Cash Flows and Compound Annual Growth Rate

Exhibits 2 to 4 (pages 12 and 13 of the report) provide the estimates of EBITDA and free cash flows to be used in the DCF model, including the compound annual growth rate in free cash flows (CAGR) of 12.3 percent (1998 to 2003).

In order to estimate the terminal (or residual) value portion of the entity's total enterprise value in the year 2003, a number of estimates are required. Exhibit 4 of the report shows how the $888 million unlevered cash flow in the year 2003 was estimated. This estimated cash flow was used to compute the terminal value after an estimate of growth (g) was obtained.

Solving for the Return on Invested Capital

Exhibit 5 (page 14 of the "Fox Rocks" report) demonstrates that the return on invested capital is calculated as the ratio of the expected free cash flows to the estimated invested capital. A "haircut" of 15 percent was applied to the calculated 22 percent amount to arrive at the 18.7 percent return used to estimate growth (g).

Solving for the Required Return on Invested Capital (R)

The last paragraph before Exhibit 6 (page 15 of the report) explains that the required return on invested capital or weighted-average cost of capital (R) was the unknown variable in the DCF equation, once the future cash flows and time horizon were estimated. In using the DCF model, (R) was solved for using the estimated cash flows and the current share price of $23^1/_8$. Solving the DCF model resulted in an initial estimated (R) expected by the market of 11.9 percent (which was later determined to be too high). The perpetual expected growth rate (g) in free cash flows, beginning in year 2003, was initially estimated at 6.8 percent (18.7 percent less 11.9 percent).

Solving for the Present Values of the Free Cash Flows and Terminal Value

The next step was to use the discount rate of 11.9 percent to calculate the present value of the estimated individual cash flows for the five years (1998 to 2002) plus the present value of the terminal value ($17,016) expected in year 2003, to obtain the total fair value of the entity of $12,405 million (excluding other assets). Refer to Exhibit 7 on page 15 of the report. When other assets and debt are subtracted, and the net amount is divided by the shares of common stock outstanding, the share price of $23.13 (currently observed in the market) is obtained.

The terminal or residual value of $17,016 as shown in Exhibit 7 of the report was computed as follows:

$$\text{Terminal entity value} = \frac{\text{Cash flow in 2003}}{R - g} = \frac{888}{.119 - .067} = \$17,076$$

Where:
- Exhibits 4 and 5 estimate 2003's unlevered free cash flows of $888 million, which is what appears in the numerator.
- The rate of .119 represents the discount rate and is explained on page 15 of the report.
- The .067 represents the excess return on invested capital over the cost of capital, or growth rate, and is calculated in Exhibit 6 as the difference between the

assumed perpetual return on equity of 18.7 percent and the 11.9 percent discount rate. This is labeled as the "excess return" of 6.7 percent in Exhibit 6.

The terminal value of $17,016 shown in Exhibit 7 is different from the amount shown above ($17,076) due to rounding, since the valuation used 1/.119 −.067 as equal to 19.2. This amount then was multiplied by the $888 to arrive at an estimated terminal value of $17,016.

Next Step in the Fox Valuation, Recalculating the Discount Rate and Value of Equity

The last paragraph on page 18 and Exhibit 10 explain the economic justification for reducing the 11.9 percent estimated cost of equity to 11.2 percent. As indicated in Exhibit 11 (page 19 of the report), using this 11.2 percent discount rate generated a $30 target price per share in the DCF analysis (using the same steps as those discussed above). Review Exhibits 8, 10, and 11 (pages 16, 18, and 19, respectively). Note the following key points:

- During the years 1998 to 2003, free cash flows were unchanged.
- The discount rate had been adjusted downward from 11.9 percent to 11.2 percent to reflect that analysts' expectations that the required rate of return on equity assumed by the market was too high.
- The lowering of the discount rate also impacted the excess return or growth rate, which is now estimated to be 7.5 percent (18.7 percent less 11.2 percent). Refer to Exhibit 11 of the report.
- The capitalization rate, $1/(R - g)$, became $1/(11.2$ percent $- 7.5$ percent), or 27 (to be used to estimate the terminal value as 27 times year 2003's free cash flow in year 2003 of $888).
- The enterprise's new estimated terminal value at year 2003 was estimated to be $24,190 (27.2 × $888).[2]

The cash flows expected during the 5-year period (1998 to 2002), including the terminal value expected at the end of year 2003, were then discounted at the lower weighted cost of capital (R) of 11.2 percent to arrive at a present value of $17,021, which represents the enterprise value (excluding other assets). This amount was then reduced by debt and other assets to produce an estimate of total equity of $20,166 million, and an estimated target per-share price of $30.

Application of Price-Multiple Valuation Model to Fox

Turn to pages 19 and 20 of the "Fox Rocks" report and review the section in which Bear Stearns concludes that Fox is positioned for growth that should increase the current price multiple for the company. The current enterprise value (EV) to EBITDA multiple (EV/EBITDA) for Fox is 10.7 times the 1999 estimated EBITDA (adjusted for assets not consolidated). This multiple is lower than its competitors whose multiples are:

- Viacom @ 11.9×
- Disney @ 13.3×
- Time Warner @15.5×

The report concludes that there will be an expansion in the EV/EBITDA multiple from 11.5 to 13.7 (refer to Exhibit 12, page 20) as a result of an expected reduction in Fox's discount rate and increase in the growth rate in its free cash flows. Those changes equate to a higher enterprise value, equity value, and, hence, price per share of common stock.

The EV/EBITDA approach used here requires projections of the entity's price multiple and free cash flows. Estimates of future EBITDA and price multiples may be determined using one of the discounted cash flow approaches (free cash flow) previously discussed.

CONCLUDING REMARKS

In addition to reading the portions of the research report provided, we encourage you to obtain and analyze a complete copy of the Fox SEC filings, such as the 10K and 10Q reports that are available on the Internet at http://*biz.yahoo.com/ reports/edgar.html.*

NOTES

1. Raymond Lee Katz, Jeffrey A. Vilensky, and Victor B. Miller IV, "Fox Entertainment Group, Inc.—Fox Rocks," Bear Stearns (1998): 1–22.

2. Note that some rounding differences are present in this example; 27.24099 × 888 = $24,190.

"Fox Rocks" Valuation Illustration

BEAR STEARNS

EQUITY RESEARCH

Cable/Entertainment

Raymond Lee Katz
(212) 272-6857
Jeffrey A. Vilensky
(212) 272-5251
Victor B. Miller, IV
(212) 272-4233

December 7, 1998

Rating: Buy

52-Week Range
$26-$23

Earnings per Share
6/98: $0.32
6/99E: $0.46

EV/EBITDA (Cal. Yr.)
1998E: 11.5 x
1999E: 10.7x

Dividend
Nil

Yield
Nil

Com. Shares (mil)
672.3

Equity Market Capitalization (mil)
$15,547

Book Value per Share
$8.67

Est. 5-Yr EPS Growth Rate
33.4%

Bear, Stearns & Co. Inc.
245 Park Avenue
New York, New York 10167
(212) 272-2000

Fox Entertainment Group, Inc.§

(FOX-23$^1/_8$)

FOX ROCKS

- **NEW COVERAGE.** We initiated coverage on December 7 with a Buy rating, at an opening price of 23^5/_{16}$. In our opinion, Fox is a classic example of how vertical integration can pay off. The company effectively leverages its businesses off one another (studio, broadcast network, television stations, cable networks), creating value for the whole that is greater than the sum-of-the-parts. This is perhaps best exemplified by the $2-plus billion of projected off-network syndication revenues at the studio, with most coming from shows cleared by the Fox Television Network.

- **GROWING CASH FLOWS MEAN GROWING VALUES.** Fox is just breaking out of the early stage of its vertically integrated business plan. Benefits to the studio of the broadcast network's assured distribution will not be fully realized until calendar 2001, after which we expect pretax cash flows to quadruple. We think the current share price and EBITDA multiple understate this potential, especially given the upsides at the studio's television unit.

- **A TRIPLE PLAY.** If history is any guide, the convergence in 2000 of the Millennium, a presidential election without incumbents, and the summer Olympics could lead to a year-over-year increase in television advertising well above both the historical mean and the consensus forecasts. We consider Fox Broadcasting, which is covering 22 major markets as well as a national footprint, especially well positioned to capitalize on this phenomenon.

- **UNDERSTATED VALUE.** The current 10.7x multiple of our 1999 calendar year EBITDA estimate understates value given the back-ended syndication cash flow, in our view. Thus, we believe value is better captured in our DCF valuation, which dictates higher EBITDA multiples. Our 12-month target price of $30 reflects this analysis.

Source: Fox Entertainment Group, Inc. Reprinted with permission.

FOX ENTERTAINMENT GROUP, INC.§ (FOX-23¹/₈)

Company Description:

Fox Entertainment Group is one of the leading vertically integrated entertainment companies. The company is principally engaged in the development, production, and worldwide distribution of feature films and television programs. The synergies of the production and distribution platforms permit the retention of a significant portion of the film and programming's economic value. The company's major assets include the Twentieth Century Fox studio, The Fox Television Network, and 22 television stations, and interests in various cable networking companies including Fox News, Fox Family Worldwide, and Fox Liberty Sports.

Key Upcoming Events/Developments:

- The major Christmas theatrical release, *The Thin Red Line*, is due to open on December 25.

- Mid-season replacements (The Family Guy, Futurama, and the PJs, to be slotted mid-January) will be promoted during the 1999 Super Bowl.

- After the Super Bowl, investors will watch first-quarter pacings for signs of a more robust broadcast economy.

- Fox Family Channel will continue its rollout of family programming, and investors will be looking for evidence of ratings acceleration.

CAPITALIZATION (11/30/98)

	$ Mil.	%
Long-Term Debt	2,010	25.6
Equity	5,841	74.4
TOTAL	7,851	100.0

KEY FINANCIAL RATIOS

Debt/Equity	34.4%
Net Debt/EBITDA	1.7x

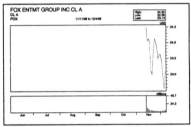

SOURCE: FACTSET RESEARCH SYSTEMS INC.

VALUATION (CALENDAR YEAR)

	1998E	1999E
Enterprise Value/EBITDA	11.5x	10.7x

QUARTERLY EARNINGS PER SHARE

	6/97	6/98	6/99E
September	NA	$0.04	$0.08A
December	NA	NA	NA
March	NA	NA	NA
June	NA	NA	NA
YEAR	$0.05	$0.32	$0.46

FINANCIAL SUMMARY
($ in millions, except per share data)

Year-End	Revenue	EBITDA Income	Margin	Operating Income	Margin	Net Income	Diluted EPS	Free Cash Flow Per Share
6/00E	$8,133	$1,111	13.7%	$845	10.4%	$390	$0.58	$0.44
6/99E	8,168	1,053	12.9	797	9.8	307	0.46	0.21
6/98	7,023	906	12.9	664	9.5	177	0.32	0.18
6/97	5,847	500	8.6	320	5.5	30	0.05	NA
6/96	4,548	578	12.7	481	10.6	411	0.75	NA

§ Within the past three years, Bear, Stearns & Co. Inc. or one of its affiliates was the manager (co-manager) of a public offering of securities of this company and/or has performed or is performing other banking services, including acting as financial advisor, for which it has received a fee.

Table of Contents

Special thanks to Adria Markus for her contributions to this report.

Fox Rocks

INVESTMENT
SUMMARY

We initiated coverage of The Fox Entertainment Group (FOX) on December 7 at an opening price of $23^5/$_{16}$, with a Buy rating and a 12-month price target of $30.

* In our opinion, this subsidiary of News Corp., Ltd. is just beginning to realize the synergies of vertically integrated manufacturing and distribution of entertainment and informational products, best exemplified by the interplay between the Twentieth Century Fox studio and The Fox Television Network. The Fox Entertainment Group is one of only four entertainment companies (along with Time Warner, Walt Disney, and Viacom) that operate a studio as well as a U.S. broadcast television network, and it is doing so most effectively. In our opinion, this vertical integration has added at least $1.3 billion to our valuation (approximately $2 per share).

While ostensibly most of the Fox Entertainment Group assets are involved with distribution, we view the company as News Corp.'s manufacturing arm, for both content and brand, for eventual worldwide distribution. For several reasons, the preponderance of distribution assets should not obscure the basic manufacturing character:

▪ Distribution must be protected (if not assured) in the competitive U.S. marketplace since the U.S. sets the value for entertainment product for the rest of the world, especially with theatrical films.

▪ The U.S.'s size, and especially the size of the English-speaking markets in aggregate, provides an economic base over which entertainment product may be amortized. In other words, controlled distribution minimizes risk.

▪ The interplay of the manufacturing and distribution assets has facilitated the establishment of an entertainment brand, nurtured in the only market where its costs can be amortized over a large enough population base.

We believe Fox Entertainment Group has been successful in creating an entertainment brand that stands for something different. News Corp. can take that brand around the world, using its satellite platforms for distribution.

Yet for the U.S. investor, Fox Entertainment Group is more than a News Corp. manufacturing arm. A strong balance sheet and the parent's backing provide a vehicle for investment in the transition of the U.S. transmission and consumption bases from analog to digital. Along the way, we would expect to find creative deal-making with joint venture partners, involving not only the cable networks but the television stations and broadcast network as well.

For all this, we believe the valuation is attractive. In many ways, Fox Entertainment Group's vertically integrated business plan is still in its infancy. The benefits of assured distribution of the Fox Television Network for the studio will not be fully felt until fiscal 2002 (late calendar 2001), at which time we expect the company's EBITDA to grow 37% from the off-network syndication of high-profile television properties. These syndication sales should produce an EBITDA compound annual growth rate of 15.1% for 1998-2004. Perhaps more important, the off-network sales should produce better than a 46% compound annual growth rate (CAGR) in free cash flow for the same period. In our opinion, the current share price and the 1999 10.7x estimated EBITDA multiple only barely reflect this growth.

At an estimated 10.7x 1999 calendar year EBITDA, Fox Entertainment Group is being priced attractively against its broadcast comparables and at a discount to its large-cap entertainment comparables. We believe there will be further multiple expansion as we get into 1999, with visibility on broadcast earnings and closer to the off-network profits in the fall of 2001. At slightly less than a 13x forward multiple, we think Fox Entertainment Group should reach $30 within 12 months and grow at a 15% rate the following year. Hence, we have initiated coverage with a Buy rating.

Company Description

As shown in the Exhibit below and in the discussion that follows, the Fox Entertainment Group consists of three major business groupings:

Exhibit 1. Fox Entertainment Group, Inc. — Organizational Chart

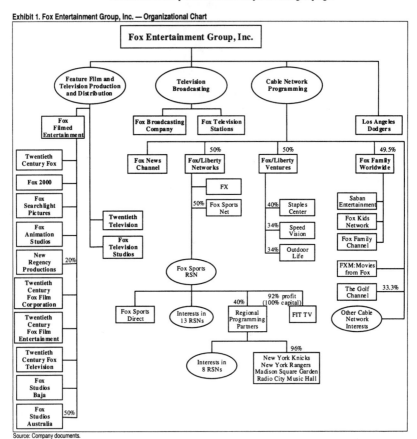

Source: Company documents.

FEATURE FILM/TV PRODUCTION AND DISTRIBUTION

Feature Film/Television Production and Distribution accounted for 1998 revenues and EBITDA of $3.9 billion and $292 million, respectively. This division is better known as the Twentieth Century Fox film studio, and is engaged in the feature film and television businesses in the following ways:

- The studio makes feature films under four imprints (20th Century Fox, Fox Searchlight, Fox 2000, and Fox Animation) and has a distribution/co-financing agreement with a fifth, New Regency Productions. Twentieth Century Fox Home Entertainment is the worldwide home video distribution subsidiary. The five feature film imprints are expected to release 25 features annually, supplying product for the home video subsidiary. Feature film product and related revenues are estimated to account for an estimated $3.0 billion in revenues, or 78% of the studio's $3.9 billion in total 1998 revenues.

- Television production and distribution are dealt with in three subsidiaries: Twentieth Century Fox Television, Twentieth Television (which, for financial reporting purposes is booked in television operations), and the Fox Television Studios. The three produce and distribute product made for primary distribution on the television screen, including first run fare for the six broadcast networks and syndication, off-network syndication, and original programming for basic and premium cable and satellite television. Television product and related revenues are estimated to account for $839 million in revenues, or 22% of the studio's $3.9 billion in total 1998 revenues.

TELEVISION BROADCASTING

Television Broadcasting had 1998 revenues and EBITDA of $3.1 billion and $727 million, respectively. This division has two major facets: The Fox Broadcasting Company, which runs the Fox Television Network (FTN), and the Fox Television Stations, which operates the 22 owned stations. They function as follows:

- The Fox Television Network (FTN) programs 15 primetime hours weekly for national distribution, with its content composed of entertainment and sports programming. Unlike the three other major networks, FTN does not program regular daytime, news, or late night. The programmed children's daypart is not part of FTN, but rather the 49.5%-owned Fox Family Worldwide (FFW). FTN represented an estimated $1.44 billion in 1998 revenues, or 47% of this segment's $3.1 billion in 1998 revenues.

- Fox Television Stations runs the 22 owned-and-operated affiliated stations. In markets covering almost 40% of U.S. television households, the stations group's markets actually account for approximately 50% of total local and national spot revenues. The television stations represented an estimated $1.39 billion in 1998 revenues, or 45% of this segment's $3.1 billion in 1998 revenues.

- The company's ownership of the Los Angeles Dodgers is booked in this line, as well as the financial impact from an indirect minority interest in the Staples center, the sports entertainment complex under construction in Los Angeles. These properties had no material impact on 1998 financial results.

<table>
<tr><td>

**CABLE NETWORK
PROGRAMMING**

</td><td>

Cable Network Programming had 1998 revenues of $72 million and an EBITDA loss of $96 million. This division has more unconsolidated than consolidated value, with the Fox News channel being the only material property consolidated for financial reporting purposes. Other properties managed in this segment include the following:

</td></tr>
</table>

- **Fox/Liberty Networks, LLC.** These are the 50%-owned and managed sports networks with TCI. The joint venture owns, manages, and has equity interests and/or affiliations with/in 21 cable regional sports networks covering more than 61 million U.S. cable and DBS households and 71 professional basketball, baseball, and hockey teams. Fox/Liberty also has a 50% interest in Fox Sports Net, a 24-hour national sports programming service. Moreover, Fox/Liberty owns and operates FX, the eighth-highest rated basic cable general entertainment network, reaching an estimated 37 million cable television households.

- **Fox Family Worldwide (FFW).** This is the 49.5%-owned family and children's programming company, distributing programming on a worldwide basis. FFW distributes its programming over-the-air through FTN affiliates both on Saturday mornings and weekday afternoons, and through the Fox Family Channel, a basic cable channel reaching over 73 million cable and DBS U.S. households. The company also owns and operates Saban Entertainment, a worldwide producer and distributor of children's programming, and operates Fox Kids channels in 28 separate countries.

- **Other.** The company also owns equity in The Golf Channel and 100% of FxM, a basic cable movie channel.

OWNERSHIP

There are 672.3 million Fox Entertainment Group shares outstanding. There are 124.8 million Class A shares held by the public, or 18.6% of the equity, and 547.5 million Class B shares beneficially held by News Corp., representing 81.4% of the equity.

Other than with respect to voting, conversion, and transfer, both classes have identical rights:

- With ten votes per share, the Class B shareholders have 97.8% of the company's vote. The Class A shareholders have one vote per share, or a total of 2.2% of the outstanding votes.

- At the option of the holder, Class B shares are convertible into Class A on a share-for-share basis.

- Class B shares will be converted into a like amount of Class A shares upon transfer to any person or entity not a permitted transferee (i.e., News Corp., direct or indirect subsidiaries, or any entity in which News Corp. directly or indirectly owns at least 50% of the equity or voting securities thereof).

It should be noted that K. Rupert Murdoch owns voting and preferred stock representing 76% of the voting power of the Fox subsidiary, Fox Television Holdings, the legal entity that owns the television stations. This structure puts the voting control for the stations into the hands of a U.S. citizen for regulatory purposes, News Corp. being an Australian company. Any impact to valuation from this structure is not material.

Valuation

**DCF IS OUR PRIMARY
VALUATION METHOD**

Our primary valuation method is discounted cash flow, which generates a risk-adjusted fair value and a 12-month price target of $30. This equates to a multiple of 1999 calendar year EBITDA of 12.9x in 12 months, or below the current average of its large-cap integrated entertainment comparables.

(Please note that, unless otherwise noted, all references are to the fiscal year. Calendar year references are duly noted, and almost always are only used in valuation discussions, unless otherwise noted.)

Why DCF?

Rather than relying primarily on a multiple of EBITDA and/or a sum-of-the-parts analysis for the company, we have chosen a discounted cash flow methodology for valuation. In our opinion, this better reflects the company's underlying economics:

- Much of the Fox Entertainment Group story is built on the synergies created through vertical integration of the broadcasting and studio assets. We believe a sum-of-the-parts analysis may understate synergies and their impact to value.

- EBITDA analysis may misrepresent the studio's underlying economics. We expect Twentieth Century Fox's cash flows to improve appreciably in fiscal 2002 from the syndication of off-network television product. A multiple of 1999 EBITDA understates that value by focusing on the near-term values, to the detriment of longer-term values. DCF captures these values. (Note that after SFAS 53 is changed, EBITDA will better reflect true cash flows. Until the rule is officially changed, we continue to present profits under the current FAS 53 method. See pages 40 to 41 for our FAS 53 discussion.)

The Mechanics

The mechanics of our model have three steps:

- Our DCF is based on first solving for the discount rate (or the market's hurdle rate) that equates our operating projections and the residual value to the current share price.

- Next, we reverse engineer the discount rate, separating it into its component parts, the cost of debt and cost of equity. The derived cost of equity is then evaluated relative to the cost of debt by comparing their spread to the historical spread between equity and fixed income returns (an average of 550 basis points between 1980 and 1997), evaluating whether it adequately reflects Fox Entertainment Group's risk to equity holders.

- Finally, we set the cost of equity equal to what we consider a fair return given our perception of the risk. This yields a new discount rate, a new residual value, and, finally, a new share price.

The Prism of Risk

Our DCF focuses as much on risk and opportunity cost as it does on potential returns. Investors have a myriad of investment choices with varying risk profiles, and we attempt to incorporate the quantification of these variables into our analysis. To evaluate the risk/reward trade-off we:

- Use the company's debt as our benchmark, since it already quantifies risk up to that point in the capital structure.

- Assume that the bond market is efficient, and that the spread between a bond's yield and a stock's implied cost of equity quantifies the excess risk incurred by the equity investor.

You Gotta Know Where You Are Before You Know Where You're Going. A basic tenet of this analysis is that before you develop a price target, you need to know what is in the current share price. The reverse engineering of the current share price (described above) provides some insight into the market's assumptions, at least through the prism of our own operating projections.

We view this as discovering not what the market is *saying*, but rather what the market *means*.

THE POT OF GOLD IS AT THE END OF THE RAINBOW

In our five-year DCF models, the residual value accounts for over 60% of the worth of Fox Entertainment Group's assets. The assumptions in its development are critical to valuation. The most critical assumption is that surrounding our assessment of return on invested capital (ROIC). To derive a residual multiple, we use projected ROIC into perpetuity. *Therefore, our residual multiple is based not on perpetual growth, but rather, perpetual returns.*

This is tricky. If it is tough to know the market's (i.e., consensus) thinking on operating projections, it is almost impossible regarding ROIC. As above, we think our model isolates what the consensus *means* as opposed to what it is *saying*. For example, a very high share price (i.e., a very high multiple) may imply a residual value built on an exceptionally high ROIC into perpetuity. A share price is the quantification of the consensus on a company's underlying economics and risk. We are confident that our methodology is directionally correct in identifying the economics and risk that underlie consensus.

The residual value is a product of a multiple applied to the last year's (2003) *normalized* unlevered free cash flow (and not EBITDA), developed through the quotient of the equation $1/(R-G)$:

- The term "R" is defined as the discount rate (i.e., marginal cost of capital).

- As we described above, our approach differs in the way we view "G." Rather than consider it as growth of unlevered free cash flow, we define it as perpetual growth in the *value* of the business (assuming unlevered free cash flow grows at a rate at least equal to the projected growth in the value of the business, at a constant discount rate).

This needs to be expanded. Given any base of invested capital, a business grows its value only by generating returns in excess of the risk-adjusted rate (i.e., the discount rate, or in our case, the marginal cost of capital).

- If returns are equal to the discount rate, then they justify claimholders' risks and there are no internally generated funds for risk-adjusted growth. In this case, growth is achieved through external investment, which in turn needs to generate incremental returns at least equal to the discount rate to justify raising the incremental capital.

- Returns below the discount rate are not sustainable in a free market. An enterprise will fail if it cannot return risk-justified rates to its investors, unless subsidized from some outside party such as the government.

- Therefore, returns above the discount (i.e., risk-adjusted) rate are necessary for *real* growth. It is this excess return, the increment above the risk-adjusted rate, that we define as "G" in our equation.

The challenge is to arrive at an analytic value for "G." Theory tells us that perpetual excess returns (a "G" greater than zero) are difficult to sustain in perfect competition; excess returns attract new entrants and are eventually driven towards zero. However, it is possible for an enterprise to generate excess returns for a period of time so that an estimate of "G" is greater than zero, especially in the absence of perfect competition.

- **The Denominator.** For Fox Entertainment Group, we define invested capital as the sum of long-term debt and the equity contributed out-of-pocket by investors (i.e., the sum of par value and additional paid-in capital). Each year, we increase the invested capital for equity contributed, and decrease it for reduction in net debt.

- **The Numerator.** This is unlevered free cash flow.

Whether viewing "G" as growth in real firm value (as we do) or as growth in free cash flow, *they are arithmetically the same*, assuming a constant discount rate. If there is real growth in firm value, there must be free cash flow growth; and if there is real (i.e., risk-adjusted) free cash flow growth, then real firm value grows as well. *Therefore, we are mathematically indifferent to whether "G" is viewed as growth in free cash flow or growth in real firm value.* However, we prefer the latter since it better focuses investors on the capital employed to generate those growth rates.

Some Caveats

Any valuation model relies as much on judgment as science, containing elements that may give pause:

- The development of the residual value involves some circularity. The discount rate is a major input in deriving a residual value that generates a share price. Yet the residual value and share price are inputs to derive the market's implied discount rate. We believe this circularity does not negate the validity of the analysis, but only dictates caution in making assumptions.

- It is impossible to know exactly what the market is thinking about ROIC into perpetuity. Our discussions with investors lead us to believe they are assuming Fox Entertainment Group is capable of "excess returns," but they still insist upon enough of a cushion in the discount rate to compensate them for uncertainty.

- We price our equity off the debt, implying an efficient bond market; that is not always the case. In addition, our definition of the marginal cost of debt may already include assumptions on refinancing. This means that future refinancing may already be in our implied discount rate, removing some of the upside from financial engineering.

- Our definition of return on invested capital (ROIC) does not dovetail with some others. We ignore some intangibles that others may consider "tangible," making our calculation of ROIC, and therefore "G," subjective.

- The 550 basis-point benchmark (the historical spread between equity and fixed income returns) is a 17-year average. Any given year has seen considerable variation from this mean, it can be argued, making comparison to the mean less meaningful.

- We do this analysis only for some of Fox Entertainment Group's assets (e.g., the studio and the television stations). Other assets (Los Angeles Dodgers, Fox/Liberty Sports equity) are valued separately using other methodologies.

RUNNING FOX   **The DCF Model.** The Fox Entertainment Group DCF model generates a risk-
THROUGH THE DCF   adjusted fair value (RAFV) price target of $30 (+30% from current levels) in 12
                     months, and $35 in 18-24 months (+15% from the 1999 target).

Solving for the Current Discount Rate. Following our model as outlined in the preceding section, we first solve for the market's implied discount rate (marginal cost of capital) and expected returns (marginal cost of equity). This can be found in Exhibits 2 through 11:

- Exhibit 2 presents our estimates for 1998-2003 fiscal year EBITDA. The CAGR for fiscal year EBITDA is estimated at 15.1%.

Exhibit 2. Given Our Estimates for FOX's EBITDA . . . (US$ millions)

Fiscal Year Ends 6/30	1998P	1999E	2000E	2001E	2002E	2003E	2004E
Television EBITDA	727	772	886	1,037	1,235	1,305	1,415
Filmed Entertainment EBITDA	292	353	283	304	550	477	525
Fox Cable	(96)	(71)	(57)	9	58	109	167
Other Charges	(17)	-	-	-	-	-	-
Total EBITDA	906	1,053	1,111	1,349	1,843	1,892	2,107
Percent Change		16.2%	5.5%	21.4%	36.6%	2.6%	11.4%
CAGR, 1998-2003	15.1%						

Source: Company documents; Bear, Stearns & Co. Inc. estimates.

- We then adjust these fiscal year EBITDA estimates and put them on a December 31 year-end basis (note that the calendarization method is taking a straight average of the two fiscal years). We remove the EBITDA from assets valued separately from the consolidated operations. These assets include (but are not limited to) Fox Cable (consisting largely of Fox News, only one of two cable properties that are consolidated) and The Fox Television Network (whose valuation discussion follows below). We also add back any capitalized interest since the DCF is unlevered. This resultant EBITDA for valuation purposes has a 1998-2003 CAGR of 10.4% (see Exhibit 3).

Exhibit 3. . . . And Our Adjustments to EBITDA for Valuation Purposes . . . (US$ millions)

	1998P	1999E	2000E	2001E	2002E	2003E	2004E
Reported Fiscal Year EBITDA	906	1,053	1,111	1,349	1,843	1,892	2,107
Less Non-Cash One-Time-Only Charges	(17)	-	-	-	-	-	-
Less Cable Network Fiscal Year EBITDA(1)	(96)	(71)	(57)	9	58	109	167
Less Fox Television Network Fiscal Year EBITDA (E)	36	6	30	74	126	118	130
Add back Fiscal Year Capitalized Interest (E)	26	26	26	26	26	26	26
Adjusted Fiscal Year EBITDA	1,009	1,145	1,164	1,292	1,685	1,690	1,836
Calendar Year EBITDA	1,077	1,155	1,228	1,489	1,687	1,763	
Percent Change		7.2%	6.4%	21.2%	13.4%	4.5%	
CAGR, 1998-2003	10.4%						

(1) Cable networks EBITDA as reported, not including the impact from amortization of carriage payments.

Source: Company documents; Bear, Stearns & Co. Inc. estimates.

- This adjusted calendar year EBITDA is then brought down to unlevered free cash flow (see Exhibit 4). One adjustment accounts for changes in operating assets and liabilities/other, and consists largely of adjustments to the P&L for off-network syndication television product; timing differences at the TV network between National Football League (NFL) rights payments and P&L amortization are a smaller element. Other adjustments are for the difference between film expenditures and amortization, capital expenditures, and unlevered cash taxes (book plus deferred). Since the analysis is unlevered, we adjust the estimated cash taxes for the interest expense tax shield. All are put on a calendar year basis.

Exhibit 4. . . . And How They Translate Into Calendar Year Unlevered Free Cash Flow . . .
(US$ millions)

Calendar Year Ends 12/31	1998E	1999E	2000E	2001E	2002E	2003E
EBITDA Used For Valuation	1,077	1,155	1,228	1,489	1,687	1,763
Change In Operating Assets & Liabilities/Other	(31)	(61)	(50)	(103)	(222)	(80)
Net Adjustment For Filmed Entert. Expenditures	(172)	(152)	(130)	(106)	(80)	(50)
Proceeds From Film Rights Agreements, net	122	-	-	-	-	-
Capital Expenditures	(252)	(259)	(193)	(164)	(165)	(158)
Unlevered Taxes	(247)	(270)	(309)	(440)	(538)	(586)
Other	-	-	-	-	-	-
Total Unlevered Free Cash Flow	497	412	546	676	684	888
Percent Change		-17.2%	32.6%	23.9%	1.1%	29.8%
CAGR, 1998-2003	12.3%					

Source: Bear, Stearns & Co. Inc. estimates.

It is important to note that the model considers the timing difference between film amortization and expenditure, and the P&L and cash flow timing differences for television syndication. Therefore, any distortion to underlying economics due to accounting treatment is removed, as per the pending change in FAS 53.

The 1998-2003 CAGR for unlevered free cash flow is estimated at 12.3%.

- To develop Fox Entertainment Group's residual multiple, we need an estimate for perpetual return on invested capital (see Exhibit 5). To do this, we use our estimate for 2003's ROIC as a guide, which is estimated at 22.0% for 2003. Our model suggests that Fox Entertainment Group's ROIC doesn't reach the current 11.9% implied marginal cost of capital until fiscal 2002. It is not coincidental that this is the first 12-month period in which the anticipated cash flows from the syndication of *King Of The Hill, Buffy The Vampire Slayer,* and *Ally McBeal* are realized. After that, we expect returns to improve considerably.

Exhibit 5. . . . And Given Our Estimate of FOX's Return on Invested Capital . . . (US$ millions)

Fiscal Year Ends 6/30	1998	1999E	2000E	2001E	2002E	2003E
TOTAL INVESTED CAPITAL						
1998 FY End Equity	5,841					
Less Book Value Of Off-Balance Sheet Assets	(791)					
1998 FY End Debt	2,010					
Total Invested Capital	7,060					
Beginning Balance		7,060	6,949	6,610	5,973	5,079
Net Of Capex & Depr. [Net Invest./(Disinvestment) In Tangible Assets]		40	(44)	(111)	(111)	(111)
Less Net Debt Reduction		(151)	(294)	(526)	(783)	(923)
Ending Balance, Invested Capital		6,949	6,610	5,973	5,079	4,045
Unlevered Free Cash Flow		412	546	676	684	888
Return On Invested Capital		5.9%	8.3%	11.3%	13.5%	22.0%
Haircut						-15%
Assumed Return On Invested Capital Into Perpetuity (Equals 2003)						18.7%

Source: Bear, Stearns & Co. Inc. estimates.

We believe the 22.0% estimate for 2003 ROIC understates Fox's economics:

1) The capital base we use to compute ROIC is the sum of total equity and long-term debt, per the estimated 1998 calendar year-end balance sheet (the equity is adjusted for the off-balance sheet assets). The equity balance is the sum of the original Fox Entertainment Group equity plus the proceeds from the November IPO. We believe the pre-IPO equity balance contains the residual effects of prior years' asset write-ups, an allowable and sometime-used practice per Australian GAAP. Therefore, we believe the equity balance is overstated relative to U.S. GAAP, overstating the invested capital and therefore understating the ROIC.

2) The invested capital base probably contains some amount attributable to the broadcast television network. While the network is not included in our consolidated DCF and is valued separately (see below), we do not break it out of the invested capital base since arriving at its invested capital base is probably impossible. Therefore, we believe the base is overstated for this variable (although we do not know by how much), understating the 2003 ROIC.

3) We estimate that television syndication product will have over $500 million of pre-tax cash flows in the post fiscal 2004 backlog (the discussion of which follows in the section on the studio and Exhibit 39). We also believe our projections could be conservative given that they do not contain any assumptions for further hits. Therefore, we are confident that ROIC in the years immediately after 2003 can improve from 2003's estimated 22.0%.

The above notwithstanding, in the interest of being conservative we have chosen to haircut the 2003 ROIC estimate 15% for an approximate 19% perpetuity number. As will be shown in Exhibits 6 and 7, this results in a terminal value based on a 19.2x multiple of unlevered free cash flow that equates to 9.7x the 2003 EBITDA estimate, and probably close to a 8.7x multiple based on calendar 2004, both reasonable figures, in our view.

- Exhibits 6 and 7 show the result of the above analysis. The metrics derived above are loaded into the unlevered DCF model and a discount rate of approximately 12% equates the cash flows and residual value to the current share price of 23^{1}/_{8}$.

Exhibit 6. . . . The Following Discount Rate and Resultant Residual Value Equate Our Projections to the Current Share Price. . . ($US millions)

Residual Value Calculation	
Assumed Perpetual Return On Invested Capital	18.7%
Discount Rate	11.9%
Excess Return (Assumed Perpetual Return Minus Discount Rate), Or G	6.7%
Residual Multiple As Applied To 2003 Unlevered Free Cash Flow (1/R-G)	19.2
Discount Rate (R)	11.9%

Source: Bear, Stearns & Co. Inc. estimates.

Exhibit 7. . . . In This DCF Model . . . (Calendar Year Estimates, US$ millions)

	1998E	1999E	2000E	2001E	2002E	2003E
Total Unlevered Free Cash Flow	497	412	546	676	684	888
Residual Value						17,016
CF Plus Residual Value To Be Discounted	497	412	546	676	684	17,904
Discount Rate	11.9%					
G (Excess return)	6.7%					
Implied Perpetual Return	18.7%					
Mult. For Last Year's Unlevered FCF	19.2					
Calendar 2003 EBITDA Mult. Implied By Res. Value	9.7					
	1998E					
NPV Of FOX Unlevered FCF	12,405					
Other Assets	5,055					
Less Net Debt	(1,909)					
Equity Value	15,550					
Shares Outstanding	672.3					
Current share Price	$ 23.13					
Note: Enterprise Value	17,460					

Source: Bear, Stearns & Co. Inc. estimates.

- When the 11.9% discount rate is disaggregated (see Exhibit 8), we find that its implied embedded cost of equity capital is 15.0%, or an 845 basis-point better return than investing in the company's debt (using a 6.55% yield for a theoretical Fox Entertainment Group ten-year non-callable debenture, or Fox Entertainment Group's marginal cost of debt).

Exhibit 8. . . . And All This Implies the Following Costs of Capital

The Following Implied Discount Rate...	11.9%
Disaggregates Into:	
Marginal Cost Of Debt (a)	6.55%
Marginal Cost Of Equity (b)	15.0%
Or A Basis Point Spread Bet. Marginal Returns For Debt & Equity Of...	845

Notes:
(a) Marginal cost of debt reflects the cost of a hypothetical non-callable 10 year senior subordinated note.
(b) Marginal cost of equity is arrived at by holding the discount rate constant at the above value and using the marginal cost of debt, above, and the weights of equity and debt in the capital structure to solve for the marginal cost of equity. Note that the equity used in the weighting is adjusted by removing the value of the assets not included in the consolidated DCF model, above (e.g., cable networks, broadcast TV network).

Source: Bear, Stearns & Co. Inc. estimates.

In the calculation deriving this equity cost, we use the sum of par value and additional paid-in capital for the equity, and book values for debt, pro forma for the equity offering. Equity book value is reduced by $791 million (6/30/98 balance), the balance in the "investments in equity affiliates," since these assets are valued separately from the consolidated DCF.

Setting the Target

Valuation always comes down to the investor's judgment. We need to analyze whether at the current return parameters and operating projections the spread between the equity and debt costs (i.e., their required returns) is in equilibrium. Given the 550 basis-point 1980-97 historical spread between equity and debt returns, the current spread of 845 basis points is 1.5 times that of the historical spread, in our opinion, higher than necessary to reflect that risk.

Fear of the impact an economic downturn would have on advertising is widening the spread (an estimated 41% of Fox Entertainment Group's revenue is derived from advertising). In 1991, during the last recession, broadcast television advertising declined 5.0%, with national network expenditures down 4.8%, national spot down 8.7%, and local spot down 3.7%. However, in the following year, TV broadcast advertising was up 8% (see Exhibit 9).

Exhibit 9. Year-over-Year Growth in Television Dollars Earned by Respective Media

	1981	1982	1983	1984	1985	1986	1987	1988	1989	1990	1991	1992	1993	1994	1995	1996	1997
Relative Growth Rates of Television Advertising Dollars																	
Network Television (ABC, CBS, NBC)	8.0%	10.9%	13.2%	19.6%	-3.1%	3.5%	1.9%	7.9%	-0.7%	3.0%	-4.8%	6.9%	-1.9%	6.3%	3.1%	11.3%	-0.9%
Local Television Stations																	
Local Spot Television	13.5%	11.8%	15.4%	17.0%	12.4%	14.0%	4.9%	6.4%	4.7%	3.2%	-3.7%	6.8%	4.4%	12.2%	5.5%	9.6%	4.5%
National Spot Television	14.6%	16.5%	10.6%	13.7%	9.4%	9.4%	4.2%	4.4%	2.9%	5.9%	-8.7%	6.2%	3.3%	15.3%	1.4%	7.5%	2.0%
Total Station Advertising Revenue	14.1%	14.3%	12.8%	15.3%	10.8%	11.7%	4.5%	5.4%	3.8%	4.5%	-6.2%	6.5%	3.9%	13.7%	3.5%	8.6%	3.3%
Cable Television																	
Cable Television (Network)	123.3%	80.6%	55.4%	62.8%	29.6%	13.9%	12.4%	23.9%	27.0%	16.4%	8.8%	10.0%	16.1%	18.0%	15.8%	26.5%	22.0%
Cable Television (Local, Non-Network)	116.7%	84.6%	58.3%	59.2%	62.0%	37.8%	13.3%	25.2%	29.8%	20.1%	17.9%	38.4%	12.1%	14.5%	25.8%	25.0%	10.5%
Total Cable Television	122.2%	81.3%	55.9%	62.2%	34.9%	18.6%	12.6%	24.2%	27.7%	17.3%	11.0%	17.3%	14.9%	17.0%	18.7%	26.0%	18.5%
Syndicated Television (Barter)	50.0%	100.0%	100.0%	40.0%	23.8%	15.4%	10.3%	13.7%	37.8%	3.1%	11.9%	7.8%	22.2%	10.0%	16.3%	10.0%	9.9%
Total Television Advertising Dollars	12.2%	14.2%	14.7%	18.7%	6.2%	9.0%	4.6%	7.7%	5.1%	5.9%	-3.0%	8.0%	4.1%	11.8%	6.8%	12.3%	4.8%
National/Local Dollar Split - Total Advertising																	
Total Local Television Advertising Dollars	26.3%	25.9%	26.2%	26.0%	27.8%	29.2%	29.4%	29.3%	29.5%	29.1%	29.3%	29.7%	30.1%	30.2%	30.6%	30.4%	30.6%
Total National Television Advertising Dollars	73.7%	74.1%	73.8%	74.0%	72.2%	70.8%	70.6%	70.7%	70.5%	70.9%	70.7%	70.3%	69.9%	69.8%	69.4%	69.6%	69.4%
National/Local Dollar Split - Station Advertising																	
Total Local Television Advertising Dollars for Station	47.3%	46.3%	47.4%	48.1%	48.8%	49.8%	50.0%	50.4%	50.9%	50.2%	51.6%	51.7%	52.0%	51.3%	52.3%	52.7%	53.4%
Total National Television Advertising Dollars for Static	52.7%	53.7%	52.6%	51.9%	51.2%	50.2%	50.0%	49.6%	49.1%	49.8%	48.4%	48.3%	48.0%	48.7%	47.7%	47.3%	46.6%
Local Dollar Split - Television Versus Cable																	
Total Local Television Advertising Dollars	99.2%	98.7%	98.3%	97.7%	96.7%	96.0%	95.7%	95.0%	93.9%	92.9%	91.5%	89.2%	88.5%	88.3%	86.4%	84.8%	84.0%
Total Local Cable Advertising Dollars	0.8%	1.3%	1.7%	2.3%	3.3%	4.0%	4.3%	5.0%	6.1%	7.1%	8.5%	10.8%	11.5%	11.7%	13.6%	15.2%	16.0%
Total Local Dollars	100.0%	100.0%	100.0%	100.0%	100.0%	100.0%	100.0%	100.0%	100.0%	100.0%	100.0%	100.0%	100.0%	100.0%	100.0%	100.0%	100.0%
National Dollar Split																	
Total Network Television Advertising Dollars	58.3%	56.4%	55.8%	56.1%	52.4%	50.8%	49.6%	49.6%	47.1%	45.5%	44.8%	44.6%	42.3%	40.3%	39.1%	38.6%	36.6%
Total Fox Television Advertising Dollars	0.0%	0.0%	0.0%	0.0%	0.0%	0.0%	0.6%	0.8%	1.3%	2.5%	3.3%	3.6%	3.8%	4.0%	5.1%	5.6%	5.5%
Total National Station Advertising Dollars	39.5%	40.0%	38.7%	37.0%	39.0%	40.0%	40.0%	38.7%	38.0%	37.8%	35.7%	35.3%	35.2%	36.4%	34.7%	33.1%	32.3%
Total National Cable Advertising Dollars	1.4%	2.2%	3.0%	4.1%	5.2%	5.5%	5.9%	6.8%	8.3%	9.0%	10.2%	10.4%	11.7%	12.3%	13.5%	15.1%	17.6%
Total Syndicated Advertising Dollars	0.8%	1.4%	2.4%	2.8%	3.4%	3.7%	3.9%	4.1%	5.4%	5.2%	6.0%	6.0%	7.1%	7.0%	7.2%	7.5%	7.9%
Total Dollars	100.0%	100.0%	100.0%	100.0%	100.0%	100.0%	100.0%	100.0%	100.0%	100.0%	100.0%	100.0%	100.0%	100.0%	100.0%	100.0%	100.0%

Source: McCann Erickson Worldwide; Bear, Stearns & Co. Inc. estimates. In 1996, McCann Erickson made revisions back to 1980 for previously reported figures for Cable TV network, Cable (non-network), Miscellaneous and the National, Local, and Grand-totals.

In 1991, this led to multiple contraction for the average broadcaster (which were then made up largely of the network-dominated stocks). Will multiples fall to the same level today? While there is nervousness that the broadcast economy is slowing, there are some important differences between 1991 and 1998:

- Concurrent with the 1991 recession was a credit crunch engendered by the Controller of the Currency's high leveraged transaction (HLT) restrictions. Leveraged broadcasters had virtually no access to capital, and equity valuations reflected this. Today's conditions in the high yield market are analogous to this 1991 condition.

- Interest rates were considerably higher in 1991. On January 1, 1991, the 30-year Treasury bond was yielding 8.25%. As of last week, the long bond's yield was $5^1/_8\%$, or 312 basis points lower than the 1991 figure.

- Both 1991 and 1999 follow years of political spending, leading to tough year-over-year comparisons. However, 1999 could see the beginnings of a flurry of Millennium advertising, which we think has the potential to be a significant element in the revenue mix.

  The year 1976 makes this point. With the concurrence of a Bicentennial, a presidential election without incumbents, and two Olympics, television advertising showed a year-over-year increase of 20.7% in constant dollars, the largest such increase in the past 35 years. With a 2000 concurrence of a Millennium, a presidential election without incumbents, and a summer Olympics, we think 1999 and 2000 could provide upside surprises.

Therefore, we believe the solved-for spread between Fox Entertainment Group's marginal costs of equity and debt is too large. Even a 100 basis-point reduction in the debt/equity spread would generate meaningful appreciation. This would bring the marginal cost of equity down from 15% to 14%, with a reduction in the discount rate to 11.2% from approximately 12% (see Exhibit 10). The result would be a RAFV and target price of $30, or 30% higher than the current share price (see Exhibit 11). Our 18- to 24-month price target with this discount rate is $35 (+15% from the 1999 target and 50% from the current share price).

Exhibit 10. However, We Are More Comfortable With the Following Metrics for Valuation . . .

A Discount Rate Of...	11.2%
Coming From:	
A Marginal Cost Of Debt Of (a)	6.6%
And A Marginal Cost Of Equity Of (b)	14.0%
For A Basis Point Spread Between Marginal Returns For Debt & Equity Of...	745

Source: Bear, Stearns & Co. Inc. estimates.

Exhibit 11. . . . Which Generate the Following Price Targets in Our DCF
(Calendar Year Estimates; US$ millions)

		1998E	1999E	2000E	2001E	2002E	2003E
Total Unlevered Free Cash Flow		497	412	546	676	684	888
Residual Value							24,190
CF Plus Residual Value To Be Discounted		497	412	546	676	684	25,078
Discount Rate		11.2%					
G (Excess return)		7.5%					
Implied Perpetual Return		18.7%					
Mult. For Last Year's Unlevered FCF		27.2					
Calendar 2003 EBITDA Mult. Implied By Res. Value		13.7					
			Targets				
			RAFV	8-24 Mo.			
NPV Of FOX Unlevered FCF			17,021	18,922			
Other Assets			5,055	5,977			
Less Net Debt			(1,909)	(1,612)			
Equity Value			20,166	23,287			
Shares Outstanding			672.3	672.3			
Risk Adjusted Fair Value		$	30.00	$34.64			
Percent Change From Current Price	$ 23.13		29.7%				
Percent Change From RAFV/Prior Year Target				15%			
Percent Change From Current Price				50%			
Note: Enterprise Value			22,076	24,899			

Source: Bear, Stearns & Co. Inc. estimates.

Talking in EBITDA

The current $23^{1}/_{8}$ share price translates into an adjusted enterprise value/EBITDA multiple of 10.7x 1999 estimated EBITDA (adjusted for valuation purposes; see Exhibit 12), and 11.5x 1998's calendar year estimate (which at this point is almost trailing 12-month cash flow). Our 1999 and 2000 DCF target prices translate into a 13.7x multiple as applied to 1999 EBITDA and 12.9x 2000 EBITDA (see Exhibit 12).

Exhibit 12. . . . All of Which Translates Into the Following EBITDA Valuation Model (US$ millions)

	1998P	1999E	2000E
Current Share Price	$ 23.13		
Target Price (12 & 24 Months Out)		$ 30.00	$ 34.64
Percent Change Versus Current/Target		30%	15%
Shares Outstanding	672.3	672.3	672.3
Equity	15,547	20,172	23,289
Calendar Year End Net Debt	1,909	1,612	1,202
Capitalization	17,456	21,783	24,490
Less Assets Not Valued On A Consolidated EBITDA Basis	(5,055)	(5,977)	(6,807)
Adjusted Enterprise value	12,402	15,806	17,683
Calendar Year EBITDA Used For Valuation	1,077	1,155	1,228
AT THE CURRENT SHARE PRICE			
1998 Adj. Enterprise Value/Multiple Of 1998 CY EBITDA	11.5		
1998 Adjusted Enterprise Value/Multiple Of 1999 CY EBITDA	10.7		
TARGET MULTIPLES FOR CURRENT YEAR'S EBITDA		13.7	14.4
TARGET MULTIPLES FOR FORWARD YEAR'S EBITDA		12.9	11.9

Source: Bear, Stearns & Co. Inc. estimates.

These compare favorably with broadcasting and large-cap integrated entertainment names (see Exhibit 13):

Exhibit 13. Fox Entertainment Group Comparables

	Price	EBITDA Mult. 1998E	EBITDA Mult. 1999E	FOX 99 Mult. As % Of...
FOX	$23.13	11.5	10.7	
Large-Cap Entertainment				
Disney	$ 31.44	13.6	13.3	80%
Time Warner	$ 106.00	17.4	15.5	69%
Viacom	$ 65.00	13.5	11.9	90%
Average		14.8	13.6	
Broadcasters				
Sinclair	$ 13.56	10.5	9.9	108%

Source: Bear, Stearns & Co. Inc. estimates.

- Of the broadcasters, the more comparable Sinclair (in scope and exposure to the Fox Television Network) trades at 9.9x estimated 1999 EBITDA, in line with Fox Entertainment Group. Granite sells at 10.5x. These comparables are leveraged at an average of 8.4x, with their valuations affected by the contraction of the high yield market. Fox Entertainment Group, on the other hand, is leveraged at 1.7x estimated 1999 EBITDA, and does not face the same potential for reduced access to capital. Therefore, we would maintain that Fox Entertainment Group is favorably valued against its broadcasting comparables, with (we believe) better fundamentals, potential synergies, and strategic positioning (more detail on this appears in the discussion of operations, below).

- Fox Entertainment Group's 10.7x 1999 multiple is lower than that of its large-cap entertainment comparables. These comparables all have less broadcasting exposure, but not necessarily less cyclical or "event" exposure:

  1) **Viacom** (11.9x estimated 1999 EBITDA) has a continual issue with Blockbuster and the impending IPO and/or spin-off.

  2) **Disney** (13.3x estimated 1999 calendar year EBITDA) has large cyclical exposure, with over half of revenue cyclically based (e.g., theme parks, retail, broadcasting) and as much as 20% coming from advertising.

  3) **Time Warner** (15.5x estimated 1999 EBITDA) has only an estimated 15% of revenue coming from advertising, and a large part of its EBITDA is generated by less-cyclical cable operations. Yet it still wrestles with an under-performing music division and slump in theatrical films at Warner Bros.

Fox Already Appears Reasonably Priced for an Economic Slowdown

In our opinion, the above comparables imply that Fox Entertainment Group is already being priced for some economic slowdown. Therefore, we think there can be multiple expansion (a reduction in the discount rate) coming from the perceived reduction in risk. The target discount rate for our RAFV (just above 11%) translates into a 13.7x multiple of 1999 calendar EBITDA. Further reduction in perceived risk, coming from a broadcast economy that re-accelerates by the middle of 1999, could take the discount rate down further, resulting in an even higher multiple as applied to the then forward year's (2000) calendar year EBITDA. The result of the former is a $30, 12-month price target. Extension of this analysis into 2000 yields a $35 price target 24 months out, with further upside from a lower discount rate (i.e., risk).

Assets Valued Outside the Main DCF Model. We run only the studio and TV stations through our discounted cash flow model (or an estimated 71% of total Fox Entertainment Group enterprise value). All other assets, including the television network and the cable properties, are valued separately, albeit with most of them using DCF given their start-up nature. These assets valued outside of the main DCF model aggregate $5.0 billion in value, and are expected to grow at an average annual rate of 16% (see Exhibit 14).

Exhibit 14. Fox Group Assets Not Valued On a Consolidated EBITDA Basis (US$ millions)

	1998P	1999E	2000E
Cable Networks:			
Fox News	562	635	718
Fox/Liberty Networks (Includes FX)	1,404	1,813	2,139
Fox/Liberty Ventures	95	104	113
Fox Family Worldwide	704	796	899
FxM	41	46	52
Golf Channel	50	58	66
Total Cable Networks Value	2,856	3,452	3,988
Fox Television Network	1,654	1,853	2,075
Regency International	80	160	178
Sports Teams (Dodgers and options on other teams)	345	380	418
Note Receivable From FFW	119	133	148
Total	5,055	5,977	6,807
Percent Change		18.3%	13.9%

Source: Bear, Stearns & Co. Inc. estimates.

Cable Networks. Total cable network values are estimated at $2.9 billion, growing to $3.5 billion in 1999 (+21%) and $4 billion in 2000 (+15%); (see Exhibit 15). Fox's cable networks are essentially start-ups, and of the six properties, only two are consolidated (Fox News and the nascent FxM). Given that they are start-ups, estimates for perpetual ROIC, and therefore "G," could eventually be higher than we believe the market attributes to the core (and more mature) consolidated Fox Entertainment Group operations.

Exhibit 15. Fox Entertainment Group — Fox Cable: Valuation Summary (US$ millions)

	Ownership	1998E	1999E	2000E
Fox News	100.0%	562	635	718
Fox/Liberty Networks (Includes FX)	50.0%	1,404	1,813	2,139
Fox/Liberty Ventures	50.0%	95	104	113
Fox Family Worldwide	49.5%	704	796	899
FxM	100.0%	41	46	52
Golf Channel	33.0%	50	58	66
Total		2,856	3,452	3,988
Percent Change			20.9%	15.5%

Source: Bear, Stearns & Co. Inc. estimates.

Fox/Liberty Sports. This property owns equity in and/or manages 21 regional cable sports networks (RSNs), a national sports programming service, as well as other miscellaneous assets. Fox Entertainment Group's 50% equity is valued at $1.4 billion, putting the total equity value for the property at $2.8 billion and the enterprise value at $4.1 billion (including debt). With the exception of the Fox Sports Net national service, we do not value this asset on a DCF basis. Instead, we use a multiple of EBITDA for the more mature regional sports networks and a per-subscriber multiple for some of the younger properties (see Exhibit 16).

Chapter 7

Derivatives

INTRODUCTION

This chapter provides an explanation of the different types of derivative instruments and how they may be commonly used. Fundamental derivative pricing concepts also are explained.[1]

From an economic standpoint, a derivative is a contract that derives its value based on the changes in an underlying, such as a specified number of shares, a share's price, an interest rate, or a commodity price.[2] A derivative contract can utilize significant leverage, since an underlying may reference a large notional amount. For example, one may enter into a five-year swap based on a notional principal amount of $100 million and agree to receive a fixed rate of interest and to pay a variable rate of interest on the notional amount. While this arrangement could provide large cash outflows or inflows, an initial investment could be worth little or nothing. The variable rate used in swaps usually is referenced to LIBOR, although other rates may be used. The variable rate will reset periodically, as agreed on in the contract.

The derivative just mentioned can be used to hedge interest rate risk. For example, a financial institution may have invested in assets that are less responsive to interest rate changes than its liabilities. Therefore, it may choose to increase the duration (and, hence, interest rate risk) of its assets to match the liability's duration.

Next we analyze the most common types of derivative instruments.

FORWARD CONTRACTS

Forward contracts are negotiated between two parties to purchase (sell) a specific quantity of a commodity, a foreign currency, or a financial instrument at a specified price, with delivery or settlement at a specified future date. Because forward contracts are not formally regulated by or traded on an organized exchange, each party to the contract is subject to potential default risk of the other party.

How Can One Purchase or Enter into a Forward Contract? Is There an Initial Cash Payment?

Forward contracts may be entered into through an agreement without a cash payment provided the forward rate is equal to the current *at-the-money* market-forward rate. If originated off-market (e.g., the forward rate is $310 for a specified quantity of a commodity yet the contract references a different amount), some initial cash flow would be required. Usually forward contracts are entered into over the phone using banks or brokers. A compensating bank balance or margin account may be required as security.

What Are the Expected Cash Flows?

Forward contracts do not have cash flows during the contract term.

How Are Forward Contracts Settled?

At maturity, a forward contract is settled by delivering the item specified in the contract, such as a commodity, a foreign currency, or a financial instrument. Contract provisions also may permit a net cash settlement.

General Pricing Model for Forward Contracts

Valuation at Contract Inception

Forward contracts usually are priced at-the-money at origination, which means that the fair value of the contract is zero and no cash payment is made. The most important aspect of forward contract pricing entails the determination of an agreed-on forward price. Pricing concepts for forward contracts (excluding foreign exchange) are simple. The forward agreed-on price is calculated based on the existing spot price, the interest cost of carrying the item over the term of the contract, storage costs (if any), and any yield on the item. The interest cost or rate is determined by reference to the risk-free Treasury rate. The formula is:

$$\text{Forward Price} = \text{Spot price} \times (1 + \text{interest rate} + \text{carrying costs} - \text{yield})^t$$

Where:
- spot price = the current price of a commodity, financial instrument, etc.
- yield = the income that the holder of the underlying would receive (i.e., a dividend related to a common stock)
- t = the time period

For example, an entity, ActionSportsCo, is required by its supplier to lock into the price of titanium purchases that will occur in six months. At January 1, 20X1, ActionSportsCo is required to enter into a firm commitment with its supplier to purchase the titanium at the current forward price of $310 per unit on June 30, 20X1. ActionSportsCo does not want to lock into this price but prefers to pay the market price in six months, since it expects prices to fall. Therefore, at January 1, 20X1, the company enters into a forward contract to sell titanium at the forward price of $310 per unit at June 30, 20X1, to offset the January 1, 20X1, firm commitment. In this situation, the spot price is known, and it is assumed there are no carrying costs or yields involved. The forward price is calculated based on the January 1, 20X1, $300 spot price multiplied by 1 plus the risk-free rate of 6.5 percent (for 6 months) (calculator keystrokes: 300 [PV], 3.25 [i], 1 [n], [FV]). Therefore, the forward price (rounded to a whole number) is calculated as:

$$\text{Forward Price} = 300(1 + .065)^{.5} = 310$$

Foreign currency forward price calculations are complicated by the need to factor in the interest rate differential that may exist between two countries. The relationship between currency spot rates and currency forward rates is expressed by:

$$FX_t = \frac{\text{Spot}_t(1 + R_{it})^t}{(1 + R_{2t})^t}$$

Where:
- FX_t = forward foreign exchange price (FX_1/FX_2), between countries 1 and 2 in period t
- Spot_t = spot foreign exchange price (FX_1/FX_2) in the current period
- R_{1t} = interest rate for country 1 in period t
- R_{2t} = interest rate for country 2 in period t

If this relationship did not hold, arbitrage opportunities would be present. Just as arbitrage arguments dictate the relationship between forward foreign exchange prices and interest rates, those relationships also must hold true for currency prices among countries.[3] For example, assume these interest rates for 90-day Treasury instruments in the U.S. and Japan:

	U.S.	Japan
Annual rate (in percentages)	4.84%	0.48%
Quarterly rate (in percentages)	1.21%	0.12%
Spot rate	140.22 J¥/US$	

Given those assumptions, the forward foreign exchange rate of Japanese yen for U.S. dollars at the end of the first quarter must be:

$$FX = 140.22 \times (1.0012/1.0121) = 138.71 \text{ J¥/US\$}$$

If the forward foreign currency rate is higher or lower than 138.71 J¥/US$, an investor could make alternative investment decisions and obtain a risk-free incremental (arbitrage) profit.

Valuation during and at Expiration of the Forward Contract Term

The value of a forward contract after it is entered into is determined by four factors:

1. Price changes in the forward contract's underlying, such as the price of titanium for delivery at June 30, 20X1
2. The discount rate used to calculate present values
3. The time to expiration
4. The notional amount of the contract, defined in terms of the number of units, shares, dollars, or other items applied to the underlying, which is used to determine the settlement amount.

Uses of Forward Contracts

The following cases illustrate uses of forward contracts.

Fair Value Hedge of a Titanium Firm Commitment

ActionSportsCo enters into a firm commitment with its supplier to purchase 10,000 units of titanium on June 30, 20X1, at the current forward price of $310 per unit. ActionSportsCo is in a "long" firm purchase commitment, that is, the company has been economically placed in an ownership position and is locked into buying titanium at $310 per unit. ActionSportsCo does not want to be locked into this price because it expects prices to fall. Therefore, it wants to pay the market price at June 30, 20X1. As discussed earlier, ActionSportsCo takes a "short" position in titanium by entering into the forward contract on January 1, 20X1, to unlock this commitment and be able to pay the market price for titanium at June 30, 20X1. The contract allows the company to sell 10,000 units of titanium at the forward price of $310 at June 30, 20X1.

Question: At March 31, 20X1, the June 30, 20X1, forward price has dropped to $297 because of decreases in the price of titanium. What does this mean to ActionSportsCo?

Answer: ActionSportsCo has a gain of $13 per unit on the forward contract because it has locked in the sales price at the higher amount ($310) on the underlying (titanium). Because the contract is for 10,000 units (the notional), the gain is $130,000. However, recall that ActionSportsCo cannot receive this benefit until June 30, 20X1. Therefore, the March 31, 20X1, value of the forward contract is calculated as the present value of $130,000. The present value of $130,000 to be received in three months and discounted at 6 percent is $128,079 (calculator keystrokes: 130,000 [FV], 1.5 [i], 1 [n], [PV]). ActionSportsCo also has an offsetting loss on the firm commitment of $128,079.

Question: At June 30, 20X1, the spot rate is $285 per unit (i.e., the price of titanium drops further to $285). What is ActionSportsCo's total gain on the forward contract?

Answer: ActionSportsCo's total gain is $25 ($310 less $285) per unit times 10,000, or $250,000. This $250,000 gain on the forward contract offsets the $250,000 loss on the firm purchase commitment.

Foreign Currency Hedge of a Firm Purchase Commitment with a Forward Contract

The case fact pattern is as follows:

- On September 30, 2001, the GlobalTechCo firm, a U.S. company, issues a purchase order to a foreign supplier for equipment to be delivered and paid for on March 31, 2002. The price of the equipment is denominated in the foreign currency (FC), which is FC 10 million.
- At September 30, 2001, the spot rate is assumed to be FC1 = US$0.65, and the six-month forward rate is FC1 = US$0.66.
- On September 30, GlobalTechCo simultaneously enters into a forward-exchange contract that matures on March 31, 2002, in order to receive FC 10 million and pay U.S. $6.6 million ($0.66 × 10 million). This contract locks in the U.S. dollar price at $6.6 million that the company will pay to acquire the foreign currency to pay for the equipment, irrespective of FC rate movements. The company is in the position of being "long" in the forward contract, which means that it has locked in the future foreign exchange rate.

Question: At December 31, 2001, the March 31, 2002, forward exchange rate has increased to FC1 = U.S. $0.68 because of weakness with the dollar, relative to the foreign currency. What is the impact of this rate movement on the fair value of the forward contract?

Answer: The forward contract has locked in the company's right and obligation to receive FC1 = $0.66 at March 31, 2002, or $6.6 million based on the FC 10 million notional amount of the forward contract. Because the U.S. dollar is weakening relative to FC, market conditions at March 31, 2002, based on this forward rate, would have required the company to pay $6.8 million for FC 10 million (10 million times $0.68). Because the forward contract locked in the March 31, 2002, exchange rate at FC1 = U.S.$0.66 ($6.6 million for the total contract), the forward contract has a $200,000 gain ($6.8 million less $6.6 million) to be received at March 31, 2002. The present value at December 31, 2001, of receiving this amount at March 31, 2002 (assuming a 6 percent discount rate) is $197,044 (calculator keystrokes: 200,000 [FV], 1 [n], 1.5 [i], [PV]). This gain represents the forward contract's fair value at December 31, 2001.

Question: At March 31, 2002, the spot rate is FC1 = U.S. $0.69. What is the impact of this rate movement on the fair value of the forward contract?

Answer: The total gain on the forward contract is $300,000, calculated as 10 million times $0.03 (the March 31, 2002, rate of FC1 = U.S.$0.69, less the locked-in rate of FC1 = U.S.$0.66). The gain for the quarter ending March 31, 2002, comprises the time value from the December 31, 2001, gain and the rate movement in the quarter ended March 31, 2002. This gain exactly offsets the $300,000 extra cost of the equipment.

Do Forward Contracts Have Symmetric or Asymmetric Return Profiles?

Forward contracts entered into at-the-money (i.e., at a fair value equal to zero) have symmetric return profiles, meaning that the values of the forward contract (which result in gains and losses) may change equally in both directions as the price of the underlying changes. In contrast, an option contract, discussed below, has an asymmetric return profile because if the option becomes *out-of-the-money,* the holder is not obligated to exercise the option, and it expires worthless. If the option contract moves to an in-the-money position, the holder will exercise it at a gain.

What Are Common Risk Management Strategies That Employ Forward Contracts? What Risk Management Strategies Are Inconsistent with the Instrument's Return Profile?

Forward contracts often are used to hedge the entire price change of a commodity, a foreign currency, or a financial instrument. For example, in the Action-SportsCo fair value hedge of the titanium firm purchase commitment, the company was hedging the entire forward price change of titanium, irrespective of whether it increased or decreased. Because forward contracts have symmetrical return profiles, it would be ineffective to designate a forward contract to hedge the price or cash flow changes from a one-directional change, such as only a potential decrease in the price of titanium. In this case, if titanium prices increase, the forward contract to sell titanium at a fixed price would lose value because there is no option to not exercise, and this is inconsistent with a risk management strategy to hedge only for price decreases.

Also review case illustration No. 6 in Appendix F at the end of this chapter, which illustrates a forward contract used in a Treasury-rate lock hedge.

FUTURES CONTRACTS

Futures contracts are standardized forward-based contracts to make or take delivery of a specified quantity of a commodity, a foreign currency, or a financial instrument at a specified price with delivery or settlement at a future date. Futures contracts are traded on a regulated exchange and, as a result, have less credit risk than forward contracts. U.S. Treasury note (interest rate) futures, S&P futures, and Eurodollar futures contracts are examples of widely traded financial futures contracts. Generally, a forward or futures contract for the identical underlying, such as a five-year Treasury note, should produce identical economic results if the futures contract's daily settlement amounts can be reinvested at certain assumed rates.

How Do Futures Differ from Forwards?

Some important differences between forwards and futures contracts are discussed next:

- Futures are standardized contracts that are traded on an organized exchange, whereas forwards are not. Futures contracts are highly uniform contracts that specify the quantity and quality of the good that can be delivered, the delivery date(s), the method for closing the contract, and the permissible minimum and maximum price fluctuations permitted in a trading day.
- Futures contracts for bonds have optionality, since the seller will deliver, or reference, the cheapest-to-deliver bond. For example, a futures contract on a five-year Treasury note will not specify a specific note. In contrast, a forward contract references a specific bond in the case of a forward contract on a bond.
- Futures are generally more liquid and have less credit risk than forwards because organized exchanges have clearinghouses that guarantee that all of the traders in the futures market will honor their obligations. Active markets exist in the United States for most financial and commodity futures contracts.
- Futures contracts are marked to market and require initial and maintenance margin deposits. The maintenance margin is the amount that must be left on deposit throughout the life of the futures position. If the value in an equity account drops to or below the level of the required maintenance margin, a variation-margin amount must be deposited to bring it back to the required level. As a result, futures contracts require daily cash settlements for the change in the contract's value. In contrast, cash payments on forward contracts generally do not occur until the contract's maturity date. For example, assume an entity, the XYZ Company, enters into a cash flow hedge of a forecasted issuance of debt, using five-year Treasury futures. In this case, any gains on the futures are received in cash (or reflected in a margin account) over the contract term.

Types of Futures Contracts

Futures contracts fall into five fundamentally different categories[4]:

1. Agricultural and metallurgical
2. Energy
3. Interest-earning assets
4. Indexes (usually a stock index)
5. Foreign currency

Purposes of Futures Markets

The futures market, like the stock market, is efficient in that the prices of the contracts that trade on the exchanges reflect all available economic, political, and other relevant information at a given point in time.

How Can Each Counterparty to a Futures Contract Be Sure That Each Party Will Fulfill the Agreement?

Traders do not actually execute transactions directly with each other. Instead, when traders agree on price and quantity for each trade, the transactions are executed with a clearinghouse that interposes itself between the buyer and the seller to guarantee performance by both parties to the contract.

Each futures exchange is associated with a clearinghouse, which may be a separate strongly capitalized financial institution or may be part of the futures exchange. The clearinghouse:

- Guarantees that all of the traders in the futures market will honor their obligations by adopting the position of buyer to every seller and seller to every buyer.
- Takes no active position in the market except by interposing itself between all parties to every transaction. Therefore, every trader in the futures market has obligations only to the clearinghouse and, in return, expects the clearinghouse to fulfill its side of the bargain.
- Substitutes its own credibility for the promise of each trader in the market.

How Can One Purchase or Enter into a Futures Contract? Is There a Cash Payment?

A futures contract is entered into through an organized exchange using banks and brokers. Although no payment is made upon entering into the futures contract, since the underlying (i.e., interest rate, share price, or commodity price) is at-the-market, subsequent value changes require daily mark-to-marking by cash settlement.

What Are the Expected Cash Flows? What Economic Changes Impact Those Cash Flows?

Price movements in the underlying security or commodity affect futures contracts' cash flows, resulting from the periodic settlements that were discussed above. Economic conditions that cause price movements depend on the nature of the futures; for example, changing interest rates impact fixed-income security futures contracts. As stated above, all daily market value changes result in a cash settlement.

What Are Important Valuation Considerations for Futures Contracts?

The valuation concepts for a futures contract follow the same principles as for forward contracts. Similar to a forward contract, a futures contract price is calculated based on the existing spot price, a rate of interest, and the costs of carrying the item over the term of the contract, and then adjusted for any expected yield on the item. As previously discussed in pricing forward contracts, the yield relates to cash flows on the underlying security or commodity, such as dividends. Different variations of future's pricing formulas are used, depending on the referenced asset. For example, the following formula illustrates the pricing for a Treasury note futures contract:

$$\text{Futures Price} = P(1 + T (R - C))$$

Where:
- P = current cash price of a Treasury note of a certain maturity
- T = time to futures delivery in years
- R = financing rate for the financial instrument
- C = current yield on the Treasury note

For example, if we assume the information provided below, we will estimate the Treasury futures price as:

$$\text{Treasury futures price} = 100.6 = 100.5(1 + (.5(.057 - .055)))$$

Where:
- P = current cash price of a five-year Treasury note (assumed to be equal to 100.5)
- T = time to futures delivery in years (assume six months)
- R = financing rate for a five-year instrument (assumed equal to .057)
- C = current yield on a five-year Treasury note (assumed at .055)

Note that other formulas are used for different types of futures contracts.[5] In addition, most commodity contracts, such as those on corn, require delivery of a contract, which is held to settlement. If used for hedging purposes without taking delivery, the contracts are closed out prior to expiration by bringing the position to zero. This is accomplished by entering into an offsetting futures position. In contrast, a Eurodollar contract can be settled only on a net basis.

How Is the Contract Settled?

There are two ways to close a futures position:

1. Completion through delivery of the commodity

2. Completion through an "offset" or via a reversing trade, which, by far, is the most prevalent practice

To complete a futures contract obligation through an offset, the trader transacts in the futures market to bring the net position in a particular futures contract back to zero. For example, if a party bought a futures contract to purchase a commodity (i.e., wheat) at a certain price in the future, the party will take exactly the opposite position by selling an equivalent futures contract for wheat.

Do Futures Contracts Have Symmetric or Asymmetric Return Profiles?

Futures contracts have symmetric return profiles that are identical to forward contracts. That means that the value of a contract changes in both directions as the price of the underlying changes in both directions.

What Are Common Risk Management Strategies for Employing This Type of Contract? What Risk Management Strategies Are Inconsistent with the Instrument's Return Profile?

Futures contracts may be used to hedge certain price changes of a commodity, a foreign currency, or a financial instrument.

Because futures contracts have symmetric return profiles, it would be ineffective to designate a futures contract to hedge price or cash flow changes from a one-directional price change in the hedged item.

Review case study illustrations Nos. 1, 2, and 7 in Appendix F at the end of this chapter for hedges involving futures contracts.

OPTION CONTRACTS

The purchaser of an option has the right but not the obligation to buy or sell a specified quantity of a particular commodity, a foreign currency, or a financial instrument at a specified price during a specified period of time (American option) or on a specified date (European option). Two common types of option contracts are call options and *put options*. American options that can be settled at any time during the option term will be discussed.

Call Options

Call options provide the holder with the right to acquire an underlying at an exercise or strike price. The holder pays a premium for the right to benefit from the appreciation in the underlying. For example, assume that GlobalTechCo purchases a call option on five-year Treasury note futures to hedge the cash flow variability of a forecasted purchase of $100 million of 6 percent, five-year Treasury notes.

Assume that the option was purchased at-the-money, which means that the intrinsic value was zero at acquisition. This may occur because the forward market rate for five-year Treasury notes was 6 percent and the option on futures contracts was also at the same forward rate of 6 percent. If market interest rates subsequently decrease below the 6 percent Treasury forward rate, the call option becomes in-the-money as its value increases. This means that the holder can exercise the option and realize the gain from the increase in the fair value of the Treasury notes. This occurs because the prices of 6 percent, five-year Treasury notes will rise as the market yield decreases, yet the option allows the investor to buy them at the option strike price, which is $100 million par in this case. For example, if the interest rates decline and the new yield for five-year Treasury notes becomes 5 percent, an investor would pay 104.376 for a five-year, 6 percent Treasury note, or a premium of 4.376. This can be calculated as the present value of the 1 percent additional interest earned on the $100 million par value over the five-year term. Since a Treasury note pays interest on a semiannual basis, this can be calculated as 5 [PMT], 10 [n], 2.5 [i], [PV].

Therefore, the option's intrinsic value at the end of the option term is $4.376 million.

If rates increase above 6 percent, the value of the call option decreases and will become out-of-the-money, which means its exercise price exceeds the current market price. In this situation, the holder would not exercise the option and it would expire worthless. From the seller's standpoint, if rates increase, the seller has been relieved of the liability to pay for any appreciation associated with the five-year Treasuries because the option is out-of-the-money. The seller therefore has gained the entire premium charged for the call option.

Put Options

Put options provide the holder with the right to sell the underlying at an exercise or strike price throughout the option term. The holder gains as the market price of the underlying falls below the strike price. For example, assume an entity purchases a put option to hedge the fair value of 1,000 shares of ABC stock that is selling at $100 per share. Assume that the option was purchased at-the-money. That is, the intrinsic value of the option (calculated as the exercise price less the price per share of stock, times the number of shares specified in the option contract) was zero at acquisition. (Thus, the assumption is that the strike price and market price of ABC stock at the inception of the contract was $100.) If the stock price falls below $100, the put becomes in-the-money by the amount below the $100 strike price times the number of option shares. In this case, assume the price of ABC stock fell to $98. The intrinsic value gain on the put option is $2 per share.

If the stock price rises and stays above $100 for the term of the contract, the put option expires worthless to the buyer because it is out-of-the-money. However, the option seller keeps the premium.

(Note that the actual values [or premiums] of the options described above are a function of other variables in addition to those included in intrinsic value, as discussed below.)

What Is the Principal Difference between an Option Contract and Either a Futures or a Forward Contract?

The primary difference is that the purchaser will exercise an option only if exercise would be favorable. (Some options exercise automatically when they benefit the holder, for example, caps and floors.) However, performance is mandatory under a futures or forward contract. Therefore, options have asymmetric or one-sided return profiles.

What Are the Advantages of an Option to the Buyer and Seller (Writer)?

The purchaser of an option pays a premium to the writer to receive the right to profit if the price of the underlying item moves in a certain direction while limiting the potential loss to the amount of premium paid for the option. The writer of an option takes a risk that potentially may result in a profit that is limited to the premium received. The writer's loss potential, however, can be substantial (and is unlimited with a call option) because the writer is obligated to settle at the exercise price (or strike price) if and when the option is exercised (which may be significantly different from the actual price of the underlying item).

How Is the Premium (or Price) That a Writer of an Option Receives Determined?

The premium (or price) that a writer of an option receives and that a buyer pays comprises:

- Intrinsic value of the option
- Both components of time value:
  - Value associated with the effects of discounting (pure time value). This relates to the discount rate and option's term and will be discussed further below.
  - Volatility value of the option (also discussed below).

For example, the intrinsic value of a call option on common stock is equal to the excess of the market price of the stock over the exercise price, times the specified number of shares of stock that can be purchased with the option. An option purchased at- or out-of-the-money has no value from the intrinsic value component of the option because it is zero. The intrinsic value of a put option on common stock, as discussed above, is equal to the excess of the exercise price over the market price of the stock, times the specified number of shares that can be sold.

The combination of the effect of discounting for the time value of money and the volatility value of an option is commonly referred to as the time value because those components converge to a zero value as the option expires.

- The effect of discounting is due to the time value of the free financing provided by the option. This equates to the interest that could be earned by investing the dollar amount of the exercise price (which does not have to be paid today) over the time period from the day the option is purchased until its expiration date. Therefore, the higher the level of interest rates, the lower the present value of the exercise price, the higher the value of a call option, and the lower the value of a put option (everything else constant).
- The volatility value depends on the probability that the price of the underlying asset will be above the exercise price (call option) or below the exercise price (put option) at the expiration date of the option. The higher the volatility of the underlying, the higher the probability of realizing a larger payoff and, hence, the higher the value of the option.
- The longer the term of an option, the higher the value of the option.

American and European Options

An American option allows the holder to exercise at any time before expiration, whereas a European option allows exercise only at expiration of the contract. Because the American option gives its owner all the rights and privileges of a European option plus the additional right to exercise anytime before expiration, the former would be worth at least as much as the latter before the expiration date is reached and in some cases is worth more.

How Does One Purchase or Enter into an Option Contract? Is There a Cash Payment?

A traded option is purchased on exchanges. The required premium payment may be significant depending on the key option terms, as discussed in the previous section on valuation.

What Are an Option's Expected Cash Flows and What Economic Changes Impact Those Cash Flows?

An option has an initial purchase price (i.e., the premium) but does not have periodic cash flows like a futures or swap contract (discussed below). At the expiration of the option, the fair value may be settled in cash. From the holder's standpoint, if the option is out-of-the-money, the contract will expire worthless and the holder will have lost the premium paid to acquire the option.

The intrinsic value of the option depends on the strike price, the value of the underlying, and the number of options or shares. For example, assume these facts surrounding an acquisition of an option on a five-year Treasury note:

- On January 1, 20X1, XYZ purchases a one-year call option to acquire five-year Treasury note futures at the one-year forward rate of 6 percent. Assume that the Treasury notes are selling at a par of 100 (which is $100 million in this example), the option premium is $1,400,000, and the intrinsic value of the option is zero.
- During the option's one-year term, the five-year Treasury-forward rate decreases to 5 percent and the price of the 6 percent Treasury note increases to 104.376. This fair value is calculated as follows, assuming semiannual interest payments of 3 percent:

$$\frac{3_1}{(1+.025)^{.5}} + \frac{3_2}{(1+.025)^1} + \frac{3_3}{(1+.025)^{1.5}} + \ldots + \frac{103_{10}}{(1+.025)^{10}} = 104.376$$

(The subscript next to the cash flows in the numerator denotes the cash flow period; 0.025 represents the semiannual market yield used to discount the interest payments and principal on the Treasury note.)

At a market yield of 6 percent, the Treasury note price is 100 (calculator keystrokes: 6 [PMT], 6 [i], 1.012000 [ENTER], 1.012005 [f] [PRICE]).

At a market yield of 5 percent, the Treasury note price is 104.376 (calculator keystrokes: 6 [PMT], 5 [i], 1.012000 [ENTER], 1.012005 [f] [PRICE]).

XYZ is therefore buying the five-year Treasury notes at 100, when the price increases to 104.376. On a notional of $100 million, this amounts to a gain of 4.376 percent, or $4.376 million. This also can be thought of as the present value of the 1 percent rate difference on the $100 million par value, received for five years, discounted at the market's required yield of 5 percent (calculator keystrokes: 500,000 [PMT], 2.5 [i], 10 [n], [PV]).

Because this is an American option, XYZ may exercise the option at any time up until the expiration date and either take delivery of the Treasury notes or obtain a cash settlement.

The time value related to the option premium is discussed below.

How Is the Contract Settled?

An option may be settled by taking delivery of the underlying or by cash settlement.

Determinants of an Option Contract's Value

At Origination

The premium that a writer of an option receives and that the buyer pays is made up of the intrinsic value of the option and both components of the time value. The intrinsic value of a call option is equal to the excess of the market price of the underlying over the exercise price, times the number of option shares or notional amount specified in the contract. In the cash flow hedge of the forecasted Treasury note purchase, the market and exercise prices were at par, making this an at-the-money option. An option purchased at- or out-of-the-money has no value from the intrinsic value component. Alternatively, at June 30, 20X1, the market yield on the five-year Treasury note rate decreased 100 basis points to 5 percent. At this point, the intrinsic value increased by $4.376 million.

The time value components are made up as follows:

- The effect of discounting is the time value of using free financing. This is the interest that could be earned by investing the dollar amount of the exercise price (which does not have to be paid today) at the risk-free rate over the time period from the day the option is purchased until its expiration date.
- The volatility value depends on the probability that the price of the underlying asset will be above the exercise price (call option) or below the exercise price (put option) at the expiration date of the option. The higher the volatility of the underlying, the higher the probability of realizing a larger payoff and, hence, the higher the value of the option.

A common method of pricing options is to use the Black-Scholes model. That model uses a complex mathematical formula that computes the value of an option at a given point in time. It can be applied without adjustment to both European options and American call options[6] on stocks that do not pay dividends and are based on a number of highly limiting assumptions, such as:

- Price changes on financial instruments are randomly distributed in a "log-normal" fashion.
- Volatility in the underlying is constant over time.
- No dividends or interest is paid during the option period.
- The option is exercisable only on the expiration date.
- The Black-Scholes model assumes an efficient marketplace that recognizes and eliminates mispricing.

As a result of these restrictive assumptions, the original Black-Scholes model did not accurately value options on dividend-paying stock. Therefore, the model has been adjusted to reflect the impact of dividends. (However, another model, the Binomial Pricing model, more accurately values American options on dividend-paying stocks and therefore is also used to value options.) It is important to recognize that the value of an option depends on the six basic variables:

1. Market value of the underlying
2. Exercise (strike) price

3. Standard deviation (volatility) of underlying's returns (price)
4. Risk-free interest rate
5. Expiration date of the option
6. Dividends or interest payments

Exhibit 7-1 illustrates an Excel-based option pricing calculation. As can be seen, the volatility and option term variables discussed above are important determinants of an option's price. For further option pricing information, readers can obtain a booklet entitled *Financial Instruments: Stock Options, Understanding Options-Pricing Models* from Deloitte & Touche LLP.

Volatility is the main determinant of option pricing and the most difficult aspect to determine. The higher the volatility or unpredictability of the underlying, the more valuable the option becomes to the holder because the probability increases that the option will become in-the-money. Note that by using an observed price of a security, the option-pricing model can solve for (reverse engineer) the option's volatility or implied option volatility. This is because the other model inputs such as the term, risk-free rate, and strike price are known. Analysts may then use the implied volatility in pricing similar nonpublicly traded options.

Exhibit 7-2 summarizes the relationship between call and put options and underlying variables that determine their value.

Pricing during the Term and at Expiration of Option Contract Term

The intrinsic value changes are easily calculated by reference to changes in the underlying. For example, assume that ABC's stock price moves from $100 per share to $98 per share. If a put option on ABC stock was acquired at a strike price of $100, the option's intrinsic value is $2.

The present value component of the time value, not illustrated here, is basically the difference between the $2 exercise price and its present value. This will converge to zero as the contract reaches its maturity. Although pricing systems generally will provide those amounts, accountants should understand the relationships and be able to recognize if an amount simply does not make economic sense. For example, in the ABC common stock hedge, XYZ paid $15,000, representing the time value for the six-month put option on ABC stock. Three months into the option, it would not make sense if the time value decreased to $2,000 because the option has half of its original term remaining.

Does the Contract Have Symmetric or Asymmetric Return Profiles?

An option that is at- or out-of-the-money has an asymmetric return profile. If an option is out-of-the-money, the holder will not exercise at a loss and the option will expire worthless if this situation continues. This is different from futures, forwards, and swaps, which have symmetric return profiles. Note that if an option is deep-in-the-money, it will have a symmetric return profile within a certain range.

Exhibit 7-1

Implementing the Black-Scholes Model in an Excel Spreadsheet

Exhibit A

	A	B
1	**INPUT VARIABLES**	
2	Stock Price	
3	Exercise Price	
4	Term	
5	Volatility	
6	Annual Rate of Quarterly Dividends	
7	Discount Rate - Bond Equivalent Yield	
8		
9	**INTERMEDIATE COMPUTATIONS**	
10	Present Value of Stock Ex-dividend	=B2/(1+B6/4)^(B4*4)
11	Present Value of Exercise Price	=B3/(1+B7/2)^(B4*2)
12	Cumulative Volatility	=B5*SQRT(B4)
13		
14	**CALL OPTION**	
15	Proportion of Stock Present Value	=NORMSDIST(LN(B10/B11)/B12+B12/2)
16	Proportion of Exercise Price PV	=NORMSDIST(LN(B10/B11)/B12-B12/2)
17	Call Option Value	=+B10*B15+B11*B16
18		
19	**PUT OPTION**	
20	Proportion of Stock PV	=B15-1
21	Proportion of Exercise Price PV	=B16+1
22	Put Option Value	=+B10*B20+B11*B21

Most modern computer spreadsheets have the necessary mathematical and statistical functions to do the Black-Scholes model computations. The spreadsheet in exhibit A, above, shows one way to implement Black-Scholes in Microsoft Excel. The formulas for the nine computational cells are shown using Excel's notation and function names. The six cells used to enter input variables are outlined in boldface.

Textbooks often show the present values of the stock without dividends and the exercise price using a continuous compound interest formula. Since people usually measure the dividend and discount rates based on quarterly or semiannual compounding, respectively, those methods are used to compute the present values in this spreadsheet. The probability computations use the spreadsheet's natural logarithm function "LN" to convert to continuous compounding when necessary, so spreadsheet users normally don't need to do this.

The Excel function for cumulative normal probability calculates the proba-

bility of the variable being lower than the threshold. However, the Black-Scholes model uses the probability of the stock return being above the threshold. To adjust for this, $-Z$ and $-Z'$ thresholds are input instead because the bell curve is symmetric and the probability of being below $-Z$ is the same as the probability of being above Z.

For each option, the spreadsheet shows one negative probability, which indicates a short stock position or a contingent liability for the exercise price. The result of using this spreadsheet to compute the option values in the article is shown in exhibit B, at left.

Historical volatility also can be easily computed in a spreadsheet such as the one in exhibit C, below. It is easiest to use regular observation periods such as a trading day, week or month. This example uses only five data points (again, the cells used to enter input variables are outlined in boldface). To get statistically valid results, the spreadsheet should be expanded to use more data covering a period long enough to be representative.

Exhibit B

	A	B	C
1	**INPUT VARIABLES**		
2	Stock Price	$ 46.50	$ 46.50
3	Exercise Price	$ 50.00	$ 50.00
4	Term	1.00	1.00
5	Volatility	30%	30%
6	Annual Rate of Quarterly Dividends	0.00%	3.30%
7	Discount Rate - Bond Equivalent Yield	8.504%	8.504%
8			
9	**INTERMEDIATE COMPUTATIONS**		
10	Present Value of Stock Ex-dividend	$ 46.50	$ 45.00
11	Present Value of Exercise Price	$ 46.00	$ 46.00
12	Cumulative Volatility	30.00%	30.00%
13			
14	**CALL OPTION**		
15	Proportion of Stock Present Value	57.37%	53.04%
16	Proportion of Exercise Price PV	-45.45%	-41.14%
17	Call Option Value	$ 5.77	$ 4.94
18			
19	**PUT OPTION**		
20	Proportion of Stock PV	-42.63%	-46.96%
21	Proportion of Exercise Price PV	54.55%	58.86%
22	Put Option Value	$ 5.27	$ 5.94

Exhibit C

	A	B	C	D
1	**HISTORICAL VOLATILITY**			
2				
3	Computed volatility			=STDEV(D9:D27)*SQRT(D5)
4				
5	Observations per year			
6				
7	Date	Stock Price	Dividend	Continuously compounded rate of return
8	1			
9	2			=LN((C9+B9)/(B8))
10	3			=LN((C10+B10)/(B9))
11	4			=LN((C11+B11)/(B10))
12	5			=LN((C12+B12)/(B11))

Source: James R. Mountain, "FASB 123: Putting Together the Pieces," *Journal of Accountancy* (January 1996), 77.

Exhibit 7-2   Effect of Changes in Variables on Values of Call and Put Options.

Typical Variables	*As the Variable Increases, the Value of a:*	
	Call Option	*Put Option*
Market value of stock	+	−
Exercise price	−	+
Standard deviation (volatility) of underlying	+	+
Risk-free interest rate[*]	+	−
Expiration date[†]	+	+
Dividends[‡]	−	+

[*]As interest rates increase, the time value of a call option increases because the present value of the exercise price (to be paid in the future) decreases, and thus, the intrinsic value increases. This has the opposite effect on the value of a put option.

[†] European put and call options on dividend-paying stocks do not necessarily become more valuable as the time to expiration increases.

[‡] When dividends are declared (and the stock goes ex-dividend) on common stock, the price of the stock drops by an equivalent amount.

What Are Common Risk Management Strategies of Employing This Type of Contract? What Risk Management Strategies Are Inconsistent with the Instrument's Return Profile?

Generally, option contracts are used to hedge a one-directional movement in the underlying commodity, foreign currency, or financial instrument. An option would not be effective to hedge the entire price change in an item. In practice, rolling hedge strategies using options may accommodate adjustments to risk exposures in more than a single direction. Refer to Appendix G at the end of this chapter, which is a Goldman Sachs Fixed-Income Research Report on option strategies.

What Are the Major Types of Options?

Options include stock (or equity) options, foreign currency options, options on futures, caps, floors, and collars, *index options,* and debt and interest rate options. Index options, caps, floors, and collars, and interest rate options are discussed in detail below.

Index Options

Index options are based on underlyings that are indexes, for example, an index fund referencing a group of stocks. Although most index options are based on various stock indexes, a wide variety of other indexes exists, including debt and precious metals. The most active index option is the Chicago Board of Options

Exchange (CBOE) S&P 100, followed by the CBOE's S&P 500, and the American Stock Exchange's (AMEX's) Major Market Index.

Caps, Floors, and Collars

Caps, floors, collars, and variations of those instruments are options. However, instead of being indexed to an underlying security, those options are linked to a notional principal amount and an underlying referenced interest rate. As with other derivatives, those contracts are used to transfer risks from one entity to another.

What Is an Interest Rate Cap? Why Is It Used?

An *interest rate cap* is an option with these characteristics:

- If interest rates rise above a certain level, the cap holder receives the excess of the reference interest rate over a designated interest rate level (the strike or cap rate), based on a notional principal amount.
- The cap holder's loss is limited to the premium paid to the cap writer.
- The cap writer has unlimited risk from potential increases in interest rates above the specified cap rate.

A cap purchaser can use interest rate caps to limit exposure to increasing interest rates on its variable-rate debt. For example, assume that an entity issued $100 million of variable-rate debt and also purchased a $100 million notional principal interest rate cap (for a premium) with a strike price at 6 percent (the current rate). Also, assume that the cap is settled on a quarterly basis, its term matches the debt term, and the cap cash flow is determined using the interest rate at the end of each period.

Question: What is the cash flow impact of a rate increase to 7 percent at the end of the first quarter?

Answer: The purchaser of the cap will receive $250,000 as a result of the 1 percent rate increase. (This is calculated as $100 million × .01/4.) This cash flow will offset the higher variable-rate debt interest expense.

What Is an Interest Rate Floor? Why Is It Used?

An *interest rate floor* is an option with these characteristics:

- If rates decline below a specified level, the floor holder receives cash payments equal to the excess of a given rate (known as the strike rate), over a reference rate, on a notional principal amount.
- The buyer pays the writer a premium to receive this right. The floor holder's loss is limited to the premium paid.

- The floor writer faces significant risk from potential decreases in interest rates below the specified strike rate.

A floor purchaser can use interest rate floors to limit exposure to decreasing interest rates on its variable-rate investments. Buyers of both caps and floors are at risk if the interest rate being hedged does not correlate highly with movements in the cap's or floor's indexed rate.

What Is an Interest Rate Collar? Why Is It Used?

An *interest rate collar* is an option that combines a cap and a floor. The buyer of a collar acquires (long) a cap and writes (short) a floor. The writer of a collar writes a cap and buys a floor. For example, a bank holding a $100 million variable-rate, five-year loan would like to hedge against rate declines. Assume interest rates are at 6 percent and the bank buys a floor at a strike price of 6 percent and sells a cap at the identical rate with both the cap and floor contracts specifying a $100 million notional amount. The premium income from the cap sold offsets the premium paid for the floor. If rates decrease below the floor, the floor provides cash inflows that offset lower loan interest income, and the sold cap is out-of-the-money. Hence, the seller keeps the premium yet does not make payments as long as rates are below the strike rate. If rates increase and exceed the cap strike price, the higher loan interest income offsets the cash payments on the cap while the purchased floor does not provide cash flow.

For example, if rates increased to 7 percent in a given quarter, the bank would pay $250,000; if rates decreased to 5 percent, the bank would receive $250,000. The cash flows will vary each quarter over the options' terms depending on the direction of interest rates.

SWAPS

A swap is a forward-based contract or agreement generally between two counterparties to exchange streams of cash flows over a specified period in the future. The cash flow streams may be based on changes in these variables:

- *Interest rates*—an interest rate swap
- *Foreign exchange rates*—a foreign currency rate swap
- *A combination of changes in interest rates and foreign currency rates*—a foreign currency interest rate swap
- *A bond credit rating*—a credit derivative
- *A combination of a bond credit and interest rates*—a total return swap

This book illustrates the pricing of interest rate swaps. For more detailed information on swap pricing, refer to the list of reference materials at the end of the book.

How Does One Purchase or Enter into This Type of Contract? Is There a Cash Payment?

Swaps are agreed-on contracts generally entered into at-the-money or with minimal cash payments. Swap facilitators are brokers or dealers that help counterparties identify and bring prospective counterparties into contact with each other to help consummate and complete the swap. They transact for their own account or may function as agents.

Credit risk, in the case of interest rate and currency rate swaps, is at a different level of credit risk from what investors experience in bonds. This is because in a swap (excluding credit swaps), the credit exposure occurs only when the swap is in-the-money from the holder's perspective. In contrast, in the situation of a bond investment, the investor is exposed for the entire principal amount. However, a swap dealer prices the swap transaction to provide a return for its services and for bearing default risk. The pricing may take the form of an up-front cash payment or be in the form of an adjustment to the rate applicable to swap payments.

Why Has the Swap Market Grown Rapidly in Recent Years?

All swap transactions have grown sharply but interest rate swaps have grown by the largest percentage. Over-the-counter interest rate swaps have grown from $2.5 trillion in 1990 to an estimated $25 trillion in 1997. This growth has occurred because the swap market provides business entities with a private, flexible, and less expensive way to manage certain types of operating and financial risks.

- The normal business operations of some firms naturally lead to certain types of commodity, interest rate, and currency risk positions that can be managed with swaps.
- Firms can borrow in the form (variable or fixed-rate) that is cheapest and/or use swaps to change the characteristics of the borrowing to one that meets the firm's specific needs.

What Characteristics of the Swap Market Distinguish It from Either the Futures or the Options Market?

The major characteristics of the swap market may be summarized and contrasted with futures and exchange-traded options:

- Swap agreements are not necessarily standardized contracts, as are futures and exchange-traded options. Rather, they are tailored to meet the specific requirements of the counterparties. Futures markets trade highly standardized contracts, and exchange-traded options also have specified contract terms that cannot be altered.

- Swap market transactions may involve private customized agreements between counterparties that can be kept secret. In contrast, the major financial institutions that trade on the futures and options exchanges are readily identifiable. This results in a certain loss of privacy.
- Swaps do not trade on government-regulated exchanges. In contrast, futures contracts trade exclusively on futures exchanges that are regulated by the Commodity Futures Trading Commission. The exchange-traded options market is highly formalized, and the SEC regulates the options exchanged.
- The contract term for privately negotiated swap agreements can span any time horizon that is mutually agreeable to the counterparties. In contrast, futures and exchange-traded options generally have a fairly short time horizon. Most futures contracts have delivery dates from three months to three years.

What Are the Expected Cash Flows from a Swap and What Economic Variables Affect Those Cash Flows?

Swap cash flow payments generally are:

- Based on an agreed-on notional principal amount. The term "notional" is used in those transactions because swap contracts generally do not involve the exchange of principal at either the beginning or the end of the contract's term, the notable exception being currency swaps. The notional principal represents the basis for calculating the cash flow payments to be exchanged.
- Based on an agreed-on fixed rate and a variable-floating rate. Those rates are applied to a notional amount to determine the cash flows to be paid and received by both parties. The floating rate resets at agreed-on intervals to the specified market rate, or basis, such as LIBOR. In the examples discussed below, the variable rates reset at June 30, 20X1, and are effective for the payments made at December 31, 20X1.
- Calculated based on the terms to which the counterparties agree (e.g., pay fixed, and receive variable terms). A counterparty's choice of receiving or paying a fixed rate is driven by its specific risk-management needs.

The next example illustrates an application of a plain-vanilla interest rate swap.

Example 1: The XYZ Company Cash Flow Hedge of its Variable-Rate Debt

On January 1, 20X1, XYZ issued a $100 million note at LIBOR with semiannual payments and a semiannual variable-rate reset date. The debt is noncallable with a five-year term. The current LIBOR rate is 5.7 percent.

XYZ wants to lock in an annual 6 percent fixed rate, since it expects rates to increase. In this and the next example, why would XYZ simply not issue a fixed-rate or a variable-rate debt instrument, respectively? Often, an entity with a low credit rating may find it more cost-effective to issue variable-rate debt and then enter into a swap to create a fixed-rate liability than to issue a high fixed-rate debt in the first place. Likewise, an entity with a high credit rating may be able to lower its cost of debt by issuing a low fixed-rate debt instrument and then entering into a swap to let the interest payments float with market interest rates instead of issuing a variable-rate debt.

Therefore, in order to lock in an annual 6 percent fixed rate, XYZ enters into an interest-rate swap to pay 6 percent fixed and receive LIBOR. The swap terms include a $100 million notional principal, a five-year term, and a semiannual variable-rate reset date. At the hedge inception, the swap is at-the-money. This concept of an at-the-money swap will be discussed and illustrated below.

Assume that at the end of the first six-month interval on June 30, 20X1, interest rates increase and the new variable LIBOR rate is 6.7 percent. This rate will be used to determine variable debt and swap payments for the following period. The following table illustrates the swap cash flows for this hedge (a cash flow hedge). Note how the variable-rate debt and swap amounts have been reset as effective for the December 31, 20X1, payments and are being offset to achieve a net, semiannual interest expense of $3 million.

	6/30/X1	*12/31/X1*
Variable-rate debt	$100,000,000	$100,000,000
Variable rate	*5.7%*	*6.7%*
Semiannual debt payment	2,850,000	3,350,000
Swap-receive variable	(2,850,000)	(3,350,000)
Swap-fixed payment	3,000,000	3,000,000
Net interest expense	$ 3,000,000	$ 3,000,000

Note how the swap has effectively locked in the annual 6 percent rate (3 percent paid semiannually).

Example 2: Fair Value Hedge of Fixed-Rate Debt

On January 1, 20X1, GlobalTechCo issued a noncallable, five-year, $100 million note at 6 percent fixed interest, semiannual payment. GlobalTechCo wants to hedge the fair value of the entire loan by converting the loan to a floating rate.

On January 1, 20X1, GlobalTechCo enters into an interest rate swap—$100 million notional principal, pay LIBOR, receive a fixed 6 percent, semiannual payment and *reset date.* At the hedge inception, the swap is at-the-money. The net interest outflow is LIBOR.

The following table illustrates the swap's cash flows for the fair value hedge. Note how the fixed cash flows for the fixed-rate debt and the fixed payments leg of the swap offset each other to achieve a net interest expense that corresponds to the floating-rate LIBOR. The variable-rate payment is initially calculated at a 5.7 percent annual rate but then resets to a 6.7 percent annual rate at June 30, 20X1.

	6/30/X1	12/31/X1
Fixed-rate debt	$100,000,000	$100,000,000
Fixed rate	6.0%	6.0%
Semiannual debt payment	3,000,000	3,000,000
Swap-fixed receipt	(3,000,000)	(3,000,000)
Swap-variable payment	2,850,000	3,350,000
Net interest expense	$ 2,850,000	$ 3,350,000

Swap Pricing

Accountants should understand swap pricing in order to record swap activity properly. One important difference in swap pricing and bond pricing is generally that the swap does not entail a credit-risk premium because collateral is required. However, interest rate swaps are usually priced from different yield curves than bonds because of differences in sectors. For example, a LIBOR-based interest rate swap is priced using the Eurodollar futures contracts to construct a LIBOR-yield curve. A debt instrument would be priced from a yield curve applicable to its sector and credit-quality, such as a Baa industrial bond (as described in Chapters 1, 2, and 3).

Pricing a traditional interest rate swap is a process of determining the fixed rate in a swap that equates the present value of the fixed cash flows to the present value of the variable cash flows discounted using the current spot rates. The variable cash flows are determined from the forward rates implied in the current spot rates on the yield curve. Therefore, this process must take into consideration all swap contract provisions, such as:

- The swap term
- The variable-rate basis (i.e., LIBOR, prime, or commercial paper rate)
- The variable-rate reset date
- The term structure of interest rates, including zero coupon spot rates that are used for discounting the cash flows and the implied forward rates that are used in estimating the variable-rate cash flows

Swaps are popular, in part, because of the flexibility in how they can be structured. Swap contract terms are defined as follows:

- *Term.* This can be any agreed-on period. In this case, five-year terms to match the debt's term were used.

- *Basis.* This refers to the referenced rate that determines the variable rate. For example, in this case, LIBOR was used. Other rates include the commercial paper rate or a spread over LIBOR.
- *Reset date.* This refers to the date on which the variable swap rate will be changed to the prevailing market rate. For example, a semiannual reset date was chosen at June 30, 20X1, and December 31, 20X1; the variable rate to be used for the next variable-rate payment will be reset. In this example, the LIBOR rate increased 100 basis points (1 percent) from 5.7 percent at January 1, 20X1, to 6.7 percent on June 30, 20X1.

If a comparable swap was issued in the market, its fixed rate would be used to mark-to-market our existing swap.

If comparable swaps do not exist or cannot be identified, a swap-pricing methodology using the following techniques may be used.

Illustrating Key Concepts for Swap Pricing

Present Value of Fixed and Variable Cash Flows Are Equal in an At-the-Money Interest Rate Swap
Exhibit 7-3 illustrates an actual swap pricing of an interest rate swap with:

- A five-year term
- Annual interest payments
- Annual variable-rate reset dates
- A LIBOR, variable-rate basis

This was priced as of March 1998, using a brokerage firm's pricing model. This modeling system solved for the fixed rate that equated the present value of fixed-cash inflows to the present value of the variable-cash outflows ($25,182,000), discounted using the current spot rates along the current yield curve. Therefore, the fair value of the swap is zero. In this swap example, investors in the marketplace are indifferent to paying the fixed 5.947 percent rate on a notional amount of $100 million or receiving the variable-implied forward rates on this notional amount. (Note that this example ignored broker fees and any credit-related spread differences that may be factored into the cash flows.)

An entity may choose to pay a swap fixed rate because it wants to convert variable-rate debt to a fixed rate. Its variable-rate debt payments are offset by the swap's variable-rate receipts, and the net interest payment has been converted to a locked-in fixed rate (6 percent in this case).

An entity may choose to receive a swap fixed rate because it wants to convert fixed-rate debt to a variable rate. Its swap fixed-rate receipt will offset the debt fixed-rate payment, and the net interest payment has been converted to LIBOR. A variable-rate instrument has little or no exposure to price changes due to interest

Exhibit 7-3   Pricing an at-the-Money Swap.

	Period 1	*Period 2*	*Period 3*	*Period 4*	*Period 5*
Receive-fixed amounts:					
Swap notional					
principal	100,000,000	100,000,000	100,000,000	100,000,000	100,000,000
Fixed rate at 5.947%	0.05947	0.05947	0.05947	0.05947	0.05947
Receive-fixed					
amounts	5,947,000	5,947,000	5,947,000	5,947,000	5,947,000
LIBOR					
zero-coupon					
spot rate	0.05691	0.05744	0.05793	0.05830	0.05864
Present values	5,627,000	5,318,000	5,023,000	4,741,000	4,473,000
Receive-fixed					
present value	**25,182,000**				
Pay-variable amounts:					
Swap notional					
principal	100,000,000	100,000,000	100,000,000	100,000,000	100,000,000
Implied forward rates	0.05776	0.05887	0.05984	0.06038	0.06097
Estimated					
pay-variable					
amounts	5,776,300	5,887,000	5,984,000	6,038,000	6,097,000
LIBOR					
zero-coupon					
spot rate	0.05691	0.05744	0.05793	0.05830	0.05864
Present values	5,465,000	5,265,000	5,054,000	4,813,000	4,585,000
Pay-variable					
present value	**25,182,000**				
Net swap present					
value	**0**				

rate movements. (Its duration is almost zero, depending on the time between reset dates; this was discussed earlier under the duration topic.)

Variable and Fixed Cash Flows Are Discounted at the Spot Rates Observed in the Market, as Applicable to the Period of the Cash Flow
Exhibit 7-3 shows that the fixed and variable cash flows are discounted by the spot rates on the yield curve at the time when the exchange of the fixed and variable (i.e., forward rate) cash flows occur. For example, recognize how the spot

rates increase from 5.691 percent in the first period to 5.864 percent in the last period. Those rates show an upward-sloping yield curve. (Chapter 1 explained yield curve concepts.)

Expected Variable Cash Flows Are Based on Forward Rates Expected at the Future Reset Dates

Exhibit 7-3 illustrates that the variable cash flows are calculated based on the notional amount of the contract, times the expected LIBOR rates, applicable to each reset date (annual in this case). The expected LIBOR rates applicable to each period are the forward rates calculated or implied from the spot rates on the yield curve existing at appropriate times in the market. (Remember the relationships between the spot and forward rates that existed on the yield curve presented in Chapter 1.)

Comparable Marked-to-Market Swap Pricing

Accountants may better visualize swap-price changes by performing a two-part pricing process. This may be done, for example, after market yields have changed. Accountants first would obtain the fixed rate that must be offered on a swap of comparable term and credit quality, either by observing the rate in the marketplace or by calculating the rate based on spot and forward rates. They then would calculate the change in price by calculating the present value of the differences in the fixed-leg cash flows. Marking-to-market a swap is a process that is similar to pricing a noncallable bond. For example, in the interest rate swap examples presented earlier, the swap's fixed rate was 6 percent. In the first example, the company paid the fixed rate semiannually; in the second example, the company received the fixed rate semiannually. Think of this as:

- Receiving a contractual series of 10 semiannual cash flows of $3 million, beginning June 30, 20X1, for the fair value hedge
- Paying a contractual series of 10 semiannual cash flows of $3 million, beginning June 30, 20X1, for the cash flow hedge

Assume that at the end of the first period, June 30, 20X1, a comparable term interest rate swap was priced at a 7 percent fixed rate, since interest rates have increased. Nine of the original semiannual periods are left. Therefore, the company paying the 6 percent fixed rate has locked in a nine-period benefit of the 1 percent rate difference amounting to $500,000 per period ($100 million × .01/2). The gain (equivalent to the swap's price) is calculated as the present value of $500,000—payments discounted at 7 percent (assuming for simplicity that this rate approximates the applicable spot rates corresponding to the period in which cash flows occur) or $3.804 million (calculator keystrokes: 500,000 [PMT], 3.5 [i], 9 [n], [PV]). Note that this example used the 7 percent rate as an approximation; the correct method is to value each cash flow at the spot rate applicable to its time of receipt. In the second swap example, the company received the 6 percent fixed rate and pays the variable rate. Therefore, it pays the extra $500,000 interest (or 1 percent rate). This results in a loss of $3.804 million (equivalent to the swap's price).

This corresponds to the gain that an issuer of a five-year, 6 percent fixed-rate, noncallable, semiannual debt with a remaining term of 54 months would realize from the decline in the carrying value of its debt, if rates increased by 100 basis points (calculator keystrokes: 6 [PMT], 7 [i], 7.012000 [ENTER], 1.012005 [f] [PRICE]). This results in a price of 96.1962, equating to a 3.804 percent decline, or $3.804 million.

Question: Assume that one period later, at December 31, 20X1, the fixed rate for a comparable term swap remains at 7 percent. What is the fair value of the pay-fixed swap, and explain why the pay fixed-rate swap has lost value from June 30, 20X1?

Answer: The fair value is $3.437 million, calculated as the present value of $500,000 received for 8 periods and discounted at 7 percent (calculator key-strokes: 500,000 [PMT], 3.5 [i], 8 [n], [PV]). The swap has lost $367,000 of value because one less period is available to collect the 1 percent annual ($500,000 semiannual) benefit. The swap's net cash receipt was $350,000, calculated as the difference between the $3,000,000 fixed-rate payment and the $3,350,000 variable-rate receipt. Assuming that the swap is not terminated, the swap payments can be thought of as paying for the swap's fair value over the term of the swap. For example, if the swap's variable rate remains at 6.7 percent on each reset date, the $350,000 would be received for each of the remaining 7 periods.

Example of Using Eurodollar Futures Contracts to Construct a LIBOR-Yield Curve for Swap Pricing

Exhibit 1-6 from Chapter 1 illustrates the creation of the Eurodollar futures yield curve that provides the forward rates (column 6) and spot discount rates (column 7) used in calculating an interest rate swap's fixed-LIBOR rate. In that case, the fixed rate was calculated at 6.532 percent. Review the exhibit to reinforce the above concepts of swap pricing. Notice that the spreadsheet solves for the fixed rate that equates the present value of the variable and variable cash flows.

Swap Pricing—Beyond the Basic Zero-Coupon Net Present Value Model

In practice, an investor requiring an interest rate swap will shop the market to find the cheapest rate. For example, assume GlobalTechCo requires an interest rate swap that pays LIBOR and receives a fixed rate interest receipts. GlobalTechCo will contact brokers and may refer to various services that provide rates that are indicative of the market. Exhibit 7-4 illustrates swap rates as of April 8, 1999 that are provided by Swaps Monitor Publications Inc. This exhibit indicates that a five-year receive-fixed, pay-LIBOR, semiannual interest rate swap would have a bid of 5.48 representing the fixed rate that the swap dealer is willing to pay the customer. The semiannual offer of 5.52 represents the fixed rate that the customer is willing to pay the dealer. The four-basis-point spread covers the dealer's expenses and profit margin. Supply and demand forces in the market may cause the actual rate that GlobalTechCo obtains to be different.

Note the other relevant information:

- The market is also interested in the swap rate spread over Treasuries. Note that the 62 represents the five-year swap spread over Treasuries that the swap dealer is willing to pay to a customer.
- The option volatilities are reverse-engineered rates using the observed cap and floor option prices applied in an option-pricing model. The 17.7 option volatility related to the five-year cap or floor shows that volatility increases with term.

To further reinforce swap-pricing concepts, refer to the FinancialCAD website at *www.fincad.com* for actual swap-pricing applications using this Excel-based vendor application.

Does a Swap Contract Have a Symmetric or Asymmetric Return Profile?

A swap has a symmetric return profile. This can be seen from the prior case examples, in which one swap counterparty gained and the other counterparty incurred a loss of equal amounts due to an increase in interest rates.

What Are Common Risk Management Strategies That Employ Swaps?

Swap contracts are generally used to hedge all price changes related to an identified hedged risk, such as interest rate or foreign currency risk. If one wanted to hedge only one-directional changes, a plain-vanilla swap is the wrong instrument. However, swap contracts may include call features and therefore have asymmetrical risk and return profiles.

Hedge strategies using swaps should be able to minimize hedge ineffectiveness if the hedged item has exposure that is hedgeable by traditional swaps. Traditional swap terms are easy to structure to meet the parties' needs. Review case illustrations 3, 4, and 5 in Appendix F that illustrate a hedge utilizing an interest rate swap.

Swaptions

A *swaption* is an option on a swap. The option provides the holder with the right to enter into a swap at a specified future date at specified terms (stand-alone

Exhibit 7-4

SWAPS MONITOR	April 12, 1999

These indicative rates are as at 4:00 p.m., New York time, on Thursday, April 8, 1999 and are supplied by Tullett and Tokyo Forex.

U.S. Dollar Interest Rate Swaps

Term	Treasury Yield (A/365)	Fixed vs Libor		All-in Swap Rate (A/360) s.a.			annual	Eurodollar Deposits (A/360)	
2	4.86s	51	47	5.29	5.25	5.36	5.32	5 7/16	5 5/16
3	4.89s	59	55	5.40	5.36	5.47	5.43	5 9/16	5 7/16
4	4.91s	63	59	5.47	5.43	5.54	5.50	5 11/16	5 9/16
★ 5	4.93s	66	62	5.52	5.48	5.59	5.55	5 13/16	5 11/16
7	4.97s	73	69	5.62	5.58	5.70	5.66	-	-
10	5.03s	79	75	5.74	5.70	5.83	5.79	-	-

U.S. Dollar Basis Swaps

Term	Prime vs Libor		3m Libor vs 6m Libor		CP vs Libor		T-Bills vs Libor		Fed Funds vs Libor	
2	-270.0	-274.0	2	-1	12.0	8.0	83	73	28.0	24.0
3	-270.0	-274.0	2	-1	10.7	6.7	85	75	27.5	23.5
4	-270.5	-274.5	2	-1	9.7	5.7	85	75	27.0	23.0
5	-270.5	-274.5	2	-1	8.7	4.7	85	75	26.5	22.5
7	-270.5	-274.5	2	-1	7.5	3.5	82	72	26.5	22.5

Option Volatilities

US Dollar Caps and Floors				Swaptions					
Term	Volatility	Strike	Currency	Term	1yr	2yr	3yr	5yr	10yr
1	11.1	5.12	US$	1m	11.3	13.1	13.5	14.1	14.0
2	15.1	5.30	US$	6m	12.7	13.7	13.9	14.4	14.2
3	16.8	5.42	US$	1yr	15.3	15.3	15.2	15.0	14.7
4	17.5	5.51	US$	3yr	16.9	16.4	16.1	15.7	14.9
5	17.7	5.58	US$	5yr	16.4	16.0	15.6	14.9	13.9
7	17.4	5.70	US$	10yr	13.4	12.8	12.4	11.7	10.7
10	17.0	5.85	Euro	1m	17.6	17.4	17.0	16.1	14.9
15	15.4	6.03	Euro	1yr	20.3	18.7	17.3	15.4	13.4
			Euro	5yr	16.5	14.8	13.5	11.9	10.1

Currency Interest Rate Swaps

Term	Australian $		Canadian $		Danish Krone		Euro		Hong Kong $	
2	4.95	4.91q	25	21s	3.47	3.41a	2.93	2.91a	6.82	6.62q
3	5.14	5.10q	(i)33	29s	3.63	3.57a	3.08	3.07a	6.86	6.66q
4	5.30	5.26s	(i)35	31s	3.75	3.69a	3.22	3.20a	6.93	6.63q
5	5.42	5.38s	35	32s	3.95	3.89a	3.41	3.39a	6.97	6.67q
7	5.60	5.56s	(i)37	33s	4.28	4.22a	3.78	3.77a	7.00	6.70q
10	5.75	5.71s	39	35s	4.65	4.59a	4.22	4.21a	7.04	6.74q

Term	New Zealand $		Sterling		Swiss Franc		Swedish Kronor		Yen	
2	5.43	5.39q	5.24	5.21s	1.49	1.45a	3.31	3.25a	0.36	0.32s
3	5.73	5.69q	5.32	5.29s	1.78	1.74a	3.54	3.48a	0.55	0.51s
4	5.97	5.93s	5.37	5.33s	2.00	1.96a	3.76	3.70a	0.78	0.74s
5	6.19	6.15s	5.34	5.30s	2.19	2.15a	3.99	3.93a	1.01	0.97s
7	6.41	6.37s	5.30	5.26s	2.56	2.52a	4.36	4.30a	1.45	1.41s
10	6.57	6.53s	5.25	5.21s	3.07	3.03a	4.71	4.65a	1.92	1.88s

Notes: The term of all instruments is in years, except for some swaptions, which is in months. All other numbers expressed as integers (as well as US dollar caps and floors) are in basis points and (except for US dollar caps and floors) numbers expressed to one or more places of decimals are percentages. For all interest rate swaps, the left column shows the indicative rate for a fixed rate payer and the right column for a receiver of the fixed rate. Currency interest rate swaps use the following floating rate benchmarks: A$ and NZ$ - 90 day bills; C$ - 90 day BAs; CHF, HK$, £ and ¥ - 6m Libor; DKK - 6m Cibor; Euro - 6m Euribor; SEK - 3m Stibor. The day counts for the currency interest rate swaps are A/365, except for DKK, Euro, CHF and SEK, which are 30/360. All basis swaps are expressed as the margin that a payer (left column) or receiver (right column) of the index in the top line (i.e. Prime, 3m Libor, CP, T-Bills or Fed Funds) must pay in exchange for Libor flat. See *SM 2/20/89* for US dollar interest rate swap conventions. All option volatilities are mid-market on a yield basis with an at-the-money strike. For US$ caps and floors, the underlying index is 3m Libor. All swaptions are European style. **Abbreviations:** *a* or *annual*, *s* or *s.a.*, and *q* - annual, semi-annual and quarterly compounding, respectively; *i* - based on interpolated yield; *yr* - year; *m* - month.

Source: Swaps Monitor Newsletter (April 12, 1999).

option on a swap) or to extend or terminate the life of an existing swap (embedded option on a swap). This derivative has characteristics of an option and a swap.

Swaptions may be exercisable on only one date in the future, at any date in the future, or at any date after an initial period.

• As with all options, the purchaser of an option is at risk only for the premium paid to enter into the contract.

• Although swaptions are usually structured as interest rate swaps, they also may be structured as other types of swaps, such as currency or commodity swaps.

One application of a swaption is to hedge a call option that is embedded in a debt instrument. For example, assume that at January 1, 1995, XYZ issued a 10-year, callable debt instrument with these terms:

• $100 million face amount, 9.5 percent fixed-rate debt, an annual interest payment, issued at par

• Callable at the end of year 5 (January 1, 2000) at par (i.e., the call option's exercise price is par)

Assume that at January 1, 1999, interest rates have decreased to 6 percent for similar debt. The embedded call option is now worth $13.9 million (present value at January 1, 1999, of $3.5 million annual savings ((.095 − .06) x $100 million) for five years, discounted at 6 percent). XYZ wants to protect the call option's fair value in the event that interest rates increase and therefore sells a swaption with the following terms:

• The swaption premium paid to XYZ at January 1, 1999, is $13.9 million.

• The swaption provides the buyer the right to require XYZ to enter into the following swap at the expiration of the swaption as long as there exists:

  • A five-year term

  • A $100 million notional principal

  • Semiannual reset

  • The swaption's term is one year, corresponding to the period during which the debt's call option cannot be exercised

XYZ pays the counter party to this contract fixed 9.5 percent annual interest payments and receives LIBOR.

The $13.9 million value is all from the embedded call option's intrinsic value (as explained below). One would expect that a premium would be paid for the option's time value; however, since the option is so deep-in-the-money, the time value was assumed to have no value.

Question: What payment would be required if the entity receives the 9.5 percent fixed interest in the Exhibit 7-5 swap, assuming a yield curve?

Answer: Exhibit 7-5 shows the calculated required payment of $14,731,075. The present value of five annual 9.5 percent cash flows calculated on $100 million of notional principal and discounted at the spot rates applicable to the time periods of receipt is $39,913,075. Because the present value of the variable cash flows is only $25,182,000, the market would require that an additional $14,731,075 payment be made to the party agreeing to pay the above-market fixed rate of 9.5%. With this payment, the present value of the net fixed cash payments equals the present value of the receipts. This is termed a *deep-in-the-money swap.*

Question: The swaption premium in the fair value hedge was $13,900,000. Why is the premium different from the calculated swap payment needed for the deep-in-the-money swap?

Answer: The $13.9 million swaption premium represents the present value of the $14,731,075 swap value to be entered into one year later, discounted at 6 percent and rounded up to an even amount. (Note that an investment-banking firm calculated the time value component of this deep-in-the-money swaption at a zero value, assuming the 9.5 percent fixed rate. The time value of the swap began to have a positive value after the fixed rate was decreased to 8 percent.)

Question: What could happen if the forward fixed rates on a five-year interest rate swap increases 100 basis points?

Answer: The swaption gives the holder the right to require the seller to enter into a 9.5 percent pay-fixed interest rate swap. Interest rate increases will decrease the swaption seller's liability and decrease the holder's swaption value. For example, if comparable rate swaps were priced at a 9.5 percent fixed rate, the intrinsic value of the option would be zero and the option would expire worthless to the holder. A 100-basis-point rate increase in a comparable term swap equates to a $4.1 million gain to the seller (and loss to the buyer) as of December 31, 20X1 (the option's expiration date). This is calculated as the present value of $1 million received for 5 periods discounted at 7 percent (calculator keystrokes: 1 million [PMT], 7 [i], 5 [n], [PV]). Note that, in practice, each $1 million cash flow would be discounted at the spot rate related to its time of receipt. However, for the illustrative purposes here, the simplistic method used demonstrates the concepts without requiring additional yield curve assumptions.

Other Types of Swaps

Swap contracts have evolved to include other forms of swaps that are tailored to meet investors' needs. The following discussions explain other common swap

Exhibit 7-5   Pricing a Deep-in-the-Money Swap.

	Period 1	Period 2	Period 3	Period 4	Period 5
Receive-fixed amounts:					
Swap notional principal	100,000,000	100,000,000	100,000,000	100,000,000	100,000,000
Fixed rate at 9.5%	0.095	0.095	0.095	0.095	0.095
Receive-fixed amounts	9,500,000	9,500,000	9,500,000	9,500,000	9,500,000
LIBOR zero-coupon spot rate	0.05691	0.05744	0.05793	0.05830	0.05864
Present values	8,675,799	8,495,954	8,023,296	7,573,357	7,144,669
Receive-fixed present value	**39,913,075**				
Pay-variable amounts:					
Swap notional principal	100,000,000	100,000,000	100,000,000	100,000,000	100,000,000
Implied forward rates	0.05776	0.05887	0.05984	0.06038	0.06097
Estimated pay-variable amounts	5,776,300	5,887,000	5,984,000	6,038,000	6,097,000
LIBOR zero-coupon spot rate	0.05691	0.05744	0.05793	0.05830	0.05864
Present values	5,465,000	5,265,000	5,054,000	4,813,000	4,585,000
Pay-variable present value	**25,182,000**				
Net swap present value payment required	**14,731,075**				

contracts; however, an in-depth discussion of swaps is beyond the scope of this book. For a complete discussion of this subject, please refer to *Solving the Mystery of Swaps,* KPMG Peat Marwick LLP (New York: KPMG Peat Marwick LLP, 1996).

Cross-Currency Interest Rate Swaps

A cross-currency interest rate swap can be viewed as an exchange between two counterparties of fixed-rate loans referenced to different currencies. The notional amount of the currencies is exchanged at the inception and maturity of the contract (unlike interest rate swaps in which such an exchange does not occur). For example, assume that ActionSportsCo borrowed 96,098,405 EURO. The borrowing is for a 10-year period, semiannual interest payments at a 4.9125 percent fixed rate. ActionSportsCo is a U.S. entity with the dollar as its functional currency. This loan was the equivalent of borrowing $100 million U.S. at a 6.915 percent rate.

Since ActionSportsCo does not want to be exposed to the movement in EURO-currency exchange rates over the life of the loan, it enters into a fixed/fixed cross-currency swap to exchange $100 million U.S. dollars for the equivalent amount of EURO, which is 96,098,405 EURO dollars. The swap terms require ActionSportsCo to receive fixed 4.9125 percent annual interest based on 96,098,405 EURO (2,360,417 EURO on a semiannual basis) and to pay fixed 6.915 percent annual interest ($3,457,500 on a semiannual basis), based on the $100 million U.S. dollar leg of the swap. Because of the difference in currencies, a net settlement does not take place each semiannual period (as was the case in the interest rate swap example above), but, rather, the actual payments applicable to each leg of the swap are made in that currency. ActionSportsCo will then use the 2,360,417 semiannual EURO interest payment received from the swap counterparty to pay its debt interest. Hence, it has converted its interest payment to the fixed $3,457,500 semiannual swap amount. At the end of the 10-year term, the swap counterparties will exchange $100 million U.S. dollars and 96,098,405 EURO. This is illustrated in Exhibits 7-6 through 7-8.

Calculation of the Cross-Currency Fixed/ Fixed Interest Rate Swap Price

Similar to the interest rate swap calculation, a cross-currency fixed/fixed interest rate swap involves calculating a present value of the receive leg and pay leg of the swap. However, this calculation is complicated because (1) currencies are exchanged at the beginning and end of the swap term and (2) the forward rate curve used to determine the swap's cash flows is impacted by both the spot exchange rates for the currencies and the interest rates for each country. One can think of this type of swap as two capital market transactions: a pay 6.915 percent fixed-rate U.S. dollar instrument and a receive 4.1925 percent fixed-rate EURO instrument. It also may be helpful to visualize the swap as a package of forward contracts in which the forward rate of exchange of U.S. dollars for EURO currency has been set applicable to the specified periods. As each period passes, changes in the spot exchange rate and each country's interest rates will cause the forward rates to change. Thus, the swap will have a gain or loss because the counterparties initially agreed to a set of forward rates in connection with the pay and receive legs of the swap. Exhibit 7-9 illustrates a calculation of this swap's cash flows and present value. Notice that at the swap's inception, a $173,290 payment is required by ActionSportsCo because the present value of the payments of U.S. dollar cash flows exceeds the U.S. dollar value of the present value of the EURO cash flow receipts. This type of payment is common in practice.

Exhibit 7-6 Cash Flows at Origination of Cross-Currency Interest Rate Swap.

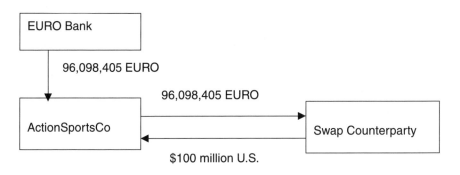

Exhibit 7-7 Semiannual Cash Flows.

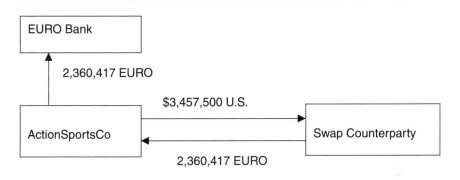

Exhibit 7-8 Cash Flows at Maturity of Cross-Currency Interest Rate Swap.

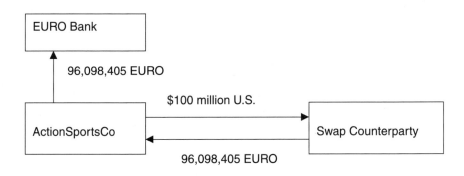

Exhibit 7-9 Fair Value of Cross Currency Swap at Inception.

EUR/USD at inception:	1.0406	Maturity:	10
USD Notional:	$100,000,000	USD Coupon Paid:	6.915%
EUR Notional:	96,098,405	EUR Coupon Received:	4.9125%

			Pay U.S. Dollar 6.915% Fixed		
Period	USD Cash Flows	Days	Forwards	DF	PV of USD Flows
6/29/99	$(100,000,000)			1.000000	(100,000,000)
12/29/99	3,457,500	183	5.447%	0.973059	3,364,350
6/29/00	3,457,500	183	5.970%	0.944398	3,265,256
12/29/00	3,457,500	183	6.305%	0.915070	3,163,856
6/29/01	3,457,500	182	6.623%	0.885426	3,061,359
12/31/01	3,457,500	185	6.740%	0.855784	2,958,874
6/28/02	3,457,500	179	6.827%	0.827687	2,861,727
12/30/02	3,457,500	185	6.857%	0.799513	2,764,316
6/30/03	3,457,500	182	6.912%	0.772518	2,670,982
12/29/03	3,457,500	182	6.872%	0.746581	2,581,304
6/29/04	3,457,500	183	6.861%	0.721420	2,494,309
12/29/04	3,457,500	183	6.949%	0.696805	2,409,204
6/29/05	3,457,500	182	7.069%	0.672762	2,326,076
12/29/05	3,457,500	183	7.087%	0.649370	2,245,196
6/29/06	3,457,500	182	7.157%	0.626694	2,166,794
12/29/06	3,457,500	183	7.128%	0.604782	2,091,032
6/29/07	3,457,500	182	7.176%	0.583609	2,017,827
12/31/07	3,457,500	185	7.150%	0.562925	1,946,314
6/30/08	3,457,500	182	7.179%	0.543210	1,878,149
12/29/08	3,457,500	182	7.171%	0.524205	1,812,439
6/29/09	103,457,500	182	7.204%	0.505784	52,327,184
				Total PV (USD): $	406,549

It is important to understand that the column entitled *forwards* represents the forward rate of exchange of EURO/U.S. dollars that is created using the spot exchange rate at the inception of the swap and the estimated zero coupon yield curve for each country's interest rates. For example, in this case, the U.S. dollar zero coupon yield curve is constructed using the EURO dollar futures curve, while the EURO zero coupon yield curve is constructed using a type of EURO futures contract. The forward rates can be calculated in various ways, and institutions may use proprietary systems to estimate the rates. As discussed earlier, the forward exchange rates for each period can be calculated as:

Exhibit 7-9 *(continued)*

Spot:	1.0406	PV of USD Flows:	$406,549
Change in USD Rates:	0.00%	PV of EUR Flows (in USD):	(233,259)
Change in EUR Rates:	0.00%	Fair Value of CCS (USD):	$173,290

Receive EURO 4.1925% Fixed

EUR Cash Flows	Forwards	Forward FX Rates	U.S. Value of CF	PV of Flows
96,098,405		1.040600	100,000,000	100,000,000
(2,360,417)	2.705%	1.054907	(2,490,019)	(2,422,935)
(2,360,417)	3.103%	1.070045	(2,525,751)	(2,385,315)
(2,360,417)	3.525%	1.084898	(2,560,812)	(2,343,323)
(2,360,417)	3.954%	1.099248	(2,594,685)	(2,297,400)
(2,360,417)	4.210%	1.113240	(2,627,711)	(2,248,754)
(2,360,417)	4.586%	1.125371	(2,656,345)	(2,198,622)
(2,360,417)	4.658%	1.137790	(2,685,658)	(2,147,219)
(2,360,417)	4.763%	1.149861	(2,714,151)	(2,096,731)
(2,360,417)	4.930%	1.160872	(2,740,143)	(2,045,739)
(2,360,417)	5.082%	1.171106	(2,764,298)	(1,994,219)
(2,360,417)	5.263%	1.180881	(2,787,373)	(1,942,256)
(2,360,417)	5.416%	1.190488	(2,810,047)	(1,890,494)
(2,360,417)	5.557%	1.199488	(2,831,293)	(1,838,556)
(2,360,417)	5.682%	1.208184	(2,851,818)	(1,787,217)
(2,360,417)	5.796%	1.216126	(2,870,564)	(1,736,064)
(2,360,417)	5.884%	1.223840	(2,888,774)	(1,685,913)
(2,360,417)	5.973%	1.231020	(2,905,720)	(1,635,703)
(2,360,417)	5.972%	1.238312	(2,922,933)	(1,587,767)
(2,360,417)	5.967%	1.245632	(2,940,211)	(1,541,273)
(98,458,822)	5.967%	1.253195	(123,388,078)	(62,407,759)

	Total PV (USD):	(233,259)
	Net PV of Cash Flows:	$173,290

$$FX_t = \frac{Spot_t(1 + R_{1t})^t}{(1 + R_{2t})^t}$$

The variables were all previously defined.

A key concept in understanding those types of swaps is that as the forward exchange rates change, the swap's fair value changes. Exhibit 7-10 illustrates that ActionSportsCo incurs a $12,718,654 loss as the fair value of its receive-U.S.-dollars-fixed, pay-EURO-fixed swap changed to a negative value of $12,545,364

Exhibit 7-10 Fair Value of Cross Currency Swap at 6 Months.

EUR/USD at inception:	1.0406			Maturity:	10
USD Notional:	$100,000,000			USD Coupon Paid:	6.915%
EUR Notional:	96,098,405			EUR Coupon Received:	4.9125%

Period	Pay U.S. Dollar 6.915% Fixed				
12/29/99	USD Cash Flows	Days	Forwards	DF	PV of USD Flows
6/29/00	3,457,500	183	6.470%	0.96815756	3,347,405
12/29/00	3,457,500	183	6.805%	0.93578753	3,235,485
6/29/01	3,457,500	182	7.123%	0.90326232	3,123,029
12/31/01	3,457,500	185	7.240%	0.87086126	3,011,003
6/28/02	3,457,500	179	7.327%	0.84024824	2,905,158
12/30/02	3,457,500	185	7.357%	0.80963752	2,799,322
6/30/03	3,457,500	182	7.412%	0.78039481	2,698,215
12/29/03	3,457,500	182	7.372%	0.75235528	2,601,268
6/29/04	3,457,500	183	7.361%	0.72521807	2,507,441
12/29/04	3,457,500	183	7.449%	0.69875873	2,415,958
6/29/05	3,457,500	182	7.569%	0.67300576	2,326,917
12/29/05	3,457,500	183	7.587%	0.64801505	2,240,512
6/29/06	3,457,500	182	7.657%	0.62386457	2,157,012
12/29/06	3,457,500	183	7.628%	0.60057807	2,076,499
6/29/07	3,457,500	182	7.676%	0.57814199	1,998,926
12/31/07	3,457,500	185	7.650%	0.55627366	1,923,316
6/30/08	3,457,500	182	7.679%	0.53548533	1,851,441
12/29/08	3,457,500	182	7.671%	0.51549313	1,782,317
6/29/09	103,457,500	182	7.704%	0.49616839	51,332,341
				Total PV (USD):	$96,333,566

Source: Bank of America, N.A. Reprinted with permission.

(loss) from a positive fair value of $173,290 in the prior period because the dollar is weakening relative to the EURO. Causes for this loss are:

• The spot EURO/U.S. dollar exchange rate changed from 1.0406 to 1.1.
• Interest rates in the United States increased 50 basis points, while interest rates related to the EURO decreased 50 basis points.
• The swap fixed rates of the receive U.S. dollars (6.0915 percent) and pay EURO (4.9125 percent) terms of the swap were locked in by the swap's terms.

Exhibit 7-10 *(continued)*

Spot:	1.1	PV of USD Flows:	$96,333,566
Change in USD Rates:	0.50%	PV of EUR Flows (in USD):	(108,878,931)
Change in EUR Rates:	–0.50%	Fair Value of CCS (USD):	$(12,545,364)

Receive EURO 4.1925% Fixed

EUR Cash Flows	Forwards	Forward FX Rates	U.S. Value of CF	PV of Flows
(2,360,417)	2.603%	1.121343	(2,646,838)	(2,562,556)
(2,360,417)	3.025%	1.142562	(2,696,922)	(2,523,746)
(2,360,417)	3.454%	1.163390	(2,746,085)	(2,480,435)
(2,360,417)	3.710%	1.184102	(2,794,974)	(2,434,034)
(2,360,417)	4.086%	1.202807	(2,839,126)	(2,385,570)
(2,360,417)	4.158%	1.222165	(2,884,819)	(2,335,658)
(2,360,417)	4.263%	1.241211	(2,929,777)	(2,286,382)
(2,360,417)	4.430%	1.259265	(2,972,390)	(2,236,293)
(2,360,417)	4.582%	1.276649	(3,013,424)	(2,185,389)
(2,360,417)	4.763%	1.293668	(3,053,596)	(2,133,727)
(2,360,417)	4.916%	1.310599	(3,093,561)	(2,081,985)
(2,360,417)	5.057%	1.327028	(3,132,340)	(2,029,803)
(2,360,417)	5.182%	1.343210	(3,170,535)	(1,977,984)
(2,360,417)	5.296%	1.358710	(3,207,122)	(1,926,127)
(2,360,417)	5.384%	1.374037	(3,243,301)	(1,875,088)
(2,360,417)	5.473%	1.388986	(3,278,585)	(1,823,791)
(2,360,417)	5.472%	1.404067	(3,314,183)	(1,774,696)
(2,360,417)	5.467%	1.419294	(3,350,126)	(1,726,967)
(98,458,822)	5.467%	1.434915	(141,280,056)	(70,098,697)

			Total PV (USD):	(108,878,931)
			Net PV of Cash Flows:	$(12,545,364)

CREDIT DERIVATIVES

Credit derivatives are an evolving product type in which credit risk is transferred from one party to another through a contract that references the actual loss in value of a specified asset as the result of a credit default or restructuring. A common credit-derivative product is a credit-default swap. In this arrangement, one party swaps the credit risk attributable to a specified entity. For example, assume that an investor holds a large portfolio of bonds that has significant credit risk to domestic automotive manufacturers and that the investor wanted to reduce this credit exposure without selling investments. The investor could enter into types of credit-default swaps in exchange for a premium that would provide cash flows in the event that the swap-specified entities suffer a credit loss. The swap can be structured in various ways to achieve the investor's risk and cost objectives. For example, a total return swap may be created to trigger a swap payment based upon a referenced peer group, index, or entity's total price change that could include interest rate, credit, and foreign exchange risks. Therefore, the pricing of such swaps takes into account various factors such as interest rate yield curves, the swap term, and pricing for credit risk.

A basic illustration of a credit default swap is a single-issuer credit default swap, such as a five-year Ford Motor Company $100 million notional amount credit default swap. In this case, the swap's price is quoted as an annual basis point charge that the buyer will pay quarterly over the five-year term. Assume in this example that the price is 75 basis points, or $187,500 per quarter ($100 million × .0075/4) and that the credit event is specified as a bankruptcy of Ford. Supply and demand conditions in the marketplace derive this price. Should Ford file for bankruptcy, the buyer will receive a payment determined by reference to a principal recovery rate that bondholders will receive.

To illustrate calculating a market value of the swap, assume that at the close of business one day after entering into the swap, its price rises to 78 basis points. The gain is calculated as follows:

$$(.0078 - .0075 \times 100{,}000{,}000)/4 = 7{,}500 \text{ quarterly savings}$$

We then present value the quarterly savings as an annuity of $7,500 received for 20 periods (5 years), discounted at the 5-year LIBOR swap rate plus the new spread price of 78 basis points (a 5.78 percent discount rate). This equals a $129,466 gain.

A more in-depth discussion of credit derivatives is beyond the scope of this book. See Robert Brooks and David Yong Yan, "Pricing Credit Default Swaps and the Implied Default Probabilities," *Derivatives Quarterly* (Winter 1998), for a complete explanation of this complex topic.

FORWARD RATE AGREEMENTS

A *forward rate agreement* (FRA) is a contract in which two parties agree on the interest rate to be paid on a notional amount at a specified future time. Principal amounts are agreed on but never exchanged, and the contracts are settled in cash. The buyer of an FRA is the party wishing to protect itself against a rise in rates, while the seller is a party protecting itself against an interest rate decline. However, FRAs have symmetrical risk profiles identical to swaps. In fact, swaps comprise a series of FRAs.

At the settlement date, the difference between the agreed-on interest rate on the FRA and the reference rate specified in the contract, usually LIBOR, is calculated. That rate difference is multiplied by the agreed principal amount and discounted to determine the amount due. If LIBOR on the settlement date is higher than the agreed rate, the buyer on the FRA receives payment of the difference from the seller; if LIBOR is lower than the agreed rate, the seller receives payment.

Forward rate agreements can be used to hedge transactions of any size or maturity and offer an alternative to interest rate futures for hedging purposes. They are not traded on commodities exchanges and therefore do not offer the liquidity or protection provided by those exchanges. Credit risk is a primary concern because the entity usually deals directly with the counterparty and is directly at risk in the event of default by the counterparty.

Derivative Pricing and Accounting Systems

Derivatives Strategy is a monthly derivatives magazine that routinely reports on derivatives' pricing and accounting systems. It periodically publishes a *Guide to Derivatives Technology* that covers over 100 products. It is published by Michael Aiken, sponsored by PricewaterhouseCoopers LLP and Compac Computer® and is an excellent reference tool. The description provided in Exhibit 7-11 is from the June 2000 issue.

Recommended Reference Materials

Accountants involved with derivatives should identify and read derivative-related periodicals that explain developments in this area on a routine basis. These periodicals are good examples of materials that will keep one informed:

- *Derivative Strategy* is published monthly by Michael Aiken. This publication also lists new system applications by company and software type (see Exhibit 7-11).
- *Derivative Quarterly* is published by Institutional Investor, Inc.
- *The Swaps Monitor* is published quarterly by Paul B. Spraos.
- *Financial Analysts Journal* is published by the AIMR.

Another excellent source of derivative (and investment) information is the research material distributed by investment banking firms. Although the distribution is generally limited to their clients, investment departments of accounting firms may receive that type of information. Appendix G at the end of this chapter provides a Goldman Sachs research report on fixed-income option applications.

Exhibit 7-11

EDITOR'S NOTE

THE 2000
GUIDE TO
DERIVATIVES
TECHNOLOGY

This is the fourth expanded edition of the guide that has changed the derivatives technology industry.

Before we published our first edition of the guide in 1997, much smaller compilations of derivatives software offerings were routinely being sold for $20,000 or more. This expanded and enhanced edition lists more than 200 products and will be distributed to more than 10,000 people—clearly the standard map to an often difficult and confusing terrain. (The software database is now available on-line at www.derivativesstrategy.com/technology/guide_dt/.)

In our efforts to go beyond publishing a simple list of features in our survey, we've once again asked industry experts to identify the key components that make software useful as well as those that are missing. Software vendors, to their credit, responded in force.

To help readers make intelligent purchasing decisions, we also asked some leading software dealers to write introductory columns about some of today's key technology issues. This forum, which begins on Page 6, allows them to air issues rarely discussed elsewhere—and to take some rather pointed jabs at their competition.

Detailed tables, beginning on Page 36, allow you to compare the features of software offerings according to a variety of criteria. Detailed textual information on each software product, beginning on Page 137, gives you contact names and numbers, product descriptions and other data.

Directories, of course, are only as accurate as the information provided by participants. In their eagerness to appeal to the widest possible audience, many—if not most—vendors boast features that may be incomplete, in "beta testing" or simply nonexistent. I encourage you to challenge vendors on the specific features they claim here.

For more detailed reporting on technology issues and in-depth reviews of individual software offerings, see our monthly Tech Notes department and our quarterly technology supplements.

Joe Kolman

Joe Kolman
Editor

Source: Kolman, Joe, "The 2000 Guide to Derivatives Technology," *Derivatives Strategy Magazine* (June 2000), p. 2.

NOTES

1. A portion of an earlier version of this chapter is available at the FASB website, where it is offered as background material for the FASB Derivatives training course.

2. For an accounting definition, see paragraph 6 of SFAS No. 133, "Accounting for Derivative Instruments and Hedging Activities."

3. As a result, prices for any three currencies (yen, deutsche mark, and U.S. dollar) must be consistent with the following relationship: J¥/DM = J¥/US$ × US$/DM.

4. This presentation is adapted from Robert Kolb, *Futures, Options, and Swaps,* 2d ed. (London: Blackwell, 1995).

5. For a complete explanation of Eurodollar futures contract pricing, refer to Burghardt, Belton, Cane, Luce, and McVey, *Eurodollar Futures and Options,* (New York: McGraw-Hill, 1991).

6. In theory, an American call option is exercisable prior to its exercise date. However, it can be shown that early exercise is never an optimal strategy. For further discussion, refer to John Hull, *Introduction to Futures and Options Markets,* Third Edition (New Jersey: Prentice Hall, 1998).

Using Pricing Concepts of Fixed-Income Investments and Derivatives to Illustrate How to Hedge the Base Rate of Interest

INTRODUCTION

Although the material presented in this appendix goes beyond the scope of investment pricing, it illustrates the use of fixed-income instruments and derivatives in developing realistic hedges of interest rate risk associated with fixed-income financial instruments. These hedging strategies are implemented within the guidelines required by SFAS 133, as amended by FASB Statement No. 138, *Accounting for Certain Derivative Instruments and Certain Hedging Activities.* Actual security prices were obtained using Bloomberg to ensure that the examples mirror real transactions. The examples reinforce pricing, hedging, and fixed-income portfolio management concepts that accountants should understand when dealing with financial instrument hedging transactions. The examples utilize terminology and price/yield relationships discussed throughout this book. Bear Stearns assisted the authors in creating the examples.

Under Statement 138, entities hedging the benchmark interest rate may specify that the hedged risk involves changes in value attributable to either the U.S. Treasury rate or the LIBOR swap rate. The examples in this appendix are intended to explain how to hedge interest rate risk and to illustrate why hedge effectiveness is, at times, not automatically assured. We provide a general discussion of hedging concepts before illustrating actual hedges. We then apply those concepts to the most basic type of interest rate hedge, a hedge of the U.S. Treasury rate associated with a five-year Treasury note investment, and progress to more complicated hedge strategies. Analysts commonly use other hedging instruments, such as cash instruments (shorting Treasuries), that do not qualify for hedge accounting. Furthermore, do not assume that all hedged strategies require the use of a duration-weighted-hedge ratio (discussed below and illustrated in some of the following examples), since certain strategies do not require this methodology. We have included certain Bloomberg screens to illustrate one type of analytical tool that investors commonly use to determine price and hedge ratios. This type of data may be useful to retain as part of a hedge documentation file.

HEDGING CONCEPTS APPLIED TO HEDGES OF INTEREST RATE RISK

Hedging interest rate risk involves obtaining a security that experiences changes in prices that offset the price changes for specified risks in another security. In the event that each security's price does not respond in the same amount to changes in the interest rate, a hedge ratio may be used. The hedge ratio represents the face amount of the hedging instrument needed to offset the price changes in a unit position in the hedged security. Investment analysts have automated tools to assist with the computations. For example, analysts may use proprietary systems, spreadsheets, or publicly available systems, such as Bloomberg. The key statistic in determining a fixed-income-related hedge ratio is the price sensitivity of the hedged item and hedging instrument to changes in yields, generally expressed as the duration (technically, the modified duration), or a related statistic, the DV01. The DV01 represents the dollar price change resulting from a one-basis-point shift in the investment's yield and may be derived using the instrument's duration, adjusted for any premium or discount associated with its current price. (If an instrument is priced at par, the instrument's DV01 equals its modified duration/100. Otherwise, the DV01 must be adjusted for changes in yields that affect the bond's price and accrued interest. Given this premise, key hedging concepts include:

- Investors sell securities short to hedge a long position and buy securities to hedge a short position (i.e., an existing borrowing).
- The hedge ratio may be calculated as the duration (or DV01 price risk) of the hedged item divided by the duration (or DV01 price risk) of the hedging instrument. The DV01 of each item must be converted to the same equivalent amount. For example, when reviewing the Bloomberg screens that illustrate the DV01 of the Treasury note and Treasury note futures contracts, the DV01 of each instrument is converted to a *risk* statistic that is comparable and can be directly used in the hedge ratio. (Note that futures contracts are issued in $100,000 amounts per contract.)
- Hedge ratios are approximations and usually require daily monitoring to ensure that the hedge remains effective. The price change or cash flow variability of the hedged item should be offset by the cash flows generated by the derivative

hedging instrument, although the offset may not be perfect due to the imprecision of the hedge ratio calculations. Furthermore, even the time of day when the hedging instrument is acquired versus the time of day when the hedged item is measured may create some ineffectiveness. As a result, entities must be careful to document the time of the hedge inception and document prices for the hedged item and hedging instrument at this point.

Exhibit F-1 summarizes the hedge strategies that are illustrated in this appendix. Compare and contrast the hedged items and hedged risks. (Note that pricing concepts are also being illustrated.)

1. Fair Value Hedge of a Treasury Note Investment—Terms: $100 Million, 6.5 Percent Coupon Rate, Due August 15, 2005, Current Price 98–28, Yield at 6.747, DV01 = 451.6/Million, Risk = 4.516 (Priced as of February 4, 2000); Hedged Risk: The Fair Value Changes Attributable to Changes in the U.S. Treasury Rate

Since a Treasury note is a default-risk-free investment (i.e., it only has interest rate risk), a hedge of changes in the U.S. Treasury rate of interest is essentially hedging the risk due to changes in the entire fair value of the Treasury note investment. To accomplish a hedge of this, investment analysts may sell a number of Treasury note futures contracts. Treasury note futures contracts are available in limited maturities—two year, five year, and 10 year—and the contracts mature quarterly. Therefore, in this case, a duration-weighted hedge ratio is needed to calculate the amount of futures contracts required because the hedged item's term and amount do not match any of the available futures contract's terms and amounts ($100,000 per futures contract).

ASSESSING HEDGE EFFECTIVENESS

Upon designating the hedging relationship, the investor must be able to justify an expectation that the hedging relationship will be highly effective over future periods in achieving offsetting changes in fair value. In this hedge, this expectation may be based on the analysis of the price changes of five-year Treasury notes and the changes in five-year Treasury note futures contracts over a moving six-month period.

The Bloomberg data shown in Exhibit F-2 illustrate the relationship between the price changes of five-year Treasury notes and five-year Treasury note futures contracts. The relationship between the price changes of these two financial instruments may be used to estimate their degree of correlation. This is determined by applying regression analyses to the price data shown in Exhibit F-2, and using it to calculate the R^2 (coefficient of determination) of the estimated regression equation. The estimated R^2 statistic may be used to illustrate whether or not the hedge is effective. The hedge will be effective if there is high correlation (i.e.,

Exhibit F-1 Summary of Hedge Case Study Illustrations.

Case No.	Type of Hedge and Hedged Item	Hedged Risk	Key Concepts and Derivative Used
1	Fair value hedge of a Treasury note investment	Fair value changes attributable to changes in the U.S. Treasury rate	Illustrate a fair value hedge, ineffectiveness, and use of Treasury futures contracts
2	Fair value hedge of a Treasury note investment	Fair value changes attributable to changes in the U.S. Treasury rate	Illustrate a fair value hedge, ineffectiveness, and use of Treasury futures contracts with different terms
3	Fair value hedge of a $100 million, 5-year, 8 percent fixed-rate, noncallable bond	Fair value changes attributable to changes in the LIBOR swap rate	Illustrate a fair value hedge that measures hedge effectiveness using the long-haul method (calculating and recording the bond's change in value)
4	Fair value hedge of a $100 million, A-quality, 10-year term bond, 7.79 percent fixed-rate, callable at the end of year 5	Fair value changes attributable to changes in the LIBOR swap rate	Illustrate the use of a callable swap to mirror and offset changes in value of the debt's embedded call option
5	Cash flow hedge of a forecasted $100 million, A-quality, 5-year, fixed-rate, noncallable bond to be issued at par	Cash flow variability of interest payments attributable to changes in the LIBOR swap rate	Illustrate a perfectly effective cash flow hedge that uses an interest rate swap
6	Cash flow hedge of a forecasted $100 million, A-quality, 5-year, fixed-rate, noncallable bond to be issued at a predetermined fixed interest rate and at a premium or discount	Cash flow variability of bond proceeds attributable to changes in the U.S. Treasury rate	Illustrate a cash flow hedge using a forward contract to sell a specific Treasury note; compare this to hedge strategy in Case 5, which use an interest rate swap
7	Fair value hedge of an FNMA 7	Fair value changes attributable to changes in the U.S. Treasury rate	Illustrate the difficulty in measuring hedge effectiveness in this type of investment hedge (uses Treasury note futures contracts)

Exhibit F-2   Historical Price Spreads—Treasury Note versus Treasury Futures.

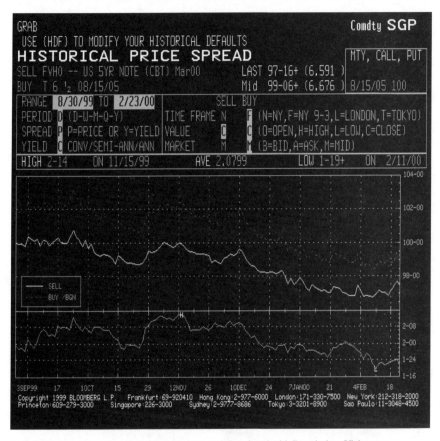

the estimated R^2 is 90 percent or more) between the hedged item (i.e., price changes in Treasury note investment) and the hedging item (i.e., price changes in Treasury note futures contracts). The entity could also base hedge effectiveness on a dollar-offset approach (discussed below).

Note that the top dotted line represents the price of the five-year Treasury note, while the white line below it represents the price of the five-year Treasury futures contract. The line on the bottom of the exhibit represents the differential between the above rates, as a percentage of the par amount.

The purpose of using price trend information to estimate R^2 statistics and changes in the values of the hedged and hedging items is to enable the investor to continuously predict whether or not at the conclusion of the hedging relationship, the hedge will produce a result that is "highly effective" on a dollar offset basis. Statement 133, Implementation Issue No. E7, "Methodologies to Assess Effectiveness of

Fair Value and Cash Flow Hedges," states that the dollar offset method is not the only required method of assessing hedge effectiveness on a period-by-period basis. However, the dollar-offset method must be used when recording hedge activity. Dollar offset means that the change in price of the hedging instrument offsets the change in price of the hedged item, attributable to the hedged risk specified.

HEDGE RATIO

Analysts generally use analytical models that calculate the duration and the associated price sensitivity that is expressed as a DV01. The DV01 of the hedged item and hedging instrument is then used to determine the hedge ratio. Software is available to calculate the hedge ratio and number of futures contracts required to be bought or sold. In this hedge, based on the Bloomberg data reproduced in Exhibit F-3, the DV01 of the Treasury note measured August 15, 2005, has been calculated at .04516, and its risk statistic used in the hedge ratio is 4.516. Another important item shown is the bond price at 98–28. This means that the bond is quoted at 98.875 percent of par. The 28 references 28/32, or .875. This equates to a quoted price of $98,875,000 for a $100 million par value, five-year Treasury note.

Exhibit F-3   Yield Analysis: Treasury Notes.

GRAB   Govt   **YA**

YIELD ANALYSIS   CUSIP   912827U83

PRICE 98-28	SETTLEMENT DATE 2/ 7/2000
YIELD MATURITY	CASHFLOW ANALYSIS
CALCULATIONS 8/15/2005	To 8/15/2005WORKOUT , 1000M FACE
STREET CONVENTION 6.747	PAYMENT INVOICE
TREASURY CONVENTION 6.746	PRINCIPAL[RND(Y/N)N] 988750.00
TRUE YIELD 6.747	176 DAYS ACCRUED INT 31086.96
EQUIVALENT 1/YEAR COMPOUND 6.861	TOTAL 1019836.96
JAPANESE YIELD (SIMPLE) 6.780	INCOME
PROCEEDS/MMKT EQUIVALENT	REDEMPTION VALUE 1000000.00
	COUPON PAYMENT 390000.00
REPO EQUIVALENT 6.235	INTEREST @ 6.669% 80099.95
EFFECTIVE @ 6.669 RATE(%) 6.734	TOTAL 1470099.95
TAXED: INC 39.60% CG 28.00% 4.104*	RETURN
ISSUE PRICE = 99.993. OID BOND WITH MARKET DISCOUNT.	GROSS PROFIT 450262.99
SENSITIVITY ANALYSIS	RETURN (SIMPLE INT) 6.734
DURATION(YEARS) 4.578	
ADJ/MOD DURATION 4.428	FURTHER ANALYSIS
RISK 4.516	
CONVEXITY 0.244	
DOLLAR VALUE OF A 0.01 0.04516	
YIELD VALUE OF A 0 32 0.00692	

Copyright 1999 BLOOMBERG L.P.   Frankfurt:69-920410 Hong Kong:2-977-6000 London:171-330-7500 New York:212-318-2000
Princeton:609-279-3000   Singapore:226-3000   Sydney:2-9777-8686   Tokyo:3-3201-8900   Sao Paulo:11-3048-4500

The DV01 of the Treasury note futures has been calculated at 394.7/million or a risk statistic of 3.947, as shown on the Bloomberg screen reproduced in Exhibit F-4. The reference to "FVHO" represents the futures contracts for March settlement. Note that the investor does not incur a cost when purchasing futures contracts; however, a margin requirement may be necessary. The futures' price referenced as of February 4, 2000, was *prc 97–01+*, which refers to the price used for the daily mark-to-market of the contract on that date (not to be confused with a cash payment required for entering into the contract). This equals 97.046875, determined as the *01* representing 1/32 and the + representing 1/64 (thus summing to .046875). Over the futures' term, the price change, as determined by changes in this amount, is used to calculate the net gain or loss on the contract. That net gain or loss equates to the cumulative net cash settlements over the contract period.

Based on these price-risk relationships, the investor will sell 1,144 Treasury note futures contracts, calculated as follows:

Hedge ratio of 5-year Treasury futures contracts = (ratio of the hedged item's risk to the risk of the hedging item) = 4.516/3.947 = 1.14416

1.14416 × 100,000,000/100,000 = 1,144 contracts sold (rounded down, since an investor cannot purchase a fraction of a contract).

Exhibit F-4   Treasury Futures Price and Risk Description (at 2/4/00).

```
GRAB                                                          Comdty DES
FVHO   prc 97-01+ Risk= 3.947 (Cheapest issue = T 5 ⅞ 11/15/04  @ 6.71%cnvYTM)
    Futures  Contract  Description                          Page 1/2
```

Exchange (CBT) Chicago Board of Trade	Related Functions	
US 5YR NOTE (CBT) Mar00	1) CT	Contract Table
FVHO <CMDTY>	2) FHG	Futures History Graph
US 5yr 6%	3) EXS	Expiration Schedule
$ 100,000	4) DLV	Cheapest to Deliver
$ 1,000	5) ECO	US Economic Releases
0-00+ (64ths)	Margin Limits	
$ 15.625	Speculator	Hedger
97-01+ pts. & 64ths	1148	850
$ 97,046.88 @ 14:59:50	850	850

Mar	Jun	Sep	Dec

Trading Hours		U.S. T-notes that have an original maturity of not
Chicago	Local	more than 5yrs and 3mo. and a remaining maturity
14:15-16:30	15:15-17:30	of not less than 4yrs and 3mo. as of the 1st day
18:00-07:00	19:00-08:00	of the delivery month. Starting with the March
07:20-14:00	08:20-15:00	2000 contract, the remaining maturity will not be
		less than 4yrs and 2mos.

		Generics Available
Wed Mar 1, 2000		
Fri Mar 31, 2000	0-00	
Wed Mar 22, 2000		
Tue Feb 29, 2000		
Tue Mar 23, 1999		

```
Copyright 1999 BLOOMBERG L.P.   Frankfurt:69-920410  Hong Kong:2-977-6000  London:171-330-7500  New York:212-318-2000
Princeton:609-279-3000        Singapore:226-3000   Sydney:2-9777-8686    Tokyo:3-3201-8900   Sao Paulo:11-3048-4500
```

COMPUTATION OF DOLLAR OFFSET

Exhibit F-5 illustrates and compares the pricing of the Treasury note and Treasury note futures contracts as of the close of business on February 10, 2000. Notice that during the five business days that the hedge was in place, the note's price declined $425,187.50 (exclusive of the changes in accrued interest), and the short position in the Treasury futures gained $320,062.50. This hedge ineffectiveness of $105,125 amounts to an under hedge of over 20 percent. This variation is due to the large amount of the hedge, the short time period, and the imprecision of the hedging ratio.

Exhibit F-5   Treasury Note and Treasury Futures Pricing.

Description	FVHO, 1144 Contracts	5-Year Treasury Note, Due 8/15/2005
Price at 2/4/00	97.046875 (stated as 97-01+)	98.875 (stated as 98-28)
Price at 2/10/00	96.765625 (stated as 96-24+)	98.453125 (stated as 98-14+)
Price change	(.28125) × (1138 × 1,000) = $320,062.50 gain	.4251875 × 1 million = $425,187.50 loss

Note that the Bloomberg screens in Exhibits F-3 and F-4 were used to obtain the February 4, 2000 prices of the Treasury note and Treasury futures contract. Exhibit F-6 below is used to obtain the February 10, 2000 Treasury note closing price. The February 10, 2000 futures' price is provided in Exhibit F-9.

Analysts indicated that they would not recalibrate the hedge ratio this early in the hedge; however, the hedge performance would be monitored. As of the close of business on February 24, 2000, the ineffectiveness had increased to $233,000 ($858,000 − $625,000) as shown in Exhibit F-7.

Analysts could indicate that they still would not change the hedge ratio because they expected the hedge would become effective on a dollar-offset basis, based on a high R^2 (not shown) from using regression analysis. Exhibits F-8 and F-9 show the February 24, 2000, prices for the Treasury note and Treasury futures contract that were used to construct the analysis presented in Exhibit F-7.

ONGOING HEDGE ACTIONS

At the end of the quarter, the investor is required to update the regression estimate of R^2, which was the specified method for measuring hedge effectiveness, to demonstrate that the hedge is effective over the specified period. Note that if the dollar-offset method was specified alone, as the measure of hedge effectiveness in the previous example, the hedge would fail to be effective due to the significant differences in price changes.

Exhibit F-6   Treasury Note Yield Analysis.

GRAB   Govt **YA**

<pre>
              YIELD ANALYSIS   CUSIP   912827U83

PRICE 98-14+   SETTLEMENT DATE 2/11/2000
YIELD   MATURITY   CASHFLOW ANALYSIS
CALCULATIONS   8/15/2005 To 8/15/2005WORKOUT , 1000M FACE
STREET CONVENTION   6.841   PAYMENT INVOICE
TREASURY CONVENTION   6.841   PRINCIPAL[RND(Y/N)N]   984531.25
TRUE YIELD   6.841   180 DAYS ACCRUED INT   31793.48
EQUIVALENT 1/YEAR COMPOUND 6.958   TOTAL   1016324.73
JAPANESE YIELD (SIMPLE)   6.887   INCOME
PROCEEDS/MMKT EQUIVALENT   REDEMPTION VALUE   1000000.00
                                    COUPON PAYMENT   390000.00
REPO EQUIVALENT   6.257   INTEREST @ 6.676%   80192.93
EFFECTIVE @ 6.676 RATE(%)   6.813   TOTAL   1470192.93
TAXED: INC 39.60% CG 28.00% 4.143•   RETURN
ISSUE PRICE = 99.993. OID BOND WITH MARKET DISCOUNT.   GROSS PROFIT   453868.20
SENSITIVITY ANALYSIS   RETURN (SIMPLE INT)   6.813
DURATION(YEARS)   4.564
ADJ/MOD DURATION   4.413   FURTHER ANALYSIS
RISK   4.485
CONVEXITY   0.243
DOLLAR VALUE OF A   0.01   0.04485
YIELD VALUE OF A   0 1/32   0.00697
</pre>

Copyright 1999 BLOOMBERG L.P.   Frankfurt:69-920410   Hong Kong:2-977-6000   London:171-330-7500   New York:212-318-2000
Princeton:609-279-3000   Singapore:226-3000   Sydney:2-9777-8686   Tokyo:3-3201-8900   Sao Paulo:11-3048-4500

Source: © 2001 Bloomberg L.P. All rights reserved. Reprinted with Permission. Visit *www. Bloomberg.com.*

Exhibit F-7   Treasury Note and Treasury Futures Pricing.

Description	FVHO, 1144 Contracts	5-Year Treasury Note, Due 8/15/2005
Price at 2/4/00	97.046875 (stated as 97-01+)	98.875 (stated as 98-28)
Price at 2/24/00	97.796875 (stated as 97-25+)	99.500 (stated as 99-16)
Price change	.75 × 1144 × 1000 = $858,000 loss	.625 × 1 million = $625,000 gain

Provided hedge effectiveness is demonstrated as the March 2000 Treasury note futures contracts expire, the investor will enter into a new quantity of contracts, using the same process as already described. Depending on the length of the hedge, the investor may periodically recalibrate the hedge ratio to ensure hedge effectiveness, because duration (and, hence, interest rate risk) changes as the time passes and as yields change. This example has been provided because it illustrates a methodology that may be utilized when hedging a bond or debt issuance's risk due to changes in the U.S. Treasury rate, which affects all yields.

Exhibit F-8   Treasury Note Yield Analysis.

```
GRAB                                                    Govt   YA
                 YIELD ANALYSIS          CUSIP     912827U83
US TREASURY N/B   T 6 ½ 08/15/05    99-13 / 99-15  ( 6.63 /62) BGN  @17:16
PRICE  99-16              SETTLEMENT DATE 2/25/2000
YIELD                  MATURITY   CASHFLOW ANALYSIS
CALCULATIONS           8/15/2005  To  8/15/2005WORKOUT , 1000M FACE
STREET CONVENTION         6.610   PAYMENT INVOICE
TREASURY CONVENTION       6.609   PRINCIPAL[RND(Y/N)N]    995000.00
TRUE YIELD                6.609    10 DAYS ACCRUED INT      1785.71
EQUIVALENT  1/YEAR COMPOUND 6.719  TOTAL                  996785.71
JAPANESE YIELD (SIMPLE)   6.624            INCOME
PROCEEDS/MMKT EQUIVALENT           REDEMPTION VALUE      1000000.00
                                   COUPON PAYMENT         357500.00
REPO EQUIVALENT           6.449    INTEREST @ 6.617%       65412.91
EFFECTIVE  @ 6.617 RATE(%) 6.611   TOTAL                 1422912.91
TAXED: INC 39.60% CG 28.00% 4.005          RETURN
                                   GROSS PROFIT           426127.20
SENSITIVITY ANALYSIS     RETURN (SIMPLE INT)    6.611
DURATION(YEARS)           4.681
ADJ/MOD DURATION          4.532    FURTHER ANALYSIS
RISK                      4.517
CONVEXITY                 0.248
DOLLAR VALUE OF A  0.01   0.04517
YIELD VALUE OF A   0 3/2  0.00692
Copyright 1999 BLOOMBERG L.P.  Frankfurt:69-920410  Hong Kong:2-977-6000  London:171-330-7500  New York:212-318-2000
Princeton:609-279-3000  Singapore:226-3000  Sydney:2-9777-8686  Tokyo:3-3201-8900  Sao Paulo:11-3048-4500
```

Source: © 2001 Bloomberg L.P. All rights reserved. Reprinted with Permission. Visit *www. Bloomberg.com.*

Exhibit F-9   Treasury Futures Prices (from 8/30/99–2/24/00).

```
GRAB                                                    Comdty HP
CLOSE/PRICE                                      Page  1 / 3
FVH0      US 5YR NOTE (CBT) Mar00   PRICE 97-25+
                                          HI 100-25    ON  9/24/99
Range  8/30/99  to  2/24/00   Period D Daily  AVE 98.751
                                          LOW 96-24+   ON  2/10/00
```

DATE	PRICE	Yield	DATE	PRICE	Yield	DATE	PRICE	Yield
			2/ 4	97-05+	6.675	1/14	97-11	6.633
2/24	97-25+	6.523	2/ 3	97-15	6.603	1/13	97-18	6.580
2/23	97-11	6.633	2/ 2	96-29	6.739	1/12	97-04+	6.682
2/22	97-22+	6.546	2/ 1	96-29	6.739	1/11	97-10	6.640
2/21			1/31	96-27+	6.751	1/10	97-23	6.542
2/18	97-04+	6.682	1/28	97-00	6.716	1/ 7	97-30	6.490
2/17	96-28	6.747	1/27	97-01+	6.705	1/ 6	97-23	6.542
2/16	97-02	6.701	1/26	97-08	6.656	1/ 5	97-17+	6.584
2/15	97-02	6.701	1/25	97-11+	6.629	1/ 4	97-29+	6.493
2/14	97-07+	6.659	1/24	97-13	6.618	1/ 3	97-19	6.572
2/11	96-30	6.732	1/21	97-02+	6.697	12/31	98-00+	6.471
2/10	L96-24+	6.773	1/20	97-02+	6.697	12/30	98-10+	6.396
2/ 9	96-26+	6.758	1/19	97-07+	6.659	12/29	98-08	6.415
2/ 8	96-27+	6.751	1/18	97-03+	6.690	12/28	98-05	6.437
2/ 7	96-26	6.762	1/17			12/27	98-09	6.407

```
Copyright 1999 BLOOMBERG L.P.  Frankfurt:69-920410  Hong Kong:2-977-6000  London:171-330-7500  New York:212-318-2000
Princeton:609-279-3000  Singapore:226-3000  Sydney:2-9777-8686  Tokyo:3-3201-8900  Sao Paulo:11-3048-4500
```

Source: © 2001 Bloomberg L.P. All rights reserved. Reprinted with Permission. Visit *www. Bloomberg.com.*

2. Fair Value Hedge of a Treasury Note Investment—Terms: $100 Million, 5.25 Percent, Due 8/15/2003, Current Price 95–15+, Yield at 6.71, DV01 = 300.4/Million (Priced as of February 4, 2000); Hedged Risk: The Fair Value Changes Attributable to Changes in the U.S. Treasury Rate

Although similar to Case 1, this hedge of the U.S. Treasury rate associated with a three-year Treasury note investment will use both two-year and five-year Treasury note futures contracts, each of which will hedge $50 million of the Treasury note investment. It is common to use different term futures contracts when the hedged item's term is split between the futures contracts' terms. The price sensitivity of each instrument is explained below. (Bloomberg screens provided this data but are not shown.)

- Three-year Treasury note investment, 5.25 percent, due August 15, 2003, yield at 6.71, DV01 = 300.4/million
- Five-year Treasury note futures expiring March 2000, DV01 = 396.60/mm
- Two-year Treasury note futures expiring March 2000, DV01 = 194.30/mm

The following calculates the hedge ratio and number of Treasury futures contracts required to be sold:

Hedge ratio of five-year Treasury note futures contracts = 300.4/394.70 = .7611
(.7611 × 50,000,000)/100,000 = 381 contracts sold
(rounded up since an investor cannot purchase a fraction of a contract)

Hedge ratio of two-year Treasury note futures contracts = 300.4/194.30 = 1.5461
(1.5461 × 50,000,000)/100,000 = 773 contracts sold
(rounded down since an investor cannot purchase a fraction of a contract).

In this example, the assessment of hedge effectiveness may be made by using an analysis of price changes in five-year Treasury note and Treasury note futures contracts. The investor also will monitor the investment's duration through time and rebalance the five-year Treasury note futures contracts hedge as necessary.

3. Fair Value Hedge of $100 Million, 5-Year, 8 Percent Fixed-Rate, Noncallable Bond; Hedged Risk: The Fair Value Changes Attributable to Changes in the LIBOR Swap Rate

On April 3, 2000, the entity issues a $100 million, 8 percent fixed-rate, five-year bond at par. The entity wants to hedge the bond's fair value changes attributable to changes in the LIBOR swap rate by converting its fixed semiannual interest payments into a LIBOR-based variable rate. Industry practice is to enter into a receive-fixed swap at a rate set equal to the debt's fixed rate, 8 percent in this case. In order to achieve an at-the-money swap, a spread over the LIBOR rate is calculated. In this case, the hedge was modeled as of April 3, 2000, to produce a 78.5-basis-point spread over LIBOR to result in an at-the-money swap. Therefore, for the first period, the entity will receive the fixed 8 percent semiannual rate and pay the LIBOR swap rate plus the 78.5-basis-point spread. The swap is assumed to reset its variable rate and settle the net interest cash flows on a semiannual basis (April 3 and October 5).

Statement 133's fair value hedge guidelines require that the hedged item's change in value be determined based on all (or a portion of) the bond's contractual cash flows, assuming that the shortcut method is not used. This means that the entity cannot measure the debt's changes in fair value attributable to changes in the LIBOR swap rate by assuming an amount equal to the swap's change in fair value (as will be illustrated in Case 5, which deals with a cash flow hedge). Therefore, the entity must measure the bond's changes in value attributable to changes in the LIBOR swap rate by discounting all the bond's remaining contractual cash flows at the reporting date, using a yield that is calculated as the debt's yield at the hedge inception, plus or minus changes in the LIBOR swap rate during the period.

The impact of this measurement requirement is that in order to minimize hedge ineffectiveness, a hedge ratio may be used to determine the swap notional amount needed to offset the debt's change in fair value attributable to changes in the LIBOR swap rate. The debt and swap have different price sensitivities to interest rate changes, as reflected in their respective DV01 calculations. To illustrate these concepts, it is assumed that the hedge is not being accounted for using the shortcut method as specified in Statement 133. Therefore, the entity will use what is termed "the long-haul" method. The duration-weighted hedge ratio calculated the swap's notional amount at $101,970,000, based on the following DV01 amounts:

- Bond's DV01 = 4.14
- Swap's DV01 = 4.06
- Hedge ratio = 4.14/4.06 = 1.0197; 1.0196 × $100,000 = $101,970,000 (rounded)

Since the price sensitivities are nearly identical, the entity may choose to obtain a $100 million swap notional amount.

At June 30, 2000, a 100-basis-point increase in the LIBOR rate produced a swap loss, excluding the swap's June 30, 2000, interest accrual, of $4,016,000. An analysis of this calculation is not provided because swap pricing is not the main concept being illustrated. However, the following calculation of the bond's fair value is provided to illustrate Statement 133's requirements:

Period	Principal Balance	Coupon Rate	Cash Flow Interest	Cash Flow Principal	Present Value
0.5	100,000,000	0.08	2,000,000		$ 1,956,464
1.5	100,000,000	0.08	4,000,000		3,744,429
2.5	100,000,000	0.08	4,000,000		3,583,185
3.5	100,000,000	0.08	4,000,000		3,428,885
4.5	100,000,000	0.08	4,000,000		3,281,230
5.5	100,000,000	0.08	4,000,000		3,139,933
6.5	100,000,000	0.08	4,000,000		3,004,721
7.5	100,000,000	0.08	4,000,000		2,875,331
8.5	100,000,000	0.08	4,000,000		2,751,513
9.5	100,000,000	0.08	4,000,000	100,000,000	68,458,689
					$96,224,380

The present value was determined using a 9% discount rate, excluding accrued interest.

The bond lost $3,775,620 in value (calculated as $100 million less $96,224,380) and this represents a gain to the issuer who owes this amount. However, since the swap lost $4.016 million in value, the hedge is ineffective by $240,380. (Note that in subsequent periods, the change in the bond's value attributable to changes in the LIBOR swap rate during the period are calculated as the difference between the bond's beginning of the period's present value, as illustrated above, less its end-of-the-period present value. Note that for hedge effectiveness purposes, the entity may assess effectiveness based on a regression analysis or dollar offset.)

4. Fair Value Hedge of a $100 Million, A-Quality, 7.79 Percent Fixed-Rate, 10-Year Term Bond, Callable at the End of Year 5; Hedged Risk: The Fair Value Changes Attributable to Changes in the LIBOR Swap Rate

This fair value hedge of the LIBOR swap rate involves an additional complexity from Case 3 because the hedged item's cash flows are less certain due to the stated call option that may be exercised by the issuer at the end of year 5. Therefore, changes in the benchmark rate (LIBOR swap rate) alter the investment's expected cash flows and the discount rate used to determine the debt's price. For example, if after year 5 the rate of interest decreases, it is likely that the issuer will call the debt and refinance at a lower rate. In that case, an effective hedge should consider the shortening of the investment's average life. Two complexities must be addressed due to the call option:

1. Determining the most viable strategy to hedge the callable bond's price change attributable to its embedded LIBOR swap rate
2. Identifying the portion of the bond's price change attributable to its embedded LIBOR swap rate, on a continual basis

Hedge Strategy

The investor has determined that the most effective method to accomplish this hedge is to enter into a receive-fixed, pay LIBOR interest rate swap that includes a call option mirroring the debt's call option. It is assumed that the hedge was transacted as of March 23, 2000, when a semiannual reset, 10-year LIBOR- based swap that is callable by the issuer at the end of year 5 was priced at a 7.79 percent fixed rate. In contrast, the fixed rate for an identical-term noncallable swap was priced at 7.31 percent. The issuer will not use a hedge ratio because the transaction qualifies for the shortcut method specified in Statement 133. Therefore, the swap's notional amount is $100 million.

5. Cash Flow Hedge of a Forecasted $100 Million, A-Quality, 5-Year, Fixed-Rate, Noncallable Bond to Be Issued at Par; Hedged Risk: The Cash Flow Variability of Interest Payments Attributable to Changes in the LIBOR Swap Rate

An issuer forecasts issuing at par a $100 million, A-quality, five-year, fixed-rate, noncallable bond at the then-market interest rate. The hedged risk is the cash flow variability of the coupon payment's LIBOR swap rate component. At hedge inception, at January 10, 2000, the issuer enters into a forward-starting five-year swap effective February 15, 2000, the date of the forecasted debt issuance. The swap terms are to pay fixed at 7.1325 percent and receive LIBOR flat (meaning no added basis point spread). This 7.1325 percent rate is the February 15, 2000 forward fixed rate applicable to the five-year swap. Because this is equal to the effective market rate at the time, the market value of the swap is zero. However, notice that the Bloomberg screen in Exhibit F-10 reflects a –$4.17 market value; this is as close to zero as the analyst could calculate the swap. Exhibit F-10 illustrates the interest rate swap characteristics (such as the fixed rate and price).

Because the swap's features mirror the debt's embedded LIBOR swap rate, the change in the mark-to-market value of the swap will be the amount that is recorded in other comprehensive income (OCI). For example, as of February 15, 2000, the market value of the pay-fixed interest rate swap decreased to $1,080,128.84, due to a rise in interest rates (see Exhibit F-11). This represents a gain of $1,080,124.67 to the party paying the fixed interest and is recorded in OCI. This amount is reclassified to earnings over the debt's term to offset the debt's price change of –$1,080,128.84, attributable to the change in the embedded LIBOR swap rate. Note that the Bloomberg screens in Exhibits F-10 and F-11 are showing the value of the swap from the counter party's perspective, who is receiving the fixed interest payments, rather than paying them.

Exhibit F-10   Swap Valuation (at 1/10/00).

```
GRAB                                                    Govt   BCSW
Curve Source: CMPN
        SWAP VALUATION                          Swap  Curve
 Settlement        1/10/00      Calculate  3    B Bid/Ask/Mid  US Curve # 23
 R Receive  Currency US      1-Fixed Coupon       BGN CURVE DATED   1/10/00
 Maturity         2/15/05     2-Spread               Rates as of   1/10/00
 Effective Date   2/15/00     3-Premium
 Notional      100,000,000                                2 Yr    6.870
         FIXED    FLOATING                               3 Yr    6.990
 Coupon            7.13250%   Index          %           4 Yr    7.050
 Nominal Payment Date 8/15 + Spread     0.0 bp           5 Yr    7.100
 First Cpn Date    8/15/00     5/15/00                      Mty    7.106
 Next to Last Cpn Dt 8/16/04   11/15/04   Reset  6.098   7 Yr    7.190
 Freq/DayCount  S   30/360    Q/Q  ACT/360             10Yr    7.290
 Business Day Adjustment:  1                            15Yr    7.410
 Swap Premium                 -0.0000                   20Yr    7.420
 Prin. Value                   -4.17                    30Yr    7.410
 Accrued                        0.00
 Market Value                  -4.17
  1=Accrued  3=Mod Dur (cnv) 5=Risk(cnv) 7=NPV    Enter:
  2=Next Pmt 4=Mod Dur (eqv) 6=Risk(eqv) 8=Prem    1 <Go> Update Swap Curve
           1              4                         2 <Go> View Cashflows
 FIXED            0.00          4.25                3 <Go> Horizon Analysis
 FLOATING         0.00         -0.10                4 <Go> To Save Swap
 NET              0.00          4.15
Copyright 1999 BLOOMBERG L.P.  Frankfurt:69-920410  Hong Kong:2-977-6000  London:171-330-7500  New York:212-318-2000
Princeton:609-279-3000    Singapore:226-3000    Sydney:2-9777-8686    Tokyo:3-3201-8900    Sao Paulo:11-3048-4500
```

Exhibit F-11   Swap Valuation (at 2/15/00).

```
GRAB                                                    Govt   BCSW
Curve Source: CMPN
        SWAP VALUATION                          Swap  Curve
 Settlement        2/15/00      Calculate  3    B Bid/Ask/Mid  US Curve # 23
 R Receive  Currency US      1-Fixed Coupon       BGN CURVE DATED   2/15/00
 Maturity         2/15/05     2-Spread               Rates as of   2/15/00
 Effective Date   2/15/00     3-Premium
 Notional      100,000,000                                2 Yr    7.150
         FIXED    FLOATING                               3 Yr    7.290
 Coupon            7.13250%   Index 6.09000%             4 Yr    7.339
 Nominal Payment Date 8/15 + Spread     0.0 bp  Reset  6.090  Mty    7.394
 First Cpn Date    8/15/00     5/15/00                      7 Yr    7.454
 Next to Last Cpn Dt 8/16/04   11/15/04                 10Yr    7.510
 Freq/DayCount  S   30/360    Q/Q  ACT/360             15Yr    7.498
 Business Day Adjustment:  1                            20Yr    7.438
 Swap Premium                 -1.0801                   30Yr    7.385
 Prin. Value            -1,080,128.84
 Accrued                        0.00
 Market Value           -1,080,128.84
  1=Accrued  3=Mod Dur (cnv) 5=Risk(cnv) 7=NPV    Enter:
  2=Next Pmt 4=Mod Dur (eqv) 6=Risk(eqv) 8=Prem    1 <Go> Update Swap Curve
           1              4                         2 <Go> View Cashflows
 FIXED            0.00          4.15                3 <Go> Horizon Analysis
 FLOATING         0.00         -0.25                4 <Go> To Save Swap
 NET              0.00          3.90
Copyright 1999 BLOOMBERG L.P.  Frankfurt:69-920410  Hong Kong:2-977-6000  London:171-330-7500  New York:212-318-2000
Princeton:609-279-3000    Singapore:226-3000    Sydney:2-9777-8686    Tokyo:3-3201-8900    Sao Paulo:11-3048-4500
```

Note that a hedge-ratio calculation was not required in this example because the LIBOR swap mirrors the debt's embedded LIBOR swap rate and the notional amounts were the same.

Other Useful Information to Note But Not Necessary for Hedge Accounting Purposes

Between January 10 and February 15, interest rates on five-year Treasury notes increased from 6.461 percent to 6.700 percent. This amounts to a 23.9 basis point increase. Refer to the five-year Treasury yield applicable to the January 10 and February 15 dates, as shown on the Bloomberg screen in Exhibit F-12.

As a result of this interest rate increase, the price of a similar quality 7.461 percent coupon corporate bond decreased from 100 to 98.94228. Its yield also increased to 7.720 percent. Review the price, yield, and coupon data for corporate bonds presented in the Bloomberg screen in Exhibit F-13. Note, however, that for purposes of determining hedge effectiveness, only the bond's price change attributable to the change of the embedded LIBOR swap rate is considered, which, in this case, is equal to $1,080,128.84.

Although not relevant to the recording of this hedge's activity, the credit spread for this issuer increased two basis points (not shown in the illustrated Bloomberg screens). Therefore, a hypothetical entity that would have issued debt at 100 basis points above the comparable Treasury at January 10 would issue debt at 102 basis points over the Treasury on February 15. This higher coupon payment from 7.461 percent on January 10 to 7.720 percent on February 15 (See Exhibit F-14), represents the increase in both the risk-free rate and the credit spread, and costs the issuer $1,057,720, as shown and calculated in the following table:

1/10/2000 bond price	100.00000
2/15/2000 bond price	98.94228
Change	1.0577
$1.0577 \times 100,000,000 = \$1,057,720$	

One Method for Assessing Hedge Effectiveness

In this example, the assessment of hedge effectiveness may state that the LIBOR swap rate of interest embedded in the forecasted debt issuance would experience identical price changes to the LIBOR-based interest rate swap. Therefore, dollar offset will occur and an assessment based on regression analysis is unnecessary. (Method 1 of Statement 133, Implementation Issue No. G7, "Measuring the Ineffectiveness of a Cash Flow Hedge under Paragraph 30(b) When the Shortcut Method is Not Applied," is used to measure ineffectiveness in this case.)

Exhibit F-12 Treasury Note Yields.

GRAB Govt HP

BGN/NY/CLOSE/MID/YTW Page 1 / 3

US TREASURY N/B T 5 7/8 11/15/04 97-8+ / 97-9 (6.56 /55) BGN @18:35

HI 6.77 ON 2/10/00

Range 8/24/99 to 2/24/00 Period D Daily AVE 6.1565

Market M Mid/Last LOW 5.61 ON 8/25/99

DATE	YIELD	DATE	YIELD	DATE	YIELD
		2/ 4	6.653	1/14	6.576
2/24	6.551	2/ 3	6.507	1/13	6.528
2/23	6.632	2/ 2	6.660	1/12	6.605
2/22	6.565	2/ 1	6.671	1/11	6.554
2/21	6.679	1/31	6.683	1/10	6.461
2/18	6.683	1/28	6.662	1/ 7	6.411
2/17	6.741	1/27	6.669	1/ 6	6.418
2/16	6.697	1/26	6.586	1/ 5	6.483
2/15	6.700	1/25	6.586	1/ 4	6.398
2/14	6.676	1/24	6.558	1/ 3	6.502
2/11	6.704	1/21	6.632	12/31	6.283
2/10 H	6.774	1/20	6.663	12/30	6.271
2/ 9	6.718	1/19	6.604	12/29	6.290
2/ 8	6.733	1/18	6.623	12/28	6.316
2/ 7	6.737	1/17	6.576	12/27	6.309

Exhibit F-13 Corporate Bond Price, Yield and Duration (at 1/10/00).

GRAB Govt BC7

CORPORATE BOND PRICE/YIELD CALCULATOR

SETTLEMENT DATE 2/15/2000

PRICE 100 MATURITY DATE 2/15/2005

YIELD CALCULATIONS	MATURITY	CALL
STREET CONVENTION	7.461	7.461
U.S. GOVT EQUIVALENT	7.461	7.461
TRUE YIELD	7.460	7.460
EQUIVALENT 1/YR COMPOUND	7.600	7.600
JAPANESE YIELD (SIMPLE)	7.461	7.461
PROCEEDS/MMKT (ACT/360)		

AFTER TAX:

INCOME 39.60% CAPITAL 20.00% 4.506 4.506

SENSITIVITY ANALYSIS

NV		
DURATION (YEARS)	4.264	4.264
ADJ/MOD DURATION	4.110	4.110
RISK	4.110	4.110
CONVEXITY	0.206	0.206
PRICE VALUE OF A 0.01	0.04110	0.04110
YIELD VALUE OF A 0 1/32	0.00760	0.00760

ISSUE DESCRIPTION

COUPON(%) 7.461 2/YR

- OPTIONAL -

ISSUE / / @ 1ST PAY / /

CALL 2/15/2005@ 100.000

CASHFLOW ANALYSIS

TO 2/15/2005 WORKOUT 1000M FACE

PAYMENT INVOICE

PRINCIPAL	1000000.00
0 DAYS ACCRUED INT	0.00
TOTAL	1000000.00

INCOME

REDEMPTION VALUE	1000000.00
COUPON PAYMENT	373050.00
INTEREST @ 7.461%	69280.25
TOTAL	1442330.25

RETURN

GROSS PROFIT	442330.25
RETURN 2 /YR COMP	7.461

Exhibit F-14   Corporate Bond Price, Yields and Duration (at 2/15/00).

```
GRAB                                                    Govt   BC7

 CORPORATE  BOND  PRICE/YIELD  CALCULATOR
                         SETTLEMENT  DATE  2/15/2000
      PRICE 98.94228           MATURITY  DATE  2/15/2005
 YIELD                         ISSUE  DESCRIPTION
 CALCULATIONS MATURITY  CALL   COUPON(%) 7.461    2/YR
 STREET CONVENTION        7.720   7.720       -   OPTIONAL   -
 U.S. GOVT EQUIVALENT     7.720   7.720   ISSUE    / /   @ 1ST PAY   / /
 TRUE YIELD               7.719   7.719   CALL 2/15/2005@        100.000
 EQUIVALENT  1/YR COMPOUND 7.869  7.869   CASHFLOW  ANALYSIS
 JAPANESE YIELD (SIMPLE)  7.754   7.754   TO  2/15/2005 WORKOUT   1000 M FACE
 PROCEEDS/MMKT  (ACT/360)                 PAYMENT  INVOICE
                                          PRINCIPAL              989422.80
                                          0 DAYS ACCRUED INT          0.00
 A F T E R   T A X :                      TOTAL                  989422.80
 INCOME 39.60% CAPITAL 20.00% 4.708  4.708    I   N   C   O   M   E
                                          REDEMPTION VALUE       1000000.00
 SENSITIVITY  ANALYSIS                    COUPON PAYMENT          373050.00
   NV    DURATION (YEARS)  4.259  4.259   INTEREST @ 7.720%       71940.85
         ADJ/MOD DURATION  4.101  4.101   TOTAL                  1444990.85
         RISK              4.057  4.057
         CONVEXITY         0.205  0.205    R   E   T   U   R   N
 PRICE VALUE OF A  0.01   0.04057 0.04057 GROSS PROFIT            455568.05
 YIELD VALUE OF A  0  32  0.00770 0.00770 RETURN       2  /YR COMP     7.720
 Copyright 1999 BLOOMBERG L.P.  Frankfurt:69-920410  Hong Kong:2-977-6000  London:171-330-7500  New York:212-318-2000
```

6. Cash Flow Hedge of a Forecasted $100 Million, A-Quality, 5-Year, Fixed-Rate, Noncallable Bond to Be Issued at a Predetermined Fixed Interest Rate and at a Premium or Discount; Hedged Risk: The Cash Flow Variability of Bond Proceeds Attributable to Changes in the Total Bond Yield (Also Referred to as a Treasury-Lock Hedge)

This is a cash flow hedge of the total proceeds of a forecasted bond issuance attributable to changes in the bond's yield. At February 4, 2000, the entity forecasts issuing a bond on February 15, 2000. The bond will be issued at a 7.611 percent coupon rate, which is the market rate at February 4, 2000. Therefore, the bond will be issued at a premium or discount depending on interest rate shifts. The hedge strategy is to enter into a forward contract to sell U.S. Treasuries in an amount that will offset the cash flow variability of debt proceeds attributable to changes in the total bond yield (not attributable only to changes in the U.S. Treasury rate).

The U.S. Treasury rate of interest associated with the corporate bond issuance is represented by the U.S. Treasury 5.875 percent of November 15, 2004, that yields 6.711 percent. This represents the on-the-run, five-year Treasury base rate. This rate is used as a spot rate from which the analysts calculate the one-month forward Treasury lock rate as follows:

Current Yield:	6.711%
Forward Carry	0.083% (This is the repo rate plus the accrued bond interest.)
Locked Yield	6.794% (This represents the one-month U.S. Treasury forward yield.)

The repo rate represents the borrowing rate that a dealer charges an investor on a short-term basis, in connection with the dealer's selling securities that the investor has agreed to sell back to the dealer at the end of the contract. The price sensitivity measure for the U.S. Treasury is calculated as the DV01 = .03872 (Bloomberg screen not shown).

Bond Issuance

To determine the price sensitivity of the bond, its total yield must be determined. (Recall that its yield affects the duration.) Therefore, one would need to determine the credit sector yield spread for the hypothetical five-year corporate issue of February 15, 2005. This is estimated at 90 basis points.

Treasury Yield:	6.711%
Credit	0.900%
Corp Yield	7.611%

The price sensitivity measure for the bond is calculated as the DV01 = .04095 percent (Bloomberg screen not shown).

Calculating Notional Amount of Treasury Rate Lock

The notional amount of the rate lock = $DV01_{CORP}/DV01_{UST} \times$ Size of the Bond Issue = .04095/.03872 × $100 million = $105,759,297 million.

In other words, a one-basis-point shift in the $100 million, 7.611 percent, corporate debt issue of February 15, 2005, equals a one-basis-point shift in $105,759,297 of 5.875 percent, U.S. Treasuries of November 15, 2004, notes. (Note that the Treasury has a 4.5-year term remaining. Therefore, its duration is lower than the five-year bond.)

In practice, risk managers sometimes choose to adjust the actual hedge ratio used to reflect the impact of anticipated Treasury note spread changes as interest rates change. Generally, this would result in a lower notional amount of the Treasury note forward contract being used. An explanation of this technique, known as generalized duration, is beyond the scope of this book. (For information concerning this and related fixed-income risk-management concepts, refer to Bennett W. Golub and Leo M. Tilman, *Risk Management Approaches for Fixed-Income Markets* [New York: John Wiley & Sons, Inc., 2000]).

ONE METHOD FOR ASSESSING HEDGE EFFECTIVENESS

This example assumes that the entity specifies a hedge effectiveness assessment based on an expected dollar offset of the changes in value of the corporate debt issuance and the one-month Treasury note forward contract. The following table illustrates the estimated price changes of the $100 million, 7.611 percent, corporate issuance of February 15, 2005, and the Treasury lock forward contract on a national amount of $105,759,297 million of corporate issue 5.875 percent U.S. Treasuries of November 15, 2004:

	Treasury Lock Value Change	Issuance Value Change	$ Difference	% Difference
+50bps	2,022,958	(2,022,133)	825	0%
+20bps	815,041	(814,919)	122	0%
+10bps	408,500	(408,478)	22	0%
−10bps	(410,468)	410,526	58	0%
−20bps	(822,915)	823,112	197	0%
−50bps	(2,072,243)	2,073,347	1,104	0%

Over the one-month hedge period, the changes in value in the forward contract will be recorded in OCI. To the extent that any differences in price changes between the hedged item and forward contract occur, some ineffectiveness may result and require an immediate reclassification to earnings. Note that only over-hedged amounts will be reclassified to earnings; underhedged amounts will not result in such a reclassification.

Statement 133 also permits hedging only the changes in cash flows attributable to changes in the U.S. Treasury rate. In this type of hedge, the notional amount of the forward contract is calculated based on the bond's embedded risk-free yield, rather than the entire yield.

7. Fair Value Hedge of an FNMA 7; Hedged Risk: Fair Value Changes Attributable to Changes in the U.S. Treasury Rate

This example was included to illustrate the difficulties in accomplishing a hedge of the embedded benchmark U.S. Treasury rate in a mortgage-backed security. Be aware that this example *is not conclusively stating that this strategy will be highly effective.* However, the example is useful because it will show the need to evaluate hedging and pricing issues that surface when hedging securities with embedded call options.

Before summarizing this hedge strategy, a brief discussion of this type of investment may be helpful. An FNMA 7.5 is a pass-through certificate, which is a type of mortgage-backed security. Mortgage-backed securities are created through a sale of assets such as the single-family residential home loans. In this example, it is assumed that they are sold to a tax-exempt trust or other form of a bankruptcy-remote, special-purpose entity, created for the benefit of the owners. The owners of the trust hold pass-through certificates that entitle them to principal and interest cash flows from the underlying assets. An investor's cash flows will vary based on the performance of the assets. Specifically, unscheduled principal payments may cause a shorter investment life and less interest income to be earned (since when the principal is repaid, it no longer earns interest at what may be higher rates than in the current market). The characteristics of this security are summarized in Exhibit F-15. The exhibit summarizes the median results of various investment bank models and is therefore a useful tool for analysts to use in evaluating such an investment. For example, the exhibit shows the following information about the investment:

- The residential mortgage pool is guaranteed as to principal and interest, since the deal is backed by the Federal National Mortgage Association. The investor in this transaction receives a pro rata distribution of the underlying mortgage's interest and principal cash flows.
- The residential mortgages have a weighted-average coupon (WAC) of 8.025 percent.
- The mortgages have a weighted-average maturity (WAM) of 29 years and 4 months.
- The average life of the investment is expected to significantly decrease as interest rates decrease by 100 to 300 basis points. The average life is a significant statistic that shows an estimate of when the present value of the mortgage principal repayments will equal one-half of the investment's fair value. This is due to the increase in unscheduled mortgage prepayments as borrowers refinance their loans at lower rates. Furthermore, if interest rates increase, the average life is expected to increase modestly. Notice the *Yield Table* information in Exhibit F-15, which shows that based on a zero shift in the yield curve, the average life of the mortgage-backed securities is expected to be 9.11 years. As rates decrease, the expected average life drops to 1.85 years. This information is important to understand as the hedging strategy is implemented and managed as time passes.

Based on the information modeled in Exhibit F-15, the investor can expect that changes in the U.S. Treasury rate will impact the investment's price because the cash flows and discount rate will change. Therefore, an investor hedging the fair value of the investment against price changes due to changes in the U.S. Treasury rate of interest will be required to adjust the amount of the hedge to mirror the changing investment balance.

HEDGE STRATEGY

This strategy is to implement a fair value hedge of a price change in a $10 million investment in the 7.5 FNCL resulting from changes in the U.S. Treasury rate of

Exhibit F-15 FANNIE MAE 7 1/2 WAC Security—Median Prepayments and Yields.

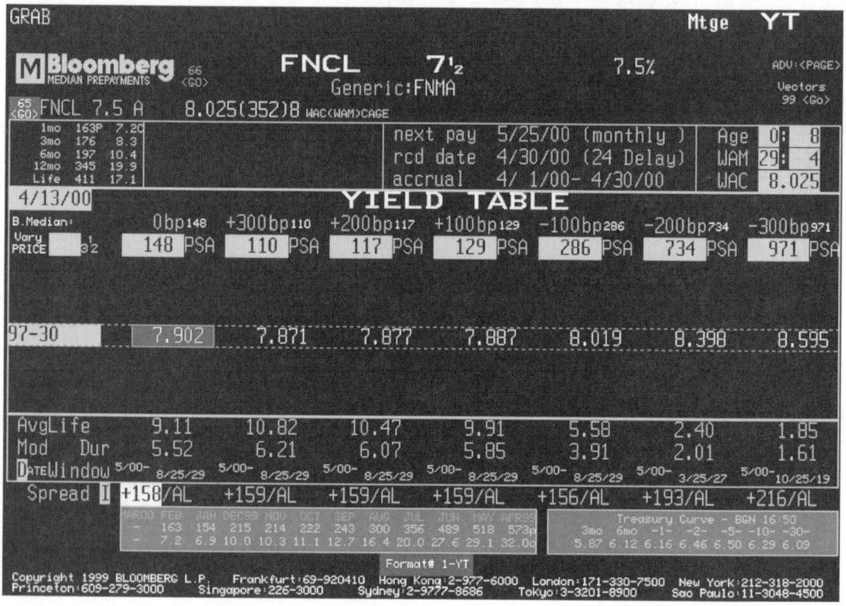

Source: © 2001 Bloomberg L.P. All rights reserved. Reprinted with Permission. Visit *www. Bloomberg.com.*

interest. The analyst has selected a short position in five-year U.S. Treasury note futures contracts as the hedging instrument. Recognize that other derivatives, such as an index-amortizing swap, also may be used in practice. The hedge strategy is to use the DV01 of the entire 7.5 FNCL in the hedge ratio, since this reflects the embedded call option impact. Based on this hedge strategy, the hedge ratio calculation is:

The DV01 of the $10 million FNCL 7.5 = modified duration × price =
5.56 × 97.9375 = 544.53, or a DV01 of 5.4453

The Bloomberg screen in Exhibit F-16 shows the modified duration (5.56) and price (97–30, or 97 30/32), assuming a zero shift in the yield curve.

The DV01 risk of the five-year Treasury note futures contracts = 3.932, as shown in Exhibit F-17.

The hedge ratio determining the number of futures contracts to sell was determined as:

Hedge ratio of five-year Treasury note futures contracts = 5.4453/3.932 = 1.3849
1.3849 × 10,000,000/100,000 = 139 contracts sold
(rounded up since an investor cannot purchase a fraction of a contract)

Exhibit F-16   Duration Analysis of FANNIE MAE 7 1/2 WAC Security.

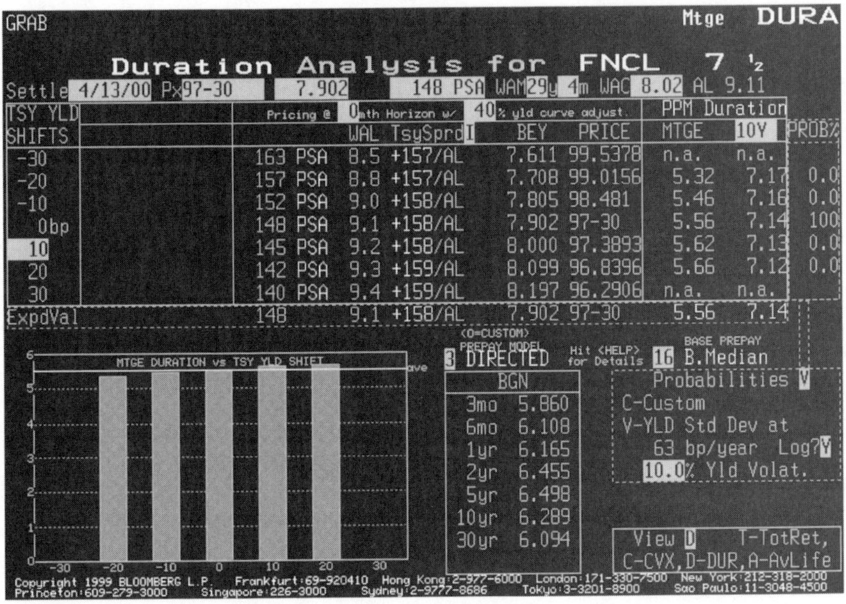

Exhibit F-17   Treasury Futures Price and Risk Description.

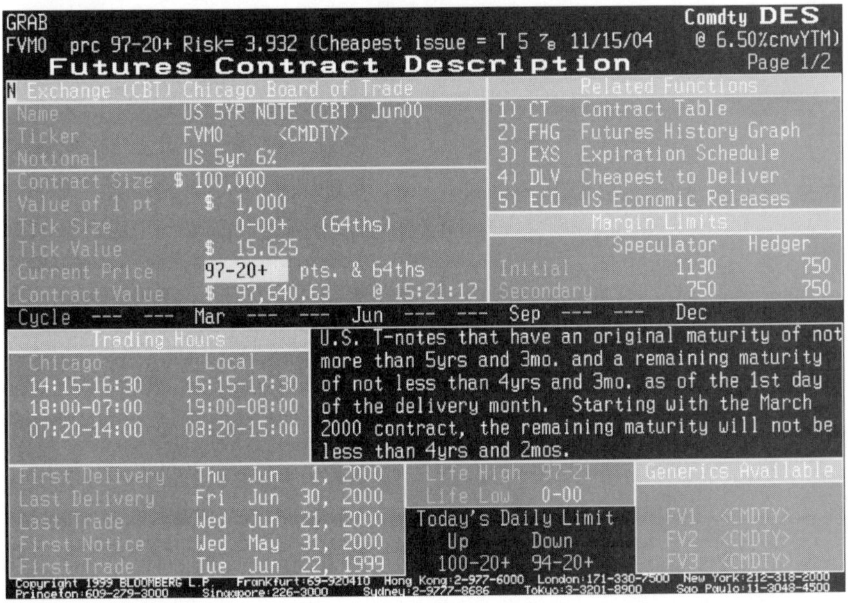

HEDGE EFFECTIVENESS ISSUES

In this example, the assessment of hedge effectiveness is complicated by the callable nature of the mortgage-backed security's collateral and the use of Treasury note futures contracts that are not callable. Therefore, the investor should monitor the investment's duration through time and rebalance or roll the five-year Treasury note futures contracts hedge as necessary in response to both yield changes and cash flow changes as prepayments occur. In assessing hedge effectiveness, Statement 133 requires the investor to perform an attribution analysis of the mortgage-backed security's price changes to determine if other factors caused the price changes. For example, if the U.S. Treasury rate decreased 300 basis points and expected prepayments did not occur because a recession eroded home-equity prices, a portion of the gain would be excluded from the hedge activity. However, a discussion of price-attribution models for mortgage-backed securities is beyond the scope of this book.

Fixed Income
Option Strategies

 Fixed Income
Research

PRIVATE CLIENT PORTFOLIOS

March 1999

Options on Fixed Income Securities: Applications for Private Clients, Part I

- Fixed income options can:
  - *enhance investment income,*
  - *express views regarding interest rates, and*
  - *manage portfolio risk.*
- **This report covers the first two uses.**
- **Sell covered options to increase portfolio yield, especially when volatility is high.**
- **Buy options to express views, especially when volatility is low.**
- **Investors can use customized options to express very specific views.**

- *In the United States, over-the-counter options may be offered only to Accredited Investors.*

Aaron S. Gurwitz
(212) 902-6705
aaron.gurwitz@gs.co

(Limited Distribution)

Goldman, Sachs & Co.   **Private Client Portfolios**   **Fixed Income Research**

Editor: Ronald A. Krieger
Production: William Tompkins

I. Introduction

Many of Goldman Sachs' private clients have used options on equity securities to manage portfolio risk or to take advantage of investment opportunities. Although puts and calls on specific stocks or on broad equity market indexes can be risky investments viewed in isolation, these instruments frequently prove to be effective tools for enhancing income, expressing views, and managing an equities portfolio. Options on fixed income instruments can serve much the same function, so individual investors should also be familiar with puts and calls on bonds.

The purpose of this report is to introduce the uses of options on fixed income securities to private clients who are already familiar with stock options. Accordingly, we will assume a basic understanding of how options work. Readers should understand terms such as *option premium, strike price, expiration, volatility, implied volatility, intrinsic value,* and *time value* and should be familiar with the way the profits or losses on long and short positions in puts and calls relate to the market price of the underlying security. We will review the definitions of some of these terms and concepts within this text, but only briefly. Readers who are interested in this subject matter but are unfamiliar with the basic concepts should consult any one of a number of basic explanations of options.[1]

Among readers who are U.S. residents, this material will be useful only to those who qualify as Accredited Investors (AIs) under regulations established by the Securities and Exchange Commission (SEC). Under current regulations, over-the-counter (OTC) options — which constitute the bulk of the types of fixed income options of interest to private clients — cannot be sold to the general public but only to AIs. U.S. residents who are not sure whether they qualify as AIs should consult their Goldman Sachs representative.

Some General Observations About Options

As noted above, options can be very risky as stand-alone investments and are not for all investors. An investor who purchases (goes long) a call or a put stands to lose all of the money invested. Taking "na-

ked" short options positions — selling (or "writing") options — can be even riskier; in this case, the potential for loss may be unlimited.

Notwithstanding these risks, options can play at least three important roles in a fixed income portfolio:

(1) **Enhancing investment income through option writing.** The most common type of transaction along these lines involves selling "covered" call options on securities the investor owns. Another application is to write puts on bonds one expects to purchase at a known time in the future.

(2) **Expressing views.** Fixed income options provide a way for an investor to express views regarding the direction of interest rates, the degree of volatility of interest rates, or the relationship (spread) between different interest rates. Expressing views with options allows the investor to take a position with known and limited downside risk. Some market expectations cannot be expressed in practice without the use of options.

(3) **Managing bond portfolio characteristics without buying or selling bonds.** Investors who have used options to reduce the risk of large single stock positions are familiar with the fact that managing portfolios in this way can be tax-efficient. Using options to manage portfolio risk can also economize on transaction costs.

We will discuss the first role in some detail in Section II of this report and the second in Section III. The third role deserves separate treatment in depth; we will cover this topic in a future publication.

Options on Bonds vs. Options on Stocks

Because this report is intended for investors who are already familiar with stock options, it will be useful to highlight the ways in which fixed income options both resemble and differ from equity options.

Options in the two markets are the same in their basic contractual terms. Each option contract will indicate whether the contract is for a put or a call, will identify a deliverable security or cash settlement formula, and will specify a strike price and expiration date. The basic determinants of an option's market value — intrinsic value, time to expiration, the short-term interest rate, and price volatility —

---

[1] See, for example, Emma B. Rasiel, *Guide to Fixed Income Options*, Goldman, Sachs & Co., Fixed Income Division, October 1995 (distribution limited to AIs).

are also the same, as are the payoff functions at expiration.

There are, however, three important differences to bear in mind.

American vs. European, Fixed Income vs. Equity. First, investors involved with longer-dated stock options must deal with uncertainties regarding the amount and timing of dividends. With options on high grade fixed income securities, there is no uncertainty regarding the timing and amount of coupon payments. On a practical level, this means that while there may be a significant difference between the value of European and American options in the equities market, the values of the two types of options will show a much smaller difference in the fixed income market.

Price Volatility vs. Yield Volatility. Second, the strike and spot levels for an equity option are always defined in terms of the *price* of a stock or a stock index, and discussions of volatility with reference to equity options invariably refer to *price volatility*. In the fixed income market, however, there can be some confusion regarding references to price and yield. The strike price of options on specific fixed income securities or futures contracts is usually specified in terms of price. However, the contract for many common fixed income options may specify a strike yield. For example, a put on a fixed income instrument — which will produce a profit for the holder of the option if interest rates rise — can also be specified contractually as a *cap* on a specific yield. In fact, caps on the London Interbank Offered Rate (LIBOR), the most popular index of short-term U.S. dollar interest rates, are among the most common varieties of fixed income options.

Furthermore, in discussions of fixed income options, the term "volatility" may also refer to movements in either prices or yields. To confuse matters further, even when referring to the value of an option with a specified strike price (rather than a strike yield) market participants will usually cite the implied yield volatility of the option. None of this reflects any conceptual difficulty; a simple formula relates the price and yield volatility of any given fixed income instrument.[2] However, investors who use fixed income options should be careful to determine whether

any mention of the implied volatility of an option premium refers to yield or price volatility.

Forward Price vs. Spot Price. When equity market participants evaluate a put or call as an in- or out-of-the-money option, they are almost invariably comparing the strike price of the option with the market price of the deliverable security *at the time of the evaluation.* But in the fixed income markets, such statements may refer either to spot prices at the time of the evaluation or to *forward prices* as of the scheduled expiration of the option. The forward price is the price that can be locked in today for purchase or sale of a bond for delivery at a date in the future. The forward price is almost always different from, and usually lower than, the current market or "spot" price. The difference between spot and forward prices depends on the difference between the yield on the bond in question and short-term interest rates, as the following example illustrates:

Consider a five-year bond with an annual 5% coupon maturing on January 1, 2005, and evaluated as of January 1, 2000, at a spot price of 100.00. Suppose the yield on one-year bonds of the same issuer is 4%. An investor would therefore be indifferent between (1) buying the 2005 bond at par today and (2) buying the one-year bond today and contracting to purchase the 2005 bond on January 1, 2001, at a price of 99.00. Under these circumstances, we say that the ("fair") forward price of the bond is 99.00. A one-year call option on the bond with a strike price of 99.50 would be in the money relative to the spot price of par and out of the money relative to the forward price of 99.00.

The pricing of an option on a fixed income security — in particular the degree to which the option is in or out of the money — depends on the forward price, *not* the spot price. Therefore, when dealing with fixed income options, investors should be aware of where the strike price or strike yield stands relative to both the spot and forward prices of the security, particularly when the slope of the yield curve is steep.

---

[2] Price Volatility = Yield Volatility × Yield × Modified Duration.

II. Using Options to Earn the Premium

Writing Covered Calls

Covered call writing involves selling options on securities the investor holds in his or her portfolio. A simple example of a covered call position appears in the exhibit below. The investor owns a five-year U.S. Treasury note on March 1, 1999, at which time the security has a spot price of 99-22 (99.6875). The investor is considering writing a one-year over-the-counter at-the-money (spot) European call option on this security. We assume that an option dealer's bid-side yield volatility for one-year at-the-money options on five-year Treasuries is 18.70%, which implies an option price of 1-08 (1.25% of the par amount). The investor will receive this option premium as an upfront payment, so the horizon total return will be augmented by the amount of the premium itself and earnings on this amount invested over the course of the year at, we assume, the short-term (repo) rate.

Because the investor owns the bond but has sold a call option against the position, the total return on the combined position over the life of the option will be greater than the total return on the bond itself *unless* the price of the bond increases by more than the option premium. Thus, writing covered calls should be an attractive tactic for investors who do not expect interest rates to decline substantially.

Many investors should be familiar with this pattern of scenario total returns; the profile for the covered call has the same shape as the return pattern for a five-year bond that is callable at the end of one year. An investor who purchases a callable bond is, in effect, writing a call option on a hypothetical underlying noncallable bond. Instead of receiving an upfront option premium payment, the holder of the callable bond will earn a higher yield than would be offered on an otherwise-identical noncallable bond of the same issuer. The return profiles of the covered call, on the one hand, and the callable bond, on the other, will be identical if the present value of the additional yield earned over the life of the option is exactly equal to the option premium.

Buying callable bonds is common for U.S. investors; most U.S. municipal bonds are callable 10 years after the date of issuance, and callable notes issued by U.S. government agencies have become very popular among private investors. Earning a higher yield as compensation for early-redemption risk is prudent, as long as it isn't taken too far. Thus, we generally recommend that private clients build fixed income portfolios with some degree of call exposure; callable bonds might reasonably account for around 25% of a well-constructed bond portfolio under "average" market conditions. Those who believe it is unlikely that interest rates will change much in either direction might hold even more call-

Example 1: One-Year At-the-Money (Spot) Covered European Call on a Five-Year U.S. Treasury Note

Term Sheet

Pricing Date	3/1/99
Deliverable Bond	
Issuer	US Treasury
Coupon	4.75%
Maturity	2/15/04
Spot price	99-22
Repo Rate	4.80%
Spot Yield	4.8211%
Forward Yield	4.8270%
Forward Price	99-23
Option	
Type	European Call
Expiration	3/15/00
Strike Price	99-22
Option Premium	01-08
Implied Yield Volatility	18.70%
Implied Price Volatility	3.93%

Payoff Diagram

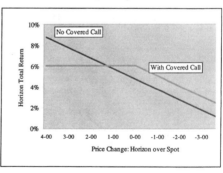

ables. Investors who routinely purchase callable bonds, accepting the risk that the redemption proceeds will have to be reinvested in a low interest rate environment in exchange for a higher yield, should not view covered call writing as a particularly aggressive or unusual investment tactic. However, investors in markets where callable bonds are common will frequently find that there is little advantage to writing covered calls relative to simply buying higher yielding bonds subject to optional early redemption.

Creating a Synthetic Callable Bond

In the European and Asian bond markets, by contrast, callable bonds are relatively uncommon. The contrast between Europe and the United States is starkest in this regard when we compare two "sister" sectors: the market for U.S. government agency notes and the German *Pfandbrief* market.[3] The former offers investors a wide variety of bond structures, the latter mainly bullets. It might be useful, therefore, to provide a second illustration of a covered call structure: a synthetic callable *Pfandbrief* that mirrors the structure of a callable U.S. government agency note.

The typical callable U.S. government agency note is structured as follows: The security has a defined maturity, usually between one and 10 years. The issuer retains the right to redeem the security at any time after the end of a specified "noncall" period, usually at a price of par plus accrued interest. The "noncall" period typically extends for as little as three months or as long as several years. Through this structure the investor has, in effect, sold a structured call option on the bond to the issuer. The option structure can be viewed as a European call struck at par expiring at the end of the noncall period, which then becomes an American call with the same strike price, expiring when the note matures.

In the case of the callable agency notes, the option-related activity is embedded in the bond's structure. Investors must go to some effort to disentangle the value of the underlying (noncallable) bond from the value of the call option. As Example 2 shows, one advantage of the covered call writing strategy is that

---

[3] *Pfandbriefe* are obligations of German commercial banks collateralized by residential mortgages and loans to governments. They resemble U.S. government agency obligations in their high degree of liquidity and their triple-A credit quality.

Example 2: Creating a Synthetic Callable *Pfandbrief*

Pricing Date	3/1/99
Deliverable Bond	
Issuer	DEPFA
Security Type	*Hypotheken Pfandbrief*
Coupon	3.50%
Maturity	11/20/02
Spot price	100.122
Spot Yield	3.4610%
Spread to Government Curve (bp)	13
Option	
Type	European Call, Converting to American Call
Expiration	11/20/02
First Exercise Date	11/20/99
Strike Price	100.000
Option Premium	1.60%
Implied Yield Volatility	14.00%
Implied Price Volatility	1.66%
Analysis	
Net Position Price	98.461
Gross Effective Yield to Maturity	3.95%
Spread to Government Curve	62
Gross Effective Yield to Worst	3.88%
Spread to Government Curve	88

the two separate components of the package's value are clearly distinguished. In terms of returns, benefits, and risks, the profile of the "synthetic" structure is identical to that of the callable agency note. The callable agency note has the edge in terms of transactional efficiency; the underlying bond and the option are offered to the investor as a single package. However, in markets where neatly packaged structures are not available, structured covered call writing may provide the only way to achieve a prudent and beneficial investment objective.

Writing Covered Puts

Being short a put obligates the option writer to purchase a specified security at a specified price on (or before) a specified future date. Such transactions can be "covered" if the investor has, or will have, sufficient cash on hand to meet the obligation to buy. There are several situations in which writing puts might make sense.

First, consider an investor with cash to put to work in the bond market, who believes it is very unlikely

Example 3: Three-Month Short Put on a 10-Year JGB Struck 30 bp Out of the Money

Term Sheet

Pricing Date	3/1/99
Deliverable Bond	
Issuer	Japan
Coupon	1.10%
Maturity	12/22/08
Spot price	93
Repo Rate	0.23%
Spot Yield	1.8850%
Forward Yield	2.0018%
Forward Price	92.7697
Option	
Type	American Put
Expiration	6/1/99
Strike Yield	2.25%
Option Premium	0.81
Implied Yield Volatility	45%
Implied Price Volatility	7.8%

Outcome Diagram

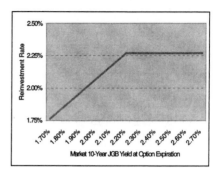

that interest rates will decline in the near future, but believes that it is possible that bond yields could rise somewhat. To make the example more concrete, imagine a Japanese investor who purchased a 10-year Japanese government bond (JGB) with a par value of ¥100 million in 1989 at a yield of 4.89%. The bond has now matured, and the investor is planning to reinvest the redemption proceeds in a new 10-year bond. Yields on 10-year JGBs are now below 2%, but within the past few weeks have been as high as 2.5%. The investor does not expect yields on JGBs to decline further, but does think there's a decent chance that yields will get back to at least 2.25% over a three-month horizon. Suppose, then, that the investor establishes the following plan: Reinvest in 10-year JGBs in three months or if the yield rises to 2.25%, whichever happens first.

This is reasonable, given the investor's objectives and views. However, the investor can enhance the return on this strategy by writing a three-month put option on a 10-year JGB with a strike yield of 2.25%. The term sheet and outcome diagram for this options application are displayed in Example 3.

The investor's concern in this example is the yield on the new 10-year bond to be purchased with the proceeds of the maturing issue — the "reinvestment rate." In this context, the option premium allows the

investor to purchase more new 10-year bonds than he or she would be able to otherwise. The outcome diagram relates the possible all-in reinvestment rates to the yield on 10-year JGBs at expiration. Writing the option can enhance the investor's reinvestment rate. However, comparing these outcomes with the case in which no options are written is less straightforward than in the previous examples.

The problem is that by writing the option, the investor gives up flexibility. Before writing the put, the investor can change course and decide, say, to wait until yields rise to 2.5% percent before buying the bond. Once the put is written, the investor loses that flexibility.

Further, the investor loses flexibility to purchase the security subject to the put before the expiration of the option. Suppose JGB yields rise to 2.25% before the end of the three-month period. Because the time value of an option is greatest when the underlying security is trading close to the strike price (or yield), it is unlikely that the holder of the option will exercise early. At that point, the option writer will have two choices. The first is to wait until expiration, taking the risk that bond yields might decline and never again rise to 2.25%. Alternatively, the option writer could buy the put back from the holder by paying the time value of the option. If a long time remains before expiration, this could result in a substantial loss on the option position.

Investors considering writing puts must decide whether the option premium received is sufficient compensation for this loss of flexibility.

Writing Caps

An *interest rate cap* is an option contract that makes a periodic payment equal to the amount, if any, by which a floating interest rate index exceeds a specified level, multiplied by a *notional principal amount*. For example, suppose an investor owns an interest rate cap with the following characteristics:

- Notional principal amount = $10 million
- Reset period = Quarterly
- Interest rate index = One-month US$ LIBOR
- Strike yield = 4.5%
- Term = Two years

Suppose that during the first quarter after the initiation of this contract, one-month US$ LIBOR averages 4.25%. If so, no payment would be due the holder of the cap. Then suppose that this particular LIBOR averages 4.85% during the second quarter. For that period, the holder of the cap would receive a quarterly payment of $8,750 [= (4.85% - 4.50%) × $10,000,000 / 4].

This two-year quarterly cap contract is equivalent to a series of eight separate "caplets," each of which is a put option on a three-month investment struck at 4.50%. In fact, the analytical models that deal with caps (and floors and collars) on floating rates treat these contracts simply as the sum of the individual put options of which they are composed.

An investor who confidently expects to hold a substantial volume of short-term or floating rate investments for a specified period is in a position to write a "covered cap" on that position. For example, consider a German investor who fully expects to hold euro 10 million in highly liquid short-term assets for the next two years. At present, three-month EURIBOR[4] is 3.125%. Assume that the investor believes it is possible that core European interest rates will decline over time and very unlikely that they will rise. Under these assumptions, the investor

might want to extend the average maturity of the euro 10 million, but suppose this is precluded by, say, a loan covenant or an established investment policy. An alternative under the circumstances would be to write a two-year EURIBOR cap, as illustrated in Example 4.

The investor who writes the cap in this example will owe the holder of the option the amount, if any, by which EURIBOR in any quarter exceeds 3.25% multiplied by euro 10 million divided by four. This obligation is "covered" in that the investor will be receiving EURIBOR multiplied by euro 10 million on a quarterly basis as a return on short-term investments. Therefore, absent any adverse credit event on the short-term investments, the funds will certainly be available to meet the cap-writer's obligations. The covered short cap position has created an investment that will pay a higher yield than a standard floating rate note unless EURIBOR rises above 3.53%. Above that level, market EURIBOR will exceed the combined value of the investor's maximum net yield on the cash investments after cap payments of 3.25% plus the periodic value of the cap premium (0.28%).

III. Using Options to Express Views

Investors who hold strong views regarding the direction of interest rates or the relationship between different bond yields will frequently find that options provide the best vehicle for expressing these opinions. Long options offer three distinct advantages in this regard: leverage, limited downside, and nearly unlimited flexibility in design. However, options will not always be the best way to express views. There are other ways than options of leveraging fixed income investments and of limiting the downside potential of such positions. In particular, at times when option prices are high — that is, when implied volatility is high — investors may prefer other ways of expressing opinions.

We illustrate these points with two examples. In Example 5, we express the view that interest rates are likely to decline in the United States. Example 6 illustrates the use of a spread option to express a view about the differential between U.S. and European bond yields.

---

[4] EURIBOR, the European interbank offered rate, is emerging as a standard short-term interest rate index for the European Economic and Monetary Union (EMU).

Example 4: Writing a Cap on a Euro LIBOR Floater

Pricing Date	3/1/99
Index Terms	
Index	EURIBOR
Term	Quarterly
Reset Period	Quarterly
Current Yield	3.125%
Repo Rate	4.80%
Option	
Type	Quarterly Cap
Expiration	3/1/01
Strike Yield	3.25%
Notional Amount	Euro 10 million
Option Premium	0.48%
Implied Yield Volatility	25.0%
Combined Investment	
Cash Yield	EURIBOR
Implied Spread	28 bp
Maximum Net Yield	3.53%

Going Long the Bond Market

In Example 5, we assume that an investor believes that bond yields in the U.S. are likely to decline substantially over the next month and wishes to invest $500,000 in the position that will perform best if this view is correct. Suppose also that the investor's bond dealer permits 10-to-1 leverage of Treasury Note positions through repurchase agreements. We compare the return on two investments: (1) purchase of a call option on the U.S. Treasury 5.25% of February 2029 with a $500,000 premium, and (2) purchase of $5,000,000 market value of U.S. Treasury Principal STRIPS maturing in November 2027, financed through a repurchase agreement. We present the particulars of these two positions in the exhibit at the top of the next page..

The analysis of this situation compares the leveraged purchase of Treasury STRIPS with call options priced at two different levels. The lower premium, 1.428% of the par value of deliverable bonds, reflects market conditions as of March 5, 1999. At that time the implied volatility of one-month at-the-money options on 30-year Treasuries was 16.2%. The higher premium reflects peak implied volatility levels of 24% experienced during the global market turmoil of late Summer 1998.

The payoff diagram illustrates the general differences between options and leveraged long positions. First, the maximum loss on the options position is limited to the premium paid, while the maximum loss on a leveraged long position held until the horizon date is essentially unlimited. This difference should not be overemphasized, however, because an investor can establish an individual maximum loss simply by determining that the long position will be liquidated as soon as mark-to-market losses reach a predetermined level. Of course, it may not be possible to unwind a position at exactly the specified level, but in a market as liquid as the Treasury market, the magnitude of such "liquidation errors" will probably be small.

More important, the leveraged long position performs better if interest rate moves are relatively small, while the option outperforms if realized interest rate volatility exceeds the level implicit in the option's pricing. In choosing between the option and the leveraged long position, the bullish investor must decide whether to establish a leveraged long position in anticipation of a relatively modest move in the expected direction or to buy a call option in expectation of a more substantial move. In this context, the pricing of the option becomes important. In this example, the less expensive option will perform better than the leveraged STRIPS position if yields decline by more than about 12.5 basis points. A 25 bp move would be required for the more expensive option to do better than the leveraged long position.

Evaluating Option Pricing

Any investor who considers options should of course be aware of the price of the instrument in terms of implied volatility. There is no "right" level of implied volatility under any given market conditions, just as there is no "right" level of interest rates. At any given time, implied volatility is what it is. However, investors can form a judgment about the pricing of options by comparing the implied volatility offered (or bid) with what historical and implied volatilities have been in the past and how implied volatility levels compare for different instruments, different terms, and different deltas. Considering the breakeven interest rate change required for the option investment to make money or to do better than some alternative position often provides a useful "gut test" of whether the pricing is consistent with the investor's expectations.

Example 5: A Call Option vs. a Leveraged Purchase of STRIPS

Option		Zero	
Pricing Date	3/1/99	Pricing Date	3/1/99
Deliverable Bond		**Bond**	
Issuer	U.S.A.	Issuer	USA
Coupon	5.25%	Coupon	0
Maturity	2/15/29	Maturity	11/15/27
Spot Yield	5.69%	Spot Yield	0.05865
Repo Rate	4.42%	Repo Rate	0.0442
Forward Yield	5.70%	Spot Price	19.026
Spot Price	93.655	Cash Requirement	10%
Forward Price	93.560	Par Amount	26,279,928
Duration	14.40135511		
Option			
Type	Call		
Expiration	4/1/99		
Strike	93.6554		
Premium	1.428%		
Implied Yield Vol.	16.20%		
Implied Price Vol.	13.30%		
Par Amount	35,000,000		
Premium Paid	499,844		
Premium @ 24%	2.125%		
Par Amount	23,500,000		
Premium Paid	499,375		

A Spread Option

Now suppose an investor believes that 10-year bond yields in the EMU are likely to rise relative to U.S. 10-year yields and wishes to express this view in a position with a known maximum downside. Simply buying a call on a U.S. 10-year Treasury note and a put on, say, the 10-year German government Bund would not work. First of all, creating the position would be expensive because it involves buying two options. Second, the position would not have the desired effect because the payoff would depend on what happened to the general level of interest rates in the two countries. If interest rates decreased in both places, the call option would pay off and the put would expire worthless, regardless of what happened to the yield spread between the two markets. If rates rose in both places, the put would pay off and the call would expire worthless, regardless of what happened to interest rates.

The solution would be to purchase an option written by a dealer directly on the spread in question. Example 6 presents one such structure. Taking the position in this way conveys two advantages. First, the option pays off in just the way the investor wants: The option holder will profit if the spread decreases by enough to offset the cost of the option regardless of what happens to the general level of interest rates. In fact, the payoff on this option is a function of the spread and only of the spread. Second, a spread option will frequently be much less expensive than the combined costs of a call and a put.

The purpose of this example is not so much to explore this specific position as to illustrate the flexibility of options as a tool for expressing opinions about relationships among interest rates. A very broad range of such views can be expressed in positions where the cost of being wrong is limited.

Example 6: Option on the Spread between U.S. and German 10-Year Government Bond Yields

Terms:	
Pricing Date:	March 1, 1999
Settlement Date:	One day after pricing date
Expiration Date:	September 1, 1999
Notional Amount:	$50,000,000
Strike:	ATM Spot = 1.20%
Premium (in US$):	0.24% = $120,000
Payoff:	MIN{0, Notional Amt. × (End Spread - Strike Spread)}
End Spread:	The difference between the yields of the on-the run 10-year U.S. Treasury and 10-year German Bund as determined by Calculation Agent at 10 a.m. N.Y. Time
Style:	European
Settlement:	Cash

IV. Summary and Conclusion

Options on fixed income securities and interest rate indexes, while quite risky, offer opportunities. These opportunities should be of particular interest to investors who already use stock and equity market index options. Writing options can enhance investment income; the additional income compensates the investor for taking the risk that the option might expire in the money. At times when the implied volatility of option prices is high, this risk may be especially worth taking. By contrast, when volatility is low, buying options provides an efficient way of expressing views about the direction of interest rates, about the future volatility of interest rates, or about the relationship between different interest rates.

Fixed Income Research

PRIVATE CLIENT PORTFOLIOS

July 1999

Options on Fixed Income Securities: Applications for Private Clients, Part II

- **Fixed income options can:**
  - *enhance investment income,*
  - *express views regarding interest rates, and*
  - *manage portfolio risk.*
- **This report covers the third use.**
- **Use options to change portfolio duration without buying or selling bonds.**
  - *Avoid short-term gain realization, and*
  - *Retain hard-to-find specific bonds.*

- *In the United States, over-the-counter options may be offered only to Accredited Investors.*

Aaron S. Gurwitz
(212) 902-6705
aaron.gurwitz@gs.com

(Limited Distribution)

Goldman, Sachs & Co.   **Private Client Portfolios**   **Fixed Income Research**

Editor: **Ronald A. Krieger**
Production: **William Tompkins**

I. Introduction[1]

Many of Goldman Sachs' private clients have used options on equity securities to manage portfolio risk or to take advantage of investment opportunities. Although puts and calls on specific stocks or on broad equity market indexes can be risky investments viewed in isolation, these instruments frequently prove to be effective tools for enhancing income, expressing views, and managing risk in an equities portfolio. Options on fixed income instruments can serve much the same function, so individual investors should also be familiar with puts and calls on bonds.

The purpose of this report is to introduce the uses of options on fixed income securities to private clients who are already familiar with stock options. Accordingly, we will assume a basic understanding of how options work. Readers should understand terms such as *option premium*, *strike price*, *expiration*, *volatility*, *implied volatility*, *intrinsic value*, and *time value* and should be familiar with the way the profits or losses on long and short positions in puts and calls relate to the market price of the underlying security. We will review the definitions of some of these terms and concepts within this text, but only briefly. Readers who are interested in this subject matter but are unfamiliar with the basic concepts should consult any one of a number of basic explanations of options.[2]

Among readers who are U.S. residents, this material will be useful only to those who qualify as Accredited Investors (AIs) under regulations established by the Securities and Exchange Commission (SEC). Under current regulations, over-the-counter (OTC) options — which constitute the bulk of the types of fixed income options of interest to private clients — cannot be sold to the general public but only to AIs. U.S. residents who are not sure whether they qualify as AIs should consult their Goldman Sachs representative.

Some General Observations About Options

As noted above, options can be very risky as stand-alone investments and are not for all investors. An investor who purchases (goes long) a call or a put stands to lose all of the money invested. Taking "na-

ked" short options positions — selling (or "writing") options — can be even riskier; in this case, the potential for loss may be unlimited.

Notwithstanding these risks, options can play at least three important roles in a fixed income portfolio:

(1) **Enhancing investment income through option writing.** The most common type of transaction along these lines involves selling "covered" call options on securities the investor owns. Another application is to write puts on bonds one expects to purchase at a known time in the future.

(2) **Expressing views.** Fixed income options provide a way for an investor to express views regarding the direction of interest rates, the degree of volatility of interest rates, or the relationship (spread) between different interest rates. Expressing views with options allows the investor to take a position with known and limited downside risk. Some market expectations cannot be expressed in practice without the use of options.

(3) **Managing bond portfolio characteristics without buying or selling bonds.** Investors who have used options to reduce the risk of large single stock positions are familiar with the fact that managing portfolios in this way can be tax-efficient. Using options to manage portfolio risk can also economize on transaction costs.

Part I of this report, dated March 1999, presented general material regarding fixed income options. It included a discussion of the ways in which options on fixed income instruments resemble and differ from options on equities and stock indexes — along with discussions of the first two of these three potential options applications. This volume — Part II of the report — considers the third use of fixed income options. It is a continuation of Part I and is not intended to be read as a separate publication.

II. A Simple Example

When an investor wishes to change the risk characteristics of a bond portfolio — to lengthen or shorten duration, to change the yield curve exposure, or to modify call risk — the most efficient way to do so will usually be simply to sell the bonds that no longer "fit" and replace them with different securities. In a "frictionless" and "tax-free" world with no

---

[1] The author thanks Paul Humphreys, Ken Gershenfeld, and Marcus Huie for their helpful comments on an earlier draft.

[2] See, for example, Emma B. Rasiel, *Guide to Fixed Income Options*, Goldman, Sachs & Co., Fixed Income Division, October 1995 (distribution limited to AIs).

transaction costs, where all bonds are readily available at all times, such straightforward "cash" transactions would almost always make sense.

However, the real world does not fit this description of a bond investor's Nirvana. Cash transactions are not costless, particularly if the sale of a security involves the realization of a taxable gain. And not all issuers' bonds are readily available in all maturities at all times. So an investor who "likes" the AT&T credit but wishes to reduce portfolio duration may find it difficult to sell 30-year Telephone bonds and replace them with five-year obligations of the same issuer. In the real world of taxes and market imperfections, the use of derivatives in general — and options in particular — is frequently the best way to accomplish a particular portfolio management goal.

We will illustrate this application of options using two examples. The first — a simple, general example — will be unrealistic, but it will highlight the basic way in which the addition of options alters a portfolio's risk characteristics. The second example will be somewhat complex and specialized. However, the complexity is essential to highlight the full range of considerations an investor needs to take into account when hedging a real portfolio with real options. And the highly specialized nature of the hypothetical situation demonstrates the broad applicability of options solutions.

Suppose an investor owns $10 million face amount of the U.S. Treasury 4.75% of November 15, 2008, priced at 91.27 to yield 5.98%. The investor decides that interest rates are substantially more likely to rise than to decline in the near term, but in any case to be quite volatile. The way to express this outlook would be to purchase, say, a three-month at-the-money put on the investor's bond position. At 15% yield volatility, such an option would cost about 1.5 points, or $200,000. Exhibit 1 depicts the total return on the combined bond + put position over the three-month life of the option as a function of the bond's yield on the expiration date. The exhibit compares three alternative strategies: (1) holding the '08 bond on an unhedged basis, (2) holding the bond and buying an at-the-money put, and (3) selling the bond and investing in a three-month Treasury bill. The three alternatives produce very different return profiles. The Treasury bill produces the best result if rates rise, and the long position performs best if the bond market rallies. The hedged strategy is never the best performer, but it will do better than the T-bill if rates decline by more than about 25 basis points and bet-

ter than the unhedged bond position if rates rise by more than the same amount. Given the expectations outlined above, the investor may reasonably conclude that the hedged (bond + put) position is the best alternative.

Exhibit 1. Returns on Three Investment Strategies as a Function of Bond Yield at the End of Three Months

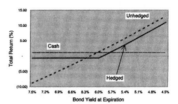

This example illustrates the simplest possible use of options to manage the risk of a bond position. The investor had a very specific point of view and could make use of a hedge vehicle — a put on the bond he happened to own — that was perfectly matched with the "portfolio." While such situations may arise from time to time, most investors find themselves in much more complex situations, in which feelings about the market outlook are inchoate while none of the available financial vehicles provides a perfect hedge.

III. A More Realistic Investment Problem

Consider a U.S. taxpayer (an AI) who resides in a "high-tax" state where in-state bonds are relatively scarce (e.g., Minnesota or Maryland). Suppose this investor acquired — for an aggregate purchase price of $10 million — a portfolio of triple-tax-exempt bonds with a relatively long weighted average maturity of 12 years, a duration of about 10 years, and an average rating of AA. Now assume that three months have passed and interest rates have declined by a dramatic 100 bp. Given the 10-year duration, the portfolio now has a market value of approximately $11 million. At this point, the investor becomes bearish on bond prices and wishes to reduce the duration of the portfolio.

The "cash" solution — replacing some of the current holdings with shorter-maturity bonds — is inefficient for two reasons. First, the sale of bonds at this point will involve realization of short-term capital gains, which will be taxed at ordinary income tax rates. Further, the most efficient way to reduce portfolio duration through a cash transaction would be to sell the longest-maturity bonds first, but these would probably be the securities with the largest gains. The sale of bonds accounting for half the gains on this portfolio would generate a federal income tax liability of $198,000 for a taxpayer in the top bracket.

Second, by assumption, this investor lives in a state where "triple-tax-exempt bonds" are hard to find.[3] As a practical matter, it may not be possible to find enough shorter-maturity bonds with the right credit quality to execute the duration-shortening transaction in a timely enough manner.

The investor knows that after the passage of nine months, the short-term gains on this portfolio will become long-term gains. And, if the investor is right about the direction of interest rates, the amount of the gain will become smaller. Further, given a bit of time to execute the shortening transaction, the investor would be able to find enough triple-tax-exempt shorter-term securities.

Under these circumstances, the best approach might be for the investor to purchase a put option. In essence, under these circumstances, a put would amount to a "casualty insurance policy" against the risk of rising interest rates. To implement this alternative, the investor must decide among several alternative specifications — none of which will be perfect — for the option to be purchased. These include:

- the appropriate *deliverable security,*
- its *par amount,*
- the *term of the option,* and
- the *strike price (or yield).*

Deliverable Security. Selecting a deliverable security involves three separate decisions. With regard to the deliverable security, the investor may choose

between exchange-traded options on interest rate futures contracts or over-the-counter options on specific securities. In most but not all cases, private clients will find that the advantage lies with OTC options because of their flexibility.[4]

If the decision is to go with an OTC contract, the next question is: "What type of bond should be the deliverable security?" The most obvious choice in this case might be simply to buy a put on the specific bonds in the investor's portfolio as in the simpler example above. That may indeed make sense, and an investor considering a hedge for a municipal bond portfolio should solicit an offering of a put on some or all of the specific bonds in the portfolio. However, the market for options on municipal bonds is almost nonexistent. To manage the portfolio's risk in this way, the investor would have to ask a dealer to offer a customized option. Although dealers might be willing to do so under some circumstances, this is unlikely to be the most cost-effective approach.

The alternative would be to buy a put on a Treasury security. The advantage of this approach would be the liquidity of the market for OTC options on Treasury securities; liquidity reduces the cost of the hedge. The disadvantage is that yields on Treasuries don't always move in synch with yields on municipals. If yields on municipals rose sharply while Treasury yields didn't move, the investor would have bought no protection at all. However, the investor might reasonably decide that the scenario in which a Treasury hedge for a municipal portfolio wouldn't work, while far from unprecedented, is unlikely, and that, if anything, Treasury yields are likely to rise relative to municipal yields as bond prices decline. We will return to this crucial issue presently.

Finally, in this regard, the investor must decide on the maturity of the deliverable bond. In this case, the average maturity of the portfolio is 12 years, but the investor might decide to use options on 10-year Treasury notes because of their greater liquidity.

In our example, we will assume that the investor has decided, taking all of the considerations into account, to buy an OTC put on 10-year Treasury notes.

---

[3] We might also consider a painstakingly assembled portfolio of "improving" corporate credits that would be hard to replace quickly. The reason for selecting the U.S. municipal bond market for our example is the fact that hedging these securities is particularly difficult, for reasons that we will discuss above. Once you understand the issues involved in using options to manage the risk characteristics of a tax-exempt bond, using similar methods with a portfolio of taxable corporate bonds will seem relatively straightforward.

[4] In this particular example, the different tax treatment of exchange-traded and OTC options may come into play. A discussion of these differences is beyond the scope of this report. Suffice it to say that investors considering the use of options or other derivatives should consult their own tax advisors regarding the advantages and disadvantages of alternative approaches.

Par Amount. The investor must also determine the volume of bonds on which the option is to be purchased. The basic idea is to estimate the par amount of bonds such that price changes on the deliverable position under the option contract will match price changes on the portfolio. In the example below, we will begin by considering a par amount such that the dollar value of one basis point (DV01) of the deliverable position matches the DV01 of the portfolio being hedged. As we explore this example more fully, we will examine the impact of changing the par amount deliverable under the options contract.

Option Term. In this case, it is relatively easy to select the right term for the option. If the investor is correct and interest rates rise, there will be gains on the value of the put option. Translating short-term gains on the bond portfolio into short-term gains on an option wouldn't make much sense. Therefore, the holding period for the option should be more than one year.

Strike Price or Yield. Decisions about the strike yield on an option used for hedging are analogous to decisions about the "deductible" on a casualty insurance policy. How much pain is the option buyer willing to live with if interest rates go up? The farther the strike yield is from spot rates — the larger the "deductible" — the lower the cost of the option but the greater the investor's maximum loss. A convinced bond market "bear" will spare no expense on the put option premium. That is what we will assume in our initial illustration for this use of options.

First Approximation: Buying an At-the-Money Put With a 100% Hedge Ratio

In this first example of an options hedge (see Exhibit 2), the investor calculates that at the end of one year's time, the DV01 of the municipal bond portfolio will be $10,663 and the DV01 of $100 par amount of the Treasury 4.75% of '08 will be $0.062. Therefore, approximately $17,200,000 par amount of the Treasury notes will have the same DV01 as the municipal bond portfolio.

So the investor decides to purchase a put option struck at the money relative to the spot yield on the Treasury note, or at 5.98%. At a market-implied yield volatility of 15%, this option has a value of 2.5% of the par amount of deliverable bonds, or $430,000.

Exhibit 2. Assumptions for Hypothetical Hedge of a Municipal Portfolio With Puts on a Treasury Note and Matching DV01s

Settlement	6/22/99
Horizon	6/22/00
Portfolio	
Par Amount	$10,000,000
Average Coupon	4.25%
Average Maturity	11/20/12
Average Price	110.00
Market Value	11,000,000
Average Market Yield	3.32%
Average Duration	10.32
DV01 @ Horizon	$10,663
Deliverable Bond	
Coupon	4.75%
Maturity	11/15/08
Price	91.27
Yield	5.98%
DV01 Per 100 @ Horizon	0.062
DV01 Equalizing Par	17,173,959
Option	
Strike Yield	5.98%
Expiration	6/23/00
Yield Volatility	15%
Premium	2.50%
Par Amount	$17,200,000
Strike Price	91.97
Short-Term Investment	
Short-Term After-Tax Yield	3.50%

Exhibit 3 represents the total returns over the one-year horizon to the expiration of the option. The payoff diagram compares the performance of the original portfolio hedged with options with that of a "cash transaction." The latter involves the sale of the original municipal bond portfolio, payment of short-term capital gains taxes, and reinvestment of the net proceeds in a new portfolio with a duration of about five years.

Consideration of this example leads quickly to the conclusion that buying an at-the-money put option on $17.2 million of Treasury notes makes sense only if the investor is strongly convinced that rates are likely to be quite volatile. The hedged portfolio is never the best performer in Exhibit 3. If rates decline, the investor is better off simply holding the unhedged position. If rates rise, a strategy of selling the municipal bonds, paying the capital gains taxes, and investing in a cash instrument does best. Indeed, the hedged portfolio is the *worst* performer unless

Goldman, Sachs & Co.   **Private Client Portfolios**   **Fixed Income Research**

**Exhibit 3. Payoff Diagram: Hedging a
Municipal Bond Portfolio With Puts on a
Treasury Note and Matching DV01s**

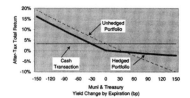

interest rates rise by more than 40 bp or decline by
more than 30 bp. Furthermore, our calculation of
these results is based on the assumption that yields
on the municipal bonds in the portfolio move by exactly the same number of basis points as do 10-year
Treasury note yields. There is no reason to expect
that this will be the case. In fact, history would lead
us to expect otherwise.

However, before we dismiss the options hedge, it
will be worth considering a couple of alternative
approaches that may produce better results.

Using a Different Hedge Ratio

This alternative approach takes into account the fact
that Treasury note yields and municipal bond yields
do not usually move together basis point for basis
point. In fact, while there have been exceptions to
this generalization, municipal yields have generally
moved by less than Treasury yields over any given
period. The relationship between municipal and
Treasury yield changes has not been stable historically, so it is impossible define a precisely "right"
hedge ratio. However, it might be reasonable to assume that if Treasury yields rise by 10 bp, yields on
municipal might rise by only 6 bp. If so, it would not
be necessary to buy puts on a full $17.2 million, but
only on 60% of that amount, or on $9.54 million.
This will reduce the option premium to $264,139.
Modifying the hedge in this way produces the payoff
diagram illustrated in Exhibit 4.

In this case, the hedge works somewhat better if municipal yields do indeed move 6 bp for every 10 bp
change in Treasury yields. When we were using a
100% hedge ratio, the hedged portfolio was the
worst performer unless yields rose by more than 40
bp or fell by more than 30 bp (+40, -30). If, in fact,

municipal bond yields do move 6 bp for every 10 bp
move by Treasuries, then the analogous figures for
the case in which we are using a 60% hedge ratio are
(+20, -20).

A lower hedge ratio is not a panacea for the high
cost of using options to hedge a bond portfolio. Exhibit 4 illustrates the payoff diagram for a municipal
bond portfolio with put options at a 60% hedge ratio

**Exhibit 4. Payoff Diagram: Hedging a Municipal
Bond Portfolio With Puts on a Treasury Note With
a 60% Hedge Ratio**

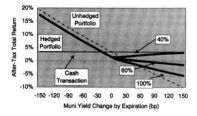

under different scenarios for how municipal bond
yields might actually move relative to Treasury note
yields. If we use a 60% hedge ratio but municipal
bond yields move by only 40% of the change in
Treasury note yields, and if interest rates rise, then
the hedged portfolio will perform quite well. In fact
there may be no interest rate scenarios in which the
portfolio generates a negative total return over the
life of the option. If, however, we use a 60% hedge
ratio but yields on municipals change basis point for
basis point with Treasury yields, then the hedged
portfolio will perform poorly when interest rates increase.

It may also be possible to improve the hedging strategy further. Specifically, suppose the investor feels
that it is too expensive to pay $262,500 to protect a
portfolio with a market yield of only $362,010. A
bearish investor who did not want to pay a large absolute option premium could reduce the out-of-
pocket cost of the hedge by giving up some of the
portfolio's upside performance potential.

Goldman, Sachs & Co.   **Private Client Portfolios**   **Fixed Income Research**

Exhibit 5. Hedging a Municipal Bond Portfolio With a U.S. Treasury Note Collar at a 60% Hedge Ratio

Settlement	6/22/99
Horizon	6/22/00
Portfolio	
Par Amount	$10,000,000
Average Coupon	4.25%
Average Maturity	11/20/12
Average Price	110.00
Market Value	11,000,000
Average Market Yield	3.320%
Average Duration	10.32
DV01 @ Horizon	10,663
Deliverable Bond	
Coupon	4.75%
Maturity	11/15/08
Price	91.27
Yield	5.98%
DV01 Per 100 @ Horizon	0.062
DV01 Equalizing Par	17,173,959
Options	
Put Option	
Strike Yield	6.08%
Expiration	6/22/00
Yield Volatility	15%
Premium	2.19%
Par Amount	$10,500,000
Strike Price	91.35
Call Option	
Strike Yield	5.73%
Expiration	6/22/00
Yield Volatility	15%
Premium	1.16%
Par Amount	$10,500,000
Strike Price	93.53
Short-Term Investment	
Short-Term After-Tax Yield	3.50%

Buying a Collar

Specifically, in addition to buying a put on Treasuries, the investor could write a call on the same deliverable security. The option premium the investor earns on the short call position will offset the premium paid on the put. The combination of long put and short call positions is referred to as a "collar" because the structure limits the investor's total return on both the upside and the downside. Exhibit 5 lays out an example of the terms for such a strategy.

In this example, the investor has decided to buy a put that is 10 bp out of the money relative to the spot yield on the deliverable bond, and sell a call option struck 25 bp out of the money. At 15% yield volatility for option pricing, the combination of the two options has a net cost to the investor of $108,404.

Exhibit 6. Payoff Diagram: Hedging a Municipal Bond Portfolio With a U.S. Treasury Note Collar at a 60% Hedge Ratio

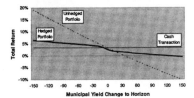

As Exhibit 6 shows, this collar produces results that, for the most part, lie in-between the unhedged portfolio and the cash transaction. The hedged portfolio is the worst performer only for a very narrow range of interest rates around current levels. The return profile of the collared position is similar to that of a bond that has a shorter duration than the underlying municipal portfolio but longer than that of the cash investment.

One difference between the collar and the other hedging strategies is that the former may involve actually selling bonds from the portfolio. If the market rallies strongly over the course of the year, the call option will expire in the money. If so, the investor may have to raise funds to meet the obligation either to deliver the Treasury securities or to finance a cash settlement. If no other sources of funds are available, it may be necessary to sell a portion of the municipal portfolio. Since, by assumption, the bonds in this portfolio are hard to find, such "forced" selling should be considered a disadvantage of the collar strategy for investors without ready alternative sources of liquidity.

Even this fairly complex example does not illuminate everything an investor needs to know about using options to hedge a fixed income portfolio. Instead, the aim has been to demonstrate two points.

First, the use of options can be the best way to manage the interest rate exposure of a bond portfolio, even when the circumstances are quite complex — particularly, but not exclusively, when tax considerations are important. Second, no hedge is ever perfect. So it is important for investors to work closely with a bond market professional to design the best hedge. The advisor, in turn, has an obligation to make it clear which risks are being reduced by the hedge and which major exposures remain uncovered.

Chapter 8

Partnerships

INTRODUCTION

Partnership valuation methods depend on the investments held in the partnership. Therefore, the assets are valued using the valuation concepts discussed in the earlier chapters. However, the special nature of a partnership ownership creates an additional layer of complexity because a partner's ability to realize the investment's return is dependent on the partnership agreement. A partnership generally involves a general partner, who is responsible for the operational management, and limited partners, who typically provide capital and are passive investors.

The partnership agreement is the key legal document that specifies the investor's rights and obligations in the investment. Its terms in addition to the characteristics of the investments in the partnership must be completely understood. Investments that may be made in a partnership are unlimited. That fact makes the partnership agreement all the more important. Assume that one has entered into an investment partnership in which $10 million was invested and that one is a limited partner. Key aspects of the partnership agreement should include:

- The purpose of the partnership and its investment risk and return parameters (e.g., private equity investing in developing countries, as opposed to Fortune 500 common stocks)
- Investment limits (e.g., limiting investments to specific asset classes, limiting each investment to no more than a specified percentage of the total partnership assets, or limiting derivative investments)
- Partner approval (e.g., a process should be in place to authorize the partnership for investments above certain risk and dollar limits)
- Authorized partnership-borrowing limits (e.g., partnership agreement prohibits borrowing)
- Identification of priority and other distributions to investors or the general partner (e.g., the first $2 million of profits first distributed to the general partners)
- Specified fee structure for the general partners
- Prohibited related-party transactions
- Exit strategy (e.g., partnership operates five years, then liquidates and distributes assets to partners)

- Identified capital-call requirements
- Information reporting requirements to partners, including frequency and depth of information
- Specified requirement for an independent yearly audit
- Identification of events that represent cause for termination of the partnership or replacement of the general partner

Key due diligence steps should include:

- Researching the general and limited partners' backgrounds to determine their financial strength and ability to fund capital calls.
- Researching the general partner track record to determine likelihood of success.
- Understanding risk characteristics of investments.
- Understanding completely all aspects of the partnership agreement.

SURFSIDE CONDOMINIUM PARTNERSHIP

To illustrate the importance of the partnership agreement, assume that an investor is a 70 percent limited partner in the hypothetical Surfside Condominium Partnership. (The general partner holds the remaining 30 percent interest.) The partnership consists of a 300-unit condominium complex located in a popular resort area. The partnership was formed to develop and sell condominium units. After four years of operation, 100 units remain unsold and the partnership liabilities amount to a $1 million mortgage. The fair value of those units is $4 million, assumed at $40,000 per unit based on sales of similar units in the marketplace. The partnership agreement provided that after the first 150 units are sold, the profits from remaining operations and sales are distributed—70 percent to the limited partner and 30 percent to the general partner. The fair value of the limited partner's interest may be calculated as follows depending on the partnership agreement.

Scenario 1: Partnership Agreement That Includes Appropriate Covenants

The partnership agreement limits general partner fees that may be charged for managing the property and specifies an exit strategy, wherein, if all units are not sold after three years, the limited partner may:

- Replace the general partner.
- Require an auction of the remaining units and a liquidating distribution after partnership liabilities are paid.
- Appoint an agent to sell the remaining units in due course.

Based on the limited partner's rights, market comparable sales at $40,000 per unit, and interim renting of unsold units producing a market return on the units, the fair value of the partnership interest would be calculated as follows:

Calculation of Limited Partnership Fair Value

100 units at $40,000	$ 4,000,000
Less sales costs at 10%	(400,000)
Less mortgage payoff	*(1,000,000)*
Total partnership net assets	2,600,000
Limited partnership interest	*0.70*
Limited partnership fair value	$ 1,820,000

Scenario 2: Partnership Agreement That Omits Appropriate Covenants

The partnership agreement does not limit general partner management fees, specify an exit strategy, or give the limited partner the right to replace the general partner. Based on those deficiencies, the limited partner has no control over the cash flow of the partnership, and the investment value is therefore negatively impacted. The extent of the discount from the $1.82 million value calculated above will depend on the facts and circumstances of the case. For example, if the general partner is charging the partnership management fees in excess of market, using related entities to perform maintenance and property improvements, and not diligently selling units, a discount of 20 to 30 percent of the investment value may be required to arrive at a fair value. In that case, the general partner has no incentive to sell units, since the units produce a cash flow that may disappear when the units are sold.

CONCLUDING REMARKS

After reading this volume, one should understand that the process of pricing an investment entails identifying the investment's basic characteristics and risks, obtaining accurate and updated financial inputs to the applicable valuation model, and, most important, understanding how the investment will generate its estimated cash flows. Investments priced using the processes described in this book, although not absolutely foolproof, will provide a reasonable measure of the asset's fair value. The fundamental valuation concepts and examples that have been analyzed should help accountants review similar and new types of investment pricings. Those concepts and examples should provide a basis for continuing development of an understanding in this area.

Glossary

This Glossary contains definitions of certain terms or phrases used in this book.

At-the-money   An option is at-the-money if the price of the underlying exactly equals the strike or exercise price.

Average life   Average life refers to the period of time it will take to receive cash flows from a fixed-income investment equal to the present value of one-half of the investment's current cost or price. This term is an important factor in evaluating a fixed-income investment that has principal cash flows throughout the investment term (as discussed in Chapter 2). An important consideration when evaluating an investment's average life is to realize that this measure is often an estimate, since the timing of cash flows may vary significantly depending on the contractual terms and economic factors.

Basis point   A basis point is equivalent to 1/100 of a percent. This term is used in the context of yields and in determining yield spreads.

Basis risk   Basis risk is the risk associated with using different indexes for the hedging instrument and the hedged item. Assume that in a cash flow hedge of a forecasted borrowing, five-year Treasury note futures are used to hedge the forecasted issuance of a B-quality note. There is basis risk in that hedge because rate movements in the five-year Treasury note and the B-quality note will be less than perfectly correlated. This is because differences in quality result in differences in coupons and yields, which result in differences in duration and interest rate risk. Another definition for basis risk, one commonly used in practice, is the risk attributable to uncertain movements in the spread between a futures price and a spot price. Within that context, basis is defined as the difference between the futures price and the spot price.

Call option   An American call option provides the holder with the right to acquire an underlying at an exercise or strike price throughout the option term. The holder pays a premium for the right to benefit from the appreciation in the underlying.

Convexity   Convexity is approximately the rate of change of duration as yields change. For all option-free bonds, duration increases as yields decline. An option-free bond is said to have positive convexity.

Cross-hedging   Cross-hedging has basis risk because the derivative and the hedged item are referenced to indexes whose changes are imperfectly correlated.

Duration   Duration provides a measure of the price sensitivity of a fixed-income security to changes in interest rates.

Forward contract   A forward contract is negotiated between two parties to purchase and sell a specific quantity of a commodity, foreign currency, or financial instrument at a specified price with delivery and/or settlement at a specified future date. Because a forward contract is not formally regulated by an organized exchange, each party to the contract is subject to the default of the other party.

Forward rate   For debt instruments, forward rate refers to a future rate of interest. It is the rate of interest between two dates in the future. The forward rate is sometimes referred to as the implied forward rate because it is computed from (e.g., implied by) spot rates. The forward rate is used to compute the theoretical spot rate for periods in which an actual security does not exist.

Forward rate agreement (FRA)   A forward rate agreement is a contract in which two parties agree on the interest rate to be paid on a notional amount at a specified future time. Principal amounts are agreed on but never exchanged, and the contracts are settled in cash. The "buyer" of an FRA is the party wishing to protect itself against a rise in interest rates, while the "seller" is a party wishing to protect itself against a decline in rates.

Futures contract   A futures contract is a forward-based contract to make or take delivery of a specified financial instrument, foreign currency, or commodity during a specified period at a specified price or yield. The contract often has provisions for cash settlement. A futures contract is traded on a regulated exchange and, as a result, has less credit risk than a forward contract.

Immunization strategies   Immunization strategies track and match asset and liability durations to eliminate the effects of interest rate volatility. As long as a portfolio's asset and liability durations are equal, the portfolio will not change in market value (excluding credit considerations) as interest rates change, since the market value changes of the asset and liability will offset.

Index option   An index option contract is based on underlyings that are indexes. Most index options are based on various stock indexes, although there is a wide variety of other indexes that include debt and precious metals.

Interest rate cap   An interest rate cap is an option with the following characteristics:

- If interest rates rise above a certain level, the cap holder receives the excess of the reference interest rate over a designated interest rate level (the strike or cap rate), based on the notional principal amount.
- The cap holder's loss is limited to the premium paid to the cap writer.
- The cap writer has unlimited risk from potential increases in interest rates above the specified cap rate.

Interest rate collar   A collar is an option that combines the strategies of a cap and a floor.

- The buyer of a collar acquires a cap and writes a floor.
- The writer of a collar writes a cap and buys a floor.

Collars fix the rate a variable-rate lender will receive or a borrower will pay between two levels (the cap and floor rate levels). Collars help reduce the cost of buying outright a cap or floor. Because a borrower or lender is usually only interested in protecting against movements in interest rates in one direction, the premium received for writing a cap or floor serves to reduce the cost of the cap or floor purchased.

Interest rate floor An interest rate floor is an option with the following characteristics:

- If rates decline below a specified level, the floor holder receives cash payments equal to the excess of a given rate (known as the strike or floor rate) over the reference rate, based on the notional principal amount.
- The buyer pays the writer a premium to receive this right.
- The floor writer faces significant risk from potential decreases in interest rates below the specified strike rate.

In-the-money A call option is in-the-money if the price of the underlying exceeds the strike or exercise price. A put option is in-the-money if the strike or exercise price exceeds the price of the underlying.

LIBOR LIBOR is the London Interbank Offered Rate. This rate is set by the British banking authority and represents an average of the short-term interest rates that AA-quality rated British banks charge each other for large Eurodollar loans in London. The rate is U.S. dollar denominated.

Notional amount Notional amount is the number of currency units, shares, bushels, pounds, or other units specified in a contract to determine settlement.

Off-the-run Off-the-run issues are those Treasury issues that have been auctioned before on-the-run issues. They tend to be less liquid and have higher bid-ask spreads.

On-the-run On-the-run issues are the most recently auctioned Treasury issues for each maturity. They are highly liquid and tend to have lower bid-ask spreads.

Out-of-the-money A call option is out-of-the-money if the strike or exercise price exceeds the price of the underlying. A put option is out-of-the-money if the price of the underlying exceeds the strike or exercise price.

Put option An American put option provides the holder the right to sell the underlying at an exercise or strike price throughout the option term. The holder gains as the market price of the underlying falls below the strike price.

Reset date Reset date is the date upon which the variable swap rate will be changed to the prevailing market rate.

Spot rate In the context of fixed-income investments, the spot rate is the prevailing rate of interest on a zero-coupon instrument for a given maturity. Spot price in the market refers to immediate, as opposed to future, delivery.

Swap A swap is a forward-based contract or agreement generally between two counterparties to exchange streams of cash flows over a specified period in the future.

Swaption   A swaption is an option on a swap that provides the holder with the right to enter into a swap at a specified future date at specified terms (free-standing option on a swap) or to extend or terminate the life of an existing swap (embedded option on a swap). A swaption has characteristics of an option and an interest rate swap.

Underlying   An underlying is a specified interest rate, security price, commodity price, foreign exchange rate, index of prices or rates, or other variable. An underlying may be a price or rate of an asset or liability but is not the asset or liability itself.

Yield curve   The yield curve refers to the relationship between interest rates and time to maturity. The yield curve is also referred to as the term structure of interest rates. It is a graph of the relationship between the yield on Treasury securities or some other homogeneous group of fixed-income securities and the time to maturity. The spot-rate term structure or spot-rate yield curve is a set of spot rates arranged by maturity.

Yield to maturity   The yield to maturity is the internal rate of return, which is the rate of interest that equates the estimated periodic future cash inflows of an instrument with its cost or cash outflows at acquisition.

References

Bookstaber, Richard. *Option Pricing and Investment Strategies.* 3rd edition. Chicago: Probus, 1996.

Burghardt, Belton, Cane, Luce, and McVey. *Eurodollar Futures and Options.* McGraw-Hill Inc., 1991.

Cox, John, and Mark Rubinstein. *Options Markets.* Englewood Cliffs, N.J.: Prentice-Hall, 1985.

Crawford, George. *Derivatives for Decision Makers: Understand and Manage Risk.* New York: John Wiley & Sons, Inc., 1996.

Deloitte & Touche LLP. *Financial Instruments: Fair Value Considerations—Implementing SFAS 107.* New York: Deloitte & Touche LLP, 1992.

———. *Fundamentals of Derivative Financial Instruments, Course 11–3080.* New York: Deloitte & Touche LLP, 1996.

Fabozzi, Frank. *The Handbook of Fixed Income Securities.* 5th edition. Chicago: Irwin Professional Publishing, 1997.

Hull, John. *Introduction to Futures and Options Markets.* 3rd edition. Upper Saddle River, N.J.: Prentice-Hall, 1998.

ICFA Continuing Education. *Derivatives in Portfolio Management.* Association for Investment Management and Research (AIMR), 1998.

Ip, Greg. "Illiquidity is Crippling Bond World." *Wall Street Journal,* October 19, 1998, p. C-1.

Jarrow, Robert, and Andrew Rudd. *Option Pricing.* Homewood, Ill.: Richard D. Irwin, 1983.

Katz, Raymond Lee, Victor B. Miller IV, and Jeffrey A. Vilensky. "Fox Entertainment Group, Inc.—Fox Rocks." *Bear Stearns & Co. Inc.,* 1998, pp. 1–22.

Kawaller, Ira. *Financial Futures and Options: Managing Risk in the Interest Rate, Currency and Equity Markets (An Institutional Investor Publication).* Chicago: Probus, 1992.

Kirkpatrick, David D. "Credit Markets: In Commercial-Mortgage Issues, Players Are Locked in a Freeze." *Wall Street Journal,* October 23, 1998, p. C-1.

Kolb, Robert. *Futures, Options and Swaps.* 2nd edition. London: Blackwell, 1995.

KPMG Peat Marwick LLP. *Solving the Mystery of Swaps.* New York: KPMG Peat Marwick LLP, 1996.

Morgenson, Gretchen. "Shrinking Treasury Debt Creates Uncertain World." *New York Times,* February 17, 2000. Available at *www.nytimes.com/00/02/17/news/financial/treasury-place.html* [February 24, 2000].

Mountain, James R. "FASB 123: Putting Together the Pieces." *Journal of Accountancy* (January 1996): 77.

Schwartz, Robert J. *Derivatives Handbook: Risk Management and Control.* New York: John Wiley & Sons, Inc., 1997.

Schwartz, Robert J., and Clifford W. Smith, Jr. *Advanced Strategies in Financial Risk Management.* New York: New York Institute of Finance, 1993.

Smithson, Charles W., Clifford W. Smith, Jr., with D. Sykes Wilford. *Managing Financial Risk: A Guide to Derivative Products, Financial Engineering, and Value Maximization.* Chicago: Irwin, 1995.

Index